A Visible Unity

A Visible Unity

Cecil Robeck and the Work of Ecumenism

Josiah Baker

LEXINGTON BOOKS/FORTRESS ACADEMIC

Lanham • Boulder • New York • London

Published by Lexington Books/Fortress Academic
Lexington Books is an imprint of The Rowman & Littlefield Publishing Group, Inc.
4501 Forbes Boulevard, Suite 200, Lanham, Maryland 20706
www.rowman.com

86-90 Paul Street, London EC2A 4NE, United Kingdom

Copyright © 2024 by The Rowman & Littlefield Publishing Group, Inc.

All rights reserved. No part of this book may be reproduced in any form or by any
electronic or mechanical means, including information storage and retrieval systems,
without written permission from the publisher, except by a reviewer who may quote
passages in a review.

British Library Cataloguing in Publication Information Available

Library of Congress Cataloging-in-Publication Data

Names: Baker, Josiah, 1994– author.
Title: A visible unity : Cecil Robeck and the work of ecumenism / Josiah Baker.
Description: Lanham : Lexington Books, Fortress Academic, [2024] | Includes
   bibliographical references and index. | Summary: "A Visible Unity is a study in
   systematic theology on the practices of the ecumenical movement, demonstrating
   how the sharing of practices between churches reconciles their ecclesiological
   differences. Josiah Baker makes his argument by studying the career and writings
   of Pentecostal ecumenist Cecil Robeck"— Provided by publisher.
Identifiers: LCCN 2024024042 (print) | LCCN 2024024043 (ebook) |
   ISBN 9781978717190 (cloth) | ISBN 9781978717206 (epub)
Subjects: LCSH: Robeck, Cecil M. | Ecumenism—United States. | Pentecostalism—
   United States. | Pentecostals—United States.
Classification: LCC BX8.3 .B33 2024 (print) | LCC BX8.3 (ebook) |
   DDC 262.001/1092—dc23/eng/20240628
LC record available at https://lccn.loc.gov/2024024042
LC ebook record available at https://lccn.loc.gov/2024024043

We have to bear in mind that we are always behind in experiencing the new gift of the Spirit to the Church. We have to catch up by making a real renewal, first in our ownselves, in our own ways of thinking and action and in our Churches. The primacy of the praxis obliges us to put the emphasis on the living tradition of the One Church rather than on local and limited confessional statements or later interpretations which caused a split in the Body of Christ. Our theology should at the same time be reoriented ecumenically as a commentary on our new experience together in the ecumenical dialogue moved by the love of the truth of the One Church and the truth which is the same for all of us and which can become a living reality amongst us only in love.

Nikos Nissiotis
"Types and Problems of Ecumenical Dialogue" (1966)

Contents

Acknowledgments	ix
Preface	xi
Introduction	1
1 Robeck's Ecclesiology amid Ecumenical and Pentecostal Conversations	27
2 Reconciling Memories of American Pentecostal Race Relations	57
3 The Push to Expand the World Council of Churches	85
4 Bilateral Dialogues as a Communal Practice of Discernment	117
5 Patristic Roots and Charismatic Controversies of Spiritual Ecumenism	147
6 Testifying to Christ within Christian Forums	179
Conclusion	213
Bibliography	225
Index	251
About the Author	265

Acknowledgments

If it takes an academy to write a book, it takes multiple academies to write an ecumenical one. A host of supporters sowed, watered, and cultivated the ideas and passions that produced the current text. The argument of this book was refined through my discussions with colleagues and mentors in the North American Academy of Ecumenists, Society for Pentecostal Studies, and American Academy of Religion. I am indebted especially to the many people who gave feedback on the material that was incorporated into the final manuscript, as well as to my editors Zachary Nycum and Gayla Freeman during the publication process. The effort that went into this book succeeded because of its many advisers (Prov. 15:22).

My research in ecumenical methodology was informed by my interactions with my co-laborers, who remain a singular source of delight in the arduous work of ecumenism. It was a joy to serve alongside my peers in the Stewards Programme of the Karlsruhe Assembly of the World Council of Churches amid our struggles with "ecumenical English," an endless sea of misdirected people, and a slate of questionable cuisine. I am grateful also for the people I have met through the Southern California Christian Forum, whose genial chaos never fails to inspire or edify. The guidance I received from Gabriel Meyer, Alexei Smith, Ray Kibler, and Michael Kinnamon will stay with me throughout my ecumenical career. I would take an underfunded project with them over tenure elsewhere any day of the week (Prov. 15:17).

The bulk of the research for this book came from my studies at North Central University (NCU) in Minneapolis, Minnesota, and at Fuller Theological Seminary in Pasadena, California. My time at NCU under Amy Anderson, Buzz Brookman, John Davenport, Phil Mayo, Glen Menzies, and Allen Tennison steeped me in the Pentecostal intellectual tradition and its place within the broader Christian church. At Fuller, the initial stages of this book benefited from the theological guidance of Veli-Matti Kärkkäinen, Kirsteen Kim, and Cheryl Peterson. My history training under Scott Sunquist and John L. Thompson, pedagogical training under Ahmi Lee, and peer mentorship under Tamisha Tyler shaped my growth as a scholar. My research would have been impossible without the master sleuths at the David Allan Hubbard Library. Unanticipated support came from Fuller's language and ethnic centers, in which my participation was the most formative part of my seminary experience. The teaching of the wise is certainly a fountain of life (Prov. 13:14).

Beyond the academy, this book was possible because of the support I received from the people in my life. I am grateful for the care shown to me by sister Candy and Miranda Houghton, along with the saints at church. I would not have made it this far without my many beloved friends, among them Irene Amon, Sheree Black, Jeremy Bone, Grace Cai, Ivy Chiu, AJ Fletcher, Jasmine Shihan Fu, Michelle Mingyue Kang, Chris Pachter, Dylan Parker, Ashni Persad, Brittany Rum, Michelle Ting, Amy Wen, Rebecca Qing Ye, and Yi Zhao. They each have been evidence that friends are given to share adversity (Prov. 17:17).

Not least am I thankful for the guidance and encouragement I received from my parents throughout my education and career. Their loving support has been constant and timely. Finally, I acknowledge the legacy of my late grandfather, who passed away while I was researching for this book and whose memory remains a blessing to many (Prov. 10:7).

Preface

Literature in systematic theology concerns the beliefs of the church, sometimes to the neglect of the people who hold these beliefs—including both author and audience. The present book's attention to a central person humanizes the discussion to demonstrate the importance and complexity of Christian theology. Along these same lines, it is helpful to insert myself here into the text for the sake of transparency. The process of researching and writing this book followed core desires of mine. I name them from the outset in hopes that they help you, the reader, understand the significance of the arguments I make in the following pages.

The first motivation in my writing this book is to honor the legacy of Cecil "Mel" Robeck. His decades of leadership shaped the practices, values, and structures of the ecumenical movement, and his example inspired countless Christians to become ecumenists—myself included. Despite this impact, however, no published literature examines his thought. My research compiled archival materials, personal interviews, and fifty years of academic literature in multiple languages by Robeck to weave together strands of his life into a portrait of the ecumenical movement. Through analyzing his career, the study puts to paper many stories never before published about developments within ecumenical circles. A goal of the book is to canonize Robeck as one of the most influential leaders of the ecumenical movement as it entered its second century.

The second motivation is to inform readers about contemporary changes in the ecumenical movement and what led us here. Public understandings of ecumenism are usually an extension of personal experiences. People often assume that the forms of church relations found in their own congregations, towns, or denominations reflect church relations at large. Even scholars of ecumenics risk becoming siloed within their portions of the academy. I wanted to study ecumenics to understand my own work better and to assist others with theirs, which depends on expanding and deepening our knowledge of ecumenism. Theological studies of the church gain credibility when they speak of the church as it exists, even when it exists in forms the author has not experienced. Good theology never results from inaccurate perceptions of reality. A goal of the book is to broaden readers' knowledge of the ecumenical movement's historical development and global diversity.

The third motivation is to push back against some claims made in ecumenical literature. Contemporary scholarship has come far in its critical understanding of epistemology and how the shaping of academic fields is a product of social forces. This is no less true for ecumenics. More than a scholastic debate, malformed ecumenical theory frustrates the inclusion of the whole Christian community within the process of theologizing. A cornerstone of ecumenical theology is the notion that Christians speak truly of God only when they speak of God together. The search for equitable ways of speaking furthers the progress of the ecumenical movement in achieving theological consensus. A goal of the book is to identify common errors in ecumenical scholarship for the sake of constructing better theory for more fruitful praxis.

The final and greatest motivation is to grow the readers' love of the church. Ecclesiology, no less than any other theological subject, concerns the orthopathic bond between belief and practice in the Christian life. A person does not need theological training to see that the divisions within the church are a perversion of Godly love, yet theology guides and grows love by speaking of God's presence within the church. While planning this book, I wanted to write systematic theology for people who "have dirt under their fingernails," people who are doing the work of uniting churches and not merely talking about it. Ecumenists live under the conviction that the love between believers calls for perseverance even when the work stops being fun. Such labor contributes to the construction of Christian theology while orienting theology toward the upbuilding of the Christian community, a task that calls for the asking of hard questions. Systematic theology plays a crucial role by interrogating beliefs that motivate ecclesial practices because theology encompasses the structures and systems of the church by which God's love is meant to be witnessed on earth. The ecumenical movement catalyzes the rigorous critical reflection that Christian love warrants. The ultimate goal of the book is to impress upon readers that to love the church is to love its people; and that love, like faith, is dead without action.

Introduction

The Karlsruhe Assembly of the World Council of Churches (WCC) in 2022 testified to the commitment of churches to each other in the face of plague, war, and environmental crises. The WCC gathered in Germany to deliberate on the needs of the world and the issues that still separated churches. It was reaffirmed that the only way to address these concerns was for churches to do so together, raising the stakes for the choices made as churches relate to each other in the future. The Assembly modeled its Message after that of the Amsterdam and Busan Assemblies. Churches in 1948 stated their intention "to stay together," and in 2013 their desire "to move together." The gathering of churches at Karlsruhe testified to their experiencing God's love in their midst, and they asked God to transform their commitment into common action. The Assembly affirmed that God had called the churches "to act together;"[1] what it did not specify, though, was *how* the churches should act together.

The work of ecumenism changes with each generation and in every location, and with these changes come new challenges. Yet, in all these variations, the goals of ecumenism remain the same. Ecumenists labor for the visible unity of the church. Church unity is not the only goal of the ecumenical movement, but it is an animating effort that enables the movement to accomplish its other goals. The means used to reach these goals are experiments under duress. Joint working groups launch campaigns to enhance churches' social witness, only to be met with resistance. Scholars author groundbreaking study documents and reports, knowing that their governing commissions likely will not read them. Financial pressure transforms ecumenical bodies into service organizations or interfaith networks. Local leaders plan elaborate ecumenical prayer services whose bricolage of spiritual traditions alienates all those in attendance. Tasked with specialized endeavors that seem divorced

1

2   *Introduction*

from the lives of churches, even the most stalwart ecumenist is left wondering
how their work could ever result in the visible unity of the church.

The perennial need for reflection on the work of ecumenism motivates the
field of ecumenical methodology. The questions seen above are not of theological method, which concerns the discernment and articulation of beliefs,
but of the discernment of praxis. This praxis is investigated in the field of ecumenics, which is the study of the church's unity, the causes of ecclesiastical
division, and the means by which division is overcome. Theologies of ecumenism inform ecumenical methods, or the means by which ecumenists seek
to overcome division together. These ecumenical methods are exercised and
altered in pursuit of church unity. The theological dimension of the pursuit is
ecclesiological convergence, which is the reconciling of doctrinal differences
that divide churches. Ecumenists distinguish between consensus—which is
the doctrinal concord needed for the desired unity—and convergence—which
is the marked progression of churches and their doctrines toward the desired
unity. Because ecumenical methodology addresses the work of ecumenists
to overcome divisions, it raises questions about the convergence of churches
toward each other.

If methodological reflection seeks ecclesiological convergence, then it
warrants discussion within the discipline of systematic theology. The present
study in systematics differs from practical theology in that it does not offer
new methods. Instead, it studies methods to determine how they result in the
reconciliation of divergent ecclesiologies. By systematic theology, I do not
present a comprehensive system of ideas as a foundation for future reflection. I study systematics here as the search for coherency and consistency
across geographic, cultural, and temporal boundaries as Christians seek to
speak of God together. Systematic theology is requisitely dialogical out of
an acknowledgment that the theologian is socially located as one small part
of the larger Christian faith. The articulation of a shared confession across
boundaries qualifies systematics as an indispensable resource for the field of
ecumenics in its search for church unity. The present study illuminates the
relation of ecumenical methodology to ecclesiological convergence, how acting together results in the churches being together.

Any plans made for future progress in the ecumenical movement need
to take seriously the developments in the movement's past century, so I
study these changes for the sake of theological reflection. This approach
distinguishes between what is already known in the field and what is yet
unclear. What is known is that ecclesiology is the elemental theological
dynamic of ecumenism. The Holy and Great Council of the Eastern Orthodox churches in 2016 even summarized the goal of the ecumenical movement as the clarification "of the whole ecclesiological question."[2] Divergent
ecclesiologies cause churches to act independently of each other. Existent

Introduction 3

ecumenical methods presume particular ecclesiological self-understandings for churches to engage in the practices. Neutrality is a fiction—and not even a useful one. To ignore the ecclesiological basis of ecumenical methodology is to overlook the reason ecumenical work is capable of spurring convergence. At the same time, churches invariably change their ecclesiologies when they develop new systems, practices, and values of relations with other churches.

What is yet unclear are the consequences of the ways that churches seek unity together for the doctrine on the church. Ecclesiological reflection on ecumenism has positioned the motivations and goals of ecumenical pursuits, the "whys" and the "whithers," as being rooted in the church's very nature and mission. The methods, or "hows," on the other hand, have often been derived from the previously determined motivations and goals. This results in a pragmatic approach to ecumenical methodology. Furthermore, without an understanding of how ecclesiology informs the derivation of shared ecumenical methods, it will remain unclear how ecumenical work can serve the reconciliation of divergent ecclesiologies. The present study elevates the theological nature of methodological questions so that ecclesiology can serve as a critical and guiding factor in methodological thinking. How do ecumenical methods result in ecclesiological convergence?

I argue that methods employed in ecumenical work are an expression of shared ecclesiology between churches. The work of uniting churches relies on ecclesiological principles of what churches are called to be and do. Churches undertake ecumenical work according to what they believe is consistent with their calling. Because ecumenical methods—by definition—are joint ventures between churches, they rely on an understanding of ecclesiology that is shared between the involved churches. Consequently, when churches further develop methods for ecumenical work, they converge in their ecclesiologies. Said differently, progress in uniting churches is seen when methods change.

The contribution of the study to the field of ecumenics is the notion that ecclesiological convergence occurs through ecumenical work. Scholars of ecclesiology who examine doctrinal convergence within the ecumenical movement more often than not rely on dialogue reports, study documents, and covenantal charters from ecumenical bodies, dialogue commissions, and church communions. They do so under the assumption that the texts measure the extent to which churches have reached a consensus on the nature of the church. They follow the timeworn pattern that scholars study scholarship. The prioritization of texts and verbal articulations of theology overshadows the equally important realms of practice and experience in Christian theologizing. The nuance and function of texts are irreplaceable in the ecumenical movement—as seen in the abundant use of texts in this book—yet they are significant only insofar as they speak of the values, practices, and structures of the ecumenical movement that make unity visible and that are the concern of systematic theology. Ecumenical texts cannot reveal convergence without these prior changes in the churches.

The argument is timely given the recent conversations surrounding the Karlsruhe Assembly of the WCC, the Catholic Church's synod on synodality, the ongoing regional tensions within Christian World Communions, and the changing relations within Eastern and Oriental Orthodox Communions that are reshaping ecclesiastical practices of communion. Such changes entail questions of ecumenical methodology to discern the next steps. The field of ecumenics will explore these questions to help divided churches pursue a common vision of the church. For theologians to prioritize texts over the changed practices of churches would be to misunderstand the nature of the ecclesiological convergence that is sought.

CONSIDERATIONS IN THE STUDY OF ECUMENICAL METHODOLOGY

Methodology is a question raised within scholarly and practical discussions on ecumenism. The latter part of the twentieth century witnessed a trend of addressing methodology within accounts of theological dialogue and ecclesiastical relations. It was increasingly recognized that the practical problems ecumenists encountered in their work required systematic thought. Because ecumenical methodology has ecclesiological implications, the practical concerns of ecumenical work inform theological reflection. Theological literature grapples with four primary considerations which also shape the present study in ecclesiological convergence, namely the historical changes in ecumenical work, social conditions of ecumenical work, internal coherency within ecumenical work, and theological construction from ecumenical work.

Historical Changes in Ecumenical Work

Even a cursory familiarity with the history of the ecumenical movement reveals that the movement is constantly changing. This could prove challenging for ecumenists because, if ecumenical efforts are to result in a common theological vision of the church, then changes in these efforts could frustrate hopes of progress. The changing nature of the ecumenical movement inspired the emergence of ecumenical methodology as a comprehensive academic subfield inclusive of particular methods that sought to understand how and why these changes occurred. An early observation from Renzo

Introduction   5

Bertalot is that methodology is not derived prior to ecumenical work but develops alongside it.[3] Kuncheria Pathil celebrates this fact when he argues that ecumenical methods, similar to the church itself, are historical, meaning they speak to changing situations and cannot be seen as timeless. The new conditions of the world and the new relations between churches require new methods. However, he is more cautious to affirm the reverse when he says that "it might also be true to a certain extent" that methodological changes change the churches.[4] In his mind, ecumenical methodology is a consequence of ecclesiology, but it is unknown whether methodology has consequences for ecumenical ecclesiology.

More recent scholarship has demonstrated the impact that methodological changes can have on churches. For example, Mary-Anne Plaatjies-Van Huffel narrates the development of the WCC's discernment practices. The historical model for WCC Assembly parliamentary processes came from Presbyterian polity before the Orthodox contingent called for more communitarian systems, seen as a more solidly ecclesiological foundation. The consultations that revised the systems drew heavily on the discernment practices of Quaker meetings, resulting in the WCC's famed consensus method. She demonstrates how the WCC changes would later impact the discernment practices of the World Communion of Reformed Churches, an example of churches changing their ecclesial practices as a result of ecumenical engagement.[5] Constitutions and policy documents remain untapped sources for ecclesiological reflection. In these ecumenical texts, churches name the practices and values by which they seek to relate to each other. The documents account for the empirical reality of churches in their geographic and compositional diversities, while efforts to revise these documents grapple with questions of authority, consensus, and finance. Theological engagement with methodology encounters these same questions.

Because ecumenism concerns visible unity, it concerns the actions of Christians and churches in history, which is where unity is seen. The notion of progress in history creates for ecumenics a distinction between methods and goals. While the culmination of the ecumenical movement occurs in history, it is still regarded as a future event and so is harder to observe. Methodology, on the other hand, is presently seen and can more readily be assessed critically. For my discussion, mission is considered a goal of unitive work insofar as churches are better capable of participating in God's mission in the world. Mission is a motivating reason rather than a temporary task, and so the various means of bearing witness to the world are not studied as part of ecumenical methodology. The methods of ecumenism are distinct from goals and thus require their own attention. Changes in ecumenical methodology are further compounded by the social contexts in which churches relate to each other.

6   *Introduction*

Social Conditions of Ecumenical Work

Theological studies on ecclesiological convergence in the ecumenical movement examine the doctrines of churches. At the same time, these doctrines
concern the social conditions in which the churches find themselves, meaning
that these conditions inform theological reflection in the ecumenical movement. The field of ecumenics has matured in its understanding of this dimension of Christian theologizing. An early conference of the Lutheran World
Federation in 1978 on ecumenical methodology reflected on new questions
of how "non-doctrinal issues" affect dialogue.[6] The term is problematic due
to the implication that doctrine could be divorced from the various aspects
of churches' lives. Peder Nørgaard-Højen would go on to write on the challenges of dialogue when it occurs across geographic, sociopolitical, and temporal boundaries. He contends that geopolitical changes during the twentieth
century increased the need to attend to matters of truth, power, and ecclesiastical structures in ecumenical discourse because of their methodological
implications.[7] Increasing attention was given to such matters in theological
construction.

The new attention to social contexts raised questions for ecumenical methodology. Konrad Raiser and Harding Meyer come to similar conclusions
when they each argue that the changing conditions of the ecumenical movement do not change the nature of the unity sought but only reveal new facets.[8]
The same cannot be said for ecumenical methods. Theological studies on
methodology are more interested in the cultural, political, and socioeconomic
conditions of the ecumenical movement than are other works on ecclesial
unity. Peter Uzochukwu demonstrates this in his study of ecumenical praxis
within African Catholicism, wherein the social contexts of congregations
have a direct bearing on their ecumenical methods.[9] Scholarship on methodology is also positioned to help diversify the broader field of ecumenics
insofar as attention to culture and politics can center voices and communities
overlooked elsewhere in the field.

Beyond the local or regional level, global conditions shape international
ecumenical concerns. The networks and organizations that function internationally serve as platforms to interrogate global ecclesiastical systems for
the sake of constructing equitable practices of communal discernment. Aram
Keshishian, in his classic monograph on conciliar fellowship, studies councils
of churches as practices of ecumenical engagement out of the experience of
Orthodox conciliarity. He argues that geopolitical changes at the end of the
twentieth century required renewed understandings and practices of transregional ecclesiastical relations.[10] Theological reflection on ecumenical methodology studies the church as it exists in society, including when churches
relate to each other across different societies.

Internal Coherency within Ecumenical Work

The plurality of ecumenical initiatives around the world results in conflict. The study of methodology seeks to preserve the integrity of the ecumenical movement through protecting its coherency.[11] Research in systematic theology on ecumenics is especially concerned with the need to hold the same beliefs regardless of situation and location. A desire for coherency in no way implies a desire for uniformity. The diverse contexts and callings of the ecumenical movement require diverse projects and methods. At the same time, ecumenists are careful to ensure their efforts do not impede each other. Carlos Cardoza-Orlandi illustrates this in his essay on the Caribbean Conference of Churches. He likens Caribbean ecumenism to the region's famed polyrhythmic music. The diversity that resulted from the indigenous communities and migrations from Europe, North America, Africa, and Asia is reflected in equally diverse churches across the islands. He argues that the task of ecumenical bodies in the Caribbean is to learn "the ability to become compatible with other rhythms without losing the beat."[12] The polyrhythmic nature of ecumenical methodology requires that efforts not compete or conflict to ensure that diversity thrives.

A recurrent struggle for theological scholarship is the ability to examine how particular methods relate to each other without being overwhelmed with data. Global analyses fail to offer granular detail, though Jill Hawkey's *Mapping the Oikoumene* remains the best resource in this direction.[13] Because of the WCC's global platform, it has fostered reflection on the synergy between methods. The WCC's Commission on Faith and Order devoted attention to methodology in the middle of the twentieth century before turning to ecclesiology.[14] Since then, the WCC has offered little expressly theological literature on the subject.

An alternative approach is to study reflection within particular churches and their participation in different ecumenical projects. Teaching documents of the Roman[15] Catholic Church have had an impact on the ecumenical movement unparalleled among other confessional bodies, including conciliar documents (*Unitatis redintegratio* [UR] and *Lumen gentium* [LG])[16] and encyclicals (*Ut unum sint* [UUS] and *Orientale lumen*).[17] More practical guidance is offered in the *Directory for the Application of Principles and Norms on Ecumenism* and *The Bishop and Christian Unity* for local Catholic communities.[18] The question I examine in this book controls how I use such literature. I have defined ecumenical methods as something that occurs between churches. Any literature that results from intra-ecclesial reflection should be understood as theological contributions to wider ecumenical discourse. Practices advocated in the texts cited above are viable only if other communities can share these practices. The search for a shared methodology is part of the

8   *Introduction*

search for a common ecclesiology, and so it would be futile to construct a
methodology that is unique to an ecclesial tradition.

Scholars go beyond studying differences in methodology toward reconciling divergent understandings of unity. Meyer explains that the work of ecumenism is effective and coherent insofar as ecumenists can hold a common,
clear expression of the goals of their work, yet he asserts that the ecumenical
movement has never been homogeneous in this regard. The multiplicity of
groups and objectives reflects diverse or competing visions of ecumenism.
Churches bring their differing beliefs about unity into the movement for them
to converge. At the same time, different theologies of ecclesial unity have
not hindered ecumenical efforts from occurring; otherwise, the ecumenical
movement would never have come into existence.[19] The movement is where
these theologies are reconciled, meaning that the practices of ecumenical
bodies are meant to foster shared understandings and models of church unity.

Theological Construction from Ecumenical Work

A goal of the ecumenical movement is the sharing of a common understanding of the church. The resultant question for theologians—and, indeed, the
question for this book—is whether the ever-changing, socially conditioned,
diverse practices of ecumenism truly give rise to a common understanding.
Authors study particular practices and what churches have learned about
ecclesiology through them. Relations between churches are a classical question for systematic theology, including topics such as conciliarity, canonical
territory, and communion between bishops. Practices and values that enact
these relations are seen as having implications for ecclesial communion, and
the practices of the ecumenical movement likewise inform the construction
of a shared ecclesiology.

Dialogue commissions serve as experiments in the derivation of ecumenical theology. Angelo Maffeis frames dialogue as a mode of relationship
between Christian communities, such that the strengthening of relationships
between churches broadens the diversity of theological languages in the conversation.[20] Elsewhere, Gillian Evans examines decades of bilateral dialogue
reports to describe the vocation of Christian theology and how ecumenical
theological construction contributes to the unity of the church.[21] Alterna-
tively, Pathil is more critical of confessionalism in dialogue—such as occurs
in bilateral commissions—because of its focus on historical conflicts and its
abstraction from present experience, which makes him opposed to authors
such as Maffeis and Evans. Ecumenists should instead judge methods by their
ability to address current questions, experiences, and contexts.[22] The desire
to work toward ecumenical ecclesiology does not preclude debates on how
divided churches should share in the endeavor.

Introduction 9

In light of this challenge, Paul Avis calls for renewed theological understandings of ecumenical methodology. The Anglican canon reflects on his career in dialogue and contemporary changes in the ecumenical movement before concluding that many ecumenical endeavors are "deficient in methodological consciousness."[23] In looking toward the future of theologies of ecumenism, he offers four criteria by which the theology should be judged—it must be coherent, credible, critical, and constructive.[24] These four criteria ensure both that the proposed methods deal with the historical reality of churches and that ecumenists can coordinate their work so that it strengthens the ecumenical movement.

Literature on methodology and ecclesiology has traced developments in the ecumenical movement to discern the theological significance of ecumenical praxis. The remaining questions include the relation of different methods to each other, the ways in which changes in the world impact the derivation of methods, and the criteria by which churches can judge the validity of methods. More importantly for the present study, there is an identified need to discern: (1) how ecumenical methods, which derive from ecclesiological principles of the church's unity, can be shared between different confessions and (2) whether changes in ecumenical methods result in ecclesiological convergence between divided churches.

BIOGRAPHICAL AND CONFESSIONAL DELINEATIONS

The driving question of this book is how ecumenical methodology results in ecclesiological convergence. The question occurs at the intersection of theory and praxis within the ecumenical movement, requiring an approach that touches on both. However, because the study examines ecumenical methodology within the field of systematic theology, it assesses the thought that informs and is informed by ecumenical praxis. Therefore, I do not focus on any one particular methodological field, as would be the approach of practical theology. I examine the ecclesiological questions and principles within various methods to assess the broader relation of ecumenical methodology to ecclesiology. I delineate the study's approach according to two pivotal choices that determine my engagement with existent literature and concerns.

The first choice is the study's biographical approach. Previous studies have examined ecumenical methodology by delineating the field according to particular methods, which limits an understanding of how methods are related to each other. I reverse this approach. Rather than studying multiple persons and ideas in one ecumenical initiative, I study one person who participates in multiple ecumenical initiatives. The ability to follow the thoughts and actions

10   *Introduction*

of one ecumenist across organizations and decades of history offers insight
into the interrelation of ecumenical methods, which addresses the previously
mentioned concerns of historical change and internal coherency.

Research on an individual person also accords with common concerns that
motivate the study of methodology. Theological reflection on ecumenical
methodology roots ecclesiology in shared experience, and experience-based
theology needfully employs narratives to structure, interpret, and interrogate
claims. Additionally, a recurrent struggle of ecumenical organizations and
initiatives is their short institutional memory. Such groups are largely staffed
with church-appointed representatives, many of whom have had no prior
experience in the ecumenical movement. The need to train new generations
of ecumenists relies on retelling the stories of the movement to offer clarity of
mission and guidance in making decisions. A common way to foster ecumenical formation is to learn from the example of iconic figures in the movement.
The field of ecumenics is replete with theological biographies of influential
leaders, including Philip Potter,[25] Sarah Chakko,[26] Dumitru Stăniloae,[27]
Willem Visser 't Hooft,[28] Chiara Lubich,[29] Paulos Mar Gregorios,[30] Emilio
Castro,[31] and Mercy Oduyoye.[32] Though the present study is not historical, it
draws on history for the sake of informing ecclesiological reflection.

A pitfall of this approach is the association of individuals and ecumenism.
The argument I make in this study is that ecumenical methods are contingent
upon shared ecclesiology between churches. As such, ecumenism is a venture of communities, not lone persons. Individuals cannot have ecumenical
methodologies, for no one can do ecumenism on their own. The value of
studying particular ecumenists lies in identifying their influences on the ecumenical movement and their reflections on different ecumenical initiatives. A
limitation of the study is the inability to go beyond the topics that the figure
addresses in their own work, leaving several crucial issues for future research.
Additionally, points of tension within the thoughts of the individual cannot
be resolved without compromising the integrity of the source material. A biographical approach offers insight into the interaction of methods within one
person's thought and ecumenical career while limiting the scope of the study
to a manageable amount of data.

The second pivotal choice for my study's method is its confessional lens.
Just as there is no generic culture or language, there is no ecclesiastically neutral vantage point for studying ecumenism. Ecumenical theory is constructed
as concrete, confessional communities operate together. Scholars of ecumenism contribute to the larger movement as they study the actions of ecclesial
traditions that are historically conditioned. Previously mentioned examples
include Uzochukwu's monograph on Catholic ecclesiology in Africa,
Keshishian's study on Orthodox conciliarity, Avis's essay on Anglican
experiences in dialogue, and Plaatjies-Van Huffel's narrative on reformed

Introduction 11

discernment practices, each of whom contributes to the field of ecumenics by studying their own ecclesial traditions.

A pitfall of this approach is the association of confessions and ecumenism. The argument I make in this study is that ecumenical methods are contingent upon shared ecclesiology between churches. As such, ecumenism is a venture across ecclesiastical boundaries. Denominations cannot have ecumenical methodologies, for no church can do ecumenism on its own. It is improper to speak of a Mennonite ecumenical methodology, or a Russian Orthodox ecumenical methodology, or a Southern Baptist ecumenical methodology. Communities participate in ecumenism insofar as they interact with each other, and so ecumenical methods requisitely are joint ventures. To say that an ecclesial tradition has a unique ecumenical methodology is tantamount to saying that a person is married without having a spouse. Nonetheless, there is a recognition that ecumenists approach practices from their confessional locations and that the wider ecumenical community benefits from the theological reflection that occurs within the still-separated churches. Ecumenism would be impossible if divided churches could not contribute to their unity from their current conditions. A confessional lens is not the only valuable way to study ecumenics, but it helps situate ecumenical theology historically in the concrete lives of churches and speaks more directly to current theological divisions as understood by churches. This approach addresses the previously mentioned concerns of social conditions and theological construction.

A limitation of the study is the inability to examine how methods shape multiple churches in a comparative sense because the approach focuses on the experience of only one confession, leaving more comprehensive accounts of methods for future research. Additionally, crucial questions for some churches are not always important for others, meaning that some questions cannot be addressed adequately through every possible confessional lens. Methodological reflection within each church aids in the derivation of shared methods.

For the present study, I examine ecumenical methodology from the vantage point of Pentecostal churches. It should be stressed from the outset that I am not making an argument about Pentecostalism directly, and so I bypass questions important for the study of that movement for the sake of focusing on ecumenical theory and praxis. The Pentecostal ecclesial tradition offers irreplaceable insight into this book's driving question.

The proposed method of study deviates from the approaches of previous analyses of the ecumenical movement, perhaps in ways that might raise concern. Why Pentecostalism? Potential concerns point to the fraught relationship between Pentecostals and other Christian communities. Pentecostalism is one of the youngest ecclesial traditions, having had less time to devote itself to matters of unity and division. The tradition is rebuffed as

12   *Introduction*

anti-intellectual with an underdeveloped ecclesiology, falling short of the need for nuanced reflection on the complexities of ecumenical theory. It is a movement as diverse as it is divided, contesting the universality of any and all definitional claims. The churches are accused of forsaking the patristic witness to the faith passed down through the centuries and of hampering the gospel's social witness. Pentecostals and their Charismatic offspring are prone to triumphalist and elitist attitudes, guilty of proselytizing other Christians wherever they spread. Pentecostalism exists at the periphery of other churches' ecumenical consciousnesses; in fact, a majority of Christians globally belong to churches that do not recognize the ecclesiality of Pentecostal communities. Regarded as outsiders, Pentecostals are labeled as either "by far the most critical challenge"[33] or an "almost insurmountable impediment"[34] to the work of ecumenism. At best, Pentecostal churches are seen as marginal to the ecumenical movement.

There is truth in many of these claims. Ecumenical relations with Pentecostal churches exhibit struggles that antagonize the movement at large. Nonetheless, seeing as how Pentecostals are, in fact, Christians, they cannot be expunged from the conceptual map of ecumenism for the sake of the convenience of others. Furthermore, as the academy is in perpetual need of remembrance, when a field seeks to reconfigure itself to meet new challenges in new situations, there is no better place to begin than from the margins. My selection of Pentecostalism as a confessional lens interrogates presuppositions in the field of ecumenics. How did the second-largest ecclesial tradition in church history come to be seen as marginal to anything? Whose narrative constructed the supposed center of ecumenism such that it was foreign to Pentecostals? Which practices hinder the equitable participation of Pentecostal churches in a movement predicated on inclusivity?

Pentecostal presence in the ecumenical movement foregrounds issues with which ecumenists grapple daily. The legitimation of ecumenical narratives and bodies defines who gets to qualify as properly ecumenical. Global shifts in ecclesial numbers undermine epistemic colonialism that fashioned many ecclesiastical networks, demanding new structures and practices to support equitable ecumenical praxis. The redrawing of communal boundaries through migration and changes in political power revise ecclesiological paradigms that once defined the field. Considered pioneering decades ago, such conversations are now normative for methodological investigations. The reconfiguration of ecumenical bodies and systems orients scholarship in the field. Pentecostalism is studied frequently by non-Pentecostals as a case study for issues of reception, representation, and recognition. The tradition has become paradigmatic for research on "newness" in the ecumenical movement— whether it be new churches, new challenges, new contexts, new voices, or new methods. Many ecumenical initiatives have identified the inclusion of

Introduction 13

Pentecostal voices as an ongoing goal; the present study furthers this agenda and so should be welcomed.

Part of the motivation to engage Pentecostal churches comes from the languishment of ecumenical work in parts of the world. Pentecostals thrive where ecumenists struggle, and so ecumenists turn to Pentecostals for support in these regions. The geographic dispersal of Pentecostal churches causes ecumenical scholarship often to conflate Pentecostalism with so-called "Majority World" Christianity. The term schematizes the diversity of the global church from the vantage point of the West, simultaneously flattening and exoticizing other communities—as though São Paulo, Kinshasa, and Jakarta have much in common. Likewise, the conflation of Pentecostalism with churches outside the West serves only to misrepresent the diversity of histories and theologies in these regions—as though Brazilian Pentecostals, Congolese Catholics, and Indonesian Evangelicals have much in common. Yet the study of Pentecostalism remains important for contemporary concerns of the ecumenical movement since it is the largest confessional body to be proportionally underrepresented within ecumenical bodies. Geographic and denominational questions for methodology are distinct and related.

Pentecostal churches are an object of inquiry in ecumenical projects when other churches seek to approach them to resolve conflict or build relationships. Mathews George Chunakara wrote of this task shortly before he was elected general secretary of the Christian Conference of Asia. He identifies the need to engage Pentecostal churches at a regional level as one of the most pressing tasks for the Conference; he looks to the Consejo Latinoamericano de Iglesias[35] as a fellow regional ecumenical organization that has historically succeeded in incorporating Pentecostals as a model for pan-Asian ecumenism.[36] Gedeon Alencar offers a counterpoint in his sociological study of ecumenical consciousness in Brazil, where ecumenical structures and Pentecostal churches often regard each other as nemeses.[37] It would be wrong to ignore other traditions that similarly have been isolated from ecumenical structures, just as it would be wrong to speak of Pentecostals always as outsiders, yet the project of strengthening relations with Pentecostal churches is a common way to frame methodological research. Whenever ecumenists ask themselves, "How do we broaden the table?", they are asking a methodological question about the very practices and self-understanding of the ecumenical movement that concern both "insiders" and "outsiders."

Dynamics of unity and division within Pentecostalism have drawn the attention of ecumenists. A Faith and Order paper from 1967 profiles, among other churches, European Pentecostalism. The editors explain that the Commission on Faith and Order narrowed the study to Europe due to the "vast, vigorous, and varied"[38] nature of the Pentecostal tradition globally. The WCC Commission upholds the tradition as an exemplar of the New Testament vision of diversity in unity, asserting that "Pentecostalism is already itself an ecumenical movement."[39] Pentecostal churches entered the consciousness of many other churches during this time as a result of the Charismatic movement's transgressing confessional boundaries. How churches responded to the movement has methodological implications. Connie Ho Yan Au studies the formation of ecumenical spaces within the Charismatic movement in England for dialogue and mutual renewal of churches, complementing institutional changes and furthering an ecumenical vision.[40] May Ling Tan-Chow published a similar study on Singapore that is more chastened than Au's. Both women agree that the Charismatic movement is a force for the unity of the church, but Tan-Chow's study is motivated by the conviction that people must confront their own internalized violence before they can contribute to the peace of society. She approaches her Pentecostal tradition with a critical lens in her construction of a Pentecostal theology of ecumenical and interfaith relations.[41] The contributions of Pentecostal churches to the unity and division of Christian communities have heightened the need for such methodological research.

The ecumenical activities of Pentecostal churches shape the work of ecumenism. It would be an overstatement to speak of a "Pentecostalization of ecumenism"—even though Kurt Koch declared the transformation over a decade ago from his vantage point as cardinal prefect of the Pontifical Council for Promoting Christian Unity[42]—but it is not improper to suggest that Pentecostals will shape the ecumenical movement as have all other traditions. Literature in this direction is more recent. Sébastien Kalombo Kapuku's two-volume work studies the impact of Pentecostal churches on ecumenism in the Democratic Republic of the Congo, arguing that the changed ecclesial landscape will require new ethical and missiological paradigms for ecumenical action to meet the needs of the country.[43] Hermen Kroesbergen similarly argues that Pentecostal ministries have altered the understanding of agency in ecumenical work among Zambian churches from being a state-sponsored effort to being a project of individuals.[44] Not every change has to be beneficial for ecumenists to recognize the value in studying these changes, which is why it is increasingly common for non-Pentecostal scholars to study Pentecostalism for its methodological implications, including the studies of the Belgian Free Church scholar Jelle Creemers on Catholic–Pentecostal dialogues.[45] Methodological investigations revise the narrative of Pentecostal churches from being mere members of ecumenical initiatives to being contributors.

I do not speak of Pentecostal churches as being outside of ecumenism. Because there is only one ecumenical movement, any unitive effort between Christian communities must be seen as part of the movement. The present study resists the ghettoization of Pentecostal thought from wider ecumenical discourse—a trend that Pentecostals and non-Pentecostals sustain alike.

The contours of global Pentecostalism will influence ongoing developments within the ecumenical movement, and so there is value in studying a Pentecostal ecumenist for methodological inquiries. Methodological questions pertaining to Pentecostalism were groundbreaking in the 1970s and have since become commonplace. The innovative aspect of the present study is not in its attention to Pentecostal churches; ecumenical literature today that fails to do more than acknowledge Pentecostalism is outdated. Rather, the study's approach offered here presupposes that Pentecostal churches will shape ecumenical methodology as all other churches do, and so attention to the ecclesial tradition benefits the wider field of ecumenics.

For the sake of the study's driving question, I also deviate from a common approach in Pentecostal literature on ecumenics. Authors often project a vision of enhanced participation in the ecumenical movement by mobilizing Pentecostal principles for a changed future. Such works border on an essentialist reading of Pentecostalism by appealing to a supposed core of Pentecostal spirituality or to an animating myth of the ecclesial tradition for the sake of identifying the ecumenical "potential" of Pentecostal churches. My study on methods does not attend to potentiality but to present realities, including those where Pentecostal churches have advanced the ecumenical movement and where they have forsaken it. This approach aligns with the claim of Nikos Nissiotis that no church is naturally ecumenical by virtue of its own background or principles, for churches learn the value of and need for unity only through the assistance of other churches.[46] Ecumenism is something that happens between Christian communities.

The selection of a Pentecostal ecumenist delineates options for the inquiry. The studied person would need to have a considerable literary output to assess their understanding of ecclesiology, and the literature would need to reach beyond Pentecostal circles to engage the wider field of ecumenics. The person would need to have an intimate knowledge of their own Pentecostal denomination as well as the expanse of global Pentecostalism. More than having good ideas, the person would need to have engaged in the work of ecumenism beyond the academy to understand the breadth of ecumenical methodology. The ecumenist would need to have decades of experience in the ecumenical movement to track its development to the present day, including a familiarity with the historical development of Pentecostal participation in ecumenism. The person would need to have been engaged in ecumenical work ranging from bilateral dialogues to councils of churches, spiritual ecumenism to local ecumenism, in order to see their interrelation. Ultimately, these decades of experience would need to inform the person's methodological reflection on enduring challenges in the ecumenical movement. Only such a person can offer insight into the ecclesiological questions that this study raises.

16   *Introduction*

LOCUS OF INQUIRY

Enter Cecil Robeck. He is the senior professor of church history and ecumenics at Fuller Theological Seminary in Pasadena, California, and an ordained minister of the Assemblies of God in the United States. He has held leadership positions in ecumenical bodies and commissions since 1985, and his career left an indelible impact on the systems, practices, and values of the ecumenical movement. Former Faith and Order moderator Mary Tanner lists Robeck alongside the likes of John Zizioulas, Geoffrey Wainwright, and Jean-Marie Tillard for their contributions to integrating disparate ecumenical conversations.[47] Veteran Catholic ecumenist Jeffrey Gros names Robeck as a mentor in his service to the ecumenical movement.[48] Brazilian sociologist Gedeon Alencar sees Robeck as a barometer in measuring the climate of Pentecostal ecumenical concern globally.[49] Ghanian statesman Opoku Onyinah venerates Robeck as an apostle of unity for his vision and work.[50] German theologian Wolfgang Vondey positions Robeck as "a dominant voice on ecclesiological and ecumenical issues among Pentecostals."[51] Even Robeck's fellow American historian and collegial critic Harold Hunter admits, "there is no Pentecostal more visible among conciliar ecumenists."[52]

Robeck's ecumenical career began with his contributions to the National Council of the Churches of Christ in the USA from 1985 to 2005 in its Commission on Faith and Order and as co-chair of its dialogue with Pentecostal churches. He has served at various times as a leader or participant of the international bilateral commissions of the Catholic–Pentecostal, Reformed–Pentecostal, and Lutheran–Pentecostal dialogues. In 1989, he was invited as an advisor to the WCC's Faith and Order Commission and has contributed to the Commission in varying capacities since then, in addition to his role as an advisor to the WCC and co-chair of its Joint Consultative Group with Pentecostals. He was present as a Pentecostal voice at the Conference of the Secretaries of Christian World Communions from 1992–2021. He was an architect of the Global Christian Forum and advised the Lausanne Committee for World Evangelization in its relations with the Vatican and Eastern Orthodox churches. He is a founding member of the Christian Unity Commissions of the Pentecostal/Charismatic Churches of North America and the Pentecostal World Fellowship, having been appointed as the Assembly of God's general liaison to Christian Communities in the United States since 2014. Since 1984, all his ecumenical activities have been conducted with the full knowledge, blessing, and support of the national Assemblies of God (AG) general superintendent and Executive Leadership Team, as well as his Southern California District superintendent.[53] He was honored in 2019 for his accomplishments by the National Workshop on Christian Unity, the body

Introduction   17

dedicated to training ecumenical officers for the United States Conference of Catholic Bishops and numerous Protestant denominations.

Robeck's scholarly contributions to ecumenics began as president of the Society for Pentecostal Studies in 1983. Since then, most of his publications have been a result of his participation in bilateral and Faith and Order dialogues at national and international levels. His career has produced more than one hundred published essays on ecumenics, in addition to dozens on Pentecostalism, patristics, and spiritual gifts. He has taught at an evangelical seminary since 1981 and held visiting instructor positions at Pentecostal and Catholic institutions. He is one of the few Pentecostals to have ever served as a professor of ecumenics; most universities with ecumenics chairs would not hire a Pentecostal, and most Pentecostal universities do not have the resources to sustain an ecumenics chair. He is a former board member and president of the North American Academy of Ecumenists, which, at the time, was a closed society to which one was invited based on one's academic contributions to the field. He is heralded as both a scholar and practitioner.

The literary impact of Robeck on ecumenical studies is demonstrated in the following chapters. More narrowly, within the corpus of anglophone Pentecostal literature on ecumenics, it is more difficult to find works that do not cite him than those that do. Nonetheless, no published works are devoted to him. Additionally, though Robeck is often cited as an authoritative source for information on historical developments in the ecumenical movement and on the progress of dialogues, he is seldom engaged as a thinker in his own right. This is likely because he has not provided a systematic account of his thought and career, yet his influence on the field has inspired students and junior colleagues to orient themselves to the field according to his example. Sherilyn Benvenuti and Mariusz Muszczyński wrote their dissertations on Robeck. The American pastor Benvenuti studied Robeck's historical research for his social ethic of racial reconciliation, which ultimately informed Benvenuti's founding of her Pentecostal university's Global Center for Women and Justice.[54] The Polish pastor Muszczyński likewise studied Robeck for the sake of constructing a Pentecostal theology of the religious Christian other, describing the project of *Pasadeńczyk* ("the Pasadenan") Robeck as a work of practical theology.[55] My study appreciatively builds on their research while expanding it by drawing on a wider array of primary source material by Robeck, studying his work within the discipline of systematic theology, and pushing the conversation beyond Pentecostal confessionalism toward the construction of a shared ecumenical ecclesiology.

Robeck should not be seen as representative of Pentecostal ecumenists— chiefly because no one can be, but also because of his frequent critiques of his own ecclesial tradition. Issues of representation shape the present study. The field of ecumenics struggles against a pervasive white normativity and privileging of male and Western voices, and, as noted above, methodological inquiries are attuned to the social conditions of ecumenical work. Additionally, the field of Pentecostal studies resists the predominance of AG narratives due to the denomination's numerical size globally, especially of the AG in the United States, due to the country's political and economic power. Robeck has pushed to address these disparities in ecumenical initiatives, and one can detect from him an arc of awareness over the decades of the need to include a more diverse representation of sources in his own literature. Nonetheless, aside from his Pentecostal confession, he, in his social location, embodies the inequalities of the field of ecumenics. Care is given in this book to oppose these trends by locating Robeck socially, naming how his vantage point shapes his thought, and placing him alongside voices often unheard in the field as equals. To uplift Robeck as a defining narrative of Pentecostal churches would be a disservice to countless other known and unknown Pentecostals who have dedicated their lives to ecumenical work, and it would misconstrue ecumenism as a project of individuals, not communities.[56]

The research question on the ecclesiological basis of ecumenical methodology constrains my use of Robeck. This book does not pretend to offer a comprehensive account of his literature or work. Numerous scholarly interests of his receive no attention here, including his writings on Pentecostal homiletics, leadership, hermeneutics, or missionary history, in addition to his work in ecumenical formation and interfaith dialogue. His understanding of the ecumenical attitude of trust also falls outside of the scope on methods. The present study in systematic theology differs from other viable approaches to Robeck that would bear fruit for the field of ecumenics, whether theological hermeneutics, practical theology, or social psychology. Future scholarship on Robeck would do well to utilize these tools.

Robeck lends himself to the research question in counterintuitive ways. He received graduate academic training neither in ecumenics nor Pentecostal studies, fields which were not afforded to him in his ecclesial circles in the 1970s. Additionally, he is a historian and not a theologian. His treatment of ecclesiological debates sometimes lacks the vocabulary needed to address the nuances of contemporary reflection in ecumenical theology. His essays on ecclesiology rely on biblical and historical theology in dialogue with Pentecostal doctrines on the church, which itself is a field that relies on experience. As a historian, he places events in their social contexts and sequences of changes while interpreting causes and consequences, factors relevant to the study of ecumenical methodology and convergence. He recounts his ecumenical work and speaks of why projects and organizations operate how they do, which also serves an apologetic function. His approach to theological construction in ecclesiology results in the use of the lived experiences of churches, a source previously noted for its central role in theological

Introduction   19

reflection on ecumenical methodology. Between his attention to the experiences of churches and his narratives of ecumenical work, his literature is unrivaled in its methodological insight, whereas most other authors are concerned primarily with doctrinal statements.

The book exists on two levels—analytic in its reading of Robeck's literature as the primary source material and synthetic in its theological understanding of ecumenical methodology. I analyze Robeck's thought according to the two key terms in the research question of ecclesiology and methodology. His ecclesiology is seen principally in his essays on Pentecostal beliefs on the church, and his understanding of methodology is discerned according to the explanations and critiques he makes of ecumenical initiatives. It is important to reiterate here that my study is not on Robeck himself but on methodology, and my argument uses Robeck as primary source material for a discussion that extends beyond him and his Pentecostal tradition. I situate Robeck within larger developments and discussions of the ecumenical movement to show how ecumenical methodology is derived from the shared ecclesiology of churches. When churches—such as Pentecostal ones—differ in the ecclesiology that is shared, different methods are needed. More importantly, by identifying the reasons for changes in methodology that occur in the movement and that Robeck promotes, I demonstrate that ecclesiological convergence occurs through the development of ecumenical methods. When churches—such as Pentecostal ones—find new ways to work toward unity with other churches, they begin to reconcile the differences that divide them.

OUTLINE OF ARGUMENT

I make my argument through the progressive study of Robeck's ecumenical career. The study begins with chapter one on Robeck's ecclesiology, in which I synthesize his ecclesiological principles as they pertain to ecumenism and introduce his ecclesial contexts of the United States and Pentecostalism. I offer three paradigms from his thought that inform his views on ecumenical methodology—the church as a divine initiative, as a historical community, and as the people of God. The goal of the chapter is to articulate an ecclesiology that guides ecumenical methods, not merely validates ecumenical goals. In each subsequent chapter, I dive into different methodological fields of Robeck's work to illustrate the ecclesiological convergence that occurs through the development of shared ecumenical methodologies.

Chapter 2 examines the method of reconciling memories. The method addresses narrative ecclesiology, or the role of communal memory in the perpetuation or healing of church divisions. The historicity of the church includes the reality of social forces within the church's life, which churches

20   *Introduction*

account for in their unitive work. Robeck's research as a historian of the Azusa Street Revival is conducted in light of the racialization of Pentecostal ecclesiastical divisions. His historical work would later inform his contributions to the founding of the Pentecostal/Charismatic Churches of North America, which is the primary framework for intra-Pentecostal ecumenism in the region. The method of reconciling memories contributes to the ability of divided communities to re-narrate their identities so that they can tell their histories in one voice.

The third chapter turns to conciliar ecumenism, one of the most institutional methods of the ecumenical movement. Ecumenical scholarship has identified conciliarity as a constitutive dimension of the church that also informs the means by which churches seek unity. I examine ecumenical methodology according to the counterpoints of Christian World Communions and councils of churches, specifically the WCC. Robeck has been involved with both the Pentecostal World Fellowship and the WCC, giving him insight into how the two forms of conciliarity contrast. The model of interchurch relations is a locus of reflection on the connection between ecumenical methodology and the nature of the church. The method spurs convergence in the church's practices of catholicity and conciliarity.

Chapter 4 looks at the scholarly realm of bilateral dialogue, a common field for ecumenists to study ecclesiological convergence. Here, I do not glean insights from statements made in dialogue reports but from the act of dialogue itself. The practice of discernment in dialogue prompts the development of communal practices and structures of discernment within and between churches. Robeck insists that communication is part of relationships, and so communication is part of the communion that constitutes the church. The method is studied as it is practiced within the international Catholic–Pentecostal, Reformed–Pentecostal, and Lutheran–Pentecostal dialogues to which Robeck contributed.

Next, the fifth chapter studies spiritual ecumenism and the church's reception of its order and charisms from the Spirit. The method of spiritual ecumenism includes more than the practice of common prayer, for the church's charismatic life contributes to its unity only when spiritual gifts are exercised rightly. Robeck's patristics research informs his understanding of ecumenism and the spiritual unity within the Charismatic movement. The ecumenical method of spiritual ecumenism results in ecclesiological convergence when churches order their gifts according to their common apostolic pattern.

Chapter 6 covers the newer method of Christian Forums and the ecclesiological questions it raises. The use of testimonies to promote recognition and reconciliation between Christians relies on the church's own function as a sign and instrument of reconciliation. Robeck was a leading voice in the planning and promotion of the Global Christian Forum, and he played a formative

Introduction 21

role in the method's implementation in his local Southern California Christian Forum. The method results in convergence in the mutual recognition of Christians even when their churches do not yet recognize each other, which prompts further ecumenical work.

In the conclusion, I return to the study's driving question to recount how ecumenical methodology results in ecclesiological convergence. Because methods rely on the ecclesiology shared between participating churches, the churches converge in their ecclesiologies as they develop their shared methods. The chapter summarizes implications for the study of ecumenical methodology that challenge common narratives and rhetoric in the field of ecumenics and that offer guidance for more fruitful lines of inquiry. I also review implications for the doctrine of ecclesiology regarding how ecumenists construct together an ecclesiology that promotes unitive work. I conclude by identifying questions the study raises for the future of methodological reflection on ecumenism.

NOTES

1. World Council of Churches, "Message of the WCC 11th Assembly, 'A Call to Act Together,'" 2022.

2. Holy and Great Council, "Relations of the Orthodox Church with the Rest of the Christian World," 2016, §6.

3. See also Giovanni Cereti around this time. Renzo Bertalot, "Metodologia ecumenica," *Studi Ecumenici* 1, no. 1 (1983): 41–60; Giovanni Cereti, *Ecumenismo: Corso di metodologia ecumenica*, 2nd ed. (Rome: Istituto di Teologia a Distanza, 1991).

4. Kuncheria Pathil, *Models in Ecumenical Dialogue: A Study of the Methodological Development in the Commission on "Faith and Order" of the World Council of Churches* (Bangalore: Dharmaram Publications, 1981), 398.

5. Mary-Anne Plaatjies-Van Huffel, "A Critical Reflection of the Role of 'Context' in Discernment, Decision-Making and Reception," in *Leaning into the Spirit: Ecumenical Perspectives on Discernment and Decision-Making in the Church*, ed. Virginia Miller, David Moxon, and Stephen Pickard, Pathways for Ecumenical and Interreligious Dialogue (Cham: Springer International, 2019), 49–64.

6. Lutheran World Federation International Consultation on Ecumenical Methodology, *Ökumenische Methodologie: Dokumentation und Bericht*, ed. Peder Nørgaard-Højen (Geneva: Lutheran World Federation, 1978).

7. Peder Nørgaard-Højen, *Ökumenisches Engagement und theologisches Erkennen: Beiträge zur ökumenischen Methodologie* (Frankfurt: Peter Lang, 1998).

8. Konrad Raiser, *Ökumene im Übergang: Paradigmenwechsel in der ökumenischen Bewegung?*, Kaiser Taschenbücher 63 (Munich, Germany: Christian Kaiser, 1989); Harding Meyer, *Ökumenische Zielvorstellungen*, Bensheimer Hefte 78, Ökumenische Studienhefte 4 (Göttingen: Vandenhoeck & Ruprecht, 1996), 12.

22 *Introduction*

9. Peter Uche Uzochukwu, *Churches in the Family of God: A Proposal for Catholic Input towards Christian Unity in Africa* (Bloomington, IN: Xlibris, 2012).

10. Aram Keshishian, *Conciliar Fellowship: A Common Goal* (Geneva: WCC Publications, 1992).

11. André Birmelé, *La communion ecclésiale : Progrès œcuméniques et enjeux méthodologiques*, Cogitatio Fidei 218 (Paris: Cerf, 2000), 375, 376.

12. Carlos F. Cardoza-Orlandi, "Caribbean," in *A History of the Ecumenical Movement, Volume 3: 1968-2000*, ed. John Briggs, Mercy Amba Oduyoye, and Georges Tsetsis (Geneva: World Council of Churches, 2004), 532.

13. Jill Hawkey, *Mapping the Oikoumene: A Study of Current Ecumenical Structures and Relationships* (Geneva: World Council of Churches, 2005).

14. World Council of Churches Commission on Faith and Order, *Social and Cultural Factors in Church Divisions*, Faith and Order Paper 40 (Geneva: World Council of Churches, 1951); World Council of Churches Commission on Faith and Order, *What Kind of Unity?*, Faith and Order Paper 69 (Geneva: World Council of Churches, 1974); World Council of Churches Commission on Faith and Order, *Councils, Conciliarity, and a Genuinely Universal Council*, Faith and Order Paper 70 (Geneva: World Council of Churches, 1974); World Council of Churches Commission on Faith and Order, *How Can Unity Be Achieved? Ecumenical Case Studies: Ghana, Korea, Rumania, Switzerland, Uruguay*, Faith and Order Paper 75 (Geneva: World Council of Churches, 1975).

15. Literature does not always differentiate Roman Catholicism within the Catholic Church, so I cannot maintain a consistent distinction in this study. Unless otherwise noted, the designator "Catholic" will refer to the Roman Catholic Church without knowledge of whether other rites are included in the discussion.

16. Paul VI, *Unitatis redintegratio*, 1964; Paul VI, *Lumen gentium*, 1964.

17. John Paul II, *Ut unum sint*, 1995; John Paul II, *Orientale lumen*, 1995.

18. Pontifical Council for Promoting Christian Unity, *Directory for the Application of Principles and Norms on Ecumenism*, 1993; Pontifical Council for Promoting Christian Unity, *The Bishop and Christian Unity: An Ecumenical Vademecum*, 2020.

19. Meyer, *Ökumenische Zielvorstellungen*.

20. Angelo Maffeis, *Il dialogo ecumenico*, Piccola Biblioteca delle Religioni 23 (Brescia, Italy: Queriniana, 2000).

21. Gillian R. Evans, *Method in Ecumenical Theology: The Lessons So Far* (Cambridge: Cambridge University Press, 1996).

22. Pathil, *Models*, 292, 441.

23. Paul Avis, "New Paths in Ecumenical Method," in *Reshaping Ecumenical Theology: The Church Made Whole?* (London: T & T Clark, 2010), 40.

24. Avis, 42, 43.

25. Michael N. Jagessar, *Full Life for All: The Work and Theology of Philip A. Potter. A Historical Survey and Systematic Analysis of Major Themes*, Serie Mission 19 (Zoetermeer, The Netherlands: Boekencentrum, 1997).

26. M. Kurian, *Sarah Chakko: A Voice of Women in the Ecumenical Movement* (Thiruvalla, India: Christhava Sahithya Samithy, 1998).

Introduction   23

27. Radu Bordeianu, *Dumitru Staniloae: An Ecumenical Ecclesiology*, Ecclesiological Investigations 13 (London: T & T Clark, 2011).

28. Michael Kinnamon, *Unity as Prophetic Witness: W. A. Visser 't Hooft and the Shaping of Ecumenical Theology*, Shapers of Ecumenical Theology (Minneapolis, MN: Fortress Press, 2018).

29. Crescencia Cabilao Gabijan, *Dialogue, Light, and Fire: Chiara Lubich and the Spirituality of Unity* (Manila, Philippines: University of Santo Tomas Publishing House, 2017).

30. Lukas Pieper, *Paulos Mar Gregorios: Imaginationen des Ostens im Zeitalter der Ökumene*, Kirche—Konfession—Religion 81 (Göttingen: Vandenhoeck & Ruprecht, 2021).

31. Carlos A. Sintado and Manuel Quintero Pérez, *Pasión y compromiso con el Reino de Dios: El testimonio ecuménico de Emilio Castro* (Buenos Aires: Kairos, 2007).

32. Oluwatomisin Olayinka Oredein, *The Theology of Mercy Amba Oduyoye: Ecumenism, Feminism, and Communal Practice* (Notre Dame, IN: University of Notre Dame Press, 2023).

33. Cardoza-Orlandi, "Caribbean," 532.

34. Anthony A. Akinwale, "Christianity without Memory: An Evaluation of Pentecostalism in Response to Emeka Nwosuh," in *Tradition and Compromises: Essays on the Challenge of Pentecostalism*, ed. Anthony A. Akinwale and Joseph Kenny, Aquinas Day Series 2 (Ibadan, Nigeria: The Michael J. Dempsey Centre for Religious and Social Research, 2004), 122.

35. In keeping with scholarly conventions, I refer to organizations and texts in their original language if the language is Western European; otherwise, I refer to them by their English names and include the original in parenthesis if the original language uses the Latin alphabet.

36. Mathews George Chunakara, *Ecumenism in Asia: Prospects and Challenges* (Tiruvalla, India: Christava Sahitya Samithi, 2014), 61.

37. Gedeon Freire de Alencar, *Ecumenismos & pentecostalismos: A relação entre o pescoço e a guilhotina?* (São Paulo: Editora Recriar, 2018).

38. World Council of Churches Commission on Faith and Order, *An Ecumenical Exercise: The Southern Baptist Convention, the Seven-Day-Adventist Church, the Kimbanguist Church in the Congo, the Pentecostal Movement in Europe*, ed. M.B. Handspicker and Lukas Vischer, Faith and Order Paper 49 (Geneva: World Council of Churches, 1967), 2.

39. *An Ecumenical Exercise*, 45, 46.

40. Connie Ho Yan Au, *Grassroots Unity in the Charismatic Renewal* (Eugene, OR: Wipf & Stock, 2011).

41. May Ling Tan-Chow, *Pentecostal Theology for the Twenty-First Century: Engaging with Multi-Faith Singapore*, Ashgate New Critical Thinking in Religion, Theology, and Biblical Studies (Aldershot, UK: Ashgate Publishing, 2007).

42. Quoted in Michael J. Miller, "God's Ecumenical Co-Pilot," The Catholic World Report, last modified January 16, 2012, https://www.catholicworldreport.com /2012/01/16/gods-ecumenical-co-pilot/.

43. Sébastien Kalombo Kapuku, *Pentecôtismes en République Démocratique du Congo, Tome 1 : Conditions et pertinence de dialogue entre églises protestantes sur la mission aujourd'hui* (Paris: Les Éditions du Panthéon, 2015); Sébastien Kalombo Kapuku, *Pentecôtismes en République Démocratique du Congo, Tome 2 : Propos et pertinence d'une éthique missionnaire* (Paris: Les Éditions du Panthéon, 2018).

44. Hermen Kroesbergen, "Radical Change in Zambia's Christian Ecumenism," *Journal of South African Studies* 44, no. 2 (2018): 331–43.

45. Jelle Creemers, "Local Dialogue as a Means to Ecumenical Reception? The International and Dutch Pentecostal-Catholic Dialogues in Close-Up," *Exchange* 42, no. 4 (2013): 366–84; Jelle Creemers, *Theological Dialogue with Classical Pentecostals: Challenges and Opportunities*, Ecclesiological Investigations 23 (London: T & T Clark, 2015).

46. Nikos A. Nissiotis, "Types and Problems of Ecumenical Dialogue," *The Ecumenical Review* 18, no. 1 (1966): 54.

47. Mary Tanner, "The Relation between Multilateral Dialogues and Their Impact on International Bilateral Dialogues and on Regional Agreements, and the Ways in Which Bilateral and Regional Agreements Impact the Faith and Order Agenda," in *Eighth Forum on Bilateral Dialogues. The Implications of Regional Bilateral Agreements for the International Dialogues of Christian World Communions, John XXIII Centre, Annecy-le-Vieux, France, 14-19 May 2001*, by World Council of Churches Commission on Faith and Order, Faith and Order Paper 190 (Geneva: World Council of Churches, 2002), 46.

48. Jeffrey Gros, "Presidential Address 2012. It Seems Good to the Holy Spirit and to Us: The Ecclesial Vocation of the Pentecostal Scholar," *Pneuma: The Journal of the Society for Pentecostal Studies* 34, no. 2 (2012): 168.

49. Alencar, *Ecumenismos*, 153.

50. Opoku Onyinah, *Apostles and Prophets: The Ministry of Apostles and Prophets throughout the Generations* (Eugene, OR: Wipf and Stock, 2022), 213, 214.

51. Wolfgang Vondey, "Preface," in *Pentecostalism and Christian Unity: Ecumenical Documents and Critical Assessments*, ed. Wolfgang Vondey (Eugene, OR: Pickwick Publications, 2010), x.

52. Harold D. Hunter, "Pentecostal Ecumenical Pioneers: Select Case Studies in Leadership," in *African Pentecostal Missions Maturing: Essays in Honor of Apostle Opoku Onyinah*, ed. Elorm Donkor and Clifton Clarke, African Christian Studies Series 14 (Eugene, OR: Pickwick Publications, 2018), 116.

53. Robeck submitted annual reports on his ecumenical activities to the Executive Leadership Team to keep them updated. The correspondence is held in a collection at the Flower Pentecostal Heritage Center in the national office of the AG in Springfield, Missouri. Cecil M. Robeck, Jr. in discussion with the author, August 16, 2023.

54. Sherilyn Rae Benvenuti, "The Reconstruction of a Pentecostal Social Ethic of Racial Reconciliation: The Work of Cecil M. Robeck, Jr., H. Vinson Synan, and Leonard Lovett" (Ph.D. dissertation, Los Angeles, University of Southern California, 2000).

55. Mariusz Muszczyński, "Ekumenizm Cecila M. Robecka" (Ph.D. dissertation, Opole, Poland, University of Opole, 2022).

56. Cheryl Bridges Johns raises these concerns within the field of Pentecostal ecumenical studies. Cheryl Bridges Johns, "Remodeling Our Ecumenical House," in *Pentecostal Theology and Ecumenical Theology: Interpretations and Intersections,* ed. Peter D. Hocken, Tony L. Richie, and Christopher A. Stephenson, Global Pentecostal and Charismatic Studies 34 (Leiden: Brill, 2019), 131–53.

Chapter 1

Robeck's Ecclesiology amid Ecumenical and Pentecostal Conversations

Ecumenism, whether as a field of inquiry or practice, is ecclesiological. The union of churches raises questions of what the church is called to be and do. Ecumenical discourse on ecclesiology has sought to discern the beliefs, structures, and practices that constitute a united church without attending as much to the process by which the churches reach these constitutive goals. I argue that the doctrine about the church informs how the churches seek unity together. When Christian communities engage in ecumenical work, the means by which they pursue unity are ecclesial acts—deeds of the church that are believed to be in accordance with the church's mission and nature. Whether a proposed ecumenical method is viable depends on how well it is in accord with an understanding of ecclesiology that is shared between the churches in question. Consequently, the task is to discern an ecclesiology that guides ecumenical work and does not merely validate ecumenical goals if the work is to result in convergence.

Such a conception of ecclesiology is necessarily contextual, taking shape according to the relations that exist between particular churches in particular times and places. No attempt will be made here at constructing a comprehensive ecclesiology. Rather, I read Robeck to discern the ecclesiological framework through which he approaches the work of ecumenism. I introduce his context of ecumenism and Pentecostalism in the United States along with his theology. His writings on ecclesiology are informed by developments in ecumenical discourse on the church, chiefly through multilateral Faith and Order dialogue and Pentecostal bilateral dialogues. Literature from these dialogues reveals the convergence reached between churches over the decades. Additionally, these texts should be read as part of larger trends in ecumenism beyond the dialogue table.

28   *Chapter 1*

Though not the focus of this book, Pentecostal engagement in ecumenism has shaped Robeck's ecclesiology. His understandings of ecclesiality and church history are at home within broader Pentecostal thought, even as he challenges it. Prevailing debates and developments within Pentecostal scholarship on the church are often a result of Pentecostal engagement with other church traditions. I periodically reference literature by other Pentecostal authors to elucidate Robeck's work—the sources of his thought, his interlocutors, and the significance of his arguments. The chapter serves as a cursory introduction for the reader unfamiliar with Pentecostal participation in ecumenism.

To limit the scope of the discussion, I address only those ecclesiological topics that Robeck examines in depth. I do not raise themes otherwise important for ecumenical ecclesiology—offices, covenants, eucharist, Israel, Mary, or liturgy, for example. I also do not address certain ecclesiological themes that Robeck examines that have few methodological implications, such as soteriology or homiletics.

Robeck has not offered a systematic outline of his ecclesiology. His doctrine of the church stems from his patristic research, his reading of scripture, and his studies of Pentecostalism. These three are his lenses when he views ecumenical ecclesiology constructively and critically. At the same time, one can see developments in his ecclesiology over the decades that have expanded his thought and brought him in alignment with convergences in ecumenical discourse. To order his thought, I offer a three-tiered framework that acknowledges ecclesiological tensions. The framework is not meant to exhaust his thought but to show the intersection of his ecclesiology with questions active in ecumenics. His ecclesiology can be divided into three principal dimensions: (1) the church is a divine initiative, making God the source of its unity and of its empowerment to pursue unity; (2) the church is a historical community, both an inheritor of Tradition and subject to social forces; (3) the church is the people of God, never existing apart from all its members in communion with each other.

THE CHURCH AS A DIVINE INITIATIVE

In one of his earliest publications, Robeck contends that the church is, "at its very heart, a movement of the Spirit."[1] The church is part of divine economy in the history of salvation. It relies on God for its origins and continuing existence, and so it precedes its members. The existence of the church as a divine initiative will stand in tension with the following section on the church's historicity, yet, for Robeck, the involvement of God in history subordinates the church's historical existence to its origins in God. As the church is a divine initiative, so is its unity. The communion of Christians with God by his Spirit results in the oneness of the church, and this same God sustains the church's work toward unity. For Robeck, the church does not gather for its own purposes but because God calls it together.[2] The act of God calling and sending the church constitutes its apostolic nature, and the continuing reliance of the church on God for its sanctification and mission is seen in the charisms given to it. Both the church's apostolicity and charisms inform the renewal of the Christian community toward unity.

Apostolicity

The church's apostolic origin is one of the four marks of the church, as something that constitutes the Christian community's ecclesiality. The origins of the church do not define it because of the acts of particular men and women in the first century but because of their being sent by the risen Christ. Robeck points to the church's being sent at Pentecost as a defining moment of the Christian community when he says the church bears the character of Pentecost.[3] At Pentecost, the church confesses the lordship of the risen Christ, and the reception of the Spirit sends the church into the world. The Pentecost event serves as a touchstone throughout Robeck's ecclesiology and his understanding of ecumenism. If the church bears the character of the Pentecost event, then studying the event contributes to an understanding of the church. It was at Pentecost that the apostles were formed into a community and empowered to participate in God's mission.

The apostolicity of the Christian community is seen in many of its aspects. Of particular importance for Robeck's ecclesiology is apostolic teaching and experience.[4] He says the teaching of the apostles consists of their memories of Jesus and the continuing guidance of the Spirit after his ascension. These teachings formed the core memory of the Christian community as it was handed down through the generations through inspired scripture and other means, a concept returned to below in the discussion on Tradition.[5] Dialogues and literature in ecumenics often study ecclesiastical offices that preserve the transmission of the apostolic deposit.

Robeck shifts the discussion from apostolic office to apostolic experience. The church preserves the continuity of the apostolic community by participating in the Spirit who formed the community at Pentecost.[6] Robeck sidesteps the significance of offices for ecumenical discussions of apostolicity, but it is meant to circumnavigate the impasse that occurs when churches do not recognize the validity of each other's ministries. More comprehensive theologies of apostolicity are needed for recognition to be reinstated. Additionally, claims of apostolic succession have not prevented schisms between bishops, meaning that succession alone does not exhaust the reality of apostolicity. Ecumenical discourse has too often treated the church's apostolicity

30   *Chapter 1*

as merely a mark of its unity rather than a resource for pursuing unity. For Robeck, if there is any hope in healing schisms, then churches must be able to recognize within each other a continuity with the apostolic community regardless of current ecclesiastical offices.

The ecumenical movement has generated a wealth of reflection on the apostolic faith. Faith and Order produced study documents on the faith as expressed in the apostolic writings of scripture and in the creeds.[7] The patristic era offers insight into the study of apostolicity. Robeck attributes his interest in ecclesiology to his patristics research. He grew in his love for the church through studying how the first Christians handed down the faith over generations and developed liturgical practices that persist to the present day.[8] Though the church's apostolicity is ever present, the church's understanding of it is informed by the church's earliest years.

The contemporary implications of the apostolic faith remain a pressing question for ecumenism because of the divergent ways that churches understand apostolicity. One of Robeck's first forays into dialogue was in the 1980s with the National Council of the Churches of Christ in the USA (NCCUSA), whose Faith and Order Commission sought to contribute to the concurrent discussion within the World Council of Churches (WCC's) Commission about the apostolic faith.[9] Under the leadership of Jeffrey Gros and Robeck as co-chairs, the NCCUSA Commission organized a consultation with Pentecostals and scholars of Pentecostalism. The consultation was the last dialogue to include the participation of South African "Mr. Pentecost" David du Plessis, known for being a founder of the Pentecostal World Conference, consort of the WCC, midwife of the Charismatic renewal, initiator of the first international Pentecostal bilateral dialogue, and the lone Pentecostal observer at the Second Vatican Council.

Robeck opens his consultation paper and his first-ever published essay on ecumenics with the assertion, "The Pentecostal Movement began in this country with a basic commitment to the Apostolic Faith, and a fundamental ecumenical optimism."[10] Early Pentecostals often used the moniker "Apostolic" to describe their community rather than "Pentecostal," believing that they were returning to apostolic sources. He argues alongside the first generation of American Pentecostals that the church's apostolicity consists—not only in its doctrine, order, and communal life—but in the indwelling of the Spirit in these other elements.[11] It was the Spirit's work that inaugurated the church at Pentecost, just as it is the Spirit's work that is discerned when churches recognize the apostolic faith in each other. Pentecostalism's theology of apostolicity is why the Faith and Order Commission consulted Pentecostal churches in their study, paving the way for future Pentecostal participation in multilateral dialogue. The larger Faith and Order discussion on the apostolic faith shaped the trajectory of Robeck's thought regarding the relationship between apostolicity, discernment, and spiritual ecumenism, as seen in the map of texts in figure 1.1.

Part of the church's apostolicity is its oneness. Robeck uses the biblical image of the church as the Body of Christ in his writings to underscore "the depth of the apostolic concern for unity."[12] Though the ecumenical movement

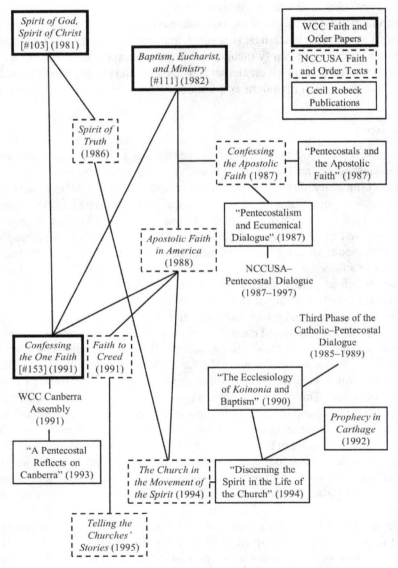

Figure 1.1 The Genesis of Robeck's Ecumenical Thought. *Source*: By the author.

32   *Chapter 1*

is a product of the twentieth century, the pursuit of church union is not a modern invention but dates to the earliest days of Christianity. It arises from the apostolic kerygma, for it bears witness to the church's being sent by the risen Christ in the power of the Spirit. Larger debates on the apostolic nature of the church detail the teachings, structures, and practices that constitute apostolicity, yet it is sufficient to note here that such elements have unitive implications. For Robeck, the church does not safeguard its unity by conforming to apostolic marks as checkboxes to be confirmed. Rather, churches believe that God gave particular teachings, structures, and practices to the Christian community to preserve the unity inaugurated among the apostles at Pentecost. To compromise these God-given elements of the church is to abandon the means by which the church maintains communion.

Charisms

The presence of God in the church is the starting point for any theological understanding of the Christian community. Gifts of divine grace are given to the community throughout its ministry and structure. Robeck defines a charism as "a manifestation of divine grace, a gift bestowed irrespective of merit or spiritual maturity . . . by the Triune God to individuals to enhance the life, worship, and service of the people of God."[13] Charisms are more than the spontaneous or dramatic manifestations of spiritual power attributed to mystics or saints; they are the numerous ways the Spirit of Christ is at work in the church to guide, comfort, and admonish. Charisms in the life of the church are the outworking of divine grace.[14]

The charismatic nature of the church consists in the transformational encounter between God and creation. Because charisms are part of the divine economy, they bear a Trinitarian structure. Robeck explains charisms by citing John 14–16, where the Son asks the Father to send the Spirit to believers. The Spirit guides Christians into truth and glorifies Jesus through divine works of grace. The charismatic nature of the church is a consequence of divine economy,[15] and the continuing role of charisms in the church's mission testifies to the unchanging nature of the Son.[16] Christ, who sent his apostles, sends the church today in the same power and with the same gospel. Charisms are given to the church to preserve its apostolic nature. The church's worship and ministry are ordered to permit the functioning of diverse works of grace, for it is through such an encounter with God that people are converted and sanctified.[17]

The experiential or visible nature of charisms in the life of the church testifies to the presence of the Spirit in its ministry. Robeck looks to the biblical witness when advocating for a "sacramental"[18] understanding of charisms. The early church expected the Spirit's work to be a normative dynamic of liturgical settings and ecclesiastical order. Whether these charisms were of a spontaneous or structural nature, they communicated divine grace to believers and permitted a form of participation within the divine life. Robeck contends that the church's ability to experience the ongoing ministry of the Spirit "points to the spiritual power that could help to unite us."[19] Charisms nourish the Christian community by drawing from the same divine source from which the church receives its unity. The charismatic nature of the church results from the presence of God within the church, and so charisms are part of the ecclesial mark of holiness.

Robeck's understanding of the church's holiness stems from Pentecostalism's inheritance of the American Holiness tradition. Originating in the nineteenth century, the Holiness movement (or "Sanctified church") inspired a greater devotion to piety and personal reform among Methodist and Baptist churches in the United States. The movement was a reaction against a perceived lapse in discipleship in many churches. Its vision for personal and ecclesial holiness stems from John Wesley, who sought to recover the Eastern patristic ascetic tradition for the English church of his day. Radical Holiness groups expanded the retrieval of patristic understandings of holiness by also retrieving patristic charismatic experience. It was believed that the church is called to and empowered for holy living through the works of grace it receives from God. Robeck alludes to the historic origins of Pentecostalism from the Holiness tradition when he describes the restoration of charisms within the church's ministry.[20]

Charisms are proclamations or manifestations of the gospel within the ministry of the church and so have ecclesiological significance. The grace given to offices and communicated through sacraments is a concern for ecumenical discussions of ecclesiology, though it is not a common topic in Robeck's literature. He alludes to 1 Corinthians 12 when describing the function of charisms and offices in church order. The Body of Christ includes many parts who serve different purposes but who all contribute to the upbuilding of the Body. Robeck's ecclesiology here spotlights the communal dimension of the church. The Spirit is not given to an abstract whole but to individual believers who constitute the church, and he is quick to add that the church precedes its members.[21] The sending of the Spirit to the church determines the functions of its members in community.

Robeck's thought here is a result of his Pentecostal upbringing, but it is also a consequence of his research as a patristics scholar. Much of his career has been spent studying the reciprocal development of pneumatology and ecclesiology in ante-Nicene North Africa. The second and third centuries were a crucible for the formulation of doctrine and ecclesial practices that still shape today's church. He studies this period to understand the relationship between the development of ecclesiastical order and the operations of charisms.[22] In patristic texts on church offices and the holiness of the church, charisms stand prominent in the church "like a diamond against a black backdrop."[23] The Spirit guides believers into truth through works of grace that edify the community, requiring practices of discernment. Robeck's theology of discernment derives from his patristics studies. The church as a whole discerns truth together to know how to live faithfully according to the Spirit's leading, a principle that will be important for the later chapter on dialogue. God sustains the church through the continuing operation of charisms throughout its ministry.

Gifts of grace also aid the sending of the church by God in mission. Robeck explains that the Spirit empowers the participation of all for ministry within and outside the church.[24] Whether in worship, evangelism, edification, or service, charisms accompany the life of the church. The charismatic nature of the church's mission is a recurring theme in bilateral dialogues with Pentecostal participation. Robeck specifically points to the report of the third round of dialogue with the World Communion of Reformed Churches, where mission was described as "an all-encompassing life ministry."[25] The report goes on to affirm that signs and wonders accompany mission.[26] Insofar as the church's ministry participates in the ongoing ministry of Christ,[27] charisms are part of the synergistic nature of mission. Any and all acts of the church rely on God's prior work, even as the church participates in this work.

Because charisms are given to the church for its mission, and ecumenism is part of the church's mission, it follows that charisms support ecumenical work. The diversity of grace gifts given to the church contributes to its functioning as a united whole. Robeck cites Pauline's theology of charisms when he notes the frequency of Paul's discussion of grace gifts within passages on the church. Three of the primary passages in the New Testament that discuss charisms are Pauline texts on the Body of Christ (Rom. 12:4-8; 1 Cor. 12:4-31; Eph. 4:1-16).[28] For Paul, God's manifest grace in the church for its upbuilding and unity is seen in the charisms given to it. A biblical theology of the church's charismatic nature goes hand in hand with a biblical theology of the church's unity. The unity of the Body of Christ depends on its members acknowledging their need for each other and on their working together. Robeck contends that the bestowal of the Spirit anticipates and enables the recognition of the Spirit's presence in the people of God.[29] He argues that charismatic ministry prompted the formation of the international Catholic–Pentecostal dialogue, including its sixth phase on spiritual gifts.[30] The ecumenical task and goal of recognition is predicated on the proper operation of grace gifts within Christian communities.

Ecumenism belongs to the charismatic nature of the Body of Christ. Robeck goes so far as to contend that ecumenical leadership requires

Robeck's Ecclesiology 35

"theological competence, holiness in life, and charismatic manifestations."[31] The work of overcoming divisions relies on God's supervening gifts of grace in the life of the church. In the same way that the ministry of the church is a result of God's active presence, so the pursuit of unity is a consequence of God's reconciling the world to himself. Gifts of grace renew the Christian community as it is sent into the world.

Renewal

The ecumenical movement has been described as a renewal movement.[32] The principle of renewal is a synthesis of the church's apostolicity and charismatic nature. Desired changes in the church rely on God for guidance and empowerment, and the changes embolden the church to be sent in mission. The ecumenical movement calls churches to a greater depth of devotion to the gospel and rekindles passion for witness. The renewal of communities is directed toward a greater measure of unity between them. Consequently, aspirations of renewal are not incidental to discussions of ecclesiology in systematic theology. To strive for renewal is to argue that churches not only can be but also must be renewed, yet such an argument could betray the notion that the church is a divine initiative. If God founded the church, but the church needs renewal, were God's acts insufficient to sustain it?

Robeck's ecclesiology revolves around the notion that the Spirit indwells the church. He states that "the work of the Spirit moves from the pages of Scripture into the ongoing life of the whole church."[33] The reality of charisms within the church's life evidences the need for renewal; otherwise, the Spirit's indwelling would have no consequence for the church. On the other hand, the direction of the Spirit's work does not move the church away from its origin but toward it. Robeck equates renewal with the concept of *aggiornamento* popularized in Catholic thought during the Second Vatican Council.[34] The proverbial "opening of the windows" of the church opens the church to receiving new winds of the Spirit. It should be remembered, nonetheless, that many of the liturgical reforms of the Council sought to recover ancient practices for the modern church as an act of *ressourcement*. There was a recognition that contemporary churches required change in order to bear witness to an ancient faith. Robeck explains that the preservation of apostolicity requires constructive and creative work, not mere repetition.[35] Adherence to the apostolic faith such that it enlivens the church and its members function as Robeck's understanding of renewal. Churches are ever called to discern how to live the faith in their present times and places. This is a bolder claim than saying churches are capable of being renewed, for, if a church never changes, it theoretically betrays its apostolic nature. Renewal, for Robeck, is at the heart of an apostolic ecclesiology.

36   Chapter 1

Talk of renewal often coincides with talk of revival, a concept more at home in Pentecostal than ecumenical discourse. Robeck understands revival as an event within the church's life that foregrounds mission.[36] It is an event that evidences the Spirit's work through charisms, resulting in the assurance of faith, healing of ailments, dedication to holiness, empowerment for witness, and upbuilding of community. Revival contributes to ecclesial renewal, but Robeck tempers some Pentecostal views on revival when he says that it is not normative.[37] The call to renewal entails periodic attention to the church's vitality, though revival is not a goal to be sought. His thought here prevents a possible conflict with ecclesiologies from non-revivalistic traditions. Revivalistic discourse, for Robeck, functions as a self-corrective to renew elements of ecclesial life rather than as a rejection of other communities as apostate. The ecclesiological concept of renewal presumes the reality of continuity in the transmission of the apostolic deposit within the community of faith; otherwise, the community would be incapable of renewal.

Robeck's ecclesiological discussions of renewal occur in his literature on the Charismatic movement. Charismatic renewal serves as a source of unity and conflict between churches, generating reflection on spiritual ecumenism. Scholarship on the Charismatic movement speaks of it as a new, innovative, forward-looking phenomenon. Pentecostals, however, assert that Charismatic renewal is worthwhile because it recovers ancient sources of the faith. Robeck argues that the driving principle of the Charismatic movement is that "ancient apostolic faith gains meaning only when it is linked to ongoing apostolic life."[38] The recovery of teaching and praxis on the charismatic nature of the church gives rise to apostolic experience, ensuring the vitality and unity of the Christian community. Because no dimension of the church exists apart from divine grace, Charismatic renewal is meant to touch the whole church. Renewed attention to Spirit baptism within ecclesial life highlights the communal dimension of the experience because it is not intended for a select few but for all.[39] For Robeck, Charismatic spirituality is normative insofar as it is apostolic, and so the promotion of this spirituality constitutes ecclesial renewal.

Pentecostal discourse on ecclesial renewal can appear to be a critique of other traditions. Admittedly, it can appear polemical because often it is polemical. At the same time, however, such vocabulary has become commonplace in ecumenical theologies of the church. The introduction to *The Church: Towards a Common Vision* (*TCTCV*) identifies renewal as the primary objective of the Faith and Order Commission in sending the document to the churches for study. The Commission hopes the convergence document will challenge churches to live the ecclesial life more fully, to recover ecclesial aspects once forgotten, and to strengthen Christian communities.[40] The ecumenical practice of receiving texts presumes an ecclesiology of renewal.

Additionally, all three facets of renewal are seen in Robeck's ecclesiology. The church's reliance on God's gifts of grace strengthens the community for its divine calling to unity. Similarly, the church is called to recover forgotten aspects of its life to return to its apostolic origins and faith. Finally, the church, through pursuing unity, is challenged to become itself more fully. In Robeck's thought, it is because the church is a divine initiative that it must always rely on God to live the ecclesial life, implying the possibility of change within the church.

THE CHURCH AS A HISTORICAL COMMUNITY

After the apostles, the church grew as part of salvation history. Ecclesiology, perhaps more than most other fields of systematic theology, is concerned with history because its subject matter is physical. Ecumenists attend to the lived dimension of the church because it determines the extent to which they can rightly say whether churches are united. Visible unity is requisitely historical. Not only a sociological discussion, historicity is also an ecclesiological concern. Robeck pushes against ethereal imaginings of the church when he argues that the true church is not invisible.[41] Because churches are divided against and grow apart from each other, theologians cannot speak as though the causes of divisions have no bearing on a theology of the church. The church's Tradition, historicity, and restoration all impact ecclesiology and, subsequently, ecumenical methodology.

Tradition

The existence of the church in history raises questions of Tradition—the faithfulness of the church to the gospel under the Spirit's guidance across time. Robeck refers to Tradition as a "tool"—not in a utilitarian sense but in the sense that it is given to benefit the church. He looks to 1 Corinthians 15:3-11 for the value of Tradition. In the passage, Paul speaks of his testifying to the Corinthian church of the risen Christ. The early church's belief in the gospel was dependent upon their receiving the testimony of those, such as Paul, to whom Christ appeared. Robeck explains that Paul understood himself as part of a line of transmission of a gospel message rooted in scripture (Old Testament prophecies of the Messiah) and experience (revelation on the road to Emmaus).[42] The early church was a product of apostolic testimony, the seed of the church's Tradition.

Robeck also takes a narrative approach when explaining Tradition. He describes it as the transmission of apostolic teaching or the apostles' testimonies of Jesus. The apostolic witness within the early church formed the

38   *Chapter 1*

collective memory of the Christian community, which was then handed down to successive generations. As the apostles told stories of Jesus and his teachings, they formed the church around the emergent Tradition. Part of this apostolic witness is recorded in scripture. The faith that the apostles and prophets handed down serves as the foundation of the church (Eph. 2:20-21). Robeck gives an image that depicts the church's living into the heritage of Tradition: Christians across time and space congregating at the feet of the apostles as they tell stories about Jesus. Tradition thereby serves a unifying function. By gathering around the apostolic witness, believers gather around the collective memory of Christ, resulting in the church of today belonging to the same community that has persisted since Pentecost.[43] The Tradition of the apostles, for Robeck, offers boundaries for the Christian community while also pointing to Jesus and the gospel.[44]

Tradition is diachronic. Though it is diverse, it is meant to serve as a consistent thread of the church throughout time. Robeck speaks of Tradition as a stabilizing element of Christian theologizing. The church's confession is not expressed apart from other Christian communities, and so the task of theologizing must not be done in isolation from the whole church. This assertion will be of particular importance for the later discussion on the church's catholicity and the chapter on dialogue. As it concerns Tradition, however, Robeck stresses the need for attending to the historical development of doctrine. Contemporary theologizing—especially within ecumenical discourse—must not seek to bypass the foundations that previous generations laid for the church.[45] Additionally, Tradition preserves the continuity of the church through worship. As Robeck explains,

> Tradition is important, because it allows those who have paved the way for us, those who have brought us to faith and nurtured us in the faith, to continue to enter into our corporate worship with us. Tradition values the experience of worship that those who have gone on before us, discovered and held sacred in their quest for God. What was good for them, we often find, is also good for us.[46]

He does not spell out a liturgical theology of Tradition, but it is noteworthy that the continuity of Tradition is more than the object and content of faith. It is also the practices of the church that preserve communal bonds across time.

Robeck's statements regarding the value of Tradition for the contemporary church and ecumenism might be surprising when the reader remembers his ecclesial affiliation. Pentecostals are hardly known for their theology of Tradition, even flaunting their disdain for anything old. If God calls the church to renewal, does not new wine require new wineskins? Robeck acknowledges that Pentecostals have a "love–hate relationship" with history and Tradition.[47] As far as Robeck is concerned, his theology of Tradition is a product of his patristics

Robeck's Ecclesiology   39

research and his dialogue with Catholics. His studies on ante-Nicene North Africa examine the relation between Tradition and revelatory experiences. The early church tested claims of revelation according to their consistency with the church's received teaching.[48] A doctrine of Tradition developed to offer stability to the church through facilitating communal meaning of symbols, ideas, and texts.[49] Tradition became a unifying force for the church as it faced doctrinal controversies and as it diversified across cultures. Because churches share a common Tradition across time and space, no church should act independently.

Robeck also acknowledges that, as a Pentecostal, he is indebted to other ecclesial traditions for passing down the faith through the centuries.[50] Had it not been for Orthodox, Catholic, and Protestant traditions, Pentecostalism today would not exist. His theology of Tradition permits him to see other churches as sharing the apostolic faith and, therefore, as viable sources of insight into the faith. He cites *Dei verbum* for its image of Tradition as the extension of the Spirit's revelation over time beyond the pages of scripture. The conciliar document describes how Tradition advanced (*proficit*) in the church through time under the leading of the Spirit as believers grew in their understanding of the apostolic message.[51] The concurrent Faith and Order study on *Tradition and Traditions* influenced *Dei verbum*, where it was affirmed that the work of the Spirit makes Christ present in the historical transmission of the apostolic deposit.[52] The study acknowledged the need for reflection on Tradition in light of the entrance of Orthodox and Pentecostal churches into the WCC at the 1961 New Delhi Assembly,[53] but the subject would lay dormant until the recent Faith and Order study on *Sources of Authority*.

Though Tradition is meant to guide and unite the church, disagreement exists over which doctrines and practices belong to the catholic Tradition. Robeck acknowledges the temptation to sanitize history to comport with authorized narratives, resulting in a revisionist account meant to justify the current views of Christian communities.[54] Consequently, he wonders whether appeals to Tradition can be attempts to maintain a status quo rather than attempts to reach a common understanding of the faith.[55] Nonetheless, churches in the ecumenical movement commit themselves to discerning how best to inhabit their received Tradition together. The goal of ecumenism is not to contrive new teachings or establish a new church but to be faithful to the teachings and church of the apostles, a task that requires attending to the transmission of the faith through history.

Historicity

Robeck's research as a historian prevents the abstraction of the church away from its existence as a living, changing community. The ability for churches

40   *Chapter 1*

to change contrasts with the previous discussion on Tradition, yet the existence of change across time can hardly be denied. Any credible theology of the church and Tradition must account for how churches preserve the faith handed down to them while living the faith differently from previous generations. The Faith and Order study on Tradition was a response to the growing recognition in ecumenical dialogue that conflicting doctrinal formulations are historically conditioned.[56] Robeck draws on historical theology when he describes the church and the methods that churches ought to use when pursuing unity together. His work as an academician and practitioner is intended to benefit real communities, and his studies of these communities inform his ecclesiology.

The history of the church is kept alive through communal memory. Robeck is sensitive to the factors that influence how communities tell their stories. The events that cause church splits embitter communities toward each other, hindering reconciliatory efforts. When churches pass on stories of these events, they hand down fears and misperceptions of other communities with each generation. Even when memories of events become distorted over time, the divisions that the events caused remain.[57] He argues that ecumenical work requires historical research to overcome divisions because it gives insight into how the divisions came about and how churches came to receive their present practices and beliefs. In this way, historical narratives can serve unitive efforts.[58] Churches are united by their shared history when they recall common periods of time or revere the same saints.

The history of the church is the constructed narratives of communities and the "non-doctrinal" dimensions of ecclesial life, and so the historicity of the church encompasses the social causes of divisions. Robeck laments that, while ecumenists define ecumenism within doctrinal or experiential paradigms, other factors often hold more sway. Ethnic and racial tensions can result in schism within churches or further divide estranged communities. Alliances to garner political power can position churches with or against each other. Even when such changes are not intentional, church traditions can drift away from each other due to independent developments that the course of history within societies causes. Social forces shape churches, thereby shaping how churches relate to each other.[59] For example, decolonial movements in early twentieth-century China coincided with the postdenominational ideals of Chinese Christianity, hastening the renunciation of ties with foreign ecclesiastical bodies; the reforms under the People's Republic of China would later determine how registered and unregistered churches interact. Geopolitical changes shaped ecclesiastical relations.

Robeck notes that a similar process occurred when American Pentecostalism negotiated its place within the changing ecclesiastical landscape of the twentieth century. Ecumenical organizations were increasingly associated

Robeck's Ecclesiology 41

with social reform movements inspired by modern thought and so came to be seen as "liberal."[60] Consequently, the vocabulary and practices of American ecumenism were sometimes defined more by political rather than confessional ideology. Pentecostals established ecclesiastical ties with churches that eschewed some of these modernist reforms and so came to be seen as anti-ecumenical. Political and social developments within the culture determined how churches understood themselves relative to other churches.

The historicity of Christian communities contributes to the construction of denominational narratives and identities. Narratives define churches and how they interact with other churches. Robeck's engagement with ecclesial narratives is rooted in his research on the Los Angeles Azusa Street Revival, which serves as the ur-myth of American Pentecostalism. The turn-of-the-twentieth-century religious revival was a catalyst of the global expansion of rhizomatic relationships that constitute global Pentecostalism. Robeck studies the revival for the way it refracts the historical development of American Pentecostalism, even as he complicates prevailing narratives on the revival.[61] He studies both the event and how others have constructed narratives around it. His historical research is part of his larger concern of ecclesiastical and racial reconciliation, for he is aware that the ways churches tell their stories affect the churches' relations with each other.

The historicity of the church holds ecclesiological and ecumenical importance. When Christian theologians speak of the church, they speak of an entity that exists amid constant change. The pursuit of church unity, consequently, occurs within sociopolitical contexts that aid and impair the work. Ecumenists do not acknowledge this ecclesial dynamic begrudgingly. In fact, they celebrate it. The earliest days of the ecumenical movement championed the cause of church union because ecumenists believed that it was bound up with the reconciliation of humanity. If the church were not part of the world, then the church could not impact the world. For Robeck, the ecumenical calling of repentance and reconciliation requires confronting the historical causes of divisions, not only doctrinal disagreements. Part of the goal of a united church is the sharing of a common narrative, or what he calls the ability to speak in one voice about divisive episodes of church history.[62] The work of overcoming divisions necessitates telling history well.[63] Ecumenism occurs in history even as it seeks to live faithfully according to the church's origins.

Restoration

There is a sense in ecumenical literature that the churches, by seeking to reverse divisions, are seeking to return to an earlier era of church history. It is debated which era is desirable, and the debate often relies on mythic accounts of history, yet ecumenism's historical consciousness informs its future vision.

Robeck's ecclesial tradition of Pentecostalism has spoken of this dynamic as the act of restoring the church. American Pentecostalism was influenced by the Stone-Campbell Movement and Landmarkism, which sought to repristinate the church in its confession, liturgy, and order. Restorationist movements naturally conflict with other church traditions that are portrayed as corrupted. Moreover, the desire to return to an earlier era seems to contradict the two previous ecclesiological themes of Tradition and historicity. If the church needs to return to its apostolic origins, then the Spirit failed to safeguard the apostolic faith as it was handed down through the generations. On the other hand, if churches can skip over centuries of history to return to apostolic origins, then churches are not historical communities shaped by the broader social forces amid which they live. How can ecumenists seek to return to an earlier era of the church without denying these two principles of ecclesiology?

Robeck acknowledges that restorationism does not always aid ecumenism. He notes that restorationist ideas prevent many churches from engaging others seen as deviating from the Christian faith.[64] Nonetheless, a desire to return to the early church need not exclude other communities. The apostolic witness to the faith includes a spirituality that renews and preserves the church for its calling.[65] Ecumenists seek to cultivate this early spirituality as a way to promote unity. As mentioned previously, Robeck turns to the Pentecost event in his ecclesiological reflection, for the church today seeks its strength, purpose, and fellowship from this early font.[66] He argues that the community formed at Pentecost was marked by a congruity between the church's nature and its visible form. Christians believed the church to be one because they experienced it as such. The call to return to this primordial unity of the church requires personal renewal and holiness.[67]

The ecclesiological concept of restoration builds on and clarifies the earlier discussion of renewal. Both restoration and renewal imply change within the church that accords with a divine purpose, and both are seen as results of God's work in the church. However, without the guiding principle of restoration, renewal could be used to describe any advocated change that is claimed to be beneficial. Such changes, nonetheless, can diverge from each other and cause even further division in the name of renewal. Not every new thing in the church accords with Tradition. Restoration, on the other hand, roots ecclesial change within the church's historical origins. Efforts of renewal are good insofar as they return the church to its apostolic font. Restorationism offers direction for divided communities as they seek renewal together by pointing to their common origins.

Eschatology bookends restoration. The church is not backward looking by focusing on the apostles to the detriment of its anticipation of the future. The ecumenical movement advances toward a greater level of unity in light of the church's expected unity after the resurrection, which is why Robeck says ecumenical work has "eschatological overtones." The act of returning to a united church accompanies a future vision that pulls the church forward.[68] His ecclesiology holds a tension between seeing the church as existing amid historical forces while being freed from them by the work of God in history. To "restore" the church, then, is to renew the church such that it can faithfully transmit the faith in new historical contexts. In a restorationist understanding, the church returns to its apostolic sources for the sake of pursuing a future unity.

While the language of restorationism might seem alien to many churches, restorationist goals are commonplace in ecumenism. For example, discussions between the Anglican and Eastern Orthodox Communions raise questions of the papacy. Though neither church is in communion with the bishop of Rome, they do not deny the validity of the papacy's claim to a form of primacy, which they see as dating back to apostolic tradition and being affirmed in the canons of the Ecumenical Councils. However, they view certain changes that have occurred over the centuries as a corruption of the papal office. In a sense, they are seeking to "restore" the office to what it was in the early church—renewing an ecclesiastical structure according to an apostolic pattern. Acts of dialogue and ecclesiastical reform are the means by which they believe God is uniting the church, and part of uniting the church is the return to an era before particular causes of division. Insofar as ecumenists believe that God is at work today in returning the church to an apostolic pattern that it had in some way betrayed previously in history, the ecumenical movement is a restorationist movement.

The church exists in a dialectic of continuity and change. Ecumenists, in seeking to remain faithful to Tradition, discern the practices and doctrines that ensure that the church remains part of the community the apostles founded. Insofar as ecumenical methods are acts of the church that support its unity, they must remain faithful to apostolic Tradition no matter how new the methods are. Ecumenical discussion of apostolic practice naturally turns to communal practice.

THE CHURCH AS THE PEOPLE OF GOD

The church is more than its members, but it never exists apart from them. People teach and believe the church's doctrine, administer and receive the church's sacraments, and proclaim and live the church's faith. Ecumenism is the pursuit of the union of ecclesiastical institutions and individual Christians. For Robeck, ecumenical work should prioritize the interpersonal nature of the church's life. Ecumenists are adamant that the church's unity, if it is to bear

44   *Chapter 1*

witness to Christ in the world, must be visible. Robeck maintains that the materiality of the church is in its people. Believers are the starting point for any visible or physical understanding of ecclesiology.[69] If the church is a fellowship of diverse persons, then ecumenism works to reconcile these persons into a diverse fellowship.

Koinonia

The significance of communion ecclesiology for ecumenism can hardly be overstated. The ecclesiological paradigm has offered a common vocabulary for ecumenists as they speak of the goals of their work, rooting the church's oneness within the divine life. The ecclesial mark of oneness, similar to the other three marks, describes a way in which the church is to reflect God, where the fellowship between believers is patterned after the fellowship between the divine Persons. For Robeck, koinonia is the communion between persons that is characterized by love and openness. The quality of love is the source for all other attitudes and actions by which a group of people can be spoken of as united. Koinonia (used hereafter synonymously with communion) is a dynamic communicated to the church through members' participation in the Spirit of God. The koinonia that believers enjoy with God is also shared between believers, including those who are departed.[70] It is a result of God's presence in the church and of the church's participation in the sending and returning of divine Persons. Because of this, koinonia is "dynamic, action-oriented, [and] charismatic."[71]

Robeck's understanding of koinonia is a product of his ecumenical work. He cites *Unitatis redintegratio* for its notion that a real, yet imperfect, communion exists between divided Christians by virtue of their common partaking in Christ through baptism.[72] This concept fed into the third phase of the Catholic–Pentecostal dialogue on koinonia, where it was recognized that the koinonia between the two communities obliges them to overcome their divisions.[73] As mentioned before, ecumenists do not seek to fabricate communion but to help churches live into a communion that already exists.

The church functions as a communion because of its order. Though the exact functions of offices change over time, Robeck sees ecclesiastical order as something that God causes and, therefore, as a result of the church's charismatic nature. The diversity of charisms and offices gives shape to communal life. For Robeck, the charismatic dimension of the church serves as the theological launch point for other discussions of diversity and order.[74] Other questions of diversity raised in ecumenical discourse are often rooted in anthropological or sociological differentiations—gender, ability, culture, race, class, or similar. Biblical images on diverse fellowship in the church, however, begin with charisms (1 Cor. 12–14). Gifts of grace operating within ecclesial offices and practices structure other forms of diversity to permit a visible form of koinonia. Charisms result from God's presence in the church and are given to order the community for fellowship; said conversely, charisms must be ordered so they can foster fellowship.[75] Social divisions in the church happen when the church does not properly exercise its charisms. Where gifts and ministries of grace are exercised rightly, other forms of diversity are preserved in fellowship. For Robeck, koinonia is a gift of grace for the church that the church must safeguard.

Communal practices safeguard communion. Robeck contends that, because koinonia is dependent on love, and love is shown through acts, so koinonia ought to be visible.[76] Such acts are illustrated in the Pentecost narrative. The formation of the new Christian community prompted believers to pray, share, and grow together (Acts 2:42-47).[77] Though Robeck does not often speak of sacraments, he says they are tangible expressions of believers being brought together into one Body.[78] He also acknowledges that, though congregations are linked by the common indwelling of the Spirit, they are linked also by human leadership. The apostles led their communities and maintained channels of communication with other regions for matters that arose, as seen in the Council of Jerusalem (Acts 15) and the preservation of New Testament texts. He adds that "any faithful reading of early Christian history" acknowledges that a line of succession extended from the apostles to the leaders of the early church for the sake of preserving the unity and well-being of Christian communities, as figures such as Irenaeus and Cyprian attest.[79] Robeck does not endorse a particular theology of contemporary apostolic succession, but he affirms the need for routinized practices between communities to ensure they preserve a living, visible koinonia across time and space.

For Robeck, one of the foremost renewal efforts that has promoted koinonia in the contemporary church is the Charismatic movement. Seldom in the history of the church has a spiritual movement dissipated across so many theologically and culturally diverse communities. He argues that, alongside an increased devotion to evangelism and social concerns, unity is a product of Charismatic renewal.[80] The spirituality of the movement trains believers in a common understanding of the faith and brings together people from churches who otherwise would have had no contact. He explains that the movement creates new commonalities and communities where previously there had been conflict or avoidance. To demonstrate the impact of the Charismatic movement, he cites a document of the Lutheran–Roman Catholic Commission on Unity that speaks of the relations between the two traditions globally.[81] The Commission refers to Charismatic renewal as offering "new ecumenical opportunities" and challenges between Lutherans and Catholics.[82] The unitive dimension of the Charismatic movement will be returned to in the chapter on

46 Chapter 1

spiritual ecumenism, yet it is here worth observing that, for Robeck, Charismatic spirituality is ecclesiologically significant because it concerns the koinonia between Christians.

Communion describes the impetus and goals of ecumenism. Because believers share in the fellowship of the Spirit, they can pursue a visible form of fellowship. The work of ecumenists discerns the necessary structures, practices, and values that manifest the church's God-given koinonia. Ecumenical methodology, therefore, concerns these structures, practices, and values to promote fellowship between divided churches. The methods that ecumenists employ, if they foster communion, are not foreign to the nature of the church. Rather, they are part of what constitutes the church's fellowship, and so they are defining markers of ecclesiality. Without practices that hold together a diverse fellowship, there is no church.

Diversity

The principle of unity implies that there is a plurality of entities being united. Additionally, the principle of diversity implies a singularity within which a plurality of entities coexists. Unity and diversity, therefore, do not stand in tension but are complementary dynamics that must occur simultaneously. Ecclesiological discussions of diversity often turn to the biblical image of the Body of Christ. Believers are united under the headship of Christ, and they work together with their diverse giftings from the Spirit. Robeck's historical approach to ecclesiology foregrounds the plurality of church practices and expressions that have existed. For example, he presented a paper with Jerry Sandidge on water baptism for the third phase of the Catholic–Pentecostal dialogue. Rather than providing a systematic account of Pentecostal baptismal theology, he details the numerous debates and practices that have occurred in Pentecostal circles globally regarding the nature of baptism.[83] At times, this prevents him from making broad-sweeping ecclesiological claims, but it is out of a commitment to recognize the diversity of the global church and his own church tradition.

The ecclesial mark of catholicity forms the identity of the church around its diversity. Christian communities are part of the church when they are in relationship with other Christian communities. The New Delhi declaration describes this as the act of the Spirit bringing together "all in each place" in visible unity with Christians "in all places and all ages."[84] An ecumenical vision of catholicity shapes Robeck's ecclesiology. He explains that the whole church throughout time and space is present with each congregation and that each congregation is present wherever the church is gathered. Catholicity underlies Robeck's work to address the persecution of Christians in some countries, and the persecution of Christians has informed much of his theology of church unity. Churches around the world should stand in solidarity with parts of the Body of Christ that suffer (1 Cor. 12:26), including when they belong to different ecclesial traditions.[85] A global vision of the church is paradigmatic for his understanding of ecumenism.

Robeck, of course, is far from the first to have called for renewed attention to transregional ecumenical engagement, yet this concern is a driving force behind his career. His work with the WCC coincided with the reforms of the Council after the Canberra Assembly to broaden its geographical and denominational scope. In a piece dating to the early stages of these reforms, he speaks of the methodological changes that would result from broadening the Council's scope. He argues that where churches are located in the world ought to determine the methods used to unite the churches. Ecclesial catholicity informs ecumenical methodology. Reform of the ecumenical movement, says Robeck, would come from outside the Global North and from among the laity, and he predicts that it would result in a "call for greater emphasis on personal spiritual renewal and responsibility and to develop more sensitive understandings of what truly constitutes Christian community."[86] Such concerns will be seen in later chapters on conciliar ecumenism and dialogue, yet it is sufficient here to note that the doctrine on the church is not indifferent to where churches are located.

The catholicity of the church also encompasses diverse communities. Ecclesial diversity is of particular importance to Robeck's work on the church and race. The racialization of the American church introduces a social division within the Christian community that ecumenists account for in their work. He appeals to the thought of Jürgen Moltmann when he says the Christian community must not legitimate such divisions.[87] The church exists as a new humanity as a product of Christ's reconciliatory work (Eph. 2:14-16).[88] Here, Robeck's understanding of ecclesial unity is not "colorblind" in the sense that it abrogates racial distinctions among Christians. Instead, he argues that such distinctions must not divide Christian communities, for this would betray the principle of a koinonia defined by love and openness.

An acknowledgment of the diversity of the church becomes the basis for mutual recognition and dialogue.[89] When one considers the confessional dimension of the church, however, the ability to recognize and dialogue requires limits to acceptable diversity. A prominent figure in Robeck's thought is his colleague, Michael Kinnamon. Robeck cites Kinnamon in his claim that two of the core values of the church—truth and community—exist in tension with each other. The diversity of the church compels believers to relate with those different from themselves for the sake of discernment and mission.[90] The tension between truth and community as an expression of diversity constitutes the church, and so this tension lays a claim on believers. As Robeck explains, "we have been placed into relationship with one another,

48   *Chapter 1*

and our role is to do the best we can at working on that relationship."[91] Diversity is a mark of the church and an impetus for unitive efforts.

Similar to renewal, the diversity of the church is not incidental to systematic theology. The practices and structures meant to preserve the unity of the church in any meaningful and visible sense must account for the diverse communities that constitute the church. For example, the ecumenical movement in India has grappled with social divisions that stem from cultural differences and the caste system. The extent to which such differences should exist within the Christian community establishes the parameters by which Christians can claim whether their churches are united. As discussed above, sociopolitical forces affect the lives of churches, but ecclesiology also determines how churches respond to these forces. The ecclesiological reflection developed in Indian ecumenism assesses what it means to be a diverse church in India, and when division exists between communities, ecumenists discern how to reconcile differences into a diverse fellowship.

Reconciliation

Reconciliation is a synthesis of the previous discussions of ecclesial koinonia and diversity. Manifestations of koinonia or diversity do not occur separately from each other, yet they are seen more clearly when one examines the process of reconciliation within the church. Robeck's understanding of reconciliation begins, not with the work of ecumenists, but with the work of Christ, who reconciles divided humanity into the temple of the Spirit by the cross (Eph. 2:14-22).[92] The Ephesian passage speaks of Christ making peace between Jews and Gentiles as a consequence of reconciling them to God. The birth of the church—in its fellowship and diversity—is an act of reconciliation. The ability of ecumenists to foster peace between divided communities is an extension of this ecclesiology. Robeck defines ecumenism as primarily relational in that it is a project of "confession, repentance, and acceptance."[93] Through overcoming divisions, Christians can build a common future as a visible expression of their being reconciled by Christ.[94]

Because reconciliation is an act of God, and Christians model Christ in their ministry of reconciliation, it is missiological. Robeck describes the dual nature of the church as that of communion and mission.[95] The reconciliatory mission in which the church participates forms a new community.[96] The making of peace between believers is a consequence of mission and serves the purposes of mission. He repeats the commonly held belief that divisions within the church impede the church's witness to the gospel message of reconciliation.[97] How can Christians preach that Christ unites humanity within himself when they themselves are not united? The bringing together of believers within the church through forgiveness is a tangible witness to the gospel.[98]

For Robeck, reconciliation begins with repentance.[99] He gives as an example the Truth and Reconciliation Commission, which sought to overcome the legacy of apartheid in South Africa. Reconciliation and healing require bringing sins into the light for believers to repent of them.[100] Ecumenism becomes a process of conversion, where Christians are transformed so they can live together in a loving communion.[101] Divided communities cannot be reconciled without changing, meaning that change is a core principle of ecclesiology insofar as the church is a reconciled community.

The reception of Christians as brothers and sisters in the faith reverses the causes of many ecclesiastical divisions. Robeck is one of the few Pentecostal ecumenists to have explicitly advocated organic union as a viable model of union. He maintains that unity must be visible for it to be a testimony of the Father's sending the Son, thus dismissing any notion of a purely spiritual union.[102] The unity of the church requires an institutional dimension. As part of a thought experiment, he wonders whether organic union would be possible within the next three centuries. The feat would require "the end of the Protestant experiment,"[103] but he does not identify any presently existing ecclesiastical communion as the future united church. The transition occurs through the convergence of doctrine and of spiritual lives of churches; Robeck points to the increasingly evangelicalized and charismaticized natures of Protestant churches in the Global South as evidence of this occurring.[104] He does not address the reciprocal influence on other churches, yet it is clear he envisions an institutional component of the process of ecclesiastical reconciliation.

The integration of diverse communities into a visible koinonia requires reconciliation. The church is a product of Christ's reconciliatory ministry, yet it also participates in this ministry. Ecumenical work brings reconciliation to the fore of ecclesiological reflection. Systematic theology does not speak of the church as a preexisting united whole but as a result of God's work in history to unite all things to himself. Ecumenists debate the character and limits of diversity that exist within a reconciled community, but the methods they employ rely on the fact that reconciliation is not ancillary to the church.

THE OUTWORKING OF ECCLESIOLOGY

The present study argues that ecumenical methodology relies on a shared ecclesiology if it results in convergence, and it argues such by examining the ecclesiological basis of Robeck's reflections on methodology. Each of the three dimensions of the church seen above is paradigmatic for Robeck's ecclesiology—the church is a divine initiative, a historical community, and the people of God. The three dimensions culminate in their respective

50 *Chapter 1*

ecclesiological principles of renewal, restoration, and reconciliation as a way of holding different aspects of ecclesiology in tension. It is noteworthy that renewal, restoration, and reconciliation are hallmarks of the two ecclesiological fields in which Robeck operates—Pentecostal ecclesiology specifically and ecumenical ecclesiology more broadly.

More important for the present study, however, is the place of renewal, restoration, and reconciliation within ecumenical methodology. The three ecclesiological concepts describe the goals of various ecumenical initiatives and explain their relation to the church's nature. Whenever ecumenists plan bilateral dialogues, promote joint service ventures, or host ecumenical prayer events, they are not embarking on enterprises foreign to the nature of the church. Because the church is a divine initiative, it relies on gifts of grace to preserve its apostolic nature. Additionally, because the church is a historical community, it seeks to remain faithful to Tradition amid constant historical change. Finally, because the church is the people of God, it seeks to be a diverse and reconciled fellowship.

The following five chapters argue the thesis from five different methodological vantage points in Robeck's ecumenical career. The chapter on *reconciling memories* touches on ecclesiological themes of historicity and reconciliation, where the church is seen as a product of historical forces that divide and unite communities. The following chapter on *conciliar ecumenism* builds on catholicity by showing how structural components of the ecumenical movement seek to facilitate the church's koinonia in visible form. Communion is strengthened through conversation, with the chapter on *bilateral dialogue* focusing on the churches' common search for renewal. Because ecumenism is more than academic, the following chapter on *spiritual ecumenism* roots the spiritual unity of believers in the church's apostolic pattern and charismatic nature. The final method chapter on *Christian Forums* addresses a newer form of ecumenical methodology that prizes the diversity and reconciliation of the church.

Each of the five chapters examines how particular ecumenical methods seek renewal, restoration, or reconciliation, resulting in ecclesiological convergence between churches through the development and refinement of methods. The chapters are structured to demonstrate the convergence, such that each chapter begins by explaining the ecclesiological nature of the particular method under examination and the questions that scholars have raised. Then, I turn to Robeck's work to narrate methodological changes and the reasons for these changes. After this, I return to ecclesiology to demonstrate the convergence that occurs in ecumenical work when churches share and change methods together. A priority for Robeck's thought is the conversion of communities toward each other, so it is helpful to begin with the ecumenical method of reconciling memories.

NOTES

1. Cecil M. Robeck, Jr., "The Church: A Unique Movement of the Spirit," *Paraclete* 16, no. 4 (1982): 1.

2. Cecil M. Robeck, Jr., "The Church," in *Pentecostals in the 21st Century: Identity, Beliefs, Praxis*, ed. Corneliu Constantineanu and Christopher J. Scobie (Eugene, OR: Cascade Books, 2018), 149.

3. Cecil M. Robeck, Jr., "Developing and Maintaining a Pentecostal Ethos," *Quadrum: Journal of the Foursquare Scholars' Fellowship* 3, no. 1 (2020): 25, 26.

4. Cecil M. Robeck, Jr., "Can We Imagine an Ecumenical Future Together? A Pentecostal Perspective," *Gregorianum* 100 (2019): 50.

5. Robeck, "The Church," 144.

6. Cecil M. Robeck, Jr., "The Holy Spirit and the Unity of the Church: The Challenge of Pentecostal, Charismatic, and Independent Movements," in *The Holy Spirit, the Church and Christian Unity: Proceedings of the Consultation Held at the Monastery of Bose, Italy (14-20 October 2002)*, ed. D. Donnelly, A. Denaux, and J. Famerée, Bibliotheca Ephemeridum Theologicarum Lovaniensium 181 (Leuven, Belgium: Leuven University Press, 2005), 378.

7. World Council of Churches Commission on Faith and Order, *The Roots of Our Common Faith: Faith in the Scriptures and in the Early Church*, ed. Hans-Georg Link, Faith and Order Paper 119 (Geneva: World Council of Churches, 1984); World Council of Churches Commission on Faith and Order, *Confessing the One Faith: An Ecumenical Explication of the Apostolic Faith as It Is Confessed in the Nicene-Constantinopolitan Creed (381)*, Faith and Order Paper 153 (Geneva: World Council of Churches, 1991).

8. Cecil M. Robeck, Jr., "When I Grow Up, I Wanna Be...," *Fuller Focus* 17, no. 3 (2009): 30.

9. Cecil M. Robeck, Jr., "The Apostolic Faith Study and the Holy Spirit," in *Ecumenical Directions in the U.S. Today: Churches on a Theological Journey*, ed. Antonios Kireopoulos and Juliana Mecera, Faith and Order Commission Theological Series (Mahwah, NJ: Paulist Press, 2012), 77–102.

10. Cecil M. Robeck, Jr., "Pentecostals and the Apostolic Faith: Implications for Ecumenism," in *Confessing the Apostolic Faith: Pentecostal Churches and the Ecumenical Movement*, ed. National Council of the Churches of Christ in the USA (Pasadena, CA: Society for Pentecostal Studies, 1987), 61.

11. Robeck, "The Holy Spirit and the Unity," 374, 379; Cecil M. Robeck, Jr., "A Pentecostal Reflects on Canberra," in *Beyond Canberra: Evangelical Responses to Contemporary Ecumenical Issues*, ed. Bruce J. Nicholls and Bong Rin Ro (Oxford: Regnum Books, 1993), 117.

12. Cecil M. Robeck, Jr., "Pentecostal Ecumenism: Overcoming the Challenges – Reaping the Benefits (Part I)," *Journal of the European Pentecostal Theological Association* 34, no. 2 (2014): 116.

13. Cecil M. Robeck, Jr., "Charism(ata)," in *Dictionary of the Ecumenical Movement*, ed. Nicholas Lossky et al., 2nd ed. (Geneva: WCC Publications, 2002), 162.

14. Robeck, "The Church: A Unique," 4.

52 *Chapter 1*

15. Cecil M. Robeck, Jr., "Discerning the Spirit in the Life of the Church," in *The Church in the Movement of the Spirit*, ed. William Barr and Rena Yocom (Grand Rapids, MI: Eerdmans, 1994), 38.

16. Robeck, "Developing," 19.

17. Robeck, 26.

18. Robeck, "Can We Imagine," 50.

19. Robeck, 49, 50.

20. Cecil M. Robeck, Jr., "Pentecostal Ecclesiology," in *T & T Clark Companion to Ecclesiology*, ed. Kimlyn J. Bender and D. Stephen Long (London: Bloomsbury, 2020), 243.

21. Robeck, "The Holy Spirit and the Unity," 365, 366, 369.

22. For a comprehensive account of his work, see Cecil M. Robeck, Jr., *Prophecy in Carthage: Perpetua, Tertullian, and Cyprian* (Cleveland, OH: Pilgrim Press, 1992).

23. Cecil M. Robeck, Jr., "Irenaeus and 'Prophetic Gifts,'" in *Essays on Apostolic Themes: Studies in Honor of Howard M. Ervin* (Peabody, MA: Hendrickson Publishers, 1985), 110.

24. Robeck, "The Holy Spirit and the Unity," 369.

25. "Called to God's Mission: Report of the Third Round of the International Dialogue Between Representatives of the World Communion of Reformed Churches and Some Classical Pentecostal Churches and Leaders 2014-2020," 2020, §14.

26. "Called to God's Mission," §56; Robeck, "Developing," 24.

27. Robeck, "Developing," 25.

28. Robeck claims that "all Pauline discussions of charismata are within the context of the metaphor of the church as the Body of Christ," but this is not entirely accurate. In addition to the three passages, Robeck notes that Paul's use of variants of *charisma* occurs in passages that speak of the upbuilding of Christians for ministry within the church (Rom. 1:11; 1 Cor. 1:7; 7:7; 2 Cor. 1:11; 1 Tim. 4:14; 2 Tim. 1:6), which could be interpreted as ecclesiologically significant. However, Paul uses the word also to refer to the free gift of salvation (Rom. 5:15, 16; 6:23; 11:29). Robeck, "Charism(ata)," 162, 163.

29. Robeck, "Can We Imagine," 67.

30. Cecil M. Robeck, Jr., "'Do Not Quench the Spirit': Some Thoughts on the International Roman Catholic – Pentecostal Dialogue," in *Pentecostalism, Catholicism, and the Spirit in the World*, ed. Stan Chu Ilo (Eugene, OR: Cascade Books, 2019), 169, 170.

31. Robeck, "Pentecostal Ecumenism Part I," 132.

32. Michael Kinnamon, *Can a Renewal Movement Be Renewed? Questions for the Future of Ecumenism* (Grand Rapids, MI: Eerdmans, 2014).

33. Robeck, "Pentecostal Ecclesiology," 253.

34. Cecil M. Robeck, Jr., "African Pentecostal Contributions to Christian Unity," in *African Pentecostal Missions Maturing: Essays in Honor of Apostle Opoku Onyinah*, ed. Elorm Donkor and Clifton R. Clarke (Eugene, OR: Wipf & Stock, 2018), 72.

35. Cecil M. Robeck, Jr., "An Emerging Magisterium? The Case of the Assemblies of God," *Pneuma* 25, no. 2 (2003): 215.

36. D. Allen Tennison and Cecil M. Robeck, Jr., "Interview with Dr. Cecil M. Robeck, Jr.," *Assemblies of God Heritage* 25, no. 4 (2006): 19.

37. Cecil M. Robeck, Jr., *The Azusa Street Mission and Revival: The Birth of the Global Pentecostal Movement* (Nashville, TN: Thomas Nelson, 2006), 321–25.

38. Cecil M. Robeck, Jr., "Charismatic Movements," in *Global Dictionary of Theology*, ed. William A. Dyrness and Veli-Matti Kärkkäinen (Downers Grove, IL: InterVarsity Press, 2008), 153.

39. Robeck, "Can We Imagine," 67; Robeck, "The Holy Spirit and the Unity," 361 n24.

40. World Council of Churches Commission on Faith and Order, *The Church: Towards a Common Vision*, Faith and Order Paper 214 (Geneva: World Council of Churches, 2013), viii.

41. Robeck, "Discerning the Spirit," 47n31.

42. Robeck, "An Emerging," 165, 166.

43. Robeck, "The Church," 144, 145.

44. Cecil M. Robeck, Jr., "Authoritative Teaching in the Church," in *Towards a Global Vision of the Church: Explorations on Global Christianity and Ecclesiology, Volume 2*, ed. Cecil M. Robeck, Jr., Sotiris Boukis, and Ani Ghazaryan Drissi, Faith and Order Paper 239 (Geneva: World Council of Churches, 2023), 203.

45. Cecil M. Robeck, Jr., "Doing Theology in Isolation," *Pneuma* 12, no. 1 (1990): 3.

46. Cecil M. Robeck, Jr., "Worship in the Evangelical Tradition," *Ecumenical Trends* 30, no. 6 (2001): 95.

47. Cecil M. Robeck, Jr., "Introducing Pentecostals to Lutherans," in *Lutherans and Pentecostals in Dialogue* (Strasbourg, France: Institute for Ecumenical Research, 2010), 41.

48. Cecil M. Robeck, Jr., "Canon, *Regulae Fidei*, and Continuing Revelation in the Early Church," in *Church, Word, and Spirit: Historical and Theological Essays in Honor of Geoffrey W. Bromiley*, ed. James E. Bradley and Richard A. Muller (Grand Rapids, MI: Eerdmans, 1987), 74.

49. Robeck, "An Emerging," 168.

50. Cecil M. Robeck, Jr., "Roman Catholic-Pentecostal Dialogue: Some Pentecostal Assumptions," *Journal of the European Pentecostal Theological Association* 21, no. 1 (2001): 4.

51. Robeck, "An Emerging," 169, 170; Paul VI, *Dei verbum*, 1965, §7–10.

52. World Council of Churches Commission on Faith and Order, *Tradition and Traditions: Fourth World Conference on Faith and Order, Montreal, Canada, 12–26 July 1963*, Faith and Order Paper 40 (Geneva: World Council of Churches, 1963), 57.

53. *Tradition and Traditions*, 25.

54. Robeck, "An Emerging," 207.

55. Cecil M. Robeck, Jr., "The Challenge Pentecostalism Poses to the Quest for Ecclesial Unity," in *Kirche en ökumenischer Perspektive*, ed. Peter Walter, Klaus Krämer, and George Augustin (Freiburg, Germany: Herder, 2003), 318.

56. *Tradition and Traditions*, 8.

54 *Chapter 1*

57. Cecil M. Robeck, Jr., "Pentecostalism and Ecumenical Dialogue: A Potential Agenda," *Ecumenical Trends* 16, no. 11 (1987): 186; Cecil M. Robeck, Jr., "Pentecostal/Charismatic Churches and Ecumenism: An Interview with Cecil M. Robeck, Jr.," *The Pneuma Review: Journal of Ministry Resources and Theology for Pentecostal and Charismatic Ministries and Leaders* 6, no. 1 (2003): 24.

58. Cecil M. Robeck, Jr., "Ecumenism," in *Studying Global Pentecostalism: Theories and Methods*, ed. Allan Anderson et al. (Berkeley: University of California Press, 2010), 294, 295.

59. Cecil M. Robeck, Jr., "Pentecostals and Visible Church Unity," *One World* 192 (1994): 12.

60. Robeck, 11.

61. Cecil M. Robeck, Jr., "*The Quiet Game*, Racism, and the Azusa Street Revival," in *The Pastor & the Kingdom: Essays Honoring Jack W. Hayford*, ed. Jon Huntzinger and S. David Moore (Southlake, TX: Gateway Academic, 2017), 65; Cecil M. Robeck, Jr., "Pentecostalism and Mission: From Azusa Street to the Ends of the Earth," *Missiology: An International Review* 35, no. 1 (2007): 75–92; Robeck, *The Azusa*.

62. Robeck, "*The Quiet*," 91.

63. Robeck, 64, 65.

64. Cecil M. Robeck, Jr., "Pentecostal Churches," in *A Handbook of Churches and Councils: Profiles of Ecumenical Relationships*, ed. Huibert van Beek (Geneva: World Council of Churches, 2006), 64.

65. Robeck, "Pentecostal Ecclesiology," 253.

66. Robeck, "The Church," 156.

67. Robeck, "The Challenge," 317.

68. Cecil M. Robeck, Jr., "The Achievements of the Pentecostal—Catholic International Dialogue," in *Celebrating a Century of Ecumenism: Exploring the Achievements of International Dialogue*, ed. John A. Radano (Grand Rapids, MI: Eerdmans, 2012), 194.

69. Robeck, "Roman Catholic-Pentecostal Dialogue: Some," 10.

70. Robeck, "Discerning the Spirit," 44; Robeck, "A Pentecostal Reflects," 112.

71. Robeck, "Pentecostal Ecclesiology," 252.

72. *UR*, §3.

73. Robeck, "'Do Not Quench,'" 161; "Perspectives on Koinonia: Report from the Third Quinquennium of the Dialogue between the Pontifical Council for Promoting Christian Unity of the Roman Catholic Church and Some Classical Pentecostal Churches and Leaders (1985-1989)," 1989, §37.

74. Robeck, "The Church," 151.

75. Robeck, "Discerning the Spirit," 38; Robeck, "The Church," 151.

76. Robeck, "The Church," 155, 156.

77. Robeck, 144, 145.

78. Cecil M. Robeck, Jr. and Jerry L. Sandidge, "The Ecclesiology of *Koinonia* and Baptism: A Pentecostal Perspective," *Journal of Ecumenical Studies* 27, no. 3 (1990): 527, 528; Robeck, "Pentecostal Ecumenism Part I," 117; Robeck, "The Church," 146.

Robeck's Ecclesiology

79. Robeck is more forceful elsewhere: "It is impossible to argue against the fact that bishops were the obvious successors to the apostles." Cecil M. Robeck, Jr., "Some Pentecostal Reflections on Current Catholic – Pentecostal Relations: What Are We Learning?," in *Towards Unity: Ecumenical Dialogue 500 Years after the Reformation. Essays in Honor of Monsignor John A. Radano*, ed. Donald Bolen, Nicholas Jesson, and Donna Geernhaert (Mahwah, NJ: Paulist Press, 2017), 230; Robeck, "Authoritative," 204.

80. Cecil M. Robeck, Jr., "The Charismatic Renewal of the Church," *Theology, News & Notes* 30, no. 1 (1983): 2.

81. Robeck, "Can We Imagine," 68.

82. "From Conflict to Communion: Lutheran–Catholic Common Commemoration of the Reformation in 2017. Report of the Lutheran–Roman Catholic Commission on Unity," 2013, §14.

83. Robeck and Sandidge, "The Ecclesiology"; Robeck, "Ecumenism," 297, 298.

84. World Council of Churches, *The New Delhi Report* (New York: Association Press, 1962), 116.

85. Cecil M. Robeck, Jr., "Christians and Persecution: Making an Appropriate Response," in *The Suffering Body: Responding to the Persecution of Christians*, ed. Harold D. Hunter and Cecil M. Robeck, Jr. (Bletchley, UK: Paternoster, 2006), 62–81; Robeck, "The Church," 153.

86. Cecil M. Robeck, Jr., "The New Ecumenism," in *The Local Church in a Global Era: Reflections for a New Century*, ed. Max Stackhouse, Tim Dearborn, and Scott Paeth (Grand Rapids, MI: Eerdmans, 2000), 174–76.

87. Cecil M. Robeck, Jr., "Pentecostal Ecumenism: Overcoming the Challenges – Reaping the Benefits (Part II)," *Journal of the European Pentecostal Theological Association* 35, no. 1 (2015): 11.

88. Cecil M. Robeck, Jr., "The Past: Historical Roots of Racial Unity and Division in American Pentecostalism," *Cyberjournal for Pentecostal-Charismatic Research* 14 (2004): 18, www.pctii.org/cyberj/cyberj14/robeck.html.

89. Cecil M. Robeck, Jr., "David du Plessis and the Challenge of Dialogue," *Pneuma* 9, no. 1 (1987): 3.

90. Robeck, "Pentecostal Ecumenism Part I," 116; Cecil M. Robeck, Jr., "Truth and Community: Insights from the Past and the Present," *Theology, News & Notes* 50, no. 1 (2003): 13, 14, 19.

91. Robeck, "Truth," 19.

92. Robeck, "The Church," 150.

93. Robeck, "Ecumenism," 293.

94. Robeck, 294.

95. Cecil M. Robeck, Jr., "On Becoming a Christian: An Important Theme in the International Roman Catholic – Pentecostal Dialogue," *PentecoStudies: Online Journal for the Interdisciplinary Study of Pentecostalism and Charismatic Movements* 8, no. 2 (2008): 15; "On Becoming a Christian: Insights from Scripture and the Patristic Writings with Some Contemporary Reflections. Report of the Fifth Phase of the International Dialogue between Some Classical Pentecostal Churches and Leaders and the Catholic Church (1998-2006)," 2006, §96.

56   *Chapter 1*

96. Robeck, "When I Grow Up," 30.

97. Robeck, "Truth," 12; Robeck, "Can We Imagine," 55.

98. Robeck, "Roman Catholic-Pentecostal Dialogue: Some," 12.

99. Robeck, "Pentecostals and Visible," 12.

100. Cecil M. Robeck, Jr., "Martin Luther King, Jr. Day, 2010," *Ecumenical Trends* 39, no. 1 (2010): 8.

101. Robeck, "Pentecostal Ecumenism Part II," 9.

102. Cecil M. Robeck, Jr., "Growing Up Pentecostal," *Theology, News & Notes* 35, no. 1 (1988): 7.

103. Robeck, "Can We Imagine," 61, 62.

104. Cecil M. Robeck, Jr., "Les pentecôtismes, entre passé et présent, et l'Église dans 300 ans," trans. P.M. Desjardins, *Istina* 59 (2014): 139–49; Robeck, "Can We Imagine," 61–63.

Chapter 2

Reconciling Memories of American Pentecostal Race Relations

The inaugural celebration of Indian Christian Day (Yeshu Bhakti Divas) in 2021 was the result of grassroots ecumenical efforts. The nationwide annual event builds on the traditional observance of St. Thomas Day, commemorating the martyrdom of the apostle who, according to an ancient tradition, first brought the gospel to India. Nearly two millennia later, the Christian community in the most populous nation in the world constitutes less than 3 percent of the country, yet it has managed to fracture along the same lines as Christians elsewhere. Centuries of competition between churches have embittered Syrian and Catholic Christians—not to mention the introduction of Protestant denominations and indigenous churches. Each of these communities has divergent visions of what it means to be the church in India. However, through their joint commemoration of Indian Christian Day, they acknowledge their common apostolic origins and history. The event brings together ecclesiastical hierarchs and community leaders as an expression of their common mission in India today, hoping such acts of unity will extend beyond an annual event.[1] By recognizing their common history, divided Christians pursue a common future.

The ecumenical method of reconciling memories acknowledges the relation of the present church to the past. As mentioned in the previous chapter, the church's diversity exists because of its existence in fellowship, though this fellowship wrestles with historical forces that threaten to break it apart. Narratives of historical conflicts can perpetuate the harm that divisive episodes of history cause between churches. Ecumenists seek to revisit these episodes and narratives to address the conflict they cause.

At first glance, the act of reconciling memories might seem to have little relation to this study's focus on ecclesiology. The ecumenical movement pursues a future union of churches rather than rehashing antiquated

58   *Chapter 2*

controversies. Furthermore, the doctrine of the church can often seem at odds with the church's lived experience. Is not the ecumenical project based on the assumption that the church's history does not reflect the ecclesial mark of oneness? How, then, can attending to historical memories inform a convergence in ecclesiology?

The mutual relation of communal identity and memory highlights the ecclesiological basis of ecumenical methodology. If the doctrine of the church reflects and informs the church's historical narrative, then the constructed narrative of the church in history functions as a form of narrative ecclesiology: the Christian community tells stories about itself for the sake of understanding itself. The figures, events, institutions, and movements honored or vilified in communal memory shape who the church believes it is called to be. The ecumenical method of reconciling memories relies upon a degree of shared memory between divided communities by which the communities see their historical relation to each other. Consequently, as communities reconcile their memories, they come to share a common historical narrative of the church, thereby converging in their ecclesiologies.

NARRATIVE ECCLESIOLOGY

The historicity of the church positions the church within salvation history. *TCTCV* opens by holding together history and reconciliation. The convergence document identifies the church as both a product of God's reconciling work in history and also as an actor in this work.[2] Theologies of reconciliation are evidenced through lived experiences and communities. Additionally, the field of ecclesiology has looked to the sacraments for a valuing of history for ecclesial life. Eucharistic *anamnesis* brings the past to the present, forming the church's identity around the historical acts of God in Christ, and the baptismal rite is an opportunity to experience the reconciliation offered through Christ's death and resurrection.[3] In terms of historicity, a doctrine of the church does not begin with a human unity that precedes the Christian community but rather sees the community as a product of God's reconciling the world to himself (2 Cor. 5:11-21).

As mentioned in the previous chapter, the church's historicity is part of ecclesiology. The church is open to social forces that shape the Christian life even as they serve to antagonize or unite Christians. Ecumenists attend to sociological differences that threaten to divide the church, with reconciliation being integral to the church's mission.[4] A focus on reconciliation clarifies the goals of the ecumenical movement, which does not seek to unite theologies but communities.[5] The unity of social diversities within the church benefits the whole, and so how churches deal with historical realities is of concern for ecumenists.

One of the ways that the church handles social diversity is through historical narratives. Richard Kearney explains the role of myths in the construction of communal identities. He borrows from Paul Ricoeur when speaking of the integrative function of social memory in that it offers an image of the community for itself and outsiders. A church's account of history reveals its worldview and perception of itself. The power of myth is seen, especially in the community's founding narrative. By repeating the story of a community's origins each generation, the community perpetuates its founding energy and purpose. Therefore, myth is both a claim about the past and a horizon for imagining the future.[6] The opening example in India employed the martyrdom of Thomas as a unifying narrative for churches, but founding myths are not always unifying. The report from the second round of the Catholic–Reformed international dialogue recognizes the value in studying the past to understand the origins of the two traditions' embitterment. Divergent historical narratives resulted in different values, institutions, and "ecclesial cultures" that have persisted centuries after the Reformation.[7]

The study of the church accounts for the church's life through time, and so ecumenism requires historical research to assess the depth of divisions between churches and the sources of the divisions. Additionally, the joint venture of studying history can reveal problems with the ways that communities have narrated episodes in their histories. The Catholic–Mennonite international dialogue describes this as the task of purifying memories. Communities are tempted to narrate events and developments to portray themselves in a positive light, yet the work of reconciling divided communities can call such false narratives into question.[8] The unity of the church, if it is from God, cannot be predicated on falsehood. The need to revisit contrasting accounts of history shaped the NCCUSA study on historiography.[9] The study was inspired by the project of the Comisión de Estudios de Historia de la Iglesia en Latinoamérica to write transdenominational history in their region. The NCCUSA study goes so far as to assert that, if ecumenical historiography is impossible, then so is ecumenism, for both require ways of talking about divisions, assessing the nature of conflicts, and recognizing fellow Christians as Christians.[10]

Because history is not confined to the academy, ecumenists are not content to leave their work to the written page. Churches commemorate their histories at sites and events as ways to pass on their stories to successive generations. Many of these sites extol heroes of the faith as exemplars for pilgrims, who are formed according to the site's message of what the faith asks of believers.[11] Commemorative sites can help unite communities when memories are shared between them. However, such sites and stories can also perpetuate conflict when they touch on events that divided churches. Ecumenical work requires attention to the ways that churches pass on their stories, lest they also

60   *Chapter 2*

pass on their divisions. The Lutheran–Mennonite international dialogue gives as an example a commemorative event of the Augsburg Confession, where Mennonites declined the invitation to attend because of the events associated with the Confession. The International Study Commission was formed to address these historical tensions between the two communities. As a result of the dialogue, the Mennonite World Conference implemented changes at historical sites to reflect an accurate account of history and to share about contemporary reconciliatory efforts with Lutherans.[12] The ecumenical method of reconciling memories changes how churches tell their stories within their own communities.

Nonetheless, the question remains how reconciled memories result in a convergence in ecclesiologies. Churches can change their understandings of the past, but they cannot change the past. If churches are products of history, how does the sharing of memories help unite divided communities? Robeck's work in this field addresses the history of denominations in the United States, specifically the divisions between Pentecostal churches over race and the relations of Pentecostalism to the ecumenical movement. He demonstrates the value of attending to historical episodes in encouraging ecumenical work—including events that inspire believers or that bring them to repentance. The ability to reconcile memories between communities relies on an understanding that they share history together, and as they come to share a common account of history, they come to see themselves as part of the same community.

HISTORY OF RACIAL DIVISIONS IN AMERICAN PENTECOSTALISM

The American church has witnessed divisions over doctrinal, political, and social issues, resulting in thousands of denominations that have proliferated globally. One of the issues to have received the most attention from American ecumenists is that of race. The ecumenical movement in the United States has spawned models of interchurch engagement to reverse ecclesiastical segregation, even experimenting with attempts to merge historically Black and white denominations, such as the Consultation on Church Union. Ecumenists recognize the social forces behind divisions and account for them when devising methods for reconciling churches. The unity of the church presumes the existence of social diversity within it. Insofar as racialization shapes the practices and values of interchurch relationships, ecumenical methodology concerns race.

Ecumenical work dealing with race devotes attention to history in addition to justice and doctrine. The task of reconciling estranged communities requires revisiting the events that divided them and the constructed narratives that keep them apart. Much of Robeck's research examines the history of race relations for the sake of encouraging intra-Pentecostal ecumenism. He describes racism as the "open secret" of American Pentecostalism, a pervasive presence that leaders and members would rather avoid.[13] His research in the field began with coursework under Russell Spittler in 1972, where Robeck discovered that the history of American Pentecostal race relations up till then was "almost unequivocally abysmal."[14] Entire denominations can be categorized as historically white, Black, or Latino. Robeck's historical research informs his ecclesiology and understanding of ecumenical methodology. Historical narratives are more than the backdrop of ecumenical work; they are unitive or divisive elements of Christian communities. Narrative and communal memory are part of ecclesiology, and so they are also part of ecumenical methodology.

Historiography of the Azusa Street Revival

How divided communities narrate the historical causes of their division reinforces their relationship—whether resolving or perpetuating conflict. The historiographical concerns of intra-Pentecostal ecumenism begin with the Azusa Street Revival of Los Angeles, California, in 1906–1909. What is important for the discussion here is not the story itself but why the story is told, so I do not spend time summarizing the event. As mentioned in the previous chapter, the revival is widely heralded as the origin of American Pentecostalism. The claim is motivated as much by historical facts as it is by political sensitivities. No denomination descended directly from the Los Angeles revival, and so the historical narrative of Azusa Street is common ground on which divided Pentecostal communities can meet.

Robeck himself uses the word "myth" when speaking of Azusa Street. He justifies the term when saying animating narratives drive all successful movements.[15] For Robeck, the Azusa Street Revival is the story of American Pentecostalism. His scholarship stresses the need to move beyond simplistic accounts that have been passed down through generations while also highlighting the value of the event for contemporary Pentecostal ministry.[16] He attends to the congregation that sustained the revival, the spread of the revival through missionaries, and the revival's leadership. Pentecostalism cannot trace its origins to an individual, as is the case for Lutheranism or Methodism, yet William Seymour is venerated for pastoring the Azusa Street Revival. A child of formerly enslaved parents, Seymour ministered to people for whom emancipation was a recent memory. It is difficult to find an account of his life that is anything less than hagiographic. For Robeck,

62   *Chapter 2*

the story of Azusa Street embodies the aspirations of what American Pentecostals believe they are called to be and do.

The multivalent significance of the event for Pentecostalism can be observed within Pentecostal discourse. Depending on the context, the two-word phrase, "Azusa Street," can variously refer to a geographic location, physical building, gathered congregation, historical event, ethical vision, or missional impetus. Scholars debate the genetic lineage of global Pentecostalism and its relation to the United States, and no attempt is made to enter the fray here. What is not debated, however, is the prominence of Azusa Street in global Pentecostal literature on ecumenism. Pentecostal ecumenists from Brazil,[17] the Democratic Republic of the Congo,[18] South Africa,[19] Norway,[20] Hong Kong,[21] and India[22] have appealed to Azusa Street in their reflections on the unity of the church. No event in the history of Pentecostalism is more widely revered for its ecumenical import.

Robeck studies the revival for its unitive aspirations. By writing on the history, he advocates for a unifying vision of the Pentecostal movement—not only among divided Pentecostal churches but also beyond Pentecostalism. He concludes that "the same ecumenical impulses which gave birth to the World Council of Churches also gave birth to the Pentecostal Movement at the turn of this [twentieth] century."[23]

The warrant for the claim lies in Azusa Street's paired values of unity and mission. Robeck refers to the revival as a religious experiment, seeking to embody a passion for the apostolic faith that churches of the day had forsaken through their divisions.[24] Christians from across the country and a plurality of denominations visited the revival, planting the theological seeds within the fertile soil of early Pentecostalism that sprouted into its current diversity. Robeck describes how Methodist, Baptist, Holiness, Quaker, Disciples, and Alliance streams fed into the confessional identity of Pentecostalism.[25] He is also sure to mention that Seymour spent most of his life as a devout Roman Catholic;[26] in all his remaining writings, Seymour never speaks an ill word of the Catholic Church. It is not for nothing that the Azusa Street Mission described itself as a movement for "Christian Unity everywhere."[27]

Azusa Street's diversity was not only denominational but also sociological. Part of its religious experiment was its inclusion of leaders from diverse racial, cultural, socioeconomic, gender, and educational backgrounds.[28] The revival occurred during a period of mass migration to Los Angeles from the east and south.[29] The congregation served as a hub for the interactions of immigrant communities in the area, launching a transnational religious movement. Robeck echoes the language of Acts 2:1 when he describes Azusa Street as a diverse gathering of believers in "one place," correlating the multinational population of Jerusalem on the day of Pentecost with the historical origins of American Pentecostalism in Los Angeles.[30] More than an accident of history, theological significance is ascribed to the diversity of Azusa Street. Seymour believed multiculturalism was a proleptic experience of eschatological fellowship. Christian discipleship entailed the erasure of prejudice under the sanctifying work of the Spirit.[31] For the church to live the apostolic faith, it must train its members in the values of the community inaugurated at Pentecost.

Robeck also chronicles the earliest interactions of American Pentecostalism with the ecumenical movement. Coincidentally, the Azusa Street Revival began the same month as the founding of the Los Angeles Church Federation (LACF) in April 1906. The Federation was one of several local ecumenical projects across the country, soon witnessing the birth of the nationwide Federal Council of Churches of Christ in America (FCC) in 1908.[32] The LACF was led by Methodist pastor Edwin Ryland. He was respected so highly for his ecumenical work that, at the founding of the FCC, he served as chairman of its Committee on Local Federations. In 1913, he also organized the statewide California Church Federation. He stressed the need to incorporate whole congregations—not only ministers—in local ecumenical work, and the LACF under his leadership amplified the voices of churches in civic affairs.[33]

One of the first actions of the LACF was to publicly denounce the pandemonium happening on Azusa Street. Ryland appreciated the Pentecostals' evangelistic zeal, but he warned that the "enthusiasts" might turn "dangerous."[34] The LACF developed a plan to counter the growth of the revival, publicizing prayer and evangelistic campaigns of their own; they even fired the director of the Union Rescue Mission for his support of the revival.[35] The periodical of Azusa Street reported that, where previously there had been no unity among churches in Los Angeles, it now appeared that the churches were uniting against their own congregation.[36]

Resistance came from an additional direction. Robeck describes the existence of two Black worlds in Los Angeles at the turn of the twentieth century. The first was that of the established Methodist and Baptist communities who were upwardly mobile and politically active; the second was that of the Sanctified church that rural Southern farmers brought during the Great Migration. Seymour—as one such Sanctified Black pastor from a poor, rural Southern family—and the church he pastored were spurned by the established Black churches as uncouth.[37] At the national level, Black Methodist and Baptist denominations were founding members of the FCC and later NCCUSA, yet no Black Pentecostal denominations have joined to the present day.[38] Robeck spotlights how Pentecostals were shunned from the existent interchurch networks.

Faced with isolation, the Azusa Street Mission established its own networks. Seymour organized ministerial prayer meetings for churches willing to associate with the Mission, coordinating evangelistic campaigns in the Los

64   *Chapter 2*

Angeles metropolitan area and swapping pulpits. He used the Mission's periodical to advertise the events of other churches. Robeck reports that Seymour saw fellow congregations as part of the same revival that was occurring on Azusa Street. Seymour celebrated the success of other churches regardless of whether the success fed into his own church.[39] The ability of the Mission not only to recognize the ecclesiality of other churches but also to receive them as coworkers in mission catalyzed the spread of the revival across the city, nation, and globe.

Every Edenic myth ends with a Fall. The Azusa Street Revival concluded in 1909 after three years and multiple schisms, leaving behind the husk of a once-thriving congregation. Robeck attributes the root cause of these divisions to racism: white clergy and laity were unable to sit under the Black leadership of Seymour.[40] Gastón Espinosa notes a similar conflict between Latino revivalists at *calle Azusa* and the Mission leadership.[41] The pattern would repeat itself within emergent Pentecostal denominations. Despite the example set at Azusa Street, Pentecostals nationwide were segregated along racial lines. A further division occurred within the Azusa Street Mission over the doctrine of sanctification, a schism that has persisted to the present day. In addition to other doctrinal and social controversies that occurred, the Azusa Street Revival encapsulates the aspirations of American Pentecostals for ecclesial unity and their failures to preserve it.

Honoring a Legacy

The story of Azusa Street did not end with the revival but continued through the testimonies handed down to today. As a child of Pentecostal ministers, Robeck was raised on stories of revivals meant to inspire faith among the congregation. His academic training was in patristics, yet he broadened his focus in the 1980s to studying early American Pentecostalism. In addition to essays and podcasts, Robeck has passed on the narrative of Azusa Street through one monograph and a forthcoming three-volume *magnum opus* on the revival. These publications are more than scholarship; they are literary testimonies within the tradition of Pentecostal narrative theologizing. History serves as the context of divine economy and, therefore, as a source of revelation. Christians learn about God and their place in the world by hearing stories of the faithful over centuries. The desire to glorify God and encourage readers in the faith shapes Robeck's historiographical approach. By retelling the story of Azusa Street, he hands down the tradition and enables readers to enter its legacy.[42]

Robeck's work as a historian is not restricted to the written page. Due to his teaching position at Fuller Theological Seminary, he has lived most of his life within ten miles of Los Angeles and enjoys a more thorough familiarity with the historical sites than do other historians of the revival. His expertise caused future AG General Superintendent George Wood to ask him in 1992 for a tour of Pentecostal historical sites in the city. Wood subsequently encouraged AG denominational leaders across the country to visit Los Angeles and learn about their heritage. Robeck's work as a historian has given him a platform to instill a vision of Christian unity among Pentecostal leaders. Since that first tour, he claims to have led over 15,000 pilgrims around the city to encounter the history of Pentecostalism.[43]

People visit the house on North Bonnie Brae Street, where revival attendees danced so mightily before the Lord that the house suffered structural damage, forcing the congregation to relocate to Azusa Street. Pilgrims witness the small plot of land where the Mission once stood and listen while Robeck recounts the thousands of visitors who came in search of Holy Ghost fire. He leads the groups in discussions about racial justice and divisions between churches. Through the tour, people participate in the legacy of Azusa Street as they follow in the footsteps of revival attendees and hear their testimonies of divine encounters passed down through generations.[44]

The value of the Azusa Street story has prompted Robeck and others to recognize the need to preserve the historical site for future generations. The Mission building was demolished in 1931, and where it stood is now a Japanese-American Cultural and Community Center. Robeck led the charge to prevent the erasure of history. Changes in the urban landscape of twentieth-century Los Angeles altered historic landmarks in the area. Official maps of the city in the 1970s and 1980s no longer listed Azusa Street, leaving behind an unnamed strip of pavement on the ground used as a back alley for dumpsters. Through his archival research, he discovered where the revival occurred after that knowledge had been lost over the generations. Pentecostals today would not know where Azusa Street is located had Robeck not excavated the myth in his research.

To preserve the site, Robeck co-founded with Bill Watanabe in 1997 the Azusa Street Memorial Committee, the core of which are Black and Japanese American community leaders local to the area. The project was motivated and frustrated by contemporaneous racial tensions. Downtown Los Angeles was still recovering from the 1992 riots, which were a reaction to the acquittal of four police officers who were charged with excessive force in beating a Black man, Rodney King. The violent unrest spread throughout the city, including into neighborhoods populated by Asian communities (most prominently Koreatown [K-Town]), thereby inflaming internecine prejudices of xenophobia, classism, and racism. Azusa Street today is located in the neighborhood of Little Tokyo, the heart of the Japanese American community in Los Angeles. A ten-minute walk to the north of the street was the

Parker Center, where the riots began, and a ten-minute walk to the south of the street lies Skid Row. It was feared that if the Azusa Street site grew in prominence, then it would draw thousands of Black tourists to Little Tokyo every year shortly after the riots. Out of their collective trauma, some groups stonewalled efforts to memorialize Azusa Street, which is why so little signage exists at the physical location today. Meanwhile, other local Japanese and Black leaders, who had formed the Azusa Street Memorial Committee, worked to improve Black–Asian relations in Los Angeles, which is why there is some signage today. While the Committee was not directly in response to the riots, its leadership composition and its focus on the multiracial revival contrasted against the backdrop of downtown Los Angeles in the 1990s. The Committee operated out of the belief that commemorating the revival's history would inspire future reconciliatory work and that this work could be done only together.[45] The project is a communal act of drawing meaning from history to discern how to be the church together in Los Angeles today. The memorialization of the Azusa Street site is a testament to the efforts of Asian and Black Christians toward unity.[46]

The project is also an exercise in ecumenical cooperation, with different denominational leaders aiding different aspects of the historical preservation. The first street sign was erected with the aid of West Angeles Church of God in Christ, while the Bonnie Brae house was purchased with donations from Foursquare and Apostolic churches, among others.[47] Robeck, as a historian and AG minister, served on the planning committee for the Church of God's Azusa Street Prayer Tower, which was financed almost entirely by Indonesian Pentecostals. A Baptist community organizer chairs the Azusa Street Memorial Committee, whose base of operations is the nearby Union Church, a Japanese American congregation belonging to both the Presbyterian Church (USA) and United Church of Christ. On the other hand, Robeck asserts that some of the greatest resistance has come from local Episcopal and Methodist congregations, who detest the idea of cooperation with Pentecostals in the area.[48] Over a century after the revival, Pentecostals in Los Angeles still face racial tensions and denominational opposition; and over a century after the revival, Pentecostals in Los Angeles still work to overcome these divisions in their community. Presently, the only physical indication of the Azusa Street site's historic significance is two signs, each the size of a platter.[49] Plans exist to develop more signage in the future.[50] Robeck received commendations for his work from the City of Los Angeles.

In a limited form, Robeck has helped his denomination honor the legacy of Azusa Street. He does not teach at an AG school, nor does he serve in an ecclesiastical office aside from his ordination, so his influence has been in the scholarly realm. He has written for AG publications on the revival, not shying away from the complicity of white Pentecostals in the scandals that ended it.[51]

At the centenary of the revival, the AG rededicated the chapel of its seminary located near the denomination's headquarters in Springfield, Missouri. Symbolic of the historically white denomination's commitment to work toward racial reconciliation, the Assemblies of God Theological Seminary dedicated its William J. Seymour Chapel to the Black father of their movement. At the front of the chapel shines a stained-glass depiction of Seymour. Robeck was asked to author a plaque for the chapel's entryway, where he extolls Seymour as having "demonstrated the value of racial unity and cultural harmony [and] exhorted his congregation to seek God above all things."[52]

Embracing a Legacy

Robeck prizes the Azusa Street narrative for the reasons seen above why ecumenists employ the method of reconciling memories. Historical events and stories shape the identity of ecclesial communities, influencing their self-understanding, values, practices, and structures. More than this, Robeck describes myths as "animating narrative[s]" that motivate movements. Contrary to a postmodern devaluing of history and tradition, he argues such stories can serve as an impetus toward encounter and growth.[53] The fact that divided Pentecostal churches look to the Azusa Street Revival as an image of the Christian faith enables the churches to recognize their commonalities with each other. He adds that a concern for unity is part of remaining faithful to the legacy of Azusa Street, with reconciliation as a value taught to those who honor the event.[54] Ecumenists commemorate moments in history as a way to animate their work.

Memories, divisive or unitive, are important for ecumenical narratives, for they shape ecclesiastical relations. The unitive dimension of Azusa Street is the example it gives of Christian community across racial lines. Robeck's belief that history has relevance for the contemporary church motivates his historical research on the "radical experiment of Pentecost at the Azusa Street Mission."[55] On his tours, he impresses upon pilgrims the debt Pentecostals owe to the Black church as a way to fight racism. He also speaks of the ghettoization of Mexican migrants in early twentieth-century Los Angeles as a way to illustrate the significance of the transnational and multilingual dimension of the revival.[56] Those who claim Azusa Street as part of their community's historical identity are led to broaden their understanding of what this history demands of them, including the event's unitive values.

Ecumenists examine divisive memories that reveal sources of conflict. As mentioned above, the Azusa Street Revival ended because of racial prejudice. Robeck contends that white Pentecostals have avoided attributing much significance to the revival to avoid the legacy of racial divisions within

68   *Chapter 2*

American Pentecostalism. The contemporary prominence of Seymour and Azusa Street in Pentecostal discourse makes his claim difficult to appreciate. Espinosa outlines the historiographical developments of the past century regarding how American Pentecostals have told the story of their origins. He argues that historians who were more racially conscious were more likely to hold the revival in high esteem.[57] When Robeck began to research Pentecostal history in the 1970s, white narratives dominated the field, many of which made no mention of Azusa Street. He was part of a generation of historians who elevated Seymour and Azusa Street in the self-definition of American Pentecostalism. In reading Espinosa's timeline of authors, it is not a coincidence that many of the historians who revered Seymour were also ecumenists (Walter Hollenweger, Vinson Synan, Leonard Lovett, and Robeck). The ecumenical method of reconciling memories causes churches to confront the forces that keep them apart. Repentance of wrongdoing is a result of embracing shared historical events.

The narratives revisited in ecumenical work are selected for their contemporary relevance. Robeck responds to the fragmentation of religion into personal spirituality by elevating the Azusa Street narrative as an example of "shared experience and communal cooperation between various Christian groups."[58] Additionally, he sees value in the narrative amid anti-immigrant rhetoric and systemic racism in the United States.[59] Reconciling memories can open communities to each other. Robeck says studying the Azusa Street Revival gave him "a greater respect for people with whom I differ over the ways we talk about our encounters with God or the ways we act when we encounter God."[60] The ability of divided churches to claim common events and figures as exemplars of the faith contributes to the churches' reconciliation.

PENTECOSTAL/CHARISMATIC CHURCHES OF NORTH AMERICA

The ecumenical method of reconciling memories contributes to other ecumenical initiatives. In the same way that repentance should result in a change in behavior, historical reckonings on social divisions should result in a change in social systems. The reconciliation of communities results in adaptations in these communities' practices and structures to enable a shared life. Hugh McCullum, as part of a WCC project to chronicle ecumenical history, narrates efforts to address racial divisions in the late twentieth century. He describes WCC and NCCUSA cooperative responses to curb racial violence in the United States. As part of the concern for social change, he lists two prominent examples of organizational projects to unite denominations across racial lines—the Consultation on Church Union and the founding of the Pentecostal/Charismatic Churches of North America (PCCNA).[61]

The PCCNA is a transdenominational fellowship of Pentecostal churches in the United States, Canada, and Mexico. It is the largest organizational expression of Pentecostalism in the three countries. The body's origins were motivated by larger trends in the American church to grapple with the legacy of ecclesiastical segregation. As is common for the continent, the United States context overshadows the concerns of Mexican and Canadian churches in the organization. Robeck's contributions to the founding and work of the PCCNA reveal the ecclesiological consequences of the reconciliation of memories. Pentecostal churches, out of a recognition of their common history and the divisive episodes therein, structured their relations to foster a greater level of community between them. The ecumenical method opened the churches to each other, as seen in the aspirations of the PCCNA and the establishment of its Christian Unity Commission.

Founding and Aspirations

The PCCNA arose from the ashes of the Pentecostal Fellowship of North America (PFNA). Founded in 1948, the PFNA was originally a federation of Pentecostal denominations that were members of the National Association of Evangelicals; consequently, it was a federation of historically white denominations. The first national experiment of organizational unity among American Pentecostals operated with a white normative understanding of their movement. PFNA executives admitted later to routinely rejecting membership applications from Black Pentecostal churches.[62]

The 1990s witnessed a new wave of attention given in churches and the nation to systemic issues of racism, prompting Pentecostal leaders to revisit their complicity in sustaining these systems. A colloquy was called in 1994 to bring together scholars who would inform the ongoing reflection. Ecclesiastical hierarchs relied on historians for an approach to church relations.[63] Robeck's paper focused on the history of racism within the AG as an example of the failure of white Pentecostal churches to work for unity, and he called for concrete acts of repentance from his own denomination.[64] The reconciliation of memories did not limit ecclesial memory to one event but to the history of relations between divided Christians. He refers to the beating of Rodney King mentioned above when describing the institutional dimension of racism and arguing that solutions would need to be equally as institutional.[65] Following the colloquy, the PFNA held a gathering to determine the organization's future. In Robeck's words, denominational leaders "euthanized"[66] the PFNA to establish the PCCNA, which included Black

70   *Chapter 2*

churches in its membership and leadership. The new organization promised
new relationships and ways of relating, offering a chance for churches to
work together to root out racism.[67]

The founding documents of the PCCNA and the organization's website
point to two narratives that shape the organization's mission—the Pentecost
event and the Azusa Street Revival. Vinson Synan describes the PCCNA as
a movement of *ressourcement*, recovering the social vision of Seymour.[68]
The organization's "Racial Reconciliation Manifesto" refers to drinking
"from the well of Pentecost" embodied at Azusa Street.[69] Leonard Lovett,
former colleague of Robeck and future ecumenical officer of the Church of
God in Christ, asked Robeck to edit Lovett's initial draft of the Manifesto;
the document was then supported by Harold Hunter and Ithiel Clemmons
for adoption.[70] The document's authorship reflects a concerted effort toward
church unity.

The desire to return to the vision of Pentecost in the early church draws
on restorationist themes from the previous chapter. Ecclesial restorationism
serves as a form of self-critique within renewal efforts. Churches abandoned
the calling of God given among the apostolic community at Pentecost to preserve unity. The return to Pentecost requires embodying the tradition handed
down through history, such as was seen at Azusa Street. More than retelling
the story in one voice, embracing the story's legacy requires ecclesiastical
commitments.

Part of the recovery of Pentecost and Azusa Street is recognizing ecclesial diversity. Pentecostalism ruptures the white–Black binary of American
Protestantism with the existence of historically Latino Pentecostal denominations—Asamblea Apostólica de la Fe de Cristo Jesús, Concilio Latinoamericano de la Iglesia de Dios Pentecostal, Victory Outreach, and similar.
Many of these groups are absent from the PCCNA for historical and doctrinal
reasons, but the founding of the organization was explicitly concerned with
white–Black relations, a dynamic that was criticized almost immediately.[71]
Robeck pushed for Latino voices to be on the agenda of the organization, but
leaders responded that it could address only one issue at a time.[72] A compromise was reached eventually that Christian ministries could join alongside
denominations as members, such as the National Hispanic Christian Leadership Conference. It was recognized that the work of supporting intra-Pentecostal ecumenism required practices, policies, and structures to represent the
diversity of Pentecostal churches, ultimately enriching dialogue and common
action within the organization.

The founding of the PCCNA inspired at least five dissertations on racial
reconciliation.[73] It is noteworthy that, of those five, three are historiographical in nature, and a fourth concerns the rhetorical use of historical themes.
Scholars recognized a direct correlation between the reconciliation of

memories and interchurch relations within the PCCNA. Sherilyn Benvenuti, the first author to examine Robeck's contributions to church unity, studies him alongside Synan and Lovett to discern how historical narratives of unity and division contribute to contemporary social ethics of church unity. Derrick Rosenior argues that the PCCNA relied on a nostalgic vision of the past that mythologized the events and figures, though he affirms the value of the events for contemporary reconciliatory efforts. Russell West is more critical when he says the retrieval of historical rhetoric cannot support contemporary social reform without adaptation. Joel Newman is the most cynical when he studies the historical changes within the AG in light of the PCCNA's vision. These studies confirm Robeck's project that historical research is needed on Azusa Street to dispel myths and inform contemporary praxis. Christian unity cannot be founded on falsehood.

The PCCNA aims to give witness to unity between churches while providing a space to work through the legacy of racism within churches. Robeck refers to the mission of the organization as "reclaiming our heritage" of the reconciliatory mission of God.[74] In this, he establishes a link between the Azusa Street myth and the goals of the PCCNA. His argument exemplifies the above-mentioned Ricoeurian idea that social memory offers an image of the community for itself and outsiders. Pentecostals often tell the story of Azusa Street to depict themselves as a diverse and fraternal fellowship, but Robeck subverts the image to challenge the social memory of Pentecostal churches. He has spent decades of his life preserving a history that many would rather forget. The joint acknowledgment between Pentecostal churches of the historical wrongs that divided their communities prompts the need for ongoing work to repair their relations.

However, Robeck is less positive regarding the progress of the PCCNA in this regard. Fears of the effectiveness of the organization arose from the outset as to whether the rhetoric of goodwill would translate into action. Robeck remains loyal to the aspirations of the PCCNA when he says that people cannot criticize the organization without offering "new and accomplishable ideas" on how to advance its mission.[75] Nonetheless, his commitment to the PCCNA does not detract from his concerns over ecclesiastical leadership. He asserts that Pentecostal leaders prize too highly the value of commemorative events to the detriment of sustained action needed for reconciliation.[76] If communal memories shape the worldview of the community, then the act of reconciling memories of racial division between churches should result in changed actions and relations. David Daniels has recently appealed to the "Racial Reconciliation Manifesto" for its articulation of a Pentecostal political theology that challenges social and ecclesiastical racial injustices, but he refers the Manifesto in the past tense; it is no longer a living document in the Pentecostal imagination.[77] With little institutional attention given by

72   *Chapter 2*

churches to addressing change, Robeck laments that the PCCNA may have lost its racial edge.[78]

Christian Unity Commission

The reconciliation of historical memories resulted in new forms of inter-ecclesial relationships, ultimately establishing a platform for ecumenical engagement with the broader church. American Pentecostal participation in the ecumenical movement grew in spurts during the twentieth century, with little coordination between denominational leaders or scholars. The Society for Pentecostal Studies offered academic support for the PFNA and served as the first forum for ecumenical deliberations between Pentecostal academics, who were able to reflect on their activities and participate in ecumenical initiatives, such as the NCCUSA's Faith and Order Commission, which also launched Robeck's ecumenical career. The founding of the PCCNA in 1994 afforded an opportunity for Pentecostal ecumenists to enhance their work and garner ecclesiastical support. David Cole, Open Bible minister and former doctoral student of Robeck, served initially as PCCNA Liaison to the Greater Christian Community. Recognizing the task to be too great for one person, the PCCNA expanded the role in 2015 to include multiple Liaisons serving in its Christian Unity Commission. Robeck serves as the AG-appointed Liaison.

The existence of national confessional federations is a feature of Pentecostalism on the global ecumenical landscape, similar to diasporic Orthodox episcopal assemblies. Covered in the next chapter, Christian World Communions—such as the Baptist World Alliance or the Lutheran World Federation—gather churches of a confession internationally, yet similar structures seldom exist at the national level. On the other hand, Pentecostal churches have found value in establishing national structures to enable a common witness in society and ecumenical settings, such as the Ghana Pentecostal and Charismatic Council, Jamaica Pentecostal Union, Council of Pentecostal Churches of Tanzania (Baraza la Makanisa ya Kipentekoste Tanzania), Indonesian Pentecostal Church Fellowship (Persekutuan Gereja-Gereja Pantekosta Indonesia), or PCCNA. Comparable initiatives include the Pan-Methodist Commission in the United States and the North American Presbyterian and Reformed Council, both of which have addressed race as part of ecclesiastical relations within their own traditions.

The PCCNA Christian Unity Commission is tasked with fulfilling the PCCNA's mission of promoting dialogue and fellowship. It also builds on the Azusa Street narrative. The revival faced opposition from local ecumenical networks in Los Angeles, the first of a pattern of antagonism between American Pentecostals and segments of the American ecumenical movement. However, the PCCNA, through the Commission, has sought to recover the outward-facing dimension of the revival. Thus far, the Commission has been staffed by delegates, or "Liaisons," who are familiar with the scholarly activities of the ecumenical movement. The Commission offers updates on the numerous ecumenical initiatives to which PCCNA churches contribute and provides ecumenical formation opportunities during PCCNA gatherings.

Robeck situates the PCCNA within the broader discourse on ecumenism. He is critical of unilateral acts of churches done under the guise of prophetic leadership that disregards the wisdom of others.[79] Rather, churches ought to consult with each other when making decisions that might impact them.[80] The PCCNA points to the need for a developed and expansive ecclesiology to enable convergence between churches.[81] The work to construct an ecclesiology that overcomes racialized divisions requires an acknowledgment of the ecclesiality of other churches. A church cannot disregard the concerns of another church while pressing into a shared ecclesial life.

Through the work of the Christian Unity Commission, the PCCNA functions comparably to the Standing Conference of Oriental Orthodox Churches in America or the Assembly of Canonical (Eastern) Orthodox Bishops of the United States of America, both of which serve as platforms for ecumenical engagement with external church traditions. The North American Baptist Fellowship is currently exploring a similar arrangement. Churches of a common confession structure their relations with each other, including the coordination of their relations with external Christian bodies. Pentecostal churches federate within the PCCNA around a common historical narrative, resulting in an awareness of how churches' decisions affect each other.

The future of American Pentecostal ecumenical relations remains open. The Christian Unity Commission of the PCCNA initiated an exploratory conversation with the United States Conference of Catholic Bishops in 2021 in hopes of establishing a national dialogue. Robeck blames the delay of the dialogue's formation on the Conference's previous failure to distinguish Pentecostal churches from evangelicalism, and he attributes the breakthrough to the work of Harold Hunter.[82] The venture marks a shift in the Christian Unity Commission's function. Previously, the Commission was tasked with internal matters of the PCCNA for ecumenical formation and communication. Now, the Commission is tasked with guiding PCCNA member churches on their relations with Catholics. It is yet unknown how such ecumenical engagement will shape relations between Pentecostal churches.

74   *Chapter 2*

NARRATIVE ECUMENICAL METHODOLOGY

Robeck's historical research on the Azusa Street Revival and his participation in the PCCNA illustrate my argument on ecclesiology. The ecumenical method of reconciling memories relies upon a degree of shared memory between divided communities. Consequently, as communities reconcile their memories, they come to share a common historical narrative of the church, thereby converging in their ecclesiologies. Ecumenists cannot change the past, nor can they change the fact that churches are products of history. Nonetheless, they revisit history for the sake of changing the narratives that define churches. Robeck refers to this as the use of history to open the future, resisting the captivity of the past that isolates communities from each other.[83]

If the ecumenical method of reconciling memories contributes to the unity of the church, it must address history as more than the backdrop of ecumenical work. Communal memory serves as a form of narrative ecclesiology, whereby churches tell stories as a way of understanding themselves. The task of telling history well is part of ecumenism because it contributes to the convergence of churches in their historical narratives.

Narrative Communities

A reciprocal relationship exists between ecclesiology and the writing of church history. Beliefs concerning the nature of the church and its historical development influence the selection of individuals, movements, and events within the narrative. Similarly, how one reads history influences how one understands the historicity of the church and its relation to the world. Robeck acknowledges several theological questions that arise in historiography, including divine economy, supernatural intervention, and ecclesial identity.[84] Events in church history gain meaning when they are seen as acts of God. As such, historical narratives, in the form of communal memory, function as hermeneutical frameworks through which Christian communities perceive the world and themselves.[85] Robeck's work on reconciling memories concerns relations between American Pentecostal denominations and between Pentecostal churches and the ecumenical movement. The historical experience of rejection between communities and the existence of differences between these communities' accounts of historical events isolate them from each other. The rift between communities cannot be healed without the two reconciling their memories.[86]

Though Robeck's historical research includes the patristic era, his engagement with narrative ecclesiology centers on the Azusa Street myth. Pentecostals in the United States, and often outside, prize the revival because it shapes the self-image of Pentecostal churches. The narrative guides how Pentecostal churches relate to other churches, and renewal efforts among Pentecostals seek to rise to the legacy of Azusa Street. This is not meant to produce a short-sighted view of history among Pentecostals, as though God's church began in 1906 in Los Angeles. As mentioned in the previous chapter, for Robeck, the church bears the character of the Pentecost event because it began there. Insofar as the Azusa Street Revival embodied the values of the Pentecost event, Pentecostal churches seek to pattern themselves after the revival. Robeck's work on the revival employs narrative ecclesiology while dispelling false understandings of the history. He acknowledges that churches are tempted to sanitize history to comport with authorized narratives.[87] Myths are too powerful for ecclesiologists to ignore in their reflections on the church.

Historical narratives are powerful because they shape communal practices, values, and structures. A culture's songs, literature, and traditions pass on the identity of the society while offering cohesion and direction.[88] The same is true for churches. Robeck gives as an example the Waldensian community in Italy, which preserves its identity every generation by repeating stories of oppression and survival amid a Catholic majority. He compares the phenomenon to eucharistic *anamnēsis*, whereby believers relive the paschal event.[89] He adds, however, that not all stories comport with reality: "The continued propagation of time worn stereotypes, the *anamnēsis* of ancient divisions, the failure to investigate fresh evidences, and to allow in others the opportunity for growth and change, perpetuates the bearing of false witness."[90] Divided communities risk passing on such false narratives when they shun each other.

Because myths and other forms of communal narratives are part of ecclesiology, they serve either to unite or divide the church. Historical memories are places where identities are contested, resulting from differing interpretations of events.[91] Divergent narratives can result in divergent ecclesiologies. The "Called Together to be Peacemakers" report of the Catholic–Mennonite dialogue illustrates this when, in each section, before examining differences in ecclesiology, extended accounts of history are given that narrate how the differences came to be. The report shows how relations between the two churches are a consequence of the historical events and how the events are told.[92] Likewise, the contemporary racialization of ecclesiastical divisions within American Pentecostalism motivates Robeck to study history and how churches have spoken of or ignored history. One could question whether he goes too far in saying history accounts for the "most substantive differences" between churches,[93] but he is highlighting the historical nature of the church for the sake of resisting ethereal understandings of its unity. Christian theology knows of no church that is ahistorical. Even when events caused bitter antagonism, they must not be forgotten so that their wounds can be healed.[94] If history influences ecclesiology, it is of concern for ecumenists.

76   *Chapter 2*

Ecumenical methods, as argued in the book's introduction, are requisitely shared between ecclesial communities. The task of reconciling memories must be a joint venture. The aforementioned Catholic–Mennonite dialogue advances the idea that a common rereading of history between the two communities will form a common memory of their history, aiding ecumenical relations.[95] The ability for the two to enter into this process came as a result of *Unitatis redintegratio*, which Robeck appreciates for its acknowledgment of fault on the sides of Catholics and Protestants.[96] Changes in communal understandings of history can call into question the judgments and views that believers have received from their predecessors.[97] The purification of memories entails narrating history such that all communities involved can recognize themselves in it, even when it leads to repentance. The historical narrative of Azusa Street, for example, spurs the need for confession and repentance between divided Pentecostal communities within the PCCNA and similar venues. Had the communities not studied the event together, they would not have been forced to confront the causes of their division.

Changes in historical narratives do not occur instantaneously, for such narratives are embodied in social practices and institutions. The reconciliation of memories—as an act of repentance—happens over time as churches reform their understanding of themselves. The Lutheran–Mennonite dialogue describes the importance of sustained reflection on reconciling memories. Each community's perception of the other spread with them wherever Mennonite and Lutheran churches traveled. Events in sixteenth-century Germany did not stay in sixteenth-century Germany, for they persist within the communal memories of contemporary Mennonites and Lutherans around the world.[98] Similarly, Robeck publicizes the Azusa Street myth widely in his scholarship because he believes it supports the unitive work of contemporary Pentecostals wherever they are found. Believers need not let the divisions of the past determine their future.[99] Ecumenists encourage members of their own churches to revisit their history for the sake of changing their understanding of who they are as a community and how they should be reconciled to other communities.

Reconciled Communities

The unity of the church concerns more than the church's rhetoric or stories. For churches to be reconciled, they must also change their systems of relations. The ecumenical method of reconciling memories, if it results in a convergence in ecclesiology, must result in a shared community. The principle of reconciliation is not an addendum to ecclesiology. As seen in the first chapter, the church is a product of God's reconciliatory work in the world, and the church's ministry of reconciliation participates in this work. Insofar as the church is missional by its very nature, it is also reconciliatory. Robeck associates the ecumenical movement with the ministry of reconciliation (2 Cor. 5:11-21).[100] The new community the gospel forms offers a tangible example of forgiveness and unity, which is why he argues that the improper treatment of Black Pentecostals by white Pentecostal churches "contaminates" the church's gospel message.[101] The work of reconciling these two communities requires ecclesiological reflection because of the ecclesiological nature of reconciliation.

The ecumenical method of reconciling memories relies on a degree of shared narrative ecclesiology, meaning that churches must remember the same events for a convergence to occur. Ecumenists employ the Azusa Street myth not only because it speaks of Christians living out unity together but also because divided communities share the story. The historical event shaped Pentecostal ecclesiology, and so a convergence between Pentecostal churches builds on their shared history. Said a different way, events that are not part of communities' histories cannot influence their relations. For example, the Lutheran–Mennonite dialogue's attempts to reconcile memories do not speak of events within Methodist history because these events are not shared between Lutherans and Mennonites. The same could be said for the virtual absence of history after the Council of Chalcedon in discussions of Chalcedonian churches with the Oriental Orthodox Communion. After Chalcedon, the divided churches did not share much history, resulting in divergent ecclesiologies. The ecumenical method of reconciling memories relies on shared experiences.

The commonality does not guarantee that the communities agree on the facts of the events. Historical research within ecumenical ventures can lead to repentance when communities realize they were in the wrong. The founding of the PCCNA is commemorated in Pentecostal literature because it was a penitential act between white and Black Pentecostal churches. The place of Latino and other Pentecostals within the history and organization is an increasingly important dynamic for scholars, yet it accords with other historical themes already seen on exclusion. Robeck identifies the role of self-awareness within ecumenical work, which enables people to listen and receive.[102] He writes for AG periodicals on the nature of the Azusa Street Revival and its racial dynamic to foster contemporary reconciliation.

The revisiting of historical narratives also broadens a church's narrative, often by including figures and events that other churches have prized as a way to receive these churches.[103] The earlier mention of the Assemblies of God Theological Seminary's William J. Seymour Chapel is an example of this. The AG seminary's honoring of Seymour is part of their honoring of Azusa Street, but it also broadens the denomination's historical narrative. As mentioned earlier, no denomination descended directly from the revival.

78 Chapter 2

Seymour was never a member of the AG. In fact, there are numerous points of doctrine, liturgy, and church polity on which Seymour disagreed with the AG. Nonetheless, by identifying with Seymour and Azusa Street, the AG identifies itself within the larger Pentecostal movement and with other churches that also honor Seymour.

The reconciliation of memories enables divided churches to see themselves as part of the same community. This does not gloss over other differences that exist between churches, but it brings the churches together to deal with their differences. Ecumenical historiography situates the divisions and unity of the church within salvation history.[104] Churches come to see themselves as products of God's reconciling work in the world. The aforementioned white PFNA formed during a time when Pentecostals attributed little significance to Azusa Street, and the revival's growing prominence in the self-definition of American Pentecostalism enabled the formation of the multiracial PCCNA. Even today, the ubiquity of the revival myth in American Pentecostal historiography testifies to the vital function of narrative ecclesiology for the work of uniting churches.

The PCCNA's Christian Unity Commission furthers the organization's mission in ways that contradict potential interpretations of the Azusa Street myth. As mentioned above, early ecumenical movements in Los Angeles shunned the Azusa Street Mission. Many Pentecostal churches are a historic result of congregations being kicked out of their denominations. If the Pentecostal tradition's narrative is one of perseverance amid opposition from other churches, why should Pentecostals bother fostering relations with those churches? Pentecostal ecumenists, however, have highlighted the unitive aspirations of the revival to embrace its legacy. The revisiting of history offers renewal within the ecclesial community for the sake of sharing an ecclesiology of reconciliation even with historic enemies of the community.

The ecumenical concern for history instills a unitive vision of the future. Robeck, during his Azusa Street tours, often distributes copies of the PCCNA "Racial Reconciliation Manifesto" to participants.[105] The revisiting of a painful memory between divided churches prompts the need for reconciled narratives, spurring the work toward reconciling the divided communities. This reveals a clear relation between narrative and ecclesiastical systems. He notes the skepticism common among Black American ecumenists of the language of "spiritual unity," for it ignores the sociopolitical realities that pertain to unity.[106] The work of reconciling communities entails changing systems and practices of relations that divide them. Robeck uses this to highlight an inconsistency that is prevalent among Pentecostal voices on ecumenism and their rhetoric of a spiritual unity without an institutional component. When Pentecostals were faced with their own divisions, however, they recognized that visible unity requires routinized, formalized, and institutionalized practices.[107] Without such structures as the PCCNA, churches are unable to pursue the unity that reconciled memories warrant.

The institutional consequences of narrative ecclesiology lead to the next chapter's discussion of conciliar ecumenism. The reconciliation of historical narratives re-narrates the self-understanding of divided Christian communities. Churches revisit episodes of history that estranged them from each other, prompting confession, repentance, and forgiveness that bring healing. The ecumenical method of reconciling memories relies on a shared ecclesial narrative; otherwise, there would be no common period of history for the divided churches to claim together. More than this, as churches reconcile their shared memories, they converge in a common ecclesial narrative; otherwise, their memories would not, in fact, be reconciled. Churches are enabled to speak in one voice on the history of their communities, paving the way for churches to live and act together through ventures such as the PCCNA. The ecumenical work to reconcile (from *reconciliare*)—literally, to "re-council"—churches consequently raises questions of conciliar ecumenism through which churches live and act together.

NOTES

1. "Home," Indian Christian Day, accessed June 29, 2022, https://indianchristianday.com/.
2. *TCTCV*, §1.
3. World Council of Churches Commission on Faith and Order, *Participating in God's Mission of Reconciliation: A Resource for Churches in Situations of Conflict*, Faith and Order Paper 201 (Geneva: World Council of Churches, 2006), §112.
4. *Participating in God's Mission*, §159, 160.
5. Mark Santer, "The Reconciliation of Memories," in *Reconciling Memories*, ed. Alan D. Falconer and Joseph Liechty, 2nd ed. (Dublin: The Columba Press, 1998), 32; Paolo Salvatore Nicosia, *Riconciliazione: Esperienze e modelli in contesti ecumenici* (Rome: Aracne Editrice, 2020), 261.
6. Richard Kearney, "Myth and the Critique of Tradition," in *Reconciling Memories*, ed. Alan D. Falconer and Joseph Liechty, 2nd ed. (Dublin: The Columba Press, 1998), 44–47.
7. "Towards a Common Understanding of the Church: Reformed/Roman Catholic International Dialogue. Second Phase (1984–1990)," 1990, §62.
8. "Called Together to Be Peacemakers: Report of the International Dialogue between the Catholic Church and Mennonite World Conference 1998–2003," 2003, §191.
9. Thomas Finger, "Reflections on an Ecumenical-Historical Experiment," in *Telling the Churches' Stories: Ecumenical Perspectives on Writing Christian History*, ed. Timothy J. Wengert and Charles W. Brockwell, Jr. (Grand Rapids, MI: Eerdmans, 1995), 106, 107.

80 *Chapter 2*

10. Timothy J. Wengert and Charles W. Brockwell, Jr., eds., "Preface," in *Telling the Churches' Stories: Ecumenical Perspectives on Writing Christian History* (Grand Rapids, MI: Eerdmans, 1995), xvi, xvii, xx.

11. Hans Uytenbogaardt and Guido Dotti, "Places of Memory," in *A Cloud of Witnesses: Opportunities for Ecumenical Commemoration. Proceedings of the International Ecumenical Symposium, Monastery of Bose, 29 October – 2 November 2008*, by World Council of Churches Commission on Faith and Order, ed. Tamara Grdzelidze and Guido Dotti, Faith and Order Paper 209 (Geneva: World Council of Churches, 2009), 200–209.

12. "Healing Memories: Reconciling in Christ. Report of the Lutheran-Mennonite International Study Commission," 2010, 11; "Bearing Fruit: Implications of the 2010 Reconciliation between Lutherans and Mennonites/Anabaptists. Report of the Lutheran World Federation Task Force to Follow Up the 'Mennonite Action' at the LWF Eleventh Assembly in 2010," 2016, 13, 14.

13. Robeck, *"The Quiet,"* 64.

14. Robeck, "The Past," 2.

15. Robeck, *The Azusa*, 10.

16. Robeck, *"The Quiet,"* 65.

17. Wallace de Góis Silva, "Igreja de Cristo Pentecostal no Brasil e unidade: Cooperação e tensões com grupos cristãos nos documentos históricos e teológicos," in *Pentecostalismos e unidade: Desafios institucionais, teológicos e sociais*, ed. David Mesquiati de Oliveira (São Paulo: Fonte Editorial, 2015), 90, 91.

18. Kalombo Kapuku, *Pentecôtismes Tome 1*, 95.

19. Japie Jimmy Lapoorta, *Unity or Division? The Unity Struggles of the Black Churches within the Apostolic Faith Mission of South Africa* (Kuils River, South Africa: J.J. Lapoorta, 1996), 23–47, 157, 160, 161, 177, 178.

20. Terje Hegertun, *Det brodersind som pinseaanden nødvendigvis maa føde: Analyse av økumeniske posisjoner i norsk pinsebevegelse med henblikk på utviklingen av en pentekostal økumenikk og fornyelse av økumeniske arbeidsformer* (Trondheim, Norway: Tapir Akademisk, 2009), 25–33.

21. 戴觀豪，"「我將澆灌我靈予所有人」：西摩的靈洗教義與普世合一，" 華文五旬宗研究期刊 [David Kwun-Ho Tai, "I Will Pour Out of My Spirit upon All Flesh: Seymour's Doctrine of Spirit Baptism and Ecumenism," *Chinese Journal of Pentecostal Studies*] 3 (2019): 56–79.

22. Alan Varghese, *Pentecostal Churches and Ecumenism in India* (New Delhi: Indian Society for Promoting Christian Knowledge, 2015), 39.

23. Cecil M. Robeck, Jr., "A Pentecostal Assessment of 'Towards a Common Understanding and Vision' of the WCC," *Midstream: The Ecumenical Movement Today* 37, no. 1 (1998): 12.

24. Tennison and Robeck, "Interview," 18.

25. Robeck, *The Azusa*, 28, 36, 121, 232, 233.

26. Robeck, 17–25.

27. "The Apostolic Faith Movement," *The Apostolic Faith*, September 1906, vol. 1, no. 1, p. 2.

28. Cecil M. Robeck, Jr., "William J. Seymour: An Early Model of Pentecostal Leadership," *Enrichment* 1, no. 2 (2006): 50.

29. Cecil M. Robeck, Jr., "Pentecostal Origins in Global Perspective," in *All Together in One Place: Theological Papers from the Brighton Conference on World Evangelization*, ed. Harold D. Hunter and Peter D. Hocken (Sheffield, UK: Sheffield Academic, 1993), 172.

30. Robeck, *The Azusa*, 1.

31. Cecil M. Robeck, Jr., "The Leadership Legacy of William J. Seymour," in *We've Come This Far: Reflections on the Pentecostal Tradition and Racial Reconciliation*, ed. Byron D. Klaus, The Pentecostal Ministry Series 2 (Springfield, MO: Assemblies of God Theological Seminary, 2007), 40; Robeck, *The Azusa*, 30.

32. Robeck, "*The Quiet*," 73, 74.

33. Ross W. Sanderson, *Church Cooperation in the United States: The Nation-Wide Backgrounds and Ecumenical Significance of State and Local Councils of Churches in Their Historical Perspective* (Hartford, CT: Finlay Brothers Press, 1960), 69, 84; Gene Boutilier, "Rev. Gene Boutilier Remarks, Centennial of Southern California Ecumenical Council, Thursday, September 27, 2012, Pasadena, California" (Southern California Christian Forum internal document, 2012), 1.

34. "Young Girl Given Gift of Tongues," *Los Angeles Express*, July 20, 1906, p. 1; quoted in Robeck, "Discerning the Spirit," 31; Robeck, *The Azusa*, 84.

35. Robeck, "The Holy Spirit and the Unity," 355; Robeck, *The Azusa*, 83–86, 188.

36. "Spreads the Fire," *The Apostolic Faith*, October 1906, vol. 1, no. 2, p. 4.

37. Cecil M. Robeck, Jr., "The Azusa Street Mission and the Historic Black Churches: Two Worlds in Conflict in Los Angeles' African American Community," in *Afro-Pentecostalism: Black Pentecostal and Charismatic Christianity in History and Culture*, ed. Amos Yong and Estrelda Y. Alexander (New York: New York University Press, 2011), 21–41.

38. Research on the Latino and other ethnic groups' presence at the revival is sparse. It is yet unknown how these communities in Los Angeles responded to the revival.

39. Robeck, "William J. Seymour: An Early," 51; Robeck, "The Leadership," 56; Cecil M. Robeck, Jr., "Early Pentecostal Visions in the United States of Christian Unity, Retrenchment, and Evangelical Influences," in *Pentecostal Theology and Ecumenical Theology: Interpretation and Intersections*, ed. Peter D. Hocken, Tony L. Richie, and Christopher A. Stephenson (Leiden: Brill, 2019), 11; Robeck, *The Azusa*, 94–96.

40. Cecil M. Robeck, Jr., "Azusa Street Revival," in *The New International Dictionary of Pentecostal and Charismatic Movements*, ed. Stanley M. Burgess and Eduard M. van der Maas, 2nd ed. (Grand Rapids, MI: Zondervan, 2003), 349.

41. Gastón Espinosa, *William J. Seymour and the Origins of Global Pentecostalism: A Biography and Documentary History* (Durham, NC: Duke University Press, 2014), 117–21.

42. Robeck, *The Azusa*, x, 3.

43. Cecil M. Robeck, Jr. in discussion with the author, April 14, 2022.

44. Robeck hosted numerous ecumenical consultations at Fuller Theological Seminary across decades. During these meetings, he led the participants on his Azusa

82 *Chapter 2*

Street tour. Through his scholarship, ecumenical work, and tours, Robeck promoted the Azusa Street myth as a defining narrative of Pentecostalism for a global audience.

45. Cecil M. Robeck, Jr. in discussion with the author, August 16, 2023. Details of this story were also confirmed by a member of the Committee who asked to remain anonymous.

46. This story deserves further examination from someone more qualified than me to tell it. However, it was important to mention it here to frame properly Robeck's role in the history. The memorialization of Azusa Street is not the tale of a white scholar but the tale of local communities of color, whose labors were supported by a scholar with access to institutional resources and specialized training.

47. Cecil M. Robeck, Jr. in discussion with the author, April 14, 2022.

48. Cecil M. Robeck, Jr. in discussion with the author, August 16, 2023.

49. The Committee has also repeatedly attempted to plant a grapefruit tree on the plaza where the Mission building stood. The saplings come from a grove that originally surrounded Azusa Street at the turn of the twentieth century. However, tourists strip the planted tree of fruit, leaves, and bark once they learn of the tree's connection to the revival, which has killed every tree that the Committee planted.

50. "The Project," Azusa Street Mission, accessed July 2, 2022, https://312azusa .com/the-project/.

51. Cecil M. Robeck, Jr., "The Earliest Pentecostal Missions of Los Angeles," *Assemblies of God Heritage* 3, no. 3 (1983): 3–4, 12; Cecil M. Robeck, Jr., "Uncovering the Forgotten Story of the Azusa Street Mission," *Assemblies of God Heritage* 25, no. 4 (2006): 12–15; Robeck, "The Leadership"; Robeck, "William J. Seymour: An Early"; Cecil M. Robeck, Jr., "Azusa Street: 100 Years Later," *Enrichment* 11, no. 2 (2006): 26–42.

52. Robeck, "The Leadership," 65.

53. Robeck, *The Azusa*, 10.

54. Harold D. Hunter and Cecil M. Robeck, Jr., eds., "Introduction," in *The Azusa Street Revival and Its Legacy* (Cleveland, TN: Pathway Press, 2006), 15.

55. Robeck, "*The Quiet*," 87.

56. Cecil M. Robeck, Jr. in discussion with the author, April 14, 2022.

57. Espinosa, *William J. Seymour*, 8–18.

58. Robeck, *The Azusa*, 8, 9.

59. Robeck, 13.

60. Tennison and Robeck, "Interview," 17.

61. Hugh McCullum, "Racism and Ethnicity," in *A History of the Ecumenical Movement, Volume 3: 1968-2000*, ed. John Briggs, Mercy Amba Oduyoye, and Georges Tsetsis (Geneva: World Council of Churches, 2004), 364.

62. Robeck, "The Past," 58.

63. Benvenuti, "Reconstruction," 1, 2.

64. The paper was published as Robeck, "The Past."

65. Robeck, "The Past," 7, 8.

66. Cecil M. Robeck, Jr., "Racial Reconciliation at Memphis: Some Personal Reflections," *Pneuma* 18, no. 1 (1996): 135.

67. Robeck, 136.

68. Vinson Synan, "Memphis 1994: Miracle and Mandate," 1997, https://pccna.org/documents/1994Memphis.pdf.

69. "Racial Reconciliation Manifesto," 1994, https://pccna.org/documents/1994manifesto.pdf.

70. Harold D. Hunter, "Attacking Systemic Racism for the Common Good: Excerpts from the History of the 'Racial Reconciliation Manifesto,'" in *The Politics of the Spirit: Pentecostal Reflections on Public Responsibility and the Common Good*, ed. Daniela C. Augustine and Chris E.W. Green (Lanham, MD: Seymour Press, 2022), 39–50.

71. David Leon Cole, "Pentecostal Koinonia: An Emerging Ecumenical Ecclesiology among Pentecostals" (Ph.D. dissertation, Pasadena, CA, Fuller Theological Seminary, 1998), 239–43.

72. Cole, 243 n122.

73. Russell Wade West, "That His People May Be One: An Interpretive Study of the Pentecostal Leadership's Quest for Racial Unity" (Ph.D. dissertation, Virginia Beach, VI, Regent University, 1997); Benvenuti, "Reconstruction"; Maryalice Newsome, "The Impact of the Miracle in Memphis on the Racial Reconciliation Initiatives of the Assemblies of God Churches in the Greater Kansas City Area" (Ph.D. dissertation, Kansas City, MO, University of Missouri - Kansas City, 2004); Joe Newman, *Race and the Assemblies of God Church: The Journey from Azusa Street to the "Miracle of Memphis"* (Youngstown, NY: Cambria Press, 2007); Derrick Rosenior, *Toward Racial Reconciliation: Collective Memory, Myth, and Nostalgia in American Pentecostalism* (Saarbrücken: VDM Verlag Dr. Müller, 2009).

74. Robeck, "The Past," 68.

75. Robeck, "Racial," 140.

76. Robeck, 138.

77. David D. Daniels, III, "Future of North American Pentecostalism: Contemporary Diasporas, New Denominationalism, Inclusive Racial Politics, and Post-Secular Sensibilities," *Pneuma* 42, no. 3–4 (2020): 401–404; David D. Daniels, III, "Engaging Racial Equity: Toward a Pentecostal Political Theology of Race," *Pneuma* 44, no. 3–4 (2022): 372.

78. Cecil M. Robeck, Jr. in discussion with the author, April 14, 2022.

79. Robeck, "Ecumenism," 294.

80. Cecil M. Robeck, Jr., "Facing Our Past," *Ministries Today* 13, no. 1 (1995): 40.

81. Robeck, "Racial," 139.

82. Cecil M. Robeck, Jr. in discussion with the author, April 14, 2022.

83. Robeck, "Ecumenism," 295.

84. Cecil M. Robeck, Jr., "The Origins of Modern Pentecostalism: Some Historiographical Issues," in *The Cambridge Companion to Pentecostalism*, ed. Cecil M. Robeck, Jr. and Amos Yong (Cambridge: Cambridge University Press, 2014), 13.

85. Alan D. Falconer, "Remembering," in *Reconciling Memories*, ed. Alan D. Falconer and Joseph Liechty, 2nd ed. (Dublin: The Columba Press, 1998), 15.

86. Cecil M. Robeck, Jr., "My Call to Ecumenism," in *Global Christian Forum: Transforming Ecumenism*, ed. Richard Howell (New Delhi: Evangelical Fellowship

of India, 2007), 70, 71; Cecil M. Robeck, Jr., "Lessons from the International Roman Catholic–Pentecostal Dialogue," in *Pentecostalism and Christian Unity: Ecumenical Documents and Critical Assessments*, ed. Wolfgang Vondey (Eugene, OR: Pickwick Publications, 2010), 94; Robeck, "A Pentecostal Assessment," 13.

87. Robeck, "An Emerging," 207.

88. Falconer, "Remembering," 12.

89. Robeck, "Some Pentecostal," 244, 245.

90. Robeck, "Pentecostals and the Apostolic," 71.

91. World Council of Churches Commission on Faith and Order, *Participating in God's Mission*, §150.

92. "Called Together to Be Peacemakers," §30–68.

93. Robeck, "Pentecostal/Charismatic," 24.

94. Robeck, "Lessons," 93.

95. "Called Together to Be Peacemakers," §27.

96. Robeck, "Lessons," 94; *UR*, §3.

97. Robeck, "Lessons," 85.

98. "Bearing Fruit," 8, 9.

99. Cecil M. Robeck, Jr., "Fuller's Ecumenical Vision," *Theology, News & Notes* 57, no. 2 (2010): 20.

100. Robeck, "Roman Catholic-Pentecostal Dialogue: Some," 12; Robeck, "When I Grow Up," 30, 31.

101. Robeck, "Facing," 40.

102. Robeck, "Ecumenism," 293, 294.

103. Mary Tanner, "The Achievement of Bilateral Dialogues and Some Implications for a Common Martyrology," in *A Cloud of Witnesses: Opportunities for Ecumenical Commemoration. Proceedings of the International Ecumenical Symposium, Monastery of Bose, 29 October – 2 November 2008*, by World Council of Churches Commission on Faith and Order, ed. Tamara Grdzelidze and Guido Dotti, Faith and Order Paper 209 (Geneva: World Council of Churches, 2009), 45; Cecil M. Robeck, Jr., "Taking Stock of Pentecostalism: The Personal Reflections of a Retiring Editor," *Pneuma* 15, no. 1 (1993): 51.

104. Lionel Chircop, "Re-Membering the Future," in *Reconciling Memories*, ed. Alan D. Falconer and Joseph Liechty, 2nd ed. (Dublin: The Columba Press, 1998), 24.

105. Cecil M. Robeck, Jr. in discussion with the author, April 14, 2022.

106. Robeck, "The Apostolic," 81.

107. Robeck, "The Challenge," 320.

Chapter 3

The Push to Expand the World Council of Churches

The violence that erupted in Kenya after the 2007 presidential election bordered on genocide. Accusations of electoral manipulation undermined confidence in governance structures, and the ensuant economic impact rippled throughout East Africa. Power differentials between ethnic groups aggravated tensions, with particular organizations and regions associated with particular tribes. Even Christian denominations were concentrated in different regions, so they struggled to gain credibility in the eyes of the public. One of the social structures that was positioned to broker peace talks in the country was the National Council of Churches of Kenya (Baraza la Kitaifa la Makanisa Nchini [NCCK]). The coalition of churches within the NCCK spanned ethnic groups and regions, and its national platform permitted it to receive assistance from the All Africa Conference of Churches.[1] The NCCK functioned as a neutral party between groups. Since then, the NCCK has amplified its voice in civic affairs as one of the few pan-ethnic entities in Kenya. The NCCK today trains women as dialogue facilitators in villages and cities.[2] The Council has strengthened Kenyan churches in a mission they otherwise would have been unable to fulfill.

Conciliar methodology touches on ecclesiological themes already examined. The fellowship between member churches reflects a diverse and catholic communion that spans social divisions. Covenanted together, the churches seek unity through renewal and a common life. Councils of churches proliferated globally during the twentieth century, becoming the iconic structural form of the ecumenical movement. The ecumenical movement has been described as a "conciliar renaissance," with councils forming within and between churches.[3] The health of a council in a nation or city has even been used to gauge the health of ecumenism in that locality.

86   *Chapter 3*

Ecumenical scholarship has grappled with the theological significance of councils of churches, a new ecclesiological manifestation that straddles the distinction between church and parachurch. The interstitial nature of conciliar ecumenism illustrates the ecclesiological basis of ecumenical methodology. Councils of churches operate on a shared understanding of how churches relate to each other, and as churches develop shared practices and relationships within councils, they converge in their ecclesiologies.

CONCILIAR ECCLESIOLOGY

The participation of churches in councils is a prominent example of the way that ecumenical methodology has informed the emergent consensus on ecclesiology. Churches recognize the conciliar nature of the church because they have experienced it. The Faith and Order paper *Councils, Conciliarity, and a Genuinely Universal Council* roots conciliarity in the presence of Christ within the church.[4] As mentioned in the first chapter, the fellowship of believers with God is the basis for communion ecclesiology. The Spirit of Christ draws churches out of their particularity into communion with each other and God.[5] Church councils are one way in which the fellowship of believers is preserved, with the structures and practices of conciliarity serving as instruments of the Spirit.[6] Conciliarity, as a consequence of God's indwelling the church, is part of the church's given nature rather than an aspiration.[7] The church does not have councils; the church itself is a conciliar fellowship.

Ecclesial communion takes historical form in conciliar practices.[8] Christian communities worship, dialogue, and act together as an expression of their partaking in the same Spirit. Jean-Marie Tillard identifies the sacramental basis of councils of churches. Christians are incorporated through baptism into the Body of Christ, with their communion as a fruit of the Spirit's work.[9] For this, he describes councils of churches as "charismatic institutions" that are part of "the great charisma of the restoration of the communion of grace."[10] The presence of the Spirit in the church defines its charismatic dimension by gracing the church with its needed gifts, which are to be shared among its members. The methodology of conciliar ecumenism presumes a pneumatological ecclesiology whereby God indwells the church and brings the church to the unity that God intended for it.

Such a high theological understanding of councils can contrast with their lived experiences. The aforementioned Faith and Order paper admits that councils oscillate between being instruments of divine economy and being administrative bureaucracies.[11] Yet conciliar life requires even mundane practices to facilitate the church's God-given fellowship.

Ecclesial interactions in the ecumenical movement have challenged churches to revisit their own ecclesiologies, including the ongoing Catholic synodal reforms.[12] Dialogue between Catholic and Orthodox communities has renewed the attention of both to synodal practices that existed prior to their schism.[13] The increasing frequency of inter-Orthodox consultations is also a consequence of ecumenical experience with the Catholic Church and within various councils of churches.

The relationship between conciliar ecclesiology and ecumenical methodology raises the question of the ecclesial nature of councils of churches. Diane Kessler and Michael Kinnamon define councils of churches as voluntary associations of churches in a region that seek to live out their fellowship together and overcome their division.[14] Councils of churches are an expression of the church's present unity that compels Christians toward a fuller unity. In this way, conciliarity is both a goal and method of the ecumenical movement.[15] Ecumenists regard councils of churches, despite their value, as temporary. Membership in any given council is not the goal of ecumenists, and the purpose of councils of churches is to make themselves obsolete. A council of churches is a midwife to a united church, not the embryo. The parallel assertions are hard to reconcile: the ecumenical method of councils of churches comports with the ecumenical goal of conciliarity, yet councils of churches are not the goal of ecumenism.

The association between conciliarism and ecclesiology is partially a consequence of language. Aram Keshishian begins his classic study on conciliar fellowship by identifying the confusion that the term "council" causes in ecumenical discourse. The English term denotes a variety of ecclesiastical gatherings whose theological self-understandings diverge. On one hand, councils can be an intra-ecclesiastical gathering of leaders presently in full communion, such as the Second Vatican Council. On the other hand, councils can be a cooperative enterprise of divided churches for a common purpose, such as the World Council of Churches. Keshishian lists examples of languages that distinguish between these two entities, including *concilio–consejo* (Spanish), *concile–conseil* (French), *Konzil–Rat* (German), σύνοδος–συμβούλιο (Greek), собор–совет (Russian), and مجمع – مجلس (Arabic).[16] One could add to his list: 协会 – 联合会 (Chinese), *konseho–sangguniáng* (Tagalog), ጉባኤ—ምክር ቤት (Amharic), *konsili–dewan* (Bahasa Indonesian), സുന്നഹദോസ് – സഭായോഗം (Malayalam), and *mtaguso–baraza* (Swahili).[17] The dominance of English as the medium of ecumenical discourse globally obfuscates a doctrinal clarity that many non-anglophone communities have found useful.

An example closer to Robeck's context would be the General Council of the Assemblies of God (the formal name of Robeck's denomination [AG]) and the National Council of the Churches of Christ in the USA (NCCUSA).

88   *Chapter 3*

The distinction is seen in the two entities' Spanish names—Concilio General de las Asambleas de Dios and Consejo Nacional de las Iglesias de Cristo en los Estados Unidos. Both are constituted as gatherings of churches for common worship and witness, so they are "councils." However, because the gathering of churches in the AG presumes a degree of communion by which they can be called a united whole, the AG is a *concilio*; because the gathering of churches in the NCCUSA does not share this form of communion, it is a *consejo*. The fact that such different ecclesial entities can both be called councils illustrates the questions that could emerge within conciliar ecumenism.

Notwithstanding its limitations, the English term "council" points to the interrelation of ecumenical methods and goals. The ecumenical method of councils arises from the ecumenical goal of ecclesial conciliarism. The ecclesiology of conciliar fellowship is drawn from the early church as a "converging model for church unity."[18] Again, the ecumenical movement seeks to restore ecclesial practices and structures to their pre-division reality. Part of this work is for churches to revisit their ecclesiologies together. The WCC, in its *Common Understanding and Vision of the WCC (CUV)*, claims for itself the mission of challenging member churches to reflect on the ecclesiological significance of the fellowship they enjoy in the Council.[19] The ecumenical method of councils of churches gives rise to an experience-based ecclesiology that churches work out together.

Robeck's experience in councils of churches has been as a partial outsider, never representing a member church. His inclusion testifies to the efforts of councils to expand their membership, which he has aided through his constructively critical contributions throughout the decades. Through his work, he intersected with different forms of conciliarity that clash with and inform each other in the ecumenical movement's search for convergence. His exposure to conciliar ecumenism coincided with methodological shifts in ecumenism globally, placing him amid conversations on Christian World Communions and the WCC.

CHRISTIAN WORLD COMMUNIONS

Christian World Communions (CWCs) are global bodies of churches congregated around a common heritage and vision of the Christian life for the sake of shared witness to the faith. CWCs and councils of churches seek to facilitate relations between churches in matters of faith. Though some CWCs existed earlier, they proliferated around the time of the founding of the WCC. In theory and praxis, CWCs are the methodological counterpoint to councils of churches. CWCs foster intra-confessional unity as an expression of presently existent fellowship at a global level; the WCC fosters interconfessional unity as an expression of imperfect fellowship at a global level.[20] Though Faith and Order has described CWCs as a form of conciliar fellowship,[21] it is generally held that they are not themselves councils of churches. The tension between the two ecumenical methods generates ecclesiological reflection, especially as it regards the church's catholicity.[22]

CWCs operate differently from each other according to the ecclesiologies of their respective confessions. The operative ecclesiology of the Anglican Communion results in a different organization than that of the Mennonite World Conference, yet they are both classified as CWCs. Lukas Vischer identifies the ecclesiological significance of the questions that CWCs pose to ecumenical methodology. The conditions of ecclesial unity, boundaries of legitimate diversity, and relations of the local and global church all determine the nature of CWCs and how CWCs interact with each other.[23] Harding Meyer adds to the discussion the three ecclesiological principles of CWCs—catholicity across space, continuity across time, and legitimate diversity of theology and praxis.[24] Relations between churches of a common confession influence and are influenced by relations with churches of other confessions. For Robeck, this is seen in his dealings with the Pentecostal World Fellowship and the Conference of the Secretaries of Christian World Communions.

Pentecostal World Fellowship

The Pentecostal World Fellowship (PWF) is the largest global body of Pentecostal churches. Robeck describes the PWF as an organization whose goals are visible witness, cooperation, doctrinal purity, and fellowship.[25] Functionally, it is a global parallel of the PCCNA mentioned in the previous chapter, though different historical and cultural dynamics shape its mission. It originated as the Pentecostal World Conference in 1947, a triennial gathering that met partially as a response to the formation process of the WCC in 1948. To strengthen the bonds of unity between member churches, the Conference established the PWF in 1999 as a continuation committee to carry out work between triennial conferences.

In general, the representative function of CWCs is tempered because CWCs seldom are comprised of every church of its confession. Some churches remain unaffiliated or join a competing CWC, as is the case for the World Communion of Reformed Churches and the World Reformed Fellowship. This is seen with the PWF and Apostolic World Christian Fellowship. Additionally, churches may belong to both a CWC and a smaller ecclesial global body, as is the case for the World Methodist Council and the global United Methodist Church. This is seen with the PWF and World Assemblies of God Fellowship. The PWF does not incorporate all Pentecostal churches, a limitation most CWCs face.

CWCs establish boundaries of identity between churches that do and do not belong to an ecclesial tradition. Churches can join if they share a common Baptist heritage, Adventist confession, or Anglican polity, for example. Such identity boundaries determine the nature of relations between CWCs. Historians of the ecumenical movement note that CWCs grew in importance because of the Second Vatican Council. CWCs were invited to send official observers to the Council, and they served as contacts when the Secretariat for Promoting Christian Unity began initiating bilateral dialogues.[26] The Catholic Church treated CWCs as the authoritative voices for their communions, determining which theologians can participate in dialogues and who is able to speak on behalf of member churches. Whereas councils of churches refrain from facilitating bilateral dialogues, CWCs act in this capacity.[27] CWCs became a space for global reflection on transregional confessional identities in dialogue.

The PWF differs from many other CWCs in its relation to the ecumenical movement. Prior to the founding of its Christian Unity Commission in 2019, the PWF was not involved with bilateral dialogues, and, prior to 2021, the PWF had no formal relations with other CWCs. Robeck spearheaded the effort to establish the Christian Unity Commission with the support of then-PWF Chair and Malaysian minister Prince Guneratnam. The Commission is tasked with overseeing Pentecostal bilateral dialogues and promoting ecumenical formation among PWF member churches, working alongside the World Missions Commission and World Alliance for Pentecostal Theological Education. Gedeon Alencar has argued that the growing ecumenical activities of the PWF will further isolate many non-Western Pentecostal churches from the organization,[28] though there is no reason to suggest that geography is a determinative factor in these trends. The integration of Pentecostal ecumenical work into a formalized structure will elevate concerns of professionalization, legitimacy, and authority with which other CWCs have grappled.[29]

Pentecostal participation in bilateral dialogues for half a century has occurred outside of CWC structures, a dynamic covered in the next chapter. Robeck's valuing of the PWF is not for its ability to foster external relations but internal ones. The PWF is currently the largest—if not the only major—transdenominational global body of Pentecostal churches. Robeck maintains that the unity of the Pentecostal movement requires knowledge of and dialogue with Pentecostals in other regions.[30] American Pentecostals, for example, cannot make declarations on what it means to be Pentecostal without making them alongside Pentecostals from other countries. The task of fostering transregional unity entails expressions of solidarity with foreign communities.[31] He sees the PWF as an opportunity for Pentecostal leaders to share what is happening in their countries.[32] Without such spaces, only cultural movements, migrations, and academic networks would connect Pentecostal churches internationally.

Unfortunately, the PWF has not yet risen to its aspirations. Robeck in 1995 critiqued the leadership of the (PWF precursor) Pentecostal World Conference as being too old, too male, too white, and too Western.[33] Nearly thirty years later, PWF leadership demographics have not changed substantially. Robeck laments that Western Pentecostalism—a minuscule fraction of the global movement—has dominated the doctrinal and political agenda, hindering a "creative tension and conversation" in the PWF.[34]

The Pentecostal CWC is not alone in this problem. It echoes the historic critique by the Christian Conference of Asia of confessional models of ecumenism. Initiatives such as CWCs and bilateral dialogues overlook the local dimension of ecumenical work, causing an imbalanced power dynamic between churches on the global stage.[35] For example, which should be more important for Nigerian Presbyterians—to maintain relations with Scottish Presbyterians, or to build relations with Nigerian Catholics? A focus on transnational relations with churches of a common confession could distract from ecumenical concerns at home. There remains a fear that CWCs could undermine the developing self-determination of politically disadvantaged churches.[36]

The PWF, similar to other CWCs, has yet to establish adequate practices and structures to address these concerns. André Birmelé observes the struggle of CWCs to speak or act coherently because the member national churches remain sovereign,[37] yet this is precisely the context where conciliarity is fostered. The catholicity of the church requires a global consciousness and systems of transregional relations. It is insufficient to attend to local unity while neglecting universal questions of a shared confession of faith. At the same time, the present system of global relations is skewed toward the West, requiring concerted attention to local ecumenism in conciliar structures. Attempts have been made to counter the disadvantages of CWCs.

Conference of the Secretaries of Christian World Communions

The Conference of the Secretaries of Christian World Communions (CSCWC) is an annual gathering of the heads (or their representatives) of several CWCs. The CSCWC is not a council of churches or an organization but an event that fosters communication and support. John Mackay is credited with providing the conceptual framework through which CWCs could participate in the broader ecumenical movement.[38] It was recognized that the global dimension of CWCs and their attention to confessional identity positioned them in a unique space in the ecumenical landscape.[39] Additionally, the broad inclusion of churches within CWCs expands the reach of ecumenical work.[40] Mexican Catholics, for example, might resist relations with Mexican Adventists, yet the two are brought into contact whenever the Vatican interacts with the General Conference of Seventh-day Adventists at the CSCWC. The event is currently one of the most confessionally diverse annual gatherings of Christian ecclesiastical leaders in the world.

In the early 1990s, the CSCWC invited the Pentecostal World Conference to collaborate in their gatherings but received no response. To make up for the absence of Pentecostals, Robeck was invited to contribute on an informal basis from 1992 until 2021, when the PWF vice-chairman was appointed to attend the Conference.[41] Robeck attended with the blessings of the chair of the Pentecostal World Conference and the general superintendent of the AG in the United States.[42] He offered reports on developments within global Pentecostalism and how Pentecostal churches were growing in their relations with other churches, causing leaders of CWCs to regard him as an authoritative voice on Pentecostalism. Robeck's presence at the Conference prompted CWC Secretaries to approach him and coordinate the launching of the international Reformed–Pentecostal dialogue (currently beginning its fourth round), Lutheran–Pentecostal dialogue (completing its first round), and Anglican–Pentecostal dialogue (beginning its first round), while also laying the groundwork for future dialogues with the Baptist World Alliance, Mennonite World Conference, and Salvation Army.[43] Had Robeck not participated in the annual CSCWC, it is possible that the Catholic Church would today be Pentecostals' only formal dialogue partner at the global level.[44]

Upon the conclusion of his thirty years of participation, Robeck had been the longest-serving member of the CSCWC. He describes it as one of the richest experiences of his ecumenical career and one of the most fruitful ecumenical initiatives in which he has engaged.[45] The venue affords CWC leaders the opportunity to share updates on their churches and collaborate on regional issues. The CSCWC meets regularly with government officials to hold them accountable for their treatment of religious communities in their countries. Robeck was involved in a consultation on the role of Orthodox churches in Turkish–Cypriot relations and, more recently, on the role of religious communities in peace talks in Colombia. He also used his CSCWC connections to mediate with the Argentinian government on a proposed tax that would impact Protestants there.[46]

The CSCWC and the CWCs it gathers rely on a global ecclesiology. There is a recognition that the Christian faith is not bound to any one locality, and so Christians everywhere must confess the faith together. Confessional identities are negotiated and constructed as churches of different confessions relate to each other. The limitation of confessional ecumenism is in its ability to foster a common ecclesial life. The task of ecumenism requires calling churches out of their separations into a shared community, yet confessional ecumenism hinges on a degree of insularity and focus on internal affairs. When the PWF, or any other CWC, directs its whole efforts toward upbuilding a confessional identity, can the organization ever succeed in healing rifts with different confessional identities, thereby threatening the continued existence of itself? CWCs constantly question their own self-understandings, and there is no common ecclesiastical polity that aids their relations.[47] Despite the CSCWC's accomplishments, it is a fragile gathering dependent on the goodwill of its attendees. Ecumenists have looked to other methods to vitalize their global unitive efforts.

WORLD COUNCIL OF CHURCHES

The WCC is synonymous with the ecumenical movement in the minds of many, yet the WCC has resisted this conflation. The WCC *Constitution and Rules* states the Council exists "to serve the one ecumenical movement," meaning it cannot be synonymous with that which it is meant to serve. The *Constitution and Rules* goes on to describe the WCC's role in calling churches to visible unity by fostering a "living fellowship" between churches and the "coherence of the one ecumenical movement."[48] The Porto Alegre Assembly described this work as "choreographing" the movements, organizations, and initiatives that constitute the ecumenical movement.[49] Recalling from the book's introduction Carlos Cardoza-Orlandi's polyrhythmic depiction of ecumenical methodology, the WCC is uniquely situated to help "keep the beat" of ecumenical work lest the ecumenical "dancers" crash into each other.

The multifaceted work of councils of churches models what Kuncheria Pathil calls a "synchronic pluralism of methods."[50] Ecclesiology encompasses numerous facets of ecclesial life, and so efforts to unite churches must account for the complex nature of ecclesiology. Councils of churches—including the WCC—operate as a whirlwind of related commissions, dialogues, and committees. Though the WCC is similar to CWCs in that it is a global body, it differs in that it is structured from below by churches in defined territories rather than by universal confessional identities.[51] Relations between member churches have ecclesiological significance, revealing how churches presently exist and how churches believe they ought to exist. This is seen in Robeck's reflections on the purpose of the WCC, on multilateral dialogue, and on the Joint Consultative Group between the WCC and Pentecostals.

Purpose of the Council

It would be misleading to say that Robeck became involved with the WCC while it was revisiting its methodology, for the WCC is always revisiting its methodology. Nonetheless, the conversations happening around the time he entered the ecumenical movement shaped his views on ecumenics. Leaders were anticipating the new century and witnessing geopolitical changes that were affecting relationships in the ecumenical movement, prompting new policies and programs for the WCC. Robeck describes the work of ecumenism as "theoretical, technical, and theological," requiring actions both slow and deliberate.[52] He affirms that the WCC is best understood as part of the larger whole of the ecumenical movement rather than its center.[53] He is one of countless Pentecostals who have contributed to the WCC over the years, yet his writings and career offer a valuable vantage point for the present study. Elsewhere, Pentecostal literature on councils has studied their practical value rather than their theological principles,[54] leaving Robeck as a rare insight into Pentecostal theologies of ecclesial conciliarity. While valuing conciliar methods, he remains a partial outsider, for his church belongs neither to the NCCUSA nor the WCC. What is the purpose of councils of churches even when not all eligible churches are members?

The purpose of councils is to gather churches into a relationship with each other. The member churches of the WCC—and other councils of churches— precede the councils themselves. A distinguishing mark of conciliar methodology is the role of churches as actors. The WCC is not a council of leaders or of service agencies but of churches. Christian communities gather in councils to witness and act together. Such a dynamic clarifies the distinction of the WCC as not being a church itself; rather, the WCC is the relations between member churches. It is a *consejo*, not a *concilio*. The WCC *Constitution and Rules* identifies the Assembly of gathered churches as the "supreme legislative body" of the organization, which assembles every eight years to chart the period between that Assembly and the next.[55] As conciliar ecclesiology understands the church as a gathering of Christians, conciliar ecumenism is concerned with uniting churches by gathering them.

Robeck was invited to attend the Canberra Assembly in 1991 as a Pentecostal visitor. At the Assembly, he helped draft a series of recommendations for the Central Committee to use as policy going forward when relating to non-member churches.[56] He recalls the Assembly as evidence of the WCC being at a juncture in its development. There was potential for greater inclusion of churches culturally, geographically, and confessionally, but there was also potential for the fracturing of the ecumenical movement.[57] He is not as critical of the Chung Hyun Kyung event as one would expect; he describes the event as both "genuinely prophetic" and "very uncomfortable." Nonetheless, he expresses appreciation for the objections of the Orthodox delegates, seeing their concerns as an opportunity for common witness with Pentecostals.[58] After the Assembly, he affirmed his support of and voiced his concerns about the WCC by signing the "Evangelical Perspectives from Canberra" document as a Pentecostal.[59] He reported on his experiences to American Pentecostals and pleaded with them not to rebuff the WCC.[60]

Part of the purpose of the WCC is what distinguishes it from national councils of churches—it gathers churches on a global level, raising the global consciousness of churches within the ecumenical movement. Robeck acknowledges the need for such a global vision for the American church to abandon its "ecclesiastical imperialism."[61] Instances of undue influence from Western churches on other regions fail to recognize the church's God-given diversity. A recognition of the diversity of the church locally and internationally is the basis for the recognition of other churches in communion and dialogue. Robeck values the WCC for providing a space for such a recognition to grow. Reflecting on the Canberra Assembly, he says it is helpful to hear discussions of indigenous and race relations in other countries to think through such issues in the United States.[62] His comments and the timing of events suggest his experience in Canberra might have shaped his thinking on race and church unity, with the WCC Assembly in 1991 preceding the founding of the PCCNA in 1994 that is mentioned in chapter 2. The opportunity to learn from churches elsewhere in the world informed his work to unite churches at home. Though Robeck is at times critical of acts and policies of the WCC, he never questions the irreplaceable role of the WCC in the ecumenical movement.

If Robeck values the WCC, why do other Pentecostals in his denomination not? He explains by narrating his own involvement in the WCC within the history of the AG's relation to the ecumenical movement. Robeck, in 1991, was not the first AG minister to attend a WCC Assembly. Donald Gee was present at the Amsterdam Assembly in 1948 as a journalist, and David du Plessis attended the Evanston Assembly in 1954 along with AG General Superintendent J. Roswell Flower. Flower was an early leader of the AG who sought to bring the denomination into closer relation with other churches. He helped found the Pentecostal Fellowship of North America (precursor to the PCCNA), National Association of Evangelicals (NAE), and Pentecostal World Conference (precursor to the PWF). Shortly after founding the Pentecostal World Conference in 1947, du Plessis and Flower attended the Evanston Assembly and reported their appreciation of what they witnessed. Robeck notes that Flower even encouraged Pentecostal churches to join the fledgling WCC.[63]

Estrangement between evangelical and ecumenical movements in the United States in the midcentury isolated Pentecostal churches from the WCC.

96   *Chapter 3*

Robeck explains that theological differences caused Pentecostal churches to be wary of associating with many Protestant churches that were part of the NCCUSA. It was thought the NAE would provide a better venue for pursuing unity in cooperation. He claims that Pentecostal membership in the NAE resulted in compromises,[64] but the relations of Pentecostal churches with evangelicalism are beyond the scope of the present study. As far as ecumenical methodology is concerned, he distinguishes the NAE from conciliar ecumenism in that the unity embodied in the NAE is not in common worship or ecclesial life, which are paradigmatic for councils of churches.[65] If worship is constitutive of the church, it must be part of the church's unity. He adds that cooperation does not address root causes of division or spur churches to greater measures of visible unity, a prerequisite for effective witness.[66] The unity of the evangelical movement is a real but lesser form of unity than that which conciliar ecumenism seeks.

The higher calling of councils of churches is more demanding. Robeck explains that inter-ecclesial engagement should result in the churches changing together to align closer with biblical truth.[67] The creative tension that occurs in such relationships is where "real koinonia" is found.[68] In his eyes, the challenge of the WCC is to hold together differing views on the nature of unity.[69] Faith and Order has recognized the value of conciliar ecumenism as a way of dealing with conflict that arises between churches.[70] A historic example is the entrance of the China Christian Council into the WCC. There were fears of how this would impact the WCC's relations with churches in Hong Kong and Taiwan, but Bishop K.H. Ting assured the Canberra Assembly that the China Christian Council's membership "will in no way impair the independence and integrity of any church outside mainland China."[71] Conciliar methods of ecumenism enable dialogue over doctrinal and political controversies by bringing churches together in relationship.

Commission on Faith and Order

Wherever gathered Christians have spoken of God, they have done theology together. Theological reflection is not foreign to interchurch engagement. The emergence of councils of churches in the twentieth century did not include formal dialogue as a constitutive dimension. Multilateral dialogue became associated with conciliar ecumenism at the formation of the WCC's Commission on Faith and Order in 1948. Methodological concerns of ecumenical dialogue are the concern of the next chapter, yet the place of multilateral dialogue within conciliar life warrants analysis.

Commissions on Faith and Order can exist locally, but they more typically function nationally and internationally. Synodal structures and decisions on church teaching for most churches occur at the national level—sometimes in consultation with international bodies—and so churches dialogue with each other at the national level. Chapter 1 discussed Robeck's contributions to Faith and Order in the NCCUSA's Commission as part of the consultation on apostolic faith in 1986, after which he continued to contribute to the Commission and opened the door for other Pentecostals to do so after him. In 1989, he was invited to serve as an advisor to the WCC Plenary Commission on Faith and Order. By the Harare Assembly in 1998, he was elected to the Plenary Commission and served as an advisor to its executive committee, the Standing Commission.[72] Upon his retirement in 2023, along with William Henn, he is likely tied as the longest-serving member in the WCC Commission's history and, since 2014, had been the first Pentecostal to serve on its Standing Commission.[73] To replace Robeck, the Commission received the appointment of five Pentecostals serving as official representatives—four of whom came from outside of Europe and North America, and three of whom were sent on behalf of the PWF's Christian Unity Commission. His participation testifies to the role of multilateral dialogue in expanding the reach of councils of churches beyond their own membership.[74]

Robeck entered Faith and Order while the reception of *Baptism, Eucharist, and Ministry* was underway. Responses to the convergence document affirmed the value of the dialogue while challenging its ecclesiological starting point. Many churches and ecumenical organizations struggled to recognize their experience in aspects of the document, especially those churches that did not contribute to the discussions that produced the document. Robeck explains that the dialogue Commission saw the need to enhance visible unity through the mutual recognition of churches, without which conversations on ministry and sacraments could not advance. The Fifth World Conference on Faith and Order in 1993 drew on progress in bilateral and multilateral dialogues while sharpening the focus on particular ecclesiological questions.[75] Robeck at the Conference chaired the discussion on proselytism as a pressing issue for recognition, which helped address grievances during a time when many Orthodox churches were threatening to leave the WCC.[76] As a result of the Conference, the Commission initiated two related topics—apostolic faith and ecclesiology.[77] His involvement was in the ecclesiology study group during the time it produced *The Nature and Mission of the Church* and *The Church: Towards a Common Vision* (*TCTCV*).

Church councils (*concilios*) originated as gatherings of bishops to deliberate on issues affecting their churches. The ecumenical method of councils of churches (*consejos*) likewise facilitates dialogue among gathered communities. Discernment is part of the purpose of conciliar ecumenism, and so councils require discernment structures—deliberative bodies to determine values and actions of the council as an expression of the member churches' relations with each other.[78] Conciliarity preserves the harmony of the confession of faith insofar as doctrine is an expression of the apostolic witness and a safeguard of communion.[79] Robeck does not often speak of doctrinal convergence. Instead, he speaks of the process of dialogue. He refers to dialogue as the act of redeeming the work of theology so that it builds up the church rather than demeans other communities.[80] For him, theologizing is the responsibility of the whole church. As contemporary theologians must account for centuries of Tradition, so North American theologians must be in dialogue with the rest of the Christian world.[81] The value of Faith and Order is in its creating a space for such dialogue to occur on a global, formal, and structural level.[82]

The challenge of Faith and Order is establishing communication channels for dialogue. The previously mentioned Faith and Order paper on conciliarity asserts that the conciliar act of dialogue fosters fellowship regardless of the dialogue's outcome.[83] Robeck too diminishes the significance of consensus when he says communication is "the point of all ecumenical dialogue,"[84] but this assertion highlights the ecclesiological basis of dialogue as an ecumenical method. Because the church is a conciliar fellowship, its members must dialogue with each other.

Historically, churches outside Europe and North America have done more to contribute to producing Faith and Order papers than to receiving them. This was seen in the absence of formal responses to *TCTCV* from many countries.[85] Reception of multilateral dialogue is itself a conciliar act where churches interpret, respond to, and change as a result of the process of ecumenical conversation. Churches receive dialogue reports when they care about the dialogue. If a church does not receive the report, they do not care about the conversations in which they participate. Barriers to the reception process are symptomatic of a weak conciliar consciousness among churches.[86] Faith and Order study group 2 sought to correct this imbalance by holding regional consultations on the convergence document.[87] These responses will inform decisions made at the Sixth World Conference on Faith and Order in 2025.

Robeck played a crucial role in organizing these consultations, drawing on his network of Pentecostal, Catholic, and Protestant colleagues outside Europe and North America. He was tasked with editing the two volumes of received essays alongside Ani Ghazaryan Drissi and Sotiris Boukis, his former student. The first volume compiles twenty-four of the presented papers by twenty-three authors.[88] Of those twenty-three, fifteen are Pentecostals.[89] The second volume synthesizes themes from these consultations and includes essays on dialogues with Pentecostal and Evangelical churches, which were not included in the initial harvesting of dialogue reports in the *TCTCV* text.

It also contains essays by Robeck on Pentecostal ecclesiology in light of ecumenical dialogue.[90] The geographic and confessional diversity of responses will enrich future conversations of the Commission.

Robeck oversaw the consultations in North America and Asia. After identifying more than a dozen scholars from across Asia to respond to *TCTCV*, consultation organizers were told to rescind the invitations from four presenters—from a house church in mainland China, a Pentecostal church in Hong Kong, a Catholic church in Macau, and the Presbyterian Church in Taiwan. Executives in the WCC instructed the organizers to regard the China Christian Council as the sole authority on behalf of churches in these territories despite the fact that the China Christian Council did not offer a response to *TCTCV*.[91] The silence of the China Christian Council was considered a sufficient voice for all sinophone churches. It was better to receive no input than to hear theirs. Robeck was able to find a way around this prohibition. He invited his former doctoral student, Judith Lin, to contribute an essay on persecuted churches. The essay never mentions East Asia, which is likely why the essay could be included. However, given her social location as a Taiwanese Christian, she has her ecclesial context in mind when speaking of the suffering church.[92] This decision of the WCC leadership will be returned to below, but it reveals methodological questions at play in multilateral dialogue. The choice of who is consulted in dialogue is determined by who is seen as viable partners for global ecclesial discernment. The task of dialogue is further complicated when the council looks beyond its own membership.

Joint Consultative Group between the WCC and Pentecostals

The WCC initiated a methodological shift in the 1990s. The council was never insular, but it had seen its mission primarily as fostering relations between member churches. It now saw the need to supplement this mission with an effort to reach out to non-member churches. On the surface, this could be seen as a betrayal of conciliar ecumenism. The purpose of councils of churches is to give expression to the communion churches enjoy and to spur them to greater unity. By relating to external churches, the council risks acting as an entity external to the fellowship of its churches. Councils of churches—including the WCC—exist as relations between member churches. Any associated structures support these relations.

The ecclesiological shift that occurred in this decision will be returned to below, but it is worth noting here the number of changes that were made. Before the Canberra Assembly, the WCC initiated the study that would produce the *CUV* policy statement on new questions and directions of ecumenism. Robeck was invited to the Assembly as part of these deliberations.

100   *Chapter 3*

After the Assembly, General Secretary Konrad Raiser inaugurated the Office of Church and Ecumenical Relations under Huibert van Beek to oversee the WCC's efforts to network with ecumenical organizations and non-member churches. The WCC augmented its ability to facilitate relations in the ecumenical movement without centering itself in the movement.

This change was not wholly new. The WCC, in 1965, established a Joint Working Group with the Roman Catholic Church out of a desire to strengthen relations between the two in the wake of the Second Vatican Council.[93] The WCC had been holding consultations with Latin American Pentecostal churches since 1988 under the leadership of General Secretary Emilio Castro. Later programs between Canberra and Harare Assemblies hosted consultations beginning in Latin America because of the groundwork already laid there.[94] A consultation would also be held with African Instituted Churches in 1996.[95]

As explained in the introductory chapter, questions of how to engage Pentecostal churches are questions of ecumenical methodology. The WCC borrowed the model of the Catholic Joint Working Group for relating to Pentecostal churches. Though the Catholic Church is not a member of the WCC, it contributes to the Faith and Order Commission and maintains a Joint Working Group, thereby offering a pattern for Pentecostal churches. However, the different ecclesiologies between Catholics and Pentecostals resulted in different ecumenical methods. Pentecostal churches do not have a global ecclesiology, as does the Catholic Church. Without a unified center for coordination, Pentecostal churches could not structure their engagements with the WCC according to the Joint Working Group model. The WCC could not "work" with Pentecostals, only "consult." The Joint Consultative Group (JCG) was formed at the Harare Assembly in 1998 with Robeck as co-chair after he helped plan the initiative with van Beek.[96]

Robeck had recently ended a similar project with the NCCUSA. His relations with NCCUSA Faith and Order Director Jeffrey Gros—whom Robeck refers to as a mentor[97]—led him to co-chair the 1986 consultation on apostolic faith mentioned in chapter 1. Catholic scholar Gros, himself part of a non-NCCUSA member church, was dedicated to incorporating non-member churches into conciliar deliberations because, in Robeck's words, Gros "was a real ecumenist."[98] Gros and Robeck pioneered a dialogue between the NCCUSA and Pentecostals from 1987 through 1997.[99] The project was terminated by the new director, William Rusch, who believed it to be of insufficient value to justify its expense and effort.[100] The year after this similar enterprise, Robeck stepped into his JCG role.

A comprehensive history of Pentecostal relations with the WCC remains to be written—including, of course, the story of the Pentecostal churches that have joined. Harold Hunter's work to archive materials from the consultations remains the most thorough resource.[101] Daniel Buda and Martin Robra narrate the history from the vantage point of their WCC offices.[102] The JCG advances WCC goals of conciliar ecumenism by implementing them within relations with Pentecostal churches. Reports from the consultations encourage dialogue between WCC member churches and Pentecostal churches, along with finding opportunities for ecumenical formation.[103] They encourage incorporating Pentecostal leaders within WCC commissions, an arrangement that similarly has enhanced Catholic participation. The gatherings serve as platforms for churches to update each other on their ecumenical activities. The consultations are more than dialogues; they feature opportunities for team building, sharing personal stories, and prayer. The JCG operates on principles of spiritual ecumenism that will be covered in chapters 5 and 6.

To promote knowledge of Pentecostalism and conciliar ecumenism, the JCG reports include brief histories of the relationship between Pentecostal churches and the WCC. The first report, along with Buda's and Robra's essays, draws almost exclusively from Robeck's accounts of history. Such a narrow selection will cause limitations in the future. Robeck is conversant with global Pentecostalism, and he has pushed for a more robust engagement with Pentecostals outside the West, but he studies primarily his own ecclesial context of the AG in the United States, which constitutes roughly one percent of the global Pentecostal population. Because of the WCC's heavy reliance on Robeck, the vast majority of Pentecostal communities fall outside the narrative offered in WCC literature. To clarify, Robeck himself has fought against this trend throughout his career, yet more work remains to be done. Future work by the JCG will have to expand its comprehension of Pentecostalism. Notwithstanding the JCG's present limitations, Robeck—through his participation in Faith and Order and leadership of the JCG—has shaped the methodology by which the WCC pursues relations with Pentecostal churches.

A primary concern of Robeck is recognition, for divided Christians to receive each other as fellow believers. His writings do not address more technical concerns of apostolic succession or the validity of sacraments but more basic concerns of prejudice. He explains that fear is often "dressed in theology to hide the cultural, class, racial and gender issues that are really the sources of the fear."[104] This notion motivated his comments on the *CUV* review process.[105] He claims that the conciliar movement is embarrassed by Pentecostals.[106] Part of the mission of the JCG is to promote recognition as a goal of conciliar ecumenism by confronting the attitudes divided churches hold toward each other. Priscille Djomhoué cites as an example the Conseil des Églises Protestantes du Cameroun, where council members refuse to accept membership applications from Pentecostal churches.[107] There are

102   *Chapter 3*

dozens of councils that include Pentecostals—including the Kenyan council mentioned in this chapter's introduction—yet there remains a need to address the prejudice behind systemic barriers in many conciliar bodies.

Robeck does not blame the WCC alone for its lack of Pentecostal membership. In fact, he is more critical of Pentecostal churches for not joining conciliar bodies. He accuses Pentecostal communities of hypocrisy for shunning ecumenical initiatives while joining evangelical ones that have many of the same goals.[108] Pentecostals have been equally arrogant toward other Christians, and their denial of other churches' ecclesiality results in proselytism. He reports that his presence in WCC spaces is welcomed and impactful. Despite his struggles, he affirms the genuineness of WCC member churches' willingness to enter into relationships with Pentecostal churches.[109] He pleads that they listen to WCC Pentecostal member churches to "hear their testimony and to re-evaluate their witness."[110]

Such thinking aligns with the methodology of conciliar ecumenism. The model of councils of churches presumes the reality that churches have problems with each other, but the model also asserts that the best way to work through these problems is by bringing the churches into relationship with each other. Avoidance and apathy cannot resolve fear, arrogance, and bitterness.

Pentecostal contributions to the WCC have grown in the twenty-first century. In 2002, the Commission on World Mission and Evangelism built on the work of the JCG by hosting a consultation with Ghanaian Pentecostals on faith, healing, and mission. In 2016, Frank Chikane was elected to serve as the new moderator of the Commission of the Churches on International Affairs, the first Commission moderator from a non-WCC member church. He is known for his supervision of the *Kairos Document* and later leadership of the South African Council of Churches. Robeck praises Chikane for his ecumenical vision.[111] Such are examples of how the WCC has implemented JCG recommendations.

Buildup to the Busan Assembly stoked hope and fear within the WCC's Permanent Committee for Consensus and Cooperation. The Committee emerged from the Special Commission on the Participation of the Orthodox churches in the WCC with the desire to address concerns that member churches raise on the operations of the WCC. In 2012, a debate arose regarding the membership criteria by which Pentecostal churches could join. Many resented the possibility of a large Pentecostal presence in the WCC based on their experiences of conflict with Pentecostal churches, while others worried how the identification of Pentecostals as non-Protestant and non-Orthodox would alter existent dynamics in the WCC. Ultimately, these discussions were unwarranted. Not a single Asian Pentecostal church applied for membership after Busan.[112]

Fruit of the JCG has been slow-coming. The PWF at the Karlsruhe Assembly assumed the position of coordinating the JCG with the WCC, potentially formalizing and broadening the voices represented. In 2022, the Apostolic Faith Mission of South Africa (Apostoliese Geloofsending [AFM]) became the eighth Pentecostal member church of the WCC. The AFM's ecumenical heritage includes such figures as Frank Chikane, David du Plessis, and Japie Lapoorta. The AFM's population dwarfs that of the other seven Pentecostal member churches combined, compounding Pentecostal presence in the WCC. Like other aspects of Pentecostal participation in the ecumenical movement, the future of Pentecostal relations with the WCC remains open.

CONCILIAR ECUMENICAL METHODOLOGY

After examining Robeck's involvement in conciliar ecumenism, themes can now be drawn regarding the ecclesiological basis of ecumenical methodology. The ecumenical method of councils of churches illustrates this study's thesis: methods of pursuing unity between churches are a consequence of shared ecclesiology between the churches, and as churches derive ecumenical methods, they converge in their ecclesiologies. Conciliar ecumenism arises from conciliar ecclesiology, albeit qualified. Conciliar ecclesiology traditionally is a consequence of sacramental theology. Christian communities gather through their assembled bishops at a eucharistic celebration, with the eucharist seen as the unitive element of the assembly (*concilio*). Councils of churches (*consejos*), however, are not gatherings of bishops, nor can all member churches presently enjoy eucharistic fellowship.

Raiser notes that this is a challenge to the ecclesiologies of some churches. Interchurch relationships have an ecclesial nature, yet, if councils of churches foster relationships without a eucharistic dimension, can one speak of ecclesiology outside the eucharist?[113] The existence of divergent answers to the question does not detract from the reality of conciliar experience within councils of churches. Member churches need not have reached an ecclesiological consensus to enact a shared methodology from their imperfectly shared ecclesiology.

Convergence in ecclesiology is part of the renewal that ecumenism seeks. Maxim Vasiljević points to this when he describes councils as an opportunity to "refresh and update the charismatic and dogmatic experience of the Church."[114] Churches revisit their theology of conciliarism as they derive ways of relating to each other. Through this, churches are renewed in the same direction as their ways of relating are necessarily shared, meaning that ecumenical practices evidence convergence. The ecclesial life of churches is renewed as they pursue a common life that is catholic and conciliar.

104   *Chapter 3*

Catholicity

The ecclesial mark of catholicity forms the church's identity around its diversity. The church's geographic and cultural inclusion constitutes its ecclesiality, and the task of fostering unity between churches in each place with churches in all places is part of catholic ecclesiology. The fact that ecumenists struggle to establish conciliar relations with other regions reveals that there were few connections previously: deficient ecclesial structures were in place to support the church's catholicity. When ecumenical methods change, it is often because the churches' understanding of catholicity changes. Councils of churches need not be catholic geographically or culturally. The WCC is the sole council that seeks to encompass the whole globe, and it is doubtful whether there are any regional councils that encompass all churches within their given regions. Nonetheless, councils of churches facilitate conversations on how churches can best foster a diverse unity.

The WCC and CWCs offer different approaches to fostering catholicity. The unity embodied in CWCs is contingent upon a degree of common ecclesiology. Not all churches in the World Methodist Council, for example, need to share an ecclesiastical polity for them to recognize each other as fellow Methodists, yet a Methodist confession would exclude Orthodox churches from membership. CWCs differ from councils of churches in that their understanding of the church's catholicity is rooted in a shared global confession. Efforts to transcend confessionalism, such as the CSCWC, affirm the global dimension of the church while struggling to articulate what the limits of ecclesial diversity ought to be. On the other hand, councils of churches are in a better position to wrestle with the present diversity of divided churches.

The desire to strengthen inter-ecclesial relations raises the perennial question of who is eligible to partake in a council. Member churches of the WCC seek to broaden the council's membership because they recognize that the church's catholicity demands it. The work of establishing conciliar relations with outside churches, however, can require changing views on which communities can be called Christian. When the WCC initiated its consultative group with Pentecostal churches and when the NCCUSA terminated its similar initiative, they each were making ecclesiological claims concerning which types of churches are worth relating to. Furthermore, as Robeck notes above, Pentecostal churches make their own ecclesiological claims when embracing or shunning other churches. Theological questions of ecclesial recognition and catholicity are not only about technical matters of sacraments but also about legitimate diversity. Ecumenical engagement spurs ecclesiological reflection on which Christian communities should or should not be included, and why.

Councils of Churches

Catholicity is more than a conscious assent to another community's ecclesiality. The koinonia that God communicates to the church is a costly fellowship. Because the same Spirit is given to all Christians, and by the Spirit, Christians are brought together into the same Body of Christ, churches do not have the option of being apathetic toward churches in other regions. Local communities within a national council of churches and national churches within the WCC commit themselves to each other as an expression of being part of the larger church. Robeck's critiques of the PWF's Western-centric ethos point to a failure to foster conciliar relations between Pentecostal churches globally. Such structures as CWCs are needed for these relations to exist, even while CWCs reformulate their practices to accord with a catholic ecclesiology, regardless of whether these CWCs are seen as having an ecclesial nature in themselves.

Likewise, membership in a council of churches signifies a church's acknowledgment of its limited place within the wider Body of Christ, and membership in the WCC is a commitment to act as part of the global church. Robeck's work in the WCC pushes this commitment forward to a greater level of commitment from the WCC and other churches to act on their understanding of catholicity. The increasing frequency of WCC consultations with Pentecostal churches indicates a growing acknowledgment both of Pentecostal churches and WCC member churches that the catholicity of the Christian faith encompasses one another.

Along these same lines, the Faith and Order geographic consultations strengthen churches' global consciousnesses as part of the task of multilateral dialogue. A common vision of the church is possible only if it is a global vision. The Faith and Order consultation in Asia raises methodological questions. As mentioned above, the consultation excluded papers from a house church in mainland China, a Pentecostal church in Hong Kong, a Catholic Church in Macau, and the Presbyterian Church in Taiwan. The geopolitical assumptions behind this decision are beyond the scope of the present study. As it regards ecumenical methodology, the exclusion of the four churches betrays the principles of conciliar ecumenism. The WCC has identified as part of its mission the facilitation of relations between member churches and with outside churches—Catholic, Pentecostal, or otherwise. The conciliar act of dialogue presumes the reality of conflict and that the only way to resolve this conflict is through communication. By silencing lines of communication, Faith and Order has severed potential relationships with these churches.

Furthermore, the WCC has hindered a conciliar relationship between the China Christian Council and the Presbyterian Church in Taiwan—both of which are WCC member churches. In effect, WCC executives have denied the significance of the fellowship they claim their respective churches

106   *Chapter 3*

experience with the Presbyterian Church in Taiwan as a result of their conciliar relations. The decision raises a host of other ecclesiological questions, but the methodological choices made going forward will shape the conciliar movement's future in East Asia.

The future work of reconfiguring global systems of ecclesiastical relations will rely on ecclesiological reflection in the ecumenical movement. Practices and structures that regulate relations between churches are ecclesiologically significant. Classical concepts of canonical territory, episcopal conferences, and the primacy of certain offices are ways that Christians have spoken of the church's catholicity in historical forms. Conciliar ecumenical methodology provides the means for Christians to discern together what forms ecclesiastical relations should take today. Ecclesial decentralization will only increase the importance of conciliarism.[115]

Conciliarity

The participation of churches in councils gives rise to an experience-based theology of conciliarity. Churches recognize the presence of Christ within the communion they enjoy with each other, revealing the need for values and practices that maintain relationships. The church exists as a conciliar fellowship because it is the gathering of Christians whom God calls and the Spirit indwells. The ecumenical movement has provided a space for separated churches to revisit their ecclesiologies together to discern how Christian communities can share a common life.

The conciliar renaissance is not limited to councils of churches but can be seen in CWCs. As mentioned before, synodal reforms in the Catholic Church are a consequence of Catholic reflection on and participation in ecumenical initiatives. The membership of Eastern and Oriental Orthodox churches in the WCC and regional ecumenical organizations strengthens the churches' relations. Likewise, the Pentecostal World Conference was partially a response to the formation of the WCC. Despite their absence from the WCC, Pentecostal churches today would likely have little institutional coordination among themselves had it not been for the WCC. Conciliar methodologies have shaped the ecclesiologies of these churches. As the divided churches find ways to participate in conciliar structures, they foster a conciliar relationship with each other.

The ecclesiological basis of conciliar ecumenism also helps explain the notable absence of some churches from the WCC. Both the WCC and national councils of churches gather national churches as the primary actors of ecumenical relations, an ecclesiological principle that guides the councils' methodologies. Whereas Catholic episcopal conferences can join their respective national councils,[116] the Catholic Church has refrained from joining the WCC

Councils of Churches 107

because of its global ecclesiology. The Catholic Church does not understand itself as a communion of national bodies, leaving the WCC to operate around an axis of Protestant and Orthodox churches. Similarly, an untold number of independent ("nondenominational") congregations of various theological traditions (Baptist, Evangelical, indigenous, and so forth) are incapable of joining the WCC because they lack a national ecclesiology. Their absence from the WCC is no more a sign of ecumenical apathy than is the Catholic Church's absence. Instead, it illustrates the fact that the ecumenical method of the WCC relies on a particular shared ecclesiology. Without a national ecclesiastical organization, churches are unable to participate.

Regardless of the council's membership, it brings churches into a relationship with each other. Conciliar relationships threaten to blur the distinction between church councils (*concilios*) and councils of churches (*consejos*). Other languages differentiate the two, while anglophone discourse on ecumenical methodology collapses methodology into ecclesiology. This is a shortcoming of the English language, but it offers insight into the ecclesial significance of conciliar methodology. The gathering of Christian communities in WCC Assemblies and similar ecumenical events reflects the basic ecclesiological claim that the church is the body of Christians God calls together. If divided churches in a council of churches experience a conciliar relationship with each other, it is not because of the existence of the council. The ecumenical movement cannot create unity between churches, for unity is a product of the Spirit of Christ's indwelling believers. Churches foster conciliar relationships because these relationships precede the churches' membership in a conciliar body. Conciliar methodology converges in conciliar ecclesiology, wherein churches develop practices of relating to each other.

A high theology of conciliarity does not overlook the reality of present disunity. Councils of churches (*consejos*) differ from church councils (*concilios*) because the gathered communities cannot yet be said to share a common life. Keshishian goes so far as to say a purpose of conciliar ecumenical methodology is to raise the awareness of how deeply divided churches are.[117] Robeck's ecumenical work testifies to the reality that separated communities encounter each other in the WCC who otherwise would have no contact. Where else would Congolese Mennonites, American Disciples, and Russian Orthodox congregate together if not at a WCC Assembly? Robeck repeats a common thought when he says that the unity of Christians in Christ precedes their unitive work, and so it is their responsibility to work out their relationship.[118] Conciliar structures are one such method.

Efforts to expand the membership of councils of churches advance the logic of conciliarism while querying some understandings of conciliarism. If councils of churches existed as the embodiment of conciliar fellowship between member churches, then efforts to expand membership would betray

108   *Chapter 3*

conciliar principles. Councils cannot act separately from member churches, and so it is questionable whether a council can pursue external relations on behalf of its members. If the WCC were the unity between member Protestants and Orthodox, why should it care about non-member Evangelicals?

On the other hand, because an imperfect communion already exists between churches before their membership in a council, then conciliar methodology demands the expansion of council membership. Councils of churches seek to foster conciliar relationships between divided churches. Faith and Order has described this as the ability of councils to "allow doctrinal formulations and secular reality to interrogate each other."[119] Current membership trends in councils of churches contrast with the claimed catholicity of ecumenical ecclesiologies. The WCC does not incorporate a mere quarter of Christians worldwide because the other three-quarters supposedly do not care about unity or lack a theology of conciliarity. Rather, the present membership of any council of churches indicates the present form of relationships between particular groups of churches. To avoid pursuing conciliar fellowship with Catholic, Pentecostal, or other non-member churches is to deny the imperfect communion that ecumenists have claimed exists. The doctrinal claims of catholicity and the reality of divisions "interrogate" each other.

If the ecumenical method of councils of churches converges in conciliar ecclesiology, then the participation of churches in a council is dependent on their conciliar consciousness—their awareness of their being in a relationship with other churches. A community that does not care about other communities will not bother to communicate with them. Conciliar practices are ecclesiological experiments in the quest to understand how Christian communities should communicate and act together. Robeck's contributions to the CSCWC and to the founding of the PWF's Christian Unity Commission were out of a concern for constructing global systems of ecclesiastical relations, just as his work to guide WCC policy and Faith and Order studies shaped the conciliar body's relations with global Pentecostalism. Questions of how churches in a council will relate to each other in the future will rely on a more developed understanding of conciliarity, or perhaps it is better to say that changes in relations will develop the churches' understanding of conciliarity. Membership in a council of churches is dependent not on recognizing the ecclesiality of other member churches but on recognizing their common belonging in Christ. However, it is also assumed that member churches' ecclesiologies will change and converge as a result of their participation in the council, enabling recognition.[120] Conciliar ecumenical methodology cannot survive by maintaining a divided status quo.

The process of change is mediated through dialogue, which is the subject of the next chapter. Participation in councils of churches extends beyond occasional gatherings of ecclesiastical leaders. Because councils of churches

Councils of Churches

incorporate whole communities, it is assumed that churches will enact their conciliar relationships with each other outside of ecumenical gatherings—whether it be in doctrinal teaching, local congregational life, social witness, or liturgical practices.[121] Additionally, conciliar structures advance the search for consensus by accounting for the historical conditioning of theology across cultural and geographic boundaries.[122] The changes within a church require discernment both within the church's community and also with other church communities. This need for theological discernment leads to the ecumenical method of dialogue.

NOTES

1. Philomena Njeri Mwaura and Constansia Mumma Martinon, "Political Violence in Kenya and Local Churches' Responses: The Case of the 2007 Post-Election Crisis," *The Review of Faith & International Affairs* 8, no. 1 (2010): 39–46.

2. "NCCK Training Mediators," National Council of Churches of Kenya, last modified December 4, 2021, http://www.ncck.org/ncck-training-mediators/.

3. Keshishian, *Conciliar Fellowship*, xiv, xv.

4. *Councils*, 9.

5. *Councils*, 17.

6. *TCTCV*, §53; *Councils*, 19.

7. Keshishian, *Conciliar Fellowship*, 5.

8. *Councils*, 3.

9. The baptismal basis of conciliarity was also discussed at the Third International Consultation for National Councils of Churches and in responses to *TCTCV*. Thomas Michel and J.M.R. Tillard, "Participation of the Roman Catholic Church in National Councils of Churches" (Federation of Asian Bishops' Conferences Paper 97, 2001), 20; Third International Consultation for NCCs, "Reports from Working Groups," *The Ecumenical Review* 45, no. 3 (1993): 291; Paul Meyendorff, "Apostolic Faith in Relation to the Historic Episcopate, Authority, and Primacy," in *Common Threads: Key Themes from Responses to* The Church: Towards a Common Vision, by World Council of Churches Commission on Faith and Order, ed. Ellen K. Wondra, Stephanie Dietrich, and Ani Ghazaryan Drissi, Faith and Order Paper 233 (Geneva: World Council of Churches, 2021), 37.

10. Michel and Tillard, "Participation," 25.

11. *Councils*, 4.

12. Janusz Bujak, "The Teaching of Pope Francis About Synodality in the Context of Contemporary Theological and Ecumenical Reflection," trans. Maciej Górnicki, *Collectanea Theologica* 91, no. 5 (2021): 148.

13. Bujak, 160.

14. Diane Kessler and Michael Kinnamon, *Councils of Churches and the Ecumenical Vision*, Risk Book Series 90 (Geneva: WCC Publications, 2000), 1.

15. Keshishian, *Conciliar Fellowship*, 4, 5.

110   *Chapter 3*

16. Keshishian, 1, 2.

17. I thank my colleagues who identified for me these pairings in their native languages. Of course, one can see colonial influence in some of these pairings. The Latinate distinction of *conciliare* and *consiliari* is preserved in Romance languages and adopted in Germanic languages, subsequently passed on through colonial transmission. The Tagalog *konseho* comes from the Spanish *consejo*, and the Bahasa Indonesian *konsili* comes from the Dutch *concilie*. Nonetheless, the indigenous adoption of the terms indicates a conceptual distinction present within their ecclesiological discourse. It is also to be observed that not all languages adopted their terms from colonial origins, discrediting any attempt to ascribe the ecclesiological distinction to the epistemic imperialism of Western Christianity. It is worth noting that, when a word is adopted, it is usually for the first of the pair to denote an intra-group gathering of the church (including the Malayalam സുന്നഹദോസ് from the Greek σύνοδος), perhaps suggesting a desire to maintain conceptual and theological continuity with received traditions across cultural divides. Insufficient information was found regarding whether the Germanic *rad* is etymologically related to the Latinate *rete*, which would offer a historical and conceptual link between conciliarity and network ecclesiology, an inquiry for future investigation along the lines of the research of my colleague, Jeremy Bone.

18. Keshishian, *Conciliar Fellowship*, xvii.

19. World Council of Churches, *Common Understanding and Vision of the WCC*, 1997, §3.4.

20. Harding Meyer, "Christian World Communions," in *A History of the Ecumenical Movement, Volume 3: 1968-2000*, ed. John Briggs, Mercy Amba Oduyoye, and Georges Tsetsis (Geneva: World Council of Churches, 2004), 115; Michael Root, "Christian World Communions and the CUV Process," *The Ecumenical Review* 50, no. 3 (1998): 333.

21. *Councils*, 18.

22. A seminal work on this tension is Ulrich Duchrow, *Konflikt um die Ökumene: Christusbekenntnis, in welcher Gestalt der ökumenischen Bewegung?* (München, Germany: Christian Kaiser, 1980). I am grateful for Michael Kinnamon in pointing me to this resource.

23. Lukas Vischer, "Comuniones mundiales, el Consejo Ecuménico de las Iglesias y el movimiento ecuménico," trans. Rosa Herrera García, *Dialogo Ecuménico* 39, no. 123 (2004): 49.

24. Meyer, "Christian," 109.

25. Robeck, "Taking Stock of Pentecostalism," 42.

26. Vischer, "Comuniones mundiales," 63.

27. Root, "Christian," 334.

28. Gedeon Freire de Alencar, "Do carisma mobilizador ao burocratismo institucional: Conferência Mundial Pentecostal realizada no Brasil em 1967 e 2016," in *Pentecostalismos em perspectiva*, ed. David Mesquiati de Oliveira, Ismael de Vasconcelos Ferreira, and Maxwell Pinheiro Fajardo (São Paulo: Edições Terceira Via, 2017), 35–56.

29. Cecil M. Robeck, Jr., "Fifty Years of Catholic-Pentecostal Dialogue, 1972–2022: A Pentecostal Assessment," *Pneuma* 44, no. 2 (2022): 220–50.

30. Cecil M. Robeck, Jr., "Southern Religion with a Latin Accent," *Pneuma* 13, no. 1 (1991): 106.

31. Robeck, "Taking Stock of Pentecostalism," 51.

32. Cecil M. Robeck, Jr., "Taking Stock," *One World* 210 (1995): 16.

33. Robeck, 16.

34. Cecil M. Robeck, Jr., "Pentecostal World Conference," in *The New International Dictionary of Pentecostal and Charismatic Movements*, ed. Stanley M. Burgess and Eduard M. van der Maas, 2nd ed. (Grand Rapids, MI: Zondervan, 2003), 974.

35. Vischer, "Comuniones mundiales," 60–62.

36. Meyer, "Christian," 106.

37. Birmelé, *Communion ecclésiale*, 315.

38. Vischer, "Comuniones mundiales," 58, 59.

39. A Joint Consultative Commission between the World Council of Churches and Christian World Communions was formed between Porto Alegre and Busan Assemblies to study their relationship, but nothing has resulted from it.

40. Jill Hawkey, *Mapping the Oikoumene: A Study of Current Ecumenical Structures and Relationships* (Geneva: World Council of Churches, 2005), 36, 37.

41. Justus (brother of David) du Plessis attended in 1991 and 1992 before his retirement. Robeck inherited some of du Plessis's responsibilities at this time, including the co-chair of the Catholic–Pentecostal dialogue discussed in the following chapter.

42. Cecil M. Robeck, Jr., "An Ecumenical Journey I Never Imagined," in *Sharing of Faith Stories: A Methodology for Promoting Unity*, ed. Richard Howell and Casely Baiden Essamuah, 2nd ed. (Farukh Nagar, India: Caleb Institute of Theology, 2018), 57.

43. Cecil M. Robeck, Jr., "Growing Opportunities for Pentecostal Ecumenical Engagement," *Pentecostal Education* 7, no. 2 (2022): 184, 185.

44. The informal conversations with the Ecumenical Patriarchate, pioneered by Harold Hunter, have yet to come to fruition in a formal dialogue due to internal struggles within the Eastern Orthodox Communion.

45. When I asked him what he believed to be the benefits of the CSCWC, he smiled and pondered aloud to himself, "Where do I start?" Cecil M. Robeck, Jr. in discussion with the author, May 25, 2022.

46. Cecil M. Robeck, Jr. in discussion with the author, May 25, 2022.

47. Vischer, "Comuniones mundiales," 47, 48; Root, "Christian," 334; Meyer, "Christian," 105.

48. World Council of Churches, "Constitution and Rules of the World Council of Churches," 2018, §III.

49. World Council of Churches, "Report of the Policy Reference Committee to the Porto Alegre Assembly," 2006, §8.

50. Pathil, *Models*, 405.

51. Vischer, "Comuniones mundiales," 53.

112 *Chapter 3*

52. Cecil M. Robeck, Jr., "Pentecostals and Ecumenism in a Pluralistic World," in *The Globalization of Pentecostalism: A Religion Made to Travel*, ed. Murray W. Dempster, Byron D. Klaus, and Douglas Petersen (Oxford: Regnum Press, 1999), 344.

53. Robeck, 348.

54. Marta Palma, "A Pentecostal Church in the Ecumenical Movement," *The Ecumenical Review* 37, no. 2 (1985): 223–29; Au, *Grassroots Unity*, 199–203; Angie Olivia Wuysang and Marthen Tahun, "Autonomy, Splintering and Growing Ecumenism: Governance and Organisation in Pentecostal and Charismatic Synods in Indonesia," in *Aspirations for Modernity and Prosperity: Symbols and Sources behind Pentecostal/Charismatic Growth in Indonesia*, ed. Christine E. Gudorf, Zainal Abidin Bagir, and Marthen Tahun, Forum for Theology in the World 1 (Adelaide, Australia: ATF Theology, 2014), 111–38; Marthen Tahun, "Fractured Ecumenism and Attempts at Fence-Mending: Relations Between Pentecostals and Non-Pentecostals in Indonesia," in *Aspirations for Modernity and Prosperity: Symbols and Sources behind Pentecostal/Charismatic Growth in Indonesia*, ed. Christine E. Gudorf, Zainal Abidin Bagir, and Marthen Tahun, Forum for Theology in the World 1 (Adelaide, Australia: ATF Theology, 2014), 139–69.

55. World Council of Churches, "Constitution and Rules," §V.1.a.

56. Robeck, "A Pentecostal Reflects," 114; World Council of Churches, *Signs of the Spirit: Official Report of the Seventh Assembly, Canberra, Australia, 7-20 February 1991*, ed. Michael Kinnamon (Geneva: WCC Publications, 1991), 107, 108.

57. Robeck, "Pentecostals and Visible," 14.

58. Robeck, "A Pentecostal Reflects," 111, 112, 120.

59. Robeck, 115; "Evangelical Perspectives from Canberra," in *Beyond Canberra: Evangelical Responses to Contemporary Issues*, ed. Bruce J. Nicholls and Bong Rin Ro (Oxford: Regnum Books, 1993), 38–43.

60. Robeck, "Taking Stock of Pentecostalism," 59.

61. Robeck, "Pentecostals and the Apostolic," 74.

62. Robeck, "A Pentecostal Reflects," 113.

63. Cecil M. Robeck, Jr., "A Pentecostal Looks at the World Council of Churches," *The Ecumenical Review* 47, no. 1 (1995): 60–62.

64. Robeck, "Pentecostals and the Apostolic," 70.

65. Robeck, "Early Pentecostal," 20, 21.

66. Robeck, "Ecumenism," 287; Cecil M. Robeck, Jr., "Christian Unity and Pentecostal Mission: A Contradiction?," in *Pentecostal Mission and Global Christianity*, ed. Wonsuk Ma, Veli-Matti Kärkkäinen, and J. Kwabena Asamoah-Gyadu, Regnum Edinburgh Centenary Series 20 (Oxford: Regnum Books International, 2014), 187, 188; Robeck, "Pentecostal/Charismatic," 24.

67. Robeck, "Pentecostals and the Apostolic," 70.

68. Robeck, "Ecumenism," 294.

69. Robeck, "Pentecostals and Ecumenism," 346.

70. *Councils*, 9.

71. Ninan Koshy, *A History of the Ecumenical Movement in Asia, Volume 1* (Hong Kong: Christian Conference of Asia, 2004), 273.

Councils of Churches 113

72. Cecil M. Robeck, Jr. and Jerry L. Sandidge, "World Council of Churches," in *The New International Dictionary of Pentecostal and Charismatic Movements*, ed. Stanley M. Burgess and Eduard M. van der Maas, 2nd ed. (Grand Rapids, MI: Zondervan, 2003), 1216.

73. Prior to Robeck, five Pentecostals had served on the Plenary Commission: the Chileans Enrique Chavez Campos (1963–1974), Daniel Palma (1968–1974), Victor Labbe Diaz (1975–1981), and Juan Sepúlveda (1985–1989); and the American Herbert Daughtry (1975–1982). Serving concurrently with Robeck on the Plenary Commission was also the Swedish Joel Halldorf (2006–2014). Several other Pentecostals have been invited to give one-time presentations to consultations.

74. Jeffrey Gros, "Fifty Years and Running: Oberlin '57, Back and Beyond," in *Ecumenical Directions in the United States Today: Churches on a Theological Journey*, ed. Antonios Kireopoulos and Juliana Mecera, Faith and Order Commission Theological Series (New York: Paulist Press, 2012), 68.

75. Cecil M. Robeck, Jr., "Panel Presentation on *The Church: Towards a Common Vision*," *Journal of Ecumenical Studies* 50, no. 2 (2015): 289.

76. Cecil M. Robeck, Jr. in discussion with the author, September 29, 2022.

77. Robeck, "Pentecostals and Ecumenism," 346, 347.

78. *Councils*, 16; Keshishian, *Conciliar Fellowship*, 62.

79. Maffeis, *Il dialogo ecumenico*, 114, 115.

80. Cecil M. Robeck, Jr., "Pentecostals and Christian Unity: Facing the Challenge," *Pneuma* 26, no. 2 (2004): 315.

81. Robeck, "Doing Theology," 3; Cecil M. Robeck, Jr., "Do Emerging Churches Have an Ecumenical Contribution to Make?" in *Towards a Global Vision of the Church: Explorations on Global Christianity and Ecclesiology, Volume 2*, ed. Cecil M. Robeck, Jr., Sotiris Boukis, and Ani Ghazaryan Drissi, Faith and Order Paper 239 (Geneva: World Council of Churches, 2023), 158.

82. Cecil M. Robeck, Jr., "Gifts (Charisms) of the Spirit," in *Towards a Global Vision of the Church: Explorations on Global Christianity and Ecclesiology, Volume 2*, ed. Cecil M. Robeck, Jr., Sotiris Boukis, and Ani Ghazaryan Drissi, Faith and Order Paper 239 (Geneva: World Council of Churches, 2023), 275.

83. *Councils*, 15.

84. Robeck, "Pentecostal/Charismatic," 27.

85. World Council of Churches Commission on Faith and Order, *Churches Respond to* The Church: Towards a Common Vision*, Volume 1*, ed. Ellen Wondra, Stephanie Dietrich, and Ani Ghazaryan Drissi, Faith and Order Paper 231 (Geneva: World Council of Churches, 2021); World Council of Churches Commission on Faith and Order, *Churches Respond to* The Church: Towards a Common Vision*, Volume 2*, ed. Ellen Wondra, Stephanie Dietrich, and Ani Ghazaryan Drissi, Faith and Order Paper 232 (Geneva: World Council of Churches, 2021); World Council of Churches Commission on Faith and Order, *What Are the Churches Saying About the Church: Key Findings and Proposals from the Responses to* The Church: Towards a Common Vision, Faith and Order Paper 236 (Geneva: World Council of Churches, 2021); World Council of Churches Commission on Faith and Order, *Common Threads: Key Themes from Responses to* The Church: Towards a Common Vision, ed. Ellen

Wondra, Stephanie Dietrich, and Ani Ghazaryan Drissi, Faith and Order Paper 233 (Geneva: World Council of Churches, 2021).

86. Ellen K. Wondra, "Ecumenical Reception," in *Common Threads: Key Themes from Responses to* The Church: Towards a Common Vision, by World Council of Churches Commission on Faith and Order, ed. Ellen K. Wondra, Stephanie Dietrich, and Ani Ghazaryan Drissi, Faith and Order Paper 233 (Geneva: World Council of Churches, 2021), 100.

87. Sotiris Boukis, Ani Ghazaryan Drissi, and Krzysztof Mielcarek, "'Towards a Global Vision of the Church': The Faith and Order Commission's Work on 'Broadening the Table of Ecclesiological Dialogue,'" *International Review of Mission* 108, no. 2 (2019): 401–14.

88. World Council of Churches Commission on Faith and Order, *Towards a Global Vision of the Church: Explorations on Global Christianity and Ecclesiology, Volume 1*, ed. Cecil M. Robeck, Jr., Sotiris Boukis, and Ani Ghazaryan Drissi, Faith and Order Paper 234 (Geneva: World Council of Churches, 2022).

89. There is a symmetry in Robeck's Faith and Order involvement. He first co-chaired a NCCUSA Faith and Order consultation in 1986 that sought to gain insight from Pentecostals, and he concluded his WCC Faith and Order position in 2023 by overseeing consultations with Pentecostals.

90. World Council of Churches Commission on Faith and Order, *Towards a Global Vision of the Church: Explorations on Global Christianity and Ecclesiology, Volume 2*, ed. Cecil M. Robeck, Jr., Sotiris Boukis, and Ani Ghazaryan Drissi, Faith and Order Paper 239 (Geneva: World Council of Churches, 2023).

91. Cecil M. Robeck, Jr. in discussion with the author, May 25, 2022.

92. Judith C.P. Lin, "The Weight of the Cross: A Response to *The Church: Towards a Common Vision* from a Perspective of Persecuted Christians," in *Towards a Global Vision of the Church: Explorations on Global Christianity and Ecclesiology, Volume 1*, by World Council of Churches Commission on Faith and Order, ed. Cecil M. Robeck, Jr., Sotiris Boukis, and Ani Ghazaryan Drissi, Faith and Order Paper 234 (Geneva: World Council of Churches, 2022), 99–102.

93. Annemarie C. Mayer, "An Instrument of the Ecumenical Movement: The Joint Working Group between the Roman Catholic Church and the World Council of Churches," *The Ecumenical Review* 70, no. 3 (2018): 526–52.

94. World Council of Churches, *Consulta con las iglesias pentecostales: Lima, Perú 14 al 19 de Noviembre de 1994, Consejo Mundial de Iglesias* (Geneva: WCC Publications, 1994); World Council of Churches, *Report of the Proceedings of the Consultation between the World Council of Churches (Office of Church and Ecumenical Relations at the General Secretariat) and African and African-Caribbean Church Leaders in Britain at the New Testament Church of God, Harebills, Leeds, England, 30 November – 2 December 1995*, ed. Roswith I.H. Gerloff and Huibert van Beek (Geneva: World Council of Churches, 1996); World Council of Churches, *Consultation with Pentecostals in the Americas: San José, Costa Rica 4–8 June 1996*, ed. Huibert van Beek (Geneva: World Council of Churches, 1996).

Councils of Churches   115

95. World Council of Churches, *Consultation with African Instituted Churches: Ogere, Nigeria, 9–14 January 1996, World Council of Churches*, ed. Huibert van Beek (Geneva: World Council of Churches, 1996).

96. Robeck, "An Ecumenical Journey," 59.

97. Robeck, "Pentecostal Ecumenism Part II," 12.

98. Cecil M. Robeck, Jr. in discussion with the author, August 16, 2023.

99. Robeck, "The Apostolic," 100 n21.

100. Cecil M. Robeck, Jr. in discussion with the author, May 25, 2022.

101. Harold D. Hunter, "WCC Consultations with Pentecostals," Pentecostal-Charismatic Theological Inquiry International, last modified January 1, 2012, http://www.pctii.org/wcc/.

102. Daniel Buda, "The World Council of Churches' Relationships with Pentecostalism: A Brief Historical Survey and Some Recent Perspectives on Membership Matters," *International Review of Mission* 107, no. 1 (2018): 81–97; Martin Robra, "The World Council of Churches and Pentecostals," *Ecumenical Review* 71, no. 1–2 (2019): 161–74.

103. Joint Consultative Group between the World Council of Churches and Pentecostals, "Report of the Joint Consultative Group (WCC–Pentecostals), 2000–2005, to the 9th Assembly of the World Council of Churches, Porto Alegre, Brazil," in *Towards a Global Vision of the Church: Explorations on Global Christianity and Ecclesiology, Volume 2*, ed. Cecil M. Robeck, Jr., Sotiris Boukis, and Ani Ghazaryan Drissi, 341–63, Faith and Order Paper 239 (Geneva: World Council of Churches, 2023); Joint Consultative Group between the World Council of Churches and Pentecostals, "Report of the Joint Consultative Group between Pentecostals and the World Council of Churches," in *Resource Book, World Council of Churches 10th Assembly, Busan, 2013* (Geneva: World Council of Churches, 2013), 151–63; Joint Consultative Group between the World Council of Churches and Pentecostals, "Report of the Joint Consultative Group between the WCC and Pentecostals," in *Resource Book, World Council of Churches, 11th Assembly, Karlsruhe, Germany 2022* (Geneva: World Council of Churches, 2022), 97–105.

104. Robeck, "A Pentecostal Reflects," 119.

105. Robeck, "A Pentecostal Assessment," 16.

106. Robeck, "Pentecostals and the Apostolic," 75; Cecil M. Robeck, Jr., "Letting the Riffraff In," in *From the Margins: A Celebration of the Theological Work of Donald W. Dayton*, ed. Christian T. Collins Winn, Princeton Theological Monograph Series (Eugene, OR: Wipf & Stock, 2007), 329.

107. Priscille Djomhoué, "Manifestations of Ecumenism in Africa Today: A Study of the Mainline and Pentecostal Churches in Cameroon," *International Journal for the Study of the Christian Church* 8, no. 4 (2008): 367.

108. Robeck, "Taking Stock of Pentecostalism," 44; Robeck, "Pentecostals and Visible," 11.

109. Robeck, "A Pentecostal Reflects," 118.

110. Robeck, "Christian Unity," 200.

116   *Chapter 3*

111. Robeck, "Pentecostals and Visible," 12; Cecil M. Robeck, Jr. and Frank Chikane, "Rebuilding a Broken Society: An Interview with Frank Chikane," *Theology, News & Notes* 48, no. 1 (2001): 20–27; Robeck, "African," 77.

112. Robra, "The World," 174; Buda, "The World," 93, 94, 97.

113. Raiser, *Ökumene im Übergang*, 175.

114. Maxim Vasiljević, "Ecumenical Councils," in *Common Threads: Key Themes from Responses to* The Church: Towards a Common Vision, by World Council of Churches Commission on Faith and Order, ed. Ellen K. Wondra, Stephanie Dietrich, and Ani Ghazaryan Drissi, Faith and Order Paper 233 (Geneva: World Council of Churches, 2021), 83.

115. Keshishian, *Conciliar Fellowship*, 25.

116. *Directory*, §168.

117. Keshishian, *Conciliar Fellowship*, 75.

118. Robeck, "Truth," 19.

119. *Councils*, 15.

120. Meyer observes that this line of thought was affirmed at the Uppsala Assembly. Common structures are needed for coordination and communication. Kessler and Kinnamon, *Councils of Churches*, 21, 22, 24, 25; Meyer, *Ökumenische Zielvorstellungen*, 69, 70.

121. *Councils*, 5.

122. Nørgaard-Højen, *Ökumenisches Engagement*, 86, 125–30.

Chapter 4

Bilateral Dialogues as a Communal Practice of Discernment

The city of Ponta Grossa, Brazil, conducted an experiment in ecumenism from 2018 to 2020. The initiative brought together local pastors, seminarians, and lay leaders to foster the practice of dialogue between Christian communities in the city. Dialogue topics were selected to help contextualize movements and questions of the past century of ecumenism within the Brazilian ecclesial landscape, an effort described as *a reconstrução do "nós"* ("the reconstruction of 'we'").[1] This search for a new collective Christian community was important for discussions on Catholic–Lutheran dialogue in the city. Local Catholic and Lutheran ministers were consulted to discern their perceptions of each other and the nature of their relations. The two groups recognized that dialogue, as an act of love, is easier to accomplish with those similar to oneself, yet the encounter between the two communities is needed to initiate the *vivência* (manifest, lived experience) of the gospel in their city.[2] The call of the gospel to the churches requires that they reconstruct themselves together through dialogue.

The ecumenical method of bilateral dialogue is a more technical form of inter-ecclesiastical engagement. Bilateral dialogue here is understood as the formal process by which two church bodies deliberate through issues that divide them. It was not unknown previously for divided Christians to speak with one another, yet the emergence of bilateral dialogue in the twentieth century required the ability for the interlocutors to approach each other as equals.[3] The method touches on the confessional nature of the church, whereby Christians discern together the doctrinal and lived dimensions of their shared faith. Yet dialogue is the method, among those studied in this book, that perhaps seems the most alien to the faith lives of local churches. Few systematic theologies would identify bilateral dialogue as a constitutive element of the church's nature. Additionally, the practice becomes

117

118   *Chapter 4*

emblematic of a scholastic ecumenism that is divorced from the lives of Christian communities. The eucharistic table might be central to the church, but the dialogue table? Not so much.

Despite the scholarly nature of dialogue, it is not wholly alien to the church. All churches have discernment practices by which they renew themselves and determine how to confess the faith. The practice of bilateral dialogue is a result of the ability to communicate and act as separated communities. As such, it intersects with ecclesiological concerns already examined. The ecumenical method of bilateral dialogue relies on common ecclesiological structures and practices between the two partners, and as churches develop dialogical methods, they converge in their discernment practices for renewal together.

DIALOGICAL ECCLESIOLOGY

If the ecumenical method of bilateral dialogue relies on a shared ecclesiology, then there must be a relationship between dialogue and ecclesiology. Ecumenists have identified the source of the church's dialogical nature as the same source of the church itself—God. Though the church's existence as communion is a consequence of its participation in the triune life, the concept of dialogue presumes the capacity for deliberation and disagreement, both of which are foreign to intertrinitarian relations. Dialogue, therefore, requires a distinction of wills. The church is a product of God's self-revelation and humanity's response, existing at the exchange between Creator and creation. The ecclesial act of dialogue participates in this exchange insofar as it participates in divine revelation and human proclamation.[4] The theological claim spotlights the relational dynamic of dialogue. Raiser appeals to the thought of John Zizioulas in arguing that dialogue is not a means to communion but is a basic expression of communion.[5] Humanity does not respond to God to establish communion with him; humanity is capable of responding because God has already established communion, and their response is part of the relationship. Similarly, dialogue between believers in the church is an expression of the communion that exists between them. Every successful relationship requires communication. Ecclesial dialogue occurs to preserve relationships across regions, between cultures, and through time.

Dialogue preserves communion through discernment, where believers think together on how to live faithfully according to the gospel in particular times and places. *TCTCV* describes this as a process of listening to the Word and each other under the guidance of the Spirit.[6] The act of dialogue, if it is a Spirit-led practice, presumes that the dialogue participants do not have foreknowledge of what the outcome will be. On the other hand, if dialogue

Bilateral Dialogues 119

is meant to help believers live according to the gospel, then it must point participants to the unchanging Word. The first chapter discussed the tension of ecclesial renewal between continuity and change. Dialogue contributes to renewal by pointing believers beyond their present circumstances while ensuring they maintain communion with previous generations of believers through Tradition.

The use of bilateral dialogue as an ecumenical method distinguishes it from other ecclesiological understandings of dialogue. The ecclesiological reflection cited above refers to dialogue as something occurring within a united community, whereas bilateral dialogue—by definition—occurs between two distinct communities that do not overlap. The difference is akin to that seen in the previous chapter on conciliar ecumenism. Councils of churches (*consejos*) reflect church councils (*concilios*), but they differ in ecclesiological self-understanding. Similarly, bilateral dialogues differ from other forms of dialogue that occur within a united church because bilateral dialogues do not occur within a gathering of Christians in an organic union with each other. William Rusch explains this difference within ecumenical theologies of reception, building on the thought of Zizioulas and André Birmelé. Classically, reception occurs within a united church as local communities interpret and implement authoritative decisions. Reception as an ecumenical process occurs between divided churches, yet both forms of reception depend on a degree of communion between the parties.[7] The ecumenical method of bilateral dialogues arises from prior ecclesiological understandings of dialogue.

Bilateral relations were not unknown prior to the 1960s, but bilateral dialogues proliferated as a result of the communication channels opened at the Second Vatican Council between the new Secretariat for Promoting Christian Unity and various Christian World Communions (CWCs). It is not a stretch to argue that dialogue is paradigmatic for the Roman Catholic Church's understanding of ecumenism. The *Directory for the Application of Principles and Norms on Ecumenism* positions dialogue as being "at the heart of ecumenical cooperation and [accompanying] all forms of it."[8] More recently, the ecumenical vademecum for bishops frames the ministry of ecumenism under the tripartite concepts of the dialogue of love, of truth, and of life.[9] It is not surprising that the Catholic Church spawned so many bilateral dialogues.

Angelo Maffeis explains the difference between the multilateral dialogue of conciliar relations and the emergent form of bilateral dialogue, drawing from his experience in the Catholic–Lutheran international dialogue and Faith and Order. He asserts that bilateral dialogue is more modest yet more demanding. It is modest because it constrains its focus on divisive issues between two communities rather than dozens. On the other hand, it is demanding because the dialogue commissions cannot bypass historic disagreements between the two communities the way that multilateral commissions often do.[10] For example, Anglican–Baptist dialogue on the sacraments assesses particular debates from the sixteenth and seventeenth centuries, whereas Faith and Order dialogue on the sacraments assesses a broader range of questions without reference to an era. Bilateral dialogues are a form of identity negotiation between the two parties as they redefine their relation to each other.

Dialogue raises methodological and ecclesiological questions. Because it occurs between two ecclesiastical partners, it relies on the ability to demarcate between the two, and binaries are difficult to define. Furthermore, because no dialogue table can accommodate millions of participants, each church must be able to provide adequate representation while ensuring that the dialogue will subsequently extend throughout the two communities by reception. These methodological considerations matter regardless of the consensus reached in dialogue. The ability of churches to communicate with each other in such a structured form requires a degree of shared theological language and communal practices. Whatever doctrinal convergence occurs through dialogical reflection, the ecumenical method itself must change the churches in order for the divided churches to be renewed together.

Robeck's understanding of the ecumenical method is a result of his forty years of leadership in international bilateral dialogues. Because he has not contributed to national or local Pentecostal dialogues,[11] I limit my study to international dialogues. Having contributed to fifty-nine sessions of international bilateral dialogue thus far, he is one of the most experienced scholars in the history of the ecumenical movement. He values the method because he believes that relationships thrive or falter according to the quality of communication between partners.[12] To improve relations, he advocates the priority of ecclesiology, saying that doctrine on the church should determine how divided churches view each other.[13] A close relationship exists in his mind between dialogical method and ecclesiology. As mentioned in the previous chapter, he was instrumental in the formation of Pentecostal bilateral dialogues with the World Alliance (now Communion) of Reformed Churches, Lutheran World Federation, and Anglican Communion, and he has co-chaired the dialogue with the Roman Catholic Church for most of its history.[14] He was not part of the planning team for the Anglican dialogue or its incipient commission,[15] so this chapter will study the other three dialogues in the order in which Robeck became involved before returning to methodology.

CATHOLIC–PENTECOSTAL DIALOGUE

The international dialogue between the Roman Catholic Church (hereafter "Catholic Church") and Pentecostals is one of the oldest and most prolific bilateral dialogues in the ecumenical movement, having released six reports

Bilateral Dialogues

since its inception in 1972. Its significance lies in its bringing together the two largest ecclesial traditions in the world. In addition to the prominence of the two communities in the global church, the dialogue has drawn attention because of the differences between the two. Scholars have described the dialogue as "improbable,"[16] "unexpected,"[17] and "extraordinary, even prophetic."[18] The project stretches the boundaries of what ecumenists expect of dialogue, defying many of the methodological principles seen above. Because the two traditions did not result from a common historical schism, the dialogue does not study the causes of their division, and because of the diverse nature of their ecclesiastical structures, the dialogue does not occur between two clearly defined partners. Such methodological dynamics have caused scholars outside of Catholicism and Pentecostalism to study the dialogue for insight into the ecumenical method.[19]

Robeck's involvement with the dialogue began in 1985 at the start of its third phase on its steering committee, his first formal role in an ecumenical endeavor; since 1991, he has served as co-chair. In 1988, after three years of involvement, he asserted that the dialogue is the ecumenical effort that has stretched him the most.[20] Nearly four decades later, one can only imagine the impact it has had on him personally. The dialogue has shaped Pentecostal engagement in ecumenism. With the possible exception of the Charismatic movement, relations with Catholicism are the most common topic in Pentecostal literature on ecumenism. Robeck's methodological reflection focuses on four dimensions of the dialogue: (1) the official status and composition of the dialogue teams, (2) the common ground between the two communities, (3) the building up of the relationship between the communities through dialogue, and (4) the publicizing of the results of the dialogue among churches.

Status and Composition

The composition and official status of the international Catholic–Pentecostal dialogue complicated methodological presuppositions of ecumenical dialogue from the project's earliest days. During the time the Catholic Church was initiating contacts with CWCs, their dialogue with Pentecostals started through other channels. David du Plessis met Kilian McDonnell at the 1968 Uppsala Assembly, after which they planned the bilateral dialogue, serving as co-chairs.[21] The Uppsala Assembly was the first WCC Assembly after the Second Vatican Council and witnessed a burgeoning of Catholic initiatives in the ecumenical movement, including the formation of the international Catholic–Reformed dialogue.

However, the process for the Catholic–Pentecostal dialogue was different from other dialogue commissions, which relied on endorsement from

122   *Chapter 4*

CWCs or churches. Du Plessis initiated the dialogue with the Secretariat for Promoting Christian Unity while he was *persona non grata* within his own Pentecostal denomination, the AG. While some participants were official representatives, others on the Pentecostal team chose to participate against the wishes of their denominational leaders or participated anonymously—the reports from the first two phases do not list the names of dialogue members, which is a practice rare among bilateral commissions. Robeck notes that some Pentecostal participants historically have suffered ridicule from their peers and have had to pay for travel expenses out of pocket.[22] Even now that the PWF Christian Unity Commission has been granted oversight of Pentecostal bilateral dialogues, participation is not limited to member churches of the PWF, nor does the PWF have programmatic oversight of the commission, meaning that the PWF cannot be seen truly as the Catholic Church's dialogue partner. The status of the Catholic–Pentecostal dialogue has never enjoyed the degree of complete official support that other commissions take for granted.

Furthermore, organizers of the dialogue wrestled with the commission's composition. The inauguration of the dialogue coincided with a global surge in the Charismatic movement in the 1970s, blurring the line between Pentecostal communities and Charismatic members of other churches. Half of the first phase's Pentecostal team consisted of Charismatic leaders from non-Pentecostal churches. Robeck explains that the range of potential participants was limited to the social circle of du Plessis.[23] The first report's notoriously convoluted title describes the dialogue as occurring between the Catholic Church and "Leaders of Some Pentecostal Churches and Participants in the Charismatic Movement within Protestant and Anglican Churches."[24] The known members of the Pentecostal team include, among others, the Lutheran pastor Arnold Bittlinger, Presbyterian elder J. Rodman Williams, Anglican cleric Michael Harper, and Antiochian Orthodox priest Athanasios Emmert. The fact that Anglican and Orthodox priests were once seen as qualified to speak on behalf of Pentecostal churches reveals the complex nature of representation and identity in the dialogue.

As mentioned above, the act of dialogue is a process of identity negotiation between the two partners. The Brazilian dialogue at the opening of the chapter saw this in the pursuit of a common communal identity among divided churches. The Catholic–Pentecostal encounter is perhaps the clearest example of identity negotiation among bilateral dialogues, which is why Silke Dangel examines the Catholic–Pentecostal dialogue in her study of the phenomenon.[25] The Catholic Church sought to narrow the conversation to the group of churches that—in the Catholic Church's eyes, at least—were "truly" Pentecostal. It was from this ecumenical encounter that the name "Classical

Pentecostal" arose, coined by Benedictine scholar Kilian McDonnell. The designator is fraught with historical, cultural, and doctrinal complications, yet it has prevailed as an ecclesiological paradigm for categorizing some Pentecostal churches apart from other Charismatic-type movements. Those Pentecostal churches that do not fit the description come to be grouped under competing labels—what sociologists call "neo-Pentecostal," Evangelicals call "Third Wave," or the Dicastery for Promoting Christian Unity (DPCU) calls "New Charismatic." The legitimacy of the distinction is beyond the scope of the present study, yet it is here worth noting that non-Pentecostal churches distinguish between Classical and other Pentecostal churches in their ecumenical relations, despite the fact that Pentecostals themselves often do not place much importance on the distinction—if they use it at all. Robeck himself sees the label as inadequate,[26] and he is attentive to include non-Classical Pentecostals within his discussion of the Pentecostal ecclesial tradition. The ecclesial identity of Classical Pentecostalism is a construct of bilateral dialogue.

The practice of bilateral dialogue presumes that participants on each side of the table represent their respective ecclesial tradition, which is why the Catholic–Pentecostal dialogue sought to restrict participation to "Classical" Pentecostals.[27] It is also widely speculated that the Pontifical Council feared that Charismatic Catholics could serve on the Pentecostal team alongside Charismatic Protestants and Orthodox, and so a stronger binary distinction was needed to ensure the viability of the ecumenical method. However, even after the second phase, the dialogue has not followed this categorization. It has remained common practice to include scholars who do not fit the strict definition of Classical Pentecostal as part of the Pentecostal team, such as the American Baptist scholar Howard Ervin and Swiss Reformed Walter Hollenweger in the Catholic–Pentecostal dialogue and Veli-Matti Kärkkäinen in the Reformed–Pentecostal dialogue after his ordination as a Finnish Lutheran minister. All three identify with Pentecostalism despite their ordination in churches that are not Pentecostal. Robeck, in his literature, has not addressed the inclusion of such figures. However, given the fact that he has served as co-chair of the Catholic dialogue since 1991, it can be assumed that he has at least condoned their inclusion as part of the Pentecostal team.

Earlier phases of the dialogue included Pentecostal ecclesiastical leaders who were ill-informed on the nature of ecumenical dialogue for the sake of elevating the status of the endeavor. Under Robeck's oversight, the commission shifted from hierarchs to scholars in order to deepen the theological reflection.[28] For Robeck, the more pressing issue of representation within the dialogue is the geographic scope of participants.[29] The

124 *Chapter 4*

ecumenical work of Pentecostals relies on knowledge of their global tradition, and so the dialogue requires teams to be diverse in terms of geography, race, and gender.[30] Geographic scope is a factor that characterizes international dialogues, similar to the discussion of the WCC in the previous chapter. The ability of the dialogue to learn from Catholic–Pentecostal relations in different parts of the world helps those regions where relations are embittered.[31]

Robeck is not indifferent to the importance of denominational support for bilateral dialogues. When inviting new team members, he regularly met with leaders of their respective denominations to explain the purpose of the dialogue and encourage financial support for participants.[32] The Pentecostal commission has never lacked official representatives, who now staff a significant portion of the commission.[33] However, the history of the Catholic–Pentecostal dialogue frustrates the prospect of garnering complete support. Robeck chronicles the attempts of PWF executives to stop the dialogue since its inception. Pentecostal hierarchs have punished dialogue participants and dissuaded non-Western churches from contributing to the endeavor.[34] He also testifies to personal encounters with Catholic hierarchs who have worked to end the dialogue. The international Catholic–Pentecostal dialogue has persisted despite half a century of institutional opposition from both sides of the table.[35]

The lack of institutional oversight of the dialogue has stirred controversy among Pentecostal ecumenists. The succession of the Pentecostal commission after the du Plessis brothers raised questions about how the commission would be staffed and led.[36] Cheryl Bridges Johns and Harold Hunter contend that the resultant practices hinder equitable representation of denominations and that the inclusion of unofficial representatives compromises the dialogue.[37] Friendships have proven to be an unstable basis for an international endeavor. Despite previous attempts by the PWF to end the dialogue, Robeck pushed for the PWF to oversee it and similar ecumenical initiatives, resulting in the Christian Unity Commission discussed in the previous chapter. The commission walks a tightrope between seeking denominational support and resisting denominational control, maintaining a "collegial and supportive but independent relationship with the PWF, providing it with purposeful accountability on the one hand and financial as well as programmatic independence from the PWF on the other."[38] Methodological questions motivate these concerns and changes. There is a recognition that the dialogue, if it is intended to speak on behalf of Pentecostal churches in their confessional and global diversity, must incorporate this diversity in its teams and receive support from Pentecostal churches. Only then can the results of the dialogue effect change in Pentecostals' relations with Catholics, recognizing their conflicts and commonalities.

Common Ground

The ecumenical method of bilateral dialogue, as explained in *Ut unum sint*, begins with the communion that exists between participants and then proceeds to disagreements.[39] Dialogues account for communion in its historical and doctrinal dimensions—what the two dialogue partners have in common. These commonalities are significant because they are not mere coincidences or shared preferences but are believed to be manifestations of the common work of God in the two communities. The second chapter saw this in the method of reconciling memories. Robeck notes the need to purify memories between Catholics and Pentecostals by finding a common approach to their shared history.[40] However, this is a departure from the approach seen previously. The ecumenical method of reconciling memories often relies on a "branch" understanding of church history, where divided Christian communities are related to each other within a series of "branches" from a historical "trunk." Under this model, however, Pentecostal churches did not emerge from the Catholic Church. Local Catholic and Pentecostal communities have their histories, but there is no universal narrative of Catholic–Pentecostal relations, which is why common memories are seldom a subject for the bilateral commission. The lack of genetic lineage between traditions requires more creative avenues for dialogue.[41] The common history for Pentecostals and Catholics is not in a past schism.

What, then, is the historical dimension of communion between Pentecostals and Catholics? Robeck points to the origins of the two in the early church. As mentioned in the first chapter, his understanding of ecclesiology values the church's handing down of the apostolic witness through Tradition. The study of the early church offers insight into the nature of the church. Robeck was influenced by the former Catholic co-chair of the dialogue, McDonnell, whom Robeck calls a mentor.[42] Robeck reports that McDonnell's patristics research helped the dialogue appreciate the common historical roots of Catholic and Pentecostal churches, especially in questions on liturgy and pneumatology.[43]

Robeck continued this focus on patristics during his tenure as co-chair, having a marked impact on the fifth phase. The phase focused on Christian initiation and drew heavily from patristic literature in the discussion. It appears that no patristic scholars have assessed the final report's reliance on the literature, though future scholarship would benefit from such a study to learn how contemporary ecumenical dialogue can receive guidance from the early church. The inclusion of patristic sources resulted in a longer report: whereas the English text of the fourth phase's report is approximately 16,000 words, and the sixth report is 13,000, the fifth report is nearly 52,000 words long (or half the length of this book).[44] The "deep affinity"[45] that Pentecostals

126   *Chapter 4*

find with the early church offers a historical common ground for dialogue with Catholics.

An additional commonality that aids dialogue is the experience of charisms within the two communities. The mutual acknowledgment of the presence of charisms allows the two to learn together through dialogue.[46] As seen in the first chapter, the charismatic nature of the church is a consequence of God's indwelling, by which he edifies and renews the church. If charisms are present in a community, then the grace gifts are given for the sake of the whole church. Such gifts do not guarantee amicable relations, though. The sixth phase of the dialogue studied charisms at the suggestion of Latin American Catholics to resolve misunderstandings with Pentecostals in their region.[47] Disagreements over what the two communities share enable and prompt the need for dialogue.

The communion between Pentecostals and Catholics has been a subject of their dialogue in large part because of the actions of each community that undermine this communion. Robeck narrates the dialogue's progression from the second phase's discussion of Mariology and the communion of saints to the third phase's focus on koinonia.[48] David Cole's dissertation—written under Robeck—describes how the third phase drew Pentecostals into the wider development of communion ecclesiology within the ecumenical movement, increasing their concern for visible unity.[49] After confirming their (imperfect) communion, the dialogue in its fourth phase addressed evangelism and proselytism.[50] Robeck and McDonnell believed the topic was too volatile, but they were outvoted by their team members, who asserted that the purpose of the dialogue was to address sources of division between the two communities.[51]

Robeck cites Gillian Evans's argument that proselytism reveals a lack of recognition of koinonia between the two parties. For koinonia to be visible, it must be seen in the practices by which churches relate to each other.[52] Because proselytism is an ecclesiological problem, the dialogue studied ecclesiology to address the problem.[53] He states that the intense discussion on proselytism relied on the trust built through prayer and time spent together over the years.[54] The common ground identified in dialogue supports the subsequent work of relationship building between the churches.

Relationship Building

As mentioned in the book's introduction, Robeck is not a systematic theologian. His conceptualization of ecumenics does not focus on the reconciliation of beliefs, and so his study of bilateral dialogue does not assess the nature of doctrinal convergence. Instead, he prizes dialogue as a relationship-building tool. Between the bilateral dialogue and various regional initiatives, he praises the Catholic Church for making a greater effort than any other ecclesial tradition to foster relations with Pentecostal churches.[55] He adopted a Christocentric understanding of ecumenical dialogue early in his career. When he explains dialogue to his Pentecostal peers, he depicts Jesus as sitting at the head of the dialogue table.[56] The presence of Christ amid the gathered believers enables the reception of the others as fellow Christians.[57] The inclusion of worship and prayer underscores dialogue's Christocentrism. The spiritual component of dialogue places participants in the presence of their common Lord, a precondition for their communion with each other. By positioning Jesus at the head of the table, Robeck addresses fears that the bilateral dialogue could be a ploy of the Catholic Church to assert dominance over Pentecostal churches. Neither Catholics nor Pentecostals are "in charge" of the dialogue; Christ is.

The need to assuage fear is not a result of Pentecostal paranoia. Part of the process of upbuilding relationships in dialogue is the overcoming of stereotypes and anonymity. Robeck contends that even misguided fears should be taken seriously because they shape how communities perceive each other.[58] Peder Nørgaard-Højen argues that a benefit of dialogue is its demonstration that divisions often result from prejudice rather than disagreement.[59] Dialogue is an opportunity for communities to question the judgments they have inherited from their predecessors.[60] However, not all suspicions are unfounded. Catholic–Pentecostal relations suffer from intimidation, suppression, and bloodshed in many parts of the world. Additionally, as noted above, proselytism erects barriers between the two communities. The two regional contexts that Robeck most often cites are Latin America and Italy, where animosity has been among the strongest. He sees it as important to listen to their witness of the harms of disunity while remembering that "apart from dialogue, healing will never take place."[61] The international scope of the bilateral dialogue includes such stories but also stories from regions where Catholics and Pentecostals enjoy fruitful relationships. The dialogue resists simplistic narratives of local experiences generalized into global realities.[62]

The inclusion of painful stories becomes a form of confrontation, an act that is needed for communion.[63] Dialogue goes beyond learning and appreciation to facilitate constructive challenging of each other regarding beliefs or practices.[64] Likely the most contentious point of confrontation was the question of proselytism. Though no universal statistics exist on the phenomenon, anecdotal evidence suggests that a sizable portion of Pentecostals globally are former Catholics, many of whom changed affiliation as a result of the evangelizing efforts of Pentecostal churches. Catholics confront Pentecostals on their disregard for the validity of Catholic ministries, and Pentecostals confront Catholics over the conditions that made people want to leave the

128   *Chapter 4*

Catholic Church. Robeck stresses that dialogue requires vulnerability and self-examination from both parties.[65] The tension that occurs in such conflict fosters koinonia when it is done out of love and a concern for the good of both communities.[66]

The process of interpersonal encounter in the dialogue requires academic preparatory work. Robeck identifies the third phase as a landmark in the dialogue's development. More Pentecostal denominations began sending participants as official representatives. Additionally, the phase transitioned from studying multiple presented papers to a singular, longer paper from each team to push the conversation forward more clearly and coherently.[67] The scholarly nature of dialogue begins before participants are seated at the table. To prepare for his leadership of the dialogue, Robeck recognized the need to study Catholic history and dogmatics, including more recent Catholic history.[68] Additionally, he sees the need to train dialogue teams in listening skills so they can grasp nuances in language that might differ from other churches.[69] The dialogue would falter if participants approached the table with ill-informed perceptions of their Catholic peers or the dialogue topic. To avoid this pitfall, Robeck built on practices that Jerry Sandidge initiated[70] and that the commission still employs:

> I have found it useful to assign a reading list to team members and to bring the Pentecostal team together one full day before a specific dialogue. By doing this, team members can get acquainted, pray together, talk about what they have learned, agree on a common language or a common approach regarding how to address the subject on the table, and bring to the surface any differences that might prove substantive in the midst of discussion. An effective methodology requires that the team have some sense of where it is going before it begins discussions and both recognizes and appreciates whatever differences of opinion there are. Nothing is more difficult to manage than a surprise that one person unleashes on his or her own team. It can scuttle days of work.[71]

As one team member reported to me after a dialogue session, "Mel [Robeck] lets you know this is not a holiday." The process of education and interaction through dialogue overcomes the fear and ignorance that each community has toward the other.[72]

Through opening each community to the other, the act of dialogue strengthens the participants' recognition of diversity in the church. Robeck identifies the acknowledgment of diversity as the basis for recognition and dialogue.[73] He says that his participation in bilateral dialogue has expanded his picture of the church.[74] It is important here to clarify the significance of his claim. He is not saying that dialogue has helped him see Catholics as part of the church. He certainly does see them as such, but the claim he is making is bigger than that. What he says is that, by acknowledging the validity of much of Catholic doctrine and practice, his ecclesiology has changed. His prior view of the church was too small, and the expanded and enriched view he now has enables him to relate more constructively with other churches. The ecumenical method of bilateral dialogue shaped his ecclesiology.

Publicizing

Literature on ecumenical dialogue follows the extension of dialogue through the process of reception, yet it often overlooks the mechanisms by which the broader church communities are incorporated into the discussion. This could be seen as a precondition of reception, for, without such mechanisms, churches would never know what they are meant to receive. The Catholic–Pentecostal dialogue began to include observers upon du Plessis's suggestion in the second phase. He reasoned that the more people who witnessed the progress of the dialogue, the quicker word would spread among churches of the dialogue's value.[75] He was likely inspired by his own attendance as an observer at the Second Vatican Council years earlier and by Pentecostal observers at WCC Assemblies. Because the goal is to publicize the dialogue among the communities involved, nearly every listed observer in the dialogue's history has identified as Pentecostal, the only exception being Jelle Creemers during his dissertation.[76] This differs from the practices of other bilateral commissions, which invite guests from outside churches or the WCC. Whereas other dialogue commissions include observers to situate their discussions within the broader ecumenical movement, the Catholic–Pentecostal dialogue has invited observers to aid reception.

An additional common practice is the release of reports at the conclusion of phases for the sake of scholarly discussion and informing educational practices. The dissemination of final reports occurs along Pentecostal scholarly communication channels. The PWF does not have a periodical similar to the World Communion of Reformed Churches's *Reformed Communiqué*, nor does its Christian Unity Commission have a bulletin similar to the DPCU's *Acta Œcumenica* (formerly *Information Service*), so Pentecostal ecumenists cannot rely on official outlets, a barrier that Robeck laments.[77] Under Robeck's editorship, the Society for Pentecostal Studies's *Pneuma* journal in 1990 began the tradition of publishing reports alongside responses from Pentecostal and Catholic scholars after each phase. The journal, since then, has become a premier outlet for discussion on ecumenics. A recent bibliometric study reports that, over the past four decades, ecumenical dialogue has been nearly the most common topic for articles published in the Pentecostal studies journal.[78]

130   Chapter 4

Attentive to the diverse populations within Catholicism and Pentecostalism, Robeck publishes summaries of the dialogue for more specialized journals whose readerships would care about the relations between the two traditions, such as the *Journal of Hispanic/Latino Theology*,[79] a Philippine Catholic journal,[80] and a Philippine Pentecostal journal,[81] in addition to articles in Romanian[82] and French.[83] In his essays, he narrates the development of the dialogue and testifies to his own encounters with his Catholic peers to illustrate the importance and possibility of resolving conflict.[84] The Eighth Forum on Bilateral Dialogues advocated for this practice to help local churches appreciate the significance of the ecumenical method and understand final reports.[85] Robeck often concludes the essays by addressing the reader directly, asking them to reflect on Catholic–Pentecostal relations in their own contexts and to pray for the success of the dialogue.[86] This incorporates the reader into the spiritual and reflective process of dialogue.

Robeck seldom speaks of the "reception" process of bilateral dialogues as such. This is likely due to his vantage point as a dialogue participant rather than being an ecclesiastical leader or local church pastor. Instead, he devotes attention to how dialogue participants can write reports so non-scholars can receive them more easily. In bilateral and multilateral dialogues, he has championed the inclusion of narrative vignettes to illustrate the topics examined in the reports.[87] The authoring of the reports should entail consultations with laypeople, clergy, ecclesiastical leaders, and scholars to ensure that the reports speak to diverse audiences within the church.[88] The publicizing of dialogues is a continual experiment in ecumenical methodology by which dialogue participants discern how best to incorporate their churches in the dialogue process, especially when it intersects with other dialogues in which churches are engaged.

REFORMED–PENTECOSTAL DIALOGUE

Robeck oversaw the beginning of bilateral dialogues with the World Alliance (later Communion) of Reformed Churches and the Lutheran World Federation. Many of the above themes apply to these dialogues with Protestant churches, including the composition and status of dialogue teams, the building of relationships from common ground, and the publicizing of the dialogue. Robeck also claims he patterned all the dialogues and consultations he has coordinated after the model of the international Catholic–Pentecostal dialogue.[89] However, Pentecostals' relations with Reformed and Lutheran churches differ from those with Catholic churches, requiring differences in dialogical method.

Bilateral Dialogues 131

The international Reformed–Pentecostal dialogue is a result of Robeck's participation in the Conference of the Secretaries of Christian World Communions (CSCWC). Milan Opočenský, general secretary of the World Alliance of Reformed Churches, proposed the dialogue in 1993 to Robeck, who initially declined the suggestion because he believed that relations between Reformed and Pentecostal churches were not strained enough to warrant a dialogue. Opočenský eventually convinced him by raising the example of South Korea. Theological controversies aggravated relations between the two traditions in the country. Even though Reformed churches were more numerous, the growing prominence of Pentecostalism in the social life of South Korea raised the stakes of misperceptions and hostility between the two communities. It was hoped that an international dialogue between Reformed and Pentecostal churches would strengthen relations between the two in a country where Christians are a minority.[90]

Robeck describes the Reformed–Pentecostal dialogue as the most difficult of the three in which he has participated.[91] Pentecostalism inherited some of its soteriology and hermeneutical principles from its Wesleyan antecedents, causing animosity toward Reformed thought. Similar to the Catholic dialogue, Robeck identifies understanding and respect as goals of the Reformed dialogue.[92] Any goal of consensus in the dialogue would not be for the sake of church union but for fostering amicable and cooperative relations, which is likely why dialogue topics have focused on ministry and missions. A recurrent point of contention is the practice of discernment, which has been examined in all three rounds.[93] There is a shift between the second and third reports. The second report identifies discernment as the most contentious topic between the two communities, with differing understandings of the purpose of the practice and conflicts over how each church engages it. Robeck recalls that the bilateral dialogue nearly fell apart due to the heated disagreement. The breakthrough came from African Reformed churches, who were able to bridge the gap between the dialogue partners on the charism.[94] By the third report, more common affirmations are found regarding the need for discernment in mission work. This change is not a sign of convergence between the two. Instead, it is an attempt to seek unity through engaging in the practice of discernment together even while the two communities disagree on the practice's nature.

Unlike the Catholic–Pentecostal dialogue, the Reformed–Pentecostal dialogue occurs between two groupings of independent denominations, causing the reception process to be more similar for each side of the dialogue table. There are no global doctrinal bodies for Pentecostal or Reformed confessions, meaning that each participating national church body receives and interprets the results of the dialogue independently. Insufficient research has been conducted thus far on the dialogue's reception, but Robeck narrates a notable parallel development of the conversations. The international dialogue was an extension of interactions that were occurring in South Korea. The increased engagement between Reformed and Pentecostal churches paved the way for the Assemblies of God of Korea to join the National Council of Churches in Korea, though timing suggests it was not a direct consequence of the international project. The Pentecostal church's membership in the council is an opportunity to strengthen their commitment to Reformed and other churches in their country, while also offering space to dialogue through misunderstandings that arise. The AG, under the leadership of Yonggi Cho and successor Young-Hoon Lee, was instrumental in the country's hosting of the Busan Assembly of the WCC in 2013.[95] The "differentiated reception"[96] of dialogue means that not all churches or countries have responded so positively, yet it is an example of how dialogue facilitates ecclesiastical relations beyond the dialogue table.

LUTHERAN–PENTECOSTAL DIALOGUE

Similar to the Reformed–Pentecostal dialogue, the Lutheran–Pentecostal dialogue began with the interactions between Robeck and Gunnar Stålsett, General Secretary of the Lutheran World Federation (LWF) within the CSCWC in 1996. However, Robeck was approached not to initiate a conversation between Lutherans and Pentecostals but to facilitate a conversation within the LWF. The leadership of the LWF was seeking to enhance the participation of member churches from outside of Europe and North America, particularly its largest member church, the Ethiopian Evangelical Church Mekane Yesus. The church differed from some other Lutheran churches due to its embrace of a wider array of charisms within the liturgical life of local congregations. Stålsett believed that a bilateral dialogue with Pentecostal churches would help Lutherans improve their relations among themselves and their understanding of spiritual gifts.[97]

The LWF at the time was busy finalizing the *Joint Declaration on the Doctrine of Justification*, and so their dialogue with Pentecostal churches began informally. The Ecumenical Institute in Strasbourg invited Robeck to co-convene an exploratory study group in 2004. The resultant five-year "proto-dialogue" identified areas of convergence and conflict between the two traditions that would be beneficial to study in the future bilateral dialogue.[98] The four topics of the proto-dialogue were ecclesiological and reflected concerns that arise between the two communities—the "pure" or "full" gospel, proclamation, sacraments, and charisms.[99] The subsequent bilateral dialogue picked up these topics within a broader concern of mission.

The report of the first round of dialogue begins with a long introduction of each community for the other. These sections rehearse the authoritative narratives of each community while addressing common stereotypes they might hold of the other.[100] Elsewhere, Robeck introduces the two by contrasting their approaches to history. While the contrast might be reductive, he compares the Lutheran paradigm of succession with the Pentecostal paradigm of restorationism. The view of each toward history is part of the self-understanding of the community toward other communities. Lutheranism's narrative situates the tradition in relationship with Catholicism and subsequent Protestant groups, while Pentecostalism's narrative places the tradition in a line of progressive restoration. Consequently, Pentecostals have a "love–hate relationship with history and Tradition."[101] This claim contrasts with his earlier assertion that Pentecostals find affinity with the patristic era, but the two statements together can be read as indicative of a tension within Pentecostal ecclesiology. Though this tension is not as strong in Lutheran ecclesiology, it would be wrong to say that it is entirely absent. Due to the recency of the dialogue's conclusion, nothing can be known yet regarding its reception, yet the future study of the reception will benefit considerations on method in bilateral dialogue.

DIALOGICAL ECUMENICAL METHODOLOGY

Bilateral dialogues illustrate this book's thesis about the reliance of ecumenical methodology on a shared ecclesiology. Each dialogue has different expectations and topics based on the participating churches, and each dialogue undergoes different processes of reception within each church. If there were no relation between ecclesiology and ecumenical methodology, then every bilateral dialogue would essentially be the same. The topics of the Reformed–Pentecostal dialogue would be similar to those of the Anglican–Reformed dialogue, and the questions of representation within the Catholic–Pentecostal dialogue would be a problem also for the Catholic–Assyrian dialogue. Yet if dialogue is to serve as a form of communication between the two parties, then the practices employed in the dialogue must be intelligible and viable for both parties. Robeck identifies the sharing of methodology as the most crucial element of a fruitful dialogue.[102]

Bilateral dialogue, as an ecumenical method, must also advance ecclesiological convergence. The method results in convergence precisely because the act of dialogue relies on shared ecclesiological principles between the two partners. The practices of discernment between the two communities enable them to be renewed together in light of how they both believe they should live faithfully according to the gospel. The pairing of discernment and renewal is

134   *Chapter 4*

common in discussions of dialogue. They are the stated twofold purpose of the Faith and Order *TCTCV* text.[103] *Unitatis redintegratio* also identifies them as the two objectives of dialogue, establishing a connection between engagement with other Christians and the ability for communities to live faithfully according to the inherited Tradition of the apostles.[104] The ecclesiological basis of bilateral dialogue is thus seen in the discernment and renewal aspects of the method.

Discernment

Bilateral dialogue is a practice of discernment. Robeck defines discernment as "prayerful reasoning" and "spiritual revelation," citing the Catholic and Reformed dialogues in their discussion of the charism's place in the Christian community.[105] Insofar as communication is part of communion, the method of dialogue encourages discernment practices that strengthen this communion. If dialogue is part of relationship, and if the church exists as a communion, then the development of dialogical practices is a form of ecclesiological convergence. Such practices are bonds of communion. Robeck goes so far as to argue that the building and maintenance of communication channels is the purpose of all ecumenical dialogues.[106] The ecumenical method relies on a preexistent relationship between participants. For any communication to occur between divided communities, there must be a common language and concepts.[107] The discernment that occurs through dialogue is an expression of this communion when it occurs within a loving context and is oriented toward the upbuilding of the Christian community.[108] The practice of dialogue informs each church's understanding of the koinonia that constitutes the church because dialogue itself is part of the koinonia. Robeck echoes Cole's argument that dialogue with the Catholic Church shaped Pentecostal theologies of communion.[109] Churches need not yet have reached a consensus on the nature of the church's communion for them to experience ongoing ecclesiological convergence on the subject.

Discernment is an ecclesial act that preserves the Christian community, which is why the Reformed–Pentecostal dialogue devoted so much attention to the topic. Robeck contends that dialogue itself is a form of community because it is a space where people listen and speak, give and receive. Community is built also when the communication is not warm. In his characteristic firm tone, Robeck declares that "dialogue is the end of fiction, and confrontation is the beginning of truth."[110] He here does not advocate confrontation for confrontation's sake but rather dispels the image of dialogue as a performance of polite half-truths. The asking of "hard questions" contributes to better relations and understanding between churches. Similar to the method of reconciling memories in the second chapter, unity between churches cannot be based on falsehood. Kuncheria Pathil acknowledges this tension when he raises concerns over whether confessional approaches to dialogue (as opposed to regional approaches) further entrench divisions in the name of seeking truth.[111] Bilateral dialogue succumbs to this potential only if it fails to develop common discernment practices, seeking instead to justify currently held beliefs. Robeck notes a growing interest in discernment as a topic within the Catholic–Pentecostal dialogue and Faith and Order.[112] Such instances demonstrate the potential to foster communication practices that are part of communion.

The contributions of bilateral dialogue grow when dialogues are conducted in view of the wider discernment process of the ecumenical movement. Birmelé raises the need for methodological research to ensure the compatibility of different dialogues.[113] The international forums on bilateral dialogues are one such way that insights on the method are gleaned and transmitted between dialogue commissions.[114] Additionally, it is common for reports to cite the work of other dialogues to measure areas of convergence or divergence, as seen in the harvesting of previous dialogue reports within *TCTCV* (despite the text's exclusion of all dialogues involving Pentecostals). The second Catholic–Evangelical round of dialogue builds on the fourth Catholic–Pentecostal report in its discussion of proselytism,[115] and the third Catholic–Reformed report speaks of the dialogues that the two communities have held with Pentecostal churches on the Kingdom of God and ecclesiology.[116] However, external citations in the ten existent dialogue reports involving Pentecostals are nearly always made by the non-Pentecostal partner. External citations have been made in joint Pentecostal–other paragraphs twice—once when the Lutheran report affirms a Lausanne Theology Working Group paper,[117] and the other when the third Reformed report quotes the Arusha Call and *Together Towards Life*.[118] Additionally, as noted above, invited observers for dialogue sessions are almost exclusively Pentecostal, whereas observers in other dialogues are invited from outside traditions to situate the conversations in the broader field. It would appear that, thus far, Pentecostal churches have not seen their dialogues as part of the larger ecumenical conversation, or, at the very least, they have seen insufficient value in studying dialogue texts to which they did not contribute.

It is not a new notion that dialogical method relies on ecclesiology. Ellen Wondra, in studying the reception process of *TCTCV*, posits that "traditional ecumenism" requires an ecclesiology that "new, emerging, non-denominational, and Pentecostal, charismatic, and fundamentalist churches" lack.[119] Barring the problematic descriptor of any ecumenical method as "traditional," her observation needs to be qualified historically. The development of ecumenical dialogue—whether bilateral or multilateral—required new structures and practices that churches did not previously have.[120] The Catholic Church established its Secretariat for Promoting Christian Unity to engage in dialogue, just as various churches and CWCs created their own ecumenical commissions. Wondra's appeal for the development of dialogical structures is applicable to all churches.[121] Pentecostal churches undergo similar changes as do others for the sake of facilitating dialogue. As Robeck notes, an ever-increasing number of Pentecostal churches embrace bilateral dialogues as official extensions of their ministries.[122] All churches change their ecclesiological self-understandings to discern with other churches.

Along these same lines, one might be tempted to discount bilateral dialogues with Pentecostal churches because of their historically tenuous claim of official representation. Even Robeck, in all his decades of work, has never served as a representative of his church. Dialogue commissions have value because they are meant to be more than merely small gatherings of scholars who like to discuss theology with each other. Commissions create spaces for Spirit-led encounters and discernment that extend from the dialogue table throughout the represented churches. To accomplish this, as Robeck himself stresses, scholars are answerable to their respective communities as they undertake a spiritual act of discernment that arises from the life of the community.[123] Dialogues with Pentecostals, nonetheless, struggle to attain this lofty goal because Pentecostal members are not always official representatives, though many or most are.[124]

The ecclesiological nature of the ecumenical method problematizes the representative dynamic of bilateral dialogues. As noted earlier, the method gained prominence after the Second Vatican Council as the Catholic Church began initiating conversations with CWCs. The Catholic Church, because of its global ecclesiology, possesses a capacity to discern authoritatively and speak with one voice internationally that other CWCs do not have—though it, too, has geographic and theological questions of representation. Creemers concludes that differences in ecclesiology require the Catholic–Pentecostal dialogue to employ alternative methods,[125] supporting the thesis that methods are constructed according to the participating churches.

On the other hand, Creemers contends that Pentecostal ecclesiology has hindered "traditional" ecumenical processes of representation and reception for discernment, as though other church traditions do not struggle with such tasks.[126] However, this is a simplistic view of other bilateral dialogues. Not all Baptist churches are members of the Baptist World Alliance, nor are all Reformed churches part of the World Communion of Reformed Churches. Regional disputes hamper deliberations within the Anglican Communion, and dialogue with Eastern Orthodox churches is plagued by their ever-changing relations among themselves. Ecumenists oversimplify the reality of contemporary ecclesiastical relations if they claim too comprehensive of a scope of their accomplishments in dialogue. Pentecostalism amplifies the methodological problems that all ecclesial traditions face when engaging in dialogue. Perhaps Pentecostals should be praised for bending the "rules" for the sake of inclusion in ways that other churches have not tried. It should be remembered that ecumenical methodology is concerned with churches as they exist rather than as ideals. Ecumenists ought not to assess churches by their ability to engage ecumenical methods but rather assess ecumenical methods by their ability to include churches. Pentecostal ecclesiology does not complicate dialogue as though dialogues precede the participating churches; Pentecostal churches along with all others shape dialogical methods.

It should also be noted that only four post-Vatican II bilateral commissions predate the formation of the Catholic–Pentecostal dialogue, with the earliest beginning in 1965. A mere seven years separated it from the start of the Catholic–Pentecostal dialogue in 1972. It is wrong to say that Pentecostal dialogues deviate from traditional dialogical methods, for Pentecostal contributions to dialogue shaped the ecumenical method during its genesis. One could just as easily say that subsequent bilateral commissions deviated from the tradition established by the Catholic–Pentecostal dialogue. It is not useful to judge the practices of one dialogue by those of another.

The development of discernment practices through dialogue is incomplete until the discernment process extends throughout the churches. Reception is not a process of affirming the decisions of scholars. It is a synodal act whereby Christians in divided churches recognize each other as possible sources of guidance from God.[127] Churches, through dialogue, expand their ecclesiology to incorporate other churches as part of their own deliberations. Whenever Pentecostal or other churches undergo structural changes to strengthen their ability to benefit from formal dialogues, they change their ecclesiological self-understanding for the sake of ecumenical engagement. In bilateral commissions, there is a desire for participants to represent their communities so that the discernment process can continue once the participants leave the table. The increase in the number of official representatives in bilateral commissions is a welcome progress in this direction. The point here is not to assess the effectiveness of official or unofficial representation in dialogues but only to affirm the value of practices that foster discernment within and between churches. Such practices are the means by which churches strengthen their relations with each other, thereby being renewed.

Renewal

As stated from the outset of this study, ecumenical methodology is distinct from ecumenical goals. Bilateral dialogue is normally studied for insight into the nature of consensus or on the particular topics of discussion within the round of dialogue. A methodological study shifts the focus to the ecclesiological convergence that occurs in the method of dialogue itself rather than the goal of consensus that results from dialogue. Renewal, in this light, is a methodological concern because it does not specify the conditions of a united church but describes the "renewing" process by which churches seek unity. The first chapter explored the ecclesiological concept of renewal as a result of God's presence in the church. Because God gives charisms, such as discernment, the church must always need renewal. Raiser sees renewal as an innate part of ecumenical work from the movement's beginning. It was recognized that churches in their current forms could not rise to the high calling of unity.[128] Membership in a council or dialogue is a call to reinterpret one's own ecclesiology to facilitate communion with other churches.[129] Bilateral dialogue similarly foregrounds the tension of continuity and change that occurs in renewal.

The tension within dialogue clarifies the method's purpose. Minna Hietamäki inverts the standard paradigm through her study of consensus in bilateral dialogues. She argues that the two interlocutors in a dialogue are not the two Christian communities on either side of the table; the interlocutors are God and the singular church of Christ. Bilateral dialogues are not primarily an act of reconciliation between the divided communities but an act of the communities receiving Tradition together from God.[130] This shift from an oppositional paradigm of dialogue positions churches as common recipients of divine revelation who are seeking how to live out the faith together. The aforementioned *Directory* affirms this image when it says that part of the discernment process is measuring the statements made in dialogue against the church's Tradition.[131] A more negative take on this imperative would be to see it as a form of magisterial control over Catholic engagement with other churches. The use of Tradition as a standard for theological discourse would anchor ecumenical construction in a preconceived notion of the past. However, the referential use of Tradition need not hinder renewal. *Lumen gentium* speaks of discernment as the application of the apostolic deposit more fully to the life of the church, a process undertaken under the Spirit's guidance for the renewal of the church.[132] Insofar as dialogue seeks to receive Tradition and preserve communion across time, churches can be renewed together according to their common apostolic source.

The retrieval of Tradition in dialogue is not meant to portray Tradition as a product of negotiation where churches "meet in the middle" of their divergent positions as though all theological positions were equally valid. Rather, the argument is that churches can pursue a more visible unity because of the elements of Tradition that they already share. Methodology is based on shared ecclesiology; otherwise, a church would deviate from Tradition when

Bilateral Dialogues   139

engaging in dialogue. The ecumenical methods of Christian communities advance toward unity when the methods accord with the one Tradition of the church. Dialogue is a means of mutual discernment between churches regarding the nature of the Tradition they are called to live out.

Renewal and Tradition are concerns that have shaped Pentecostal bilateral dialogues. The attention given in the fifth phase of the Catholic–Pentecostal dialogue to patristic sources shows a common devotion to the early church and its relevance for contemporary Christian communities. However, as Robeck notes above, Pentecostals also experience a love–hate relationship with history and Tradition. He contrasts this with Lutherans' understanding of continuity with the heritage of the church, though one must admit that Lutherans—similar to all Protestants—have their own qualms with aspects of what they received from prior generations of Christians. Creemers argues that Pentecostal restorationism clashes with a desire for continuity of Tradition in dialogue.[133] Such an assertion, however, presupposes an ahistorical understanding of Tradition. The first chapter explored the tension between historicity and Tradition in restorationist ecclesiology, where ecclesiological renewal accords with an apostolic pattern. Churches discern together how they should interpret their common heritage. Marcial Maçaneiro draws on the Catholic–Pentecostal dialogue when he says that apostolicity is not a past symbol but a present process and experience of renewal.[134] Adherence to Tradition is not a passive repetition of prior statements and actions but a constructive and creative work to preserve the church's apostolic nature.[135] Historical change is not antithetical to Tradition.

The dynamics of continuity and change within bilateral dialogue begin to reveal how the ecumenical method results in ecclesiological convergence. Renewal is a process that all churches undergo as they discern how to live the Christian life in particular contexts. Through the discernment process in bilateral dialogue, churches learn to be renewed together. Robeck affirms the value of Tradition as a form of stability and catholicity across time and space. It offers communal meaning of ideas, symbols, and acts, and so it should be preserved through the church's teaching.[136] Each church's devotion to their understanding of apostolic teaching, however, could make them shun dialogue as a form of compromise. Robeck's advocacy of dialogue distinguishes compromise from change. Representatives in dialogue need to be devoted to their particular churches, yet ecclesiological change is a goal of dialogue.[137] The recognition of common ground and the building of relationship can and should alter the churches' teachings and practices.

Bilateral dialogue results in ecclesiological convergence when churches change their relations toward each other such that they seek to be renewed together. Part of this change is identity negotiation. The Lutheran–Pentecostal dialogue saw this when the LWF sought to better engage the Ethiopian

140 Chapter 4

Evangelical Church Mekane Yesus; it was hoped that dialogue with Pentecostal churches would expand the communal identity of Lutheranism to include the Ethiopian group, though it is too soon to know what effect it will have. Similarly, Robeck reports that the dialogue with the Catholic Church has helped Pentecostal churches learn the importance of visible unity while they both learn from each other about the nature of the church's catholicity and diversity.[138] Again, it is too soon to speak of consensus on such doctrinal areas, but one can see how bilateral dialogue changes ecclesiology in that it changes communal ecclesial practices. The ecumenical method relies on shared discernment structures and practices, and as churches develop methods for dialogue, they converge in their ecclesiologies.

The renewal of churches in dialogue leads to the following chapter on spiritual ecumenism. Robeck describes dialogue as an encounter between Christians that promotes spiritual growth.[139] Dialogue, as an exercise in discernment, entails the operation of spiritual gifts, and the reliance on God for the unity of the church is cultivated through the church's worship. However, worship is also a divisive dimension of ecclesiology. Competing understandings of liturgy can determine the boundary line of when diversity becomes division, and churches today are fraught with "worship wars" and spiritual reform movements gone awry. Such struggles beg the question of how the ethereal phenomenon of spirituality can serve the concrete, visible unity of the church.

NOTES

1. Joanicio Fernando Bauwelz, *Sobre a reconstrução do "nós": Laboratório de estudos sobre ecumenismo e diálogo inter-religioso*, Série teologia em diálogo 9 (Porto Alegre: Editora Fi, 2020); Joanicio Fernando Bauwelz, "Laboratório de diálogo ecumênico e inter-religioso na Diocese de Ponta Grossa, Paraná," *Caminhos de diálogo: Revista brasileira de diálogo ecumênico e inter-religioso* 9, no. 14 (2021): 128–37.

2. Felipe Lucas Mendes, "Ecumenismo na diocese de Ponta Grossa, a partir de uma visão católica e luterana," in *Sobre a reconstrução do "nós": Laboratório de estudos sobre ecumenismo e diálogo inter-religioso*, ed. Joanicio Fernando Bauwelz, Série teologia em diálogo 9 (Porto Alegre: Editora Fi, 2020), 118.

3. Nissiotis, "Types," 43, 44.

4. Maffeis, *Il dialogo ecumenico*, 109.

5. Raiser, *Ökumene im Übergang*, 164.

6. *TCTCV*, §51.

7. William G. Rusch, *Ecumenical Reception: Its Challenge and Opportunity* (Grand Rapids, MI: Eerdmans, 2007), 55.

8. *Directory*, §172.

Bilateral Dialogues 141

9. Pontifical Council for Promoting Christian Unity, *The Bishop*.
10. Maffeis, *Il dialogo ecumenico*, 89.
11. Robeck has chaired a Catholic–Evangelical dialogue in Los Angeles as part of his faculty position at Fuller Theological Seminary since 1992, but his involvement in the Evangelical dialogue as a Pentecostal differs from the nature of Pentecostal dialogues in this chapter.
12. Cecil M. Robeck, Jr., "'The Color Line Was Washed Away in the Blood': A Pentecostal Dream for Racial Harmony" (Costa Mesa, CA, Christian Education Press, 1995), 7.
13. Cecil M. Robeck, Jr., "Roman Catholic – Pentecostal Dialogue: Challenges and Lessons for Living Together," in *Pentecostal Power: Expressions, Impact, and Faith of Latin American Pentecostalism*, ed. Calvin Smith, Global Pentecostal and Charismatic Studies 6 (Leiden: Brill, 2010), 255.
14. Robeck participated in an audience with the Ecumenical Patriarchate in 2010 that was intended to launch an Eastern Orthodox–Pentecostal dialogue, an effort overseen by Harold Hunter, but the endeavor has been delayed due to political complications in the Eastern Orthodox Communion. Additionally, Robeck co-chaired an exploratory meeting of a Baptist–Pentecostal dialogue in 2011, an endeavor that similarly fell apart due to political tensions within the Baptist World Alliance. These two are examples of how Pentecostal ecumenical engagement is sometimes hindered by other churches, a counternarrative that is often absent from literature.
15. When Robeck was approached to initiate the Anglican dialogue, he advised that a smaller, national dialogue be conducted first. David Hilborn, "Anglicans, Pentecostals, and Ecumenical Theology," in *The Many Faces of Global Pentecostalism*, ed. Harold D. Hunter and Neil Ormerod (Cleveland, TN: CPT Press, 2013), 243–63; William K. Kay, "Anglican-Pentecostal Dialogue in the UK: An Analysis and Exhortation," *Journal of the European Pentecostal Theological Association* 34, no. 2 (2014): 160–71; David Hilborn and Simo Frestadius, eds., *Anglicans and Pentecostals in Dialogue* (Eugene, OR: Wipf & Stock, 2023).
16. Kilian McDonnell, "Improbable Conversations: The International Classical Pentecostal/Roman Catholic Dialogue," *Pneuma* 17, no. 2 (1995): 163–74.
17. Michael Kinnamon, "Assessing the Ecumenical Movement," in *A History of the Ecumenical Movement, Volume 3: 1968-2000*, ed. John Briggs, Mercy Amba Oduyoye, and Georges Tsetsis (Geneva: World Council of Churches, 2004), 54.
18. John Mansford Prior, "Jesus Christ the Way to the Father: The Challenge of the Pentecostals" (Federation of Asian Bishops' Conferences Paper 119, 2006), 50.
19. Arnold Bittlinger, *Papst und Pfingstler: Der römisch katholisch-pfingstliche Dialog und seine ökumenische Relevanz*, Studien zur Interkulturellen Geschichte des Christentums 16 (Frankfurt: Peter Lang, 1978); Creemers, *Theological Dialogue*.
20. Robeck, "Growing Up Pentecostal," 26.
21. Robeck reports that McDonnell first contacted du Plessis for help with a paper on Pentecostalism in 1966, though they did not meet until two years later. Arnold Bittlinger offers a fuller account of the initiation. Robeck, "Some Pentecostal," 227; Robeck, "Fifty," 223; Bittlinger, *Papst*, 17–49.
22. Cecil M. Robeck, Jr., "When Being a 'Martyr' Is Not Enough: Catholics and Pentecostals," *Pneuma* 21, no. 1 (1999): 7.

142   Chapter 4

23. Robeck, "Fifty," 225.

24. "Final Report of the Dialogue between the Secretariat for Promoting Christian Unity of the Roman Catholic Church and Leaders of Some Pentecostal Churches and Participants in the Charismatic Movement within Protestant and Anglican Churches (1972-1976)," 1976.

25. Silke Dangel, "Die ökumenische Arbeit der Pfingstbewegung und die Frage nach der konfessionellen Identitätskonstitution," in *Konfessionelle Identität und ökumenische Prozesse: Analysen zum interkonfessionellen Diskurs des Christentums*, Theologische Bibliothek Töpelmann 168 (Berlin: De Gruyter, 2014), 237–316.

26. Cecil M. Robeck, Jr., "Pentecostals and Charismatics in America," in *The Oxford History of Protestant Dissenting Traditions: The Twentieth Century. Traditions in a Global Context*, ed. Jehu J. Hanciles, vol. 4 (Oxford: Oxford University Press, 2019), 244, 245. Cecil M. Robeck, Jr., "An Introduction to Pentecostal Identity: Ecclesiology, Pneumatology, and Spirituality," in *Towards a Global Vision of the Church: Explorations on Global Christianity and Ecclesiology, Volume 2*, ed. Cecil M. Robeck, Jr., Sotiris Boukis, and Ani Ghazaryan Drissi, 297–310, Faith and Order Paper 239 (Geneva: World Council of Churches, 2023).

27. "Final Report of the Dialogue between the Secretariat for Promoting Christian Unity of the Roman Catholic Church and Some Classical Pentecostals (1977-1982)," 1982.

28. Creemers, *Theological Dialogue*, 52, 53.

29. Robeck, "Roman Catholic-Pentecostal Dialogue: Some," 22; Creemers, *Theological Dialogue*, 79.

30. Robeck, "Ecumenism," 296, 300.

31. Robeck, "Roman Catholic—Pentecostal Dialogue: Challenges," 255, 268.

32. Robeck, "Fifty," 234.

33. Creemers, *Theological Dialogue*, 61.

34. Robeck, "Pentecostals and Christian Unity," 328 n33.

35. Robeck, "The Achievements," 165.

36. Creemers, *Theological Dialogue*, 42.

37. The exact nature of this dispute seems to be of a personal nature between the involved parties and goes beyond the scope of discussion here. Harold D. Hunter, "An Emmaus Walk That Leads to Rome? Little Known Convergences Emerge," *Plērōma: Studii Şi Cercetări Teologice* 20, no. 1 (2018): 90; Johns, "Remodeling," 145–48; Robeck, "Fifty."

38. Robeck, "Fifty," 245, 246.

39. *UUS*, §49.

40. Robeck, "Some Pentecostal," 247.

41. Evans, *Method*, 133.

42. Robeck, "Ecumenism," 300.

43. Robeck, "On Becoming a Christian," 6; Cecil M. Robeck, Jr., "Catholic-Pentecostal Dialogue: An Update on the Fifth Round of Discussions," *Boletín Eclesiástico de Filipinas* 82, no. 854 (2006): 482.

44. "Evangelization, Proselytism, and Common Witness: Report from the Fourth Phase of the International Dialogue between the Roman Catholic Church and Some

Classical Pentecostal Churches and Leaders (1990-1997)," 1997; "On Becoming a Christian: Insights from Scripture and the Patristic Writings with Some Contemporary Reflections. Report of the Fifth Phase of the International Dialogue between Some Classical Pentecostal Churches and Leaders and the Catholic Church (1998-2006)"; "'Do Not Quench the Spirit': Charisms in the Life and Mission of the Church. Report of the Sixth Phase of the International Catholic-Pentecostal Dialogue (2011-2015)," 2015.

45. Robeck, "On Becoming a Christian," 8.

46. Robeck, "The Achievements," 193.

47. Robeck, "'Do Not Quench,'" 169.

48. Cecil M. Robeck, Jr., "Do 'Good Fences Make Good Neighbors'? Evangelization, Proselytism, and Common Witness," *Asian Journal of Pentecostal Studies* 2, no. 1 (1999): 101.

49. Cole, "Pentecostal Koinonia"; "Perspectives on Koinonia."

50. The discussion coincided with that occurring within the Joint Working Group between the WCC and the Roman Catholic Church also on proselytism, both of which later contributed to reflection within the Commission on World Mission and Evangelism and with the World Evangelical Alliance. Joint Working Group between the World Council of Churches and the Roman Catholic Church, "The Challenge of Proselytism and the Calling to Common Witness: A Study Document of the Joint Working Group between the World Council of Churches and the Roman Catholic Church," 1995; World Council of Churches, *Towards Common Witness*, 1997; "Church, Evangelization, and the Bonds of *Koinonia*: A Report of the International Consultation between the Catholic Church and the Evangelical Alliance (1993-2002)," 2002; Pontifical Council for Interreligious Dialogue, World Council of Churches, and World Evangelical Alliance, *Christian Witness in a Multi-Religious World: Recommendations for Conduct*, 2011.

51. Robeck, "When Being," 6, 7.

52. Robeck, "Lessons," 86, 87; Gillian R. Evans, *The Church and the Churches: Toward an Ecumenical Ecclesiology* (Cambridge: Cambridge University Press, 1994), 70.

53. Robeck, "The Challenge," 313.

54. Robeck, "'Do Not Quench,'" 164.

55. Cecil M. Robeck, Jr., "Evangelization or Proselytism of Hispanics? A Pentecostal Perspective," *Journal of Hispanic/Latino Theology* 4, no. 4 (1997): 58.

56. Robeck, "David du Plessis," 2.

57. Cecil M. Robeck, Jr., "Specks and Logs, Catholics and Pentecostals," *Pneuma* 12, no. 2 (1990): 79, 80.

58. Robeck, "Roman Catholic-Pentecostal Dialogue: Some," 8.

59. Nørgaard-Højen, *Ökumenisches Engagement*, 57.

60. Robeck, "Lessons," 85.

61. Robeck, "Roman Catholic – Pentecostal Dialogue: Challenges," 250; Robeck, "Lessons," 93, 94.

62. Cecil M. Robeck, Jr. and Jerry L. Sandidge, "Roman Catholic and Classical Pentecostal Dialogue," in *The New International Dictionary of Pentecostal and*

144   *Chapter 4*

Charismatic Movements, ed. Stanley M. Burgess and Eduard M. van der Maas, 2nd ed. (Grand Rapids, MI: Zondervan, 2003), 581; Robeck, "Some Pentecostal," 232.

63. Robeck, "Evangelization," 56.

64. Robeck, "Pentecostal/Charismatic," 35.

65. Robeck, "David du Plessis," 1, 2.

66. Robeck, "Ecumenism," 294.

67. Robeck, "Specks," 81.

68. Cecil M. Robeck, Jr., "John Paul II: A Personal Account of His Impact and Legacy," *Pneuma* 27, no. 1 (2005): 6.

69. "The key to effective ecumenism is to listen, listen, and listen some more." Robeck, "Ecumenism," 298.

70. Creemers, *Theological Dialogue*, 185.

71. Robeck, "Ecumenism," 297.

72. Robeck, "Pentecostal/Charismatic," 30.

73. Robeck, "David du Plessis," 3.

74. Robeck, "Growing Up Pentecostal," 26.

75. Robeck and Sandidge, "Roman Catholic," 578.

76. Creemers, *Theological Dialogue*.

77. Robeck, "Pentecostal/Charismatic," 31, 32.

78. Daniel W. Eller and Daniel D. Isgrigg, "Bibliometrics and Pentecostal Scholarship: A Review of Trends in *Pneuma*," *Pneuma* 45, no. 1 (2023): 94–96.

79. Robeck, "Evangelization."

80. Robeck, "Catholic-Pentecostal."

81. Robeck, "Do 'Good Fences.'"

82. Cecil M. Robeck, Jr., "Dialogul dintre romano–catolici și penticostali: Câteva ipoteze penticostale," *Plērōma* 4, no. 1 (2002): 5–36.

83. Cecil M. Robeck, Jr., "Le dialogue entre les pentecôtistes classiques et l'Église catholique," *Istina* 59 (2014): 151–60.

84. Robeck, "Some Pentecostal," 241.

85. World Council of Churches Commission on Faith and Order, "Report of Eighth Forum on Bilateral Dialogues," in *Eighth Forum on Bilateral Dialogues. The Implications of Regional Bilateral Agreements for the International Dialogues of Christian World Communions, John XXIII Centre, Annecy-le-Vieux, France, 14-19 May 2001*, Faith and Order Paper 190 (Geneva: World Council of Churches, 2002), 62.

86. Robeck, "Do 'Good Fences,'" 102; Robeck, "Catholic-Pentecostal," 508.

87. Robeck and Sandidge, "Roman Catholic," 580; Robeck, "Panel," 292.

88. Robeck, "Ecumenism," 299.

89. Cecil M. Robeck, Jr., in discussion with the author, May 25, 2022.

90. Robeck, "Growing Opportunities," 181.

91. Cecil M. Robeck, Jr., in discussion with the author, September 29, 2022.

92. Cecil M. Robeck, Jr., "First International Reformed-Pentecostal Dialogue," *Journal of Ecumenical Studies* 33, no. 3 (1996): 442.

93. "Word and Spirit, Church and World: Final Report of the International Dialogue between Representatives of the World Alliance of Reformed Churches and Some Classical Pentecostal Churches and Leaders (1996-2000)," 2000, §42–49;

Bilateral Dialogues

"Experience in Christian Faith and Life: Worship, Discipleship, Discernment, Community, and Justice. The Report of the International Dialogue between Representatives of the World Alliance of Reformed Churches and Some Classical Pentecostal Churches and Leaders (2001-2011)," 2011, §73–116; "Called to God's Mission," §34–47.

94. Birmelé makes a similar observation when he reports that differences between Lutheran–Catholic dialogues in Germany and the United States ultimately contributed to the international project of the *Joint Declaration on the Doctrine of Justification*. Cecil M. Robeck, Jr. in discussion with the author, November 29, 2022; Birmelé, *Communion ecclésiale*, 128.

95. Cecil M. Robeck, Jr. and Young-gi Hong, "The Influence on the Churches in the World: Interview with Dr. Cecil Robeck," in *Charis and Charisma: David Yonggi Cho and the Growth of Yoido Full Gospel Church*, ed. Sung-hoon Myung and Yong-gi Hong (Oxford: Regnum Books International, 2003), 27–33; Cecil M. Robeck, Jr., "Yoido Full Gospel Church and Ecumenism," in *The Holy Spirit, Spirituality, and Leadership: Essays in Honor of Young-Hoon Lee*, ed. Wonsuk Ma and Robert Menzies (Oxford: Regnum Books International, forthcoming); Robeck, "Growing Opportunities," 182.

96. Birmelé, *Communion ecclésiale*, 387.

97. Robeck, "Growing Opportunities," 182, 183.

98. Institute for Ecumenical Research in Strasbourg, France, David du Plessis Center for Christian Spirituality in Pasadena, California, and The European Pentecostal Charismatic Research Association in Zürich, Switzerland, *Lutherans and Pentecostals in Dialogue* (Strasbourg, France: Institute for Ecumenical Research, 2010).

99. "'The Spirit of the Lord Is Upon Me': International Lutheran-Pentecostal 2016–2022 Dialogue Statement," 2022, §6.

100. "The Spirit of the Lord Is Upon Me," §8–23.

101. Robeck, "Introducing Pentecostals," 32, 35, 41.

102. Cecil M. Robeck, Jr., "Foreword," in *Grassroots Ecumenism: The Way of Local Christian Reunion*, by Karen Petersen Finch (Hyde Park, NY: New City Press, 2022), xiv.

103. *TCTCV*, viii.

104. *UR*, §4.

105. Robeck, "Authoritative," 209–14.

106. Robeck, "Pentecostal/Charismatic," 27.

107. Maffeis, *Il dialogo ecumenico*, 107.

108. Robeck, "Discerning the Spirit," 34.

109. Robeck, "On Becoming a Christian," 3.

110. Robeck, "Lessons," 96.

111. Pathil, *Models*, 292.

112. Robeck, "Fifty," 241; Robeck, "Authoritative"; "'Do Not Quench the Spirit,'" §73–98; *TCTCV*, question following §30.

113. Birmelé, *Communion ecclésiale*, 380–86.

114. See the most recent report: World Council of Churches Commission on Faith and Order, "The Dar es Salaam Report: Tenth Forum on Bilateral Dialogues, 'International Dialogues in Dialogue: Context and Reception,'" 2012.

146   *Chapter 4*

115. "Church, Evangelization, and the Bonds of *Koinonia*," §60–68, 74, 77, 78.

116. "The Church as Community of Common Witness to the Kingdom of God: Report of the Third Phase of the International Theological Dialogue between the Catholic Church and the World Alliance of Reformed Churches (1998-2005)," 2005, §162 and appendix.

117. "The Spirit of the Lord Is Upon Me," §55.

118. "Called to God's Mission," §31.

119. Wondra, "Ecumenical Reception," 103.

120. Rusch, *Ecumenical Reception*, 57.

121. Wondra, "Ecumenical Reception," 104.

122. Cecil M. Robeck, Jr., "What Catholics Should Know about Pentecostals," *The Catholic World* 238, no. 1428 (1995): 281.

123. Cecil M. Robeck, Jr., "Some Reflections from a Pentecostal/Evangelical Perspective," in *Faith and Order in Moshi: The 1996 Commission Meeting*, by World Council of Churches Commission on Faith and Order, ed. Alan Falconer, Faith and Order Paper 177 (Geneva: World Council of Churches, 1998), 136.

124. Johns offers a helpful reframing of this dimension of Pentecostal participation in ecumenical dialogue, though the details of her argument go beyond the argument here. Johns, "Remodeling," 145–48.

125. Creemers, *Theological Dialogue*, 269.

126. Creemers, 38, 264.

127. Wondra, "Ecumenical Reception," 93, 100.

128. Raiser, *Ökumene im Übergang*, 24.

129. Nissiotis, "Types," 50.

130. Minna Hietamäki, *Agreeable Agreement: An Examination of the Quest for Consensus in Ecumenical Dialogue*, Ecclesiological Investigations 8 (London: T & T Clark, 2010), 108.

131. *Directory*, §179.

132. *LG*, §12.

133. Creemers, *Theological Dialogue*, 28.

134. Marcial Maçaneiro, "Na unidade do Espírito Santo: Observações sobre o diálogo internacional católico-pentecostal," in *Pentecostalismos e unidade: Desafios institucionais, teológicos e sociais*, ed. David Mesquiati de Oliveira (São Paulo: Fonte Editorial, 2015), 103, 104.

135. *Tradition and Traditions*, 57; Robeck, "An Emerging," 215.

136. Robeck, "An Emerging," 167–70.

137. Robeck, "Pentecostals and the Apostolic," 70; Robeck, "Pentecostal Ecumenism Part II," 8.

138. Robeck, "Some Pentecostal," 231, 247.

139. Robeck and Sandidge, "Roman Catholic," 581.

Chapter 5

Patristic Roots and Charismatic Controversies of Spiritual Ecumenism

The Zambian National Day of Prayer, Fasting, Repentance, and Reconciliation is one of the only events where churches in the country cooperate. The nation's quasi-theocratic aspirations raise the importance of the churches' social presence while also making churches compete for national influence. The merger of several missionary churches after the colonial era into the United Church of Zambia centered the body within the ecclesial landscape, despite the additional presence of millions of Catholics, Adventists, Pentecostals, and other Christians. One day a year, churches set aside their conflicts to pray for their country. Committees of representatives from participating churches plan prayer services for towns and provinces. The gatherings employ liturgical practices from an array of Christian traditions, transgressing confessional boundaries and fostering new imaginations of peace. Churches in Zambia are tasked with facilitating dialogue and reconciliation due to the state's failure to do so.[1] The foremost way Zambian churches have pursued reconciliation is through common prayer.

Spiritual ecumenism foregrounds the source of the church's unity in the church's partaking in the divine life. Christians are not united by sharing a language, history, or location but by sharing a common gift of divine grace that transcends these other characteristics. The renewal of the church toward unity occurs through pointing the church to its origins in God. *Unitatis redintegratio* famously refers to spiritual ecumenism as "the soul of the whole ecumenical movement," constituted by a "change of heart and holiness of life."[2] The anthem of the movement in John 17:21 draws from Jesus' prayer to the Father. Every day of WCC Assemblies begins and ends with common prayer, and the high holy days of the ecumenical movement occur during the Week of Prayer for Christian Unity. If believers in a local congregation never experience any other form of ecumenical engagement, they have likely

147

148   *Chapter 5*

at least prayed for Christians of another church. Spiritual ecumenism is the simplest, most ubiquitous, and most highly valued ecumenical method.

The importance of the method does not prevent tensions over how the method should be implemented. There is no generic Christian spirituality. All spiritual practices and experiences are located confessionally, historically, or culturally. People tasked with planning ecumenical services know well the struggle of integrating divergent spiritual traditions and making them accessible to all attendees. The communal nature of Christian spirituality has a direct bearing on the ecclesiological themes examined in this study. The ecumenical method of spiritual ecumenism relies on shared spiritual practices of encountering God, and as churches develop common ways of communing with God, they converge in their understandings and practices of spirituality.

SPIRITUAL ECCLESIOLOGY

Individualistic frameworks for spirituality would question whether there is any relation between it and ecclesiology. The common moniker of "spiritual but not religious" drives a wedge between spiritual practices and communal identity. However, Christian theology has maintained that Christians do not exist apart from each other, binding them together in their communion with God. As described in the first chapter, God's indwelling in the church constitutes its ecclesiality. The charismatic life of the church manifests the perichoretic love between divine Persons, and believers share in the divine life more fully as they partake in the Christian community.[3] Spirituality is understood here as the practices by which Christians encounter God directly and through their fellow Christians. The church's spiritual reality precedes its expression in ministry, worship, and fellowship.[4] Such expressions are not ancillary to the church's nature. They are ways that believers maintain communion with God and other Christians across time and space.[5] The church is where Christian spirituality takes communal form.

Theologies of spirituality are as ecclesiological as they are pneumatological. The Spirit's leading in spiritual practices molds believers into the image of Christ. The oft-cited prayer of Christ in John 17 on the unity of believers in God occurs within the larger farewell discourse of John's Gospel, where Jesus says he will ask the Father to send the Spirit, who will continue Jesus' ministry after the ascension.[6] The Pentecost event is an answer to Christ's prayer for the church. *TCTCV* affirms the source of the church's ministry in the Spirit, who bestows faith and other charisms that equip the church with "essential gifts, qualities, and order."[7] The charismatic dimension of the church's life is a result of God's presence in the church, and all persons

Spiritual Ecumenism   149

within the church are called to exercise the gifts given to them as part of their membership in the church.

The charismatic nature of the church is a dimension of the church's unity. Spiritual practices accompany ecumenical projects, pointing participants to the source of their work. *Ut unum sint* advocates for the synergism of dialogue and prayer, whose pairing makes both more fruitful.[8] Yet spirituality itself is also seen as a method of ecumenical work. Walter Kasper acknowledges the unitive effect of common prayer in civic events,[9] such as the Zambian Day of Prayer mentioned above. The opportunity to share spiritual practices of other communities expresses the church's catholicity.[10] It is common for prayer and worship to be shared ventures whenever separate Christian communities seek to express solidarity. For example, the first fruit of the Joint Working Group between the Roman Catholic Church and the WCC was the agreement to produce jointly the annual materials for the Week of Prayer for Christian Unity.[11]

Spiritual practices are core to the ecumenical movement because of the movement's pursuit of spiritual renewal in the lives of churches. Insofar as churches are called to unity, ecumenism encourages renewal as an increase in fidelity to the call.[12] This has been seen already in previous chapters. The reconciliation of memories entails repentance and conversion toward others, just as the discernment in bilateral dialogue makes divided Christians attentive to the Spirit's leading. Ecumenical renewal contributes to the unity of the church when it extends beyond any one community. *TCTCV* names Roger Schütz and the Taizé community as examples of spiritual renewal that unite Christians.[13] The sharing of spiritual practices and the gathering of Christians from divided communities in prayer enable the recognition of believers as fellow members of the Body of Christ.

The ecclesiological consequences of spiritual ecumenism, however, are less apparent. Renewal movements seldom follow the prescribed projects of ecumenists, choosing instead to blow like the wind wherever they will. Despite the ecclesiological context of Christian spirituality, there is no clear relation between spirituality and divergent ecclesiologies. Because spiritual practices are not bound by church divides, and because a plurality of spiritual traditions can coexist in a church communion, it is improper to say that any particular doctrine of the church has a correlate spirituality. It is even improper to speak of "spiritualities" as discrete phenomena that can be chosen between or counted. Additionally, though it is agreed that the Spirit bestows gifts and order for the church's well-being, the divergent uses of these gifts have resulted in different patterns of ecclesial life. Believers might not always know the history of their churches or be able to articulate nuances of doctrine, but they can tell when churches worship differently from each other. Spirituality, rather than uniting the church, is often its most visible dividing factor.

150   *Chapter 5*

Robeck defines spirituality as pneumatological ecclesiology.[14] The spiritual practices in which Christians participate are a consequence of the Spirit's presence in the church. This definition delineates the discussion by focusing on the relation of the church to the Spirit as a pressing question for the method of spiritual ecumenism. Robeck argues that the charismatic dimension of the church is where the church's existence as unity in diversity is most clearly seen. The goal of spiritual ecumenism is not to fabricate a uniform spirituality but to order the gifts of the Spirit such that they fulfill their intended purpose of building up the singular body.[15] Robeck's understanding of spiritual ecumenism draws from two fields of research—the patristic era and the Charismatic movement. He sees these as complementary fields in that contemporary spiritual renewal should seek to pattern itself after the early church for the sake of revitalizing and restoring the Christian community as God intends.[16] I here do not study patristic literature or the Charismatic movement directly but only Robeck's understanding of them. Additionally, this chapter in its study of Robeck differs from previous topics in their accounting for his ecumenical work. His experience in spiritual ecumenism is not as a leader but as a participant and scholar. As such, this chapter is more text-driven in its reading of Robeck's thought on praxis. Patristic and Charismatic thought inform Robeck's promotion of spiritual ecumenism.

PATRISTIC PNEUMATOLOGY AND ECCLESIOLOGY

Charismatic patristics research uses the operation of spiritual gifts within the early church as an entry point into the development of the church's beliefs and practices. Gifts intersect with epistemological, soteriological, and liturgical questions, along with scholarly interests such as hermeneutics, gender, or power. The use and abuse of charisms fueled debates within patristic ecclesiology. Early Christians were beset with questions of authority amid waves of heresy and schism, even as they sought to distinguish the manifestations of spiritual power within their own minority communities from those in other larger religions. The church, as the "ark of salvation," became the place where gifts of grace were expected from the Holy Spirit.

Robeck's interest in patristics came after his research in Pauline's charismatic theology.[17] Patristic theologies of spiritual gifts offer a form of continuity between the apostles and the first centuries of the church. His academic training is in patristics, antedating his research in ecumenics or Pentecostal studies. These later interests built atop his prior historical knowledge. Similar to other ecumenists' patristics work, he studies the period for the sake of gaining insight into the apostolic nature of the church and how the early church preserved its unity as a religious minority amid ecclesiastical conflicts. His

Spiritual Ecumenism 151

research on the era helped him understand the differences between Pentecostal and other churches through studying the origins of doctrines and practices.[18]

Of the topics covered in this book, Robeck's patristics research is the least cited by other authors.[19] This is likely due to his interstitial place in the field. Ecumenists dealing with patristic sources of the faith seldom think to consult literature from Pentecostals, the youngest ecclesial tradition. Similarly, Pentecostals studying ecumenics typically conceive of the topic as a matter of contemporary questions, not ancient principles. Benvenuti's and Muszczyński's dissertations that examine Robeck barely acknowledge his patristics research.[20] Authors who engage Robeck's work overlook one of the most formative sources of his thought regarding the nature of church unity.

Robeck opens his *Prophecy in Carthage* with a liberative impulse. The bestowal of charisms in the church contributed to the social liberation within the Christian community of previously oppressed peoples: the Spirit's work, regardless of class, gender,[21] or lineage, subverted the existent social order. Charismatic freedom did not dispense with communal guidelines or boundaries. On the contrary, the democratization of spiritual gifts heightened the need for discernment and the maintenance of ecclesiastical order to preserve the freedom God intended.[22] Robeck's monograph is partially a response to the project of John Panagopoulos, who researched early Christian prophetism for its value for the ecumenical movement, including a consultation held at the Ecumenical Institute in Bossey.[23] The heritage of the early church belongs to all Christians, and so the study of the doctrinal and practical debates from the era informs contemporary questions of ecclesiology.[24] Robeck researches the ante-Nicene era, especially in North Africa, for the church-dividing controversies that occurred there and for the role of charisms in causing and resolving these divisions. His patristic reflections center on the two related subjects of prophecy and church unity.

Prophecy

Robeck's interest in prophetic gifts developed out of a desire to build up his Pentecostal community through the right use of the charism.[25] Prophecy, as all other charisms, is given by God to edify the church, which is why Paul pleads for its use above other gifts (1 Cor. 14). The charism provides continuity between Israel, the apostles, and the church insofar as God speaks through his Spirit.[26] Alan Humm adds that, while the titled office of apostle ceased after the first century, the title of prophet continued for centuries afterward,[27] offering greater insight into the development of the early church. Prophecy had such an impact on the early church's faith that it is the only spiritual gift mentioned in the Nicene Creed—"I believe in the Holy Spirit, . . . who has

152   *Chapter 5*

spoken through the prophets." The charism in the Creed serves as an identifier of the Third Person of the Trinity, rooting the church's creedal confession within the church's received faith and experience.

Prophecy was seen as a constitutive element of the church's nature and mission in the apostolic era. Robeck points to Peter's interpretation of the Pentecost event, where Peter alludes to Joel's promise of a prophetic outpouring of the Spirit (Joel 2:28; Acts 2:17). Prophetic gifts are a sign of the church's charismatic nature.[28] Paul's letter to the Ephesians lists prophets alongside apostles for their common ecclesiological context. The two offices are recipients of the revelation that Jews and Gentiles are united in the Body of Christ (Eph. 3:5, 6), and the two are gifts that Christ gives for the edification of the church (4:11-16). Paul even refers to apostles and prophets as the foundation of the household of God (2:19-22).[29] Post-apostolic literature, including the *Didache* and *The Shepherd of Hermas*, presumes the normalcy of prophetic activity among Christians, giving guidelines on how the gift should be shared with the community.[30]

Robeck reads patristic literature to discover the purposes for which early Christians relied on prophecies. Letters and sermons speak of the need to exhort the church to faithfulness amid persecution, as seen in *The Passion of Perpetua and Felicitas*. Ignatius's epistle, *To the Philadelphians*, likewise relays a prophetic utterance given to the congregation to "love unity [and] avoid divisions."[31] Prophetic leadership of churches influenced theological debates of the time, where visions and prophetic words were cited to support doctrinal positions and interpretations of scripture.[32] Robeck gives an example wherein Tertullian relies on a recorded oracle to affirm the inseparability of divine Persons when the North African church was combating patripassianism. Tertullian argues that the church affirms the Trinitarian principle because it accords with the church's reception of God's self-revelation in both scripture and prophecy.[33]

The operation of prophetic gifts was not without problems. In some cases, the presence of prophets validated Christian communities as orthodox over and against heretical movements. Tertullian relies on this approach in his response to Marcion; he contends that, because early catholicism had more prophets and manifestations of spiritual gifts, the community enjoyed a divine presence that was absent from Marcionite churches.[34] In other cases, however, prophetic activity did not safeguard orthodoxy. Robeck's studies include the origins of the New Prophecy (Montanism). The teachings and practices of the movement are not always clear because heresiologists handed down what little information remains, but it is clear that part of the controversy surrounded the use of prophetic gifts. Robeck explains that Montanists assumed that, because God speaks to the whole church, if other people did not agree with the prophecies that Montanists received, then those people

Spiritual Ecumenism 153

were not part of the church. He argues that the Montanists' false understanding of prophecy impaired their discernment practices, thereby rupturing their communion with other Christians.[35] This is not the only controversial aspect of the movement, but it illustrates patristic debates on spiritual gifts and their function in the faith community.

A prominent figure in Robeck's thought is Cyprian.[36] The third-century bishop of Carthage influenced later patristic thought on the nature of prophetic gifts. His influence was partially a result of his episcopal office, but also because of his personal experience with the charism. Humm relies on Robeck's study of Cyprian in saying that Cyprian had a more intimate knowledge of prophecy than did Tertullian. Tertullian wrote about prophets and prophecies, but Cyprian received visions himself and corresponded regularly with those who also did.[37] Cyprian's ministry occurred during a time of intense ecclesiastical politics and persecution, so the visions he received exhorted and guided the Christians under his see. Robeck chronicles instances where Cyprian relied on revelations to appoint candidates to offices, a politically delicate procedure that ensured the continuity of church communities.[38] It is no surprise that Cyprian—the man credited with coining the slogan that would become *extra ecclesiam nulla salus*—rejected all prophecy that occurred outside the church.[39] Nonetheless, Robeck demonstrates that Cyprian assumed the validity and value of widespread prophetic activity outside the episcopate.[40]

The abundance of prophets in the early church and the high stakes of the prophecies' validity required shared criteria by which believers could know whether a prophetic word was from God. Robeck places prophecy alongside its complementary spiritual gift of discernment in his research. Every time a person delivers a message purportedly from God, the community must test and interpret it. Post-biblical discernment criteria date back as early as the *Didache*.[41] Robeck's research on the patristic era attends to the forces of stability and adaptability within the interplay of divine revelation and community life. Charismatic activity spurred the development of guiding principles such as the biblical canon, the *regula fidei*, and the church's Tradition as sources that offered communal meaning.[42] These guides did not replace charisms. In fact, their existence presumed the continuing activity of the Spirit in transmitting revelation that would need to be tested. If a prophecy is consistent with scripture and Tradition, and if it is given for the edification of the church, then the prophecy is an act of God to preserve the transmission of the apostolic faith. Though prophecy is not a common topic for research in ecumenical ecclesiology, it is the complementary charism for discernment, a topic receiving increasingly more attention from ecumenists in dialogue, conciliar processes, and ethical deliberations. Ecumenists cannot advance in their understanding of discernment without accounting for prophecy, and as

154   Chapter 5

Robeck demonstrates, there is no better place to study charisms after scripture
than the patristic witness.

The previous chapter noted Robeck's role in the attention given to patristic theology in the fifth Catholic–Pentecostal phase, but this was not his
only influence. Robeck's research on prophetic gifts overlapped with the
beginnings of his ecumenical work in the 1980s. His participation in the
NCCUSA's Faith and Order Commission occurred during its studies on the
apostolic faith, pneumatology, and ecclesiology, molding his understanding
of discernment according to its function in the life of the church, as illustrated in figure 5.1. He also came to see it as an important topic for dialogue
between churches. Every subsequent international dialogue with Pentecostal
churches has examined discernment as a result of Robeck's influence.[43]
Harold Hunter blames Robeck for the reports' avoidance of the problematic
nature of prophetic gifts,[44] and Robert Grant likewise has accused Robeck of
overlooking the strife present in the early church,[45] but Robeck raises these
gifts for the sake of encouraging communal reflection on them because he
knows how controversial they are. Benvenuti notes that his study of prophecy
also informed his understanding of Azusa Street and racial reconciliation in
the second chapter.[46] Even when Robeck's discussions do not cite patristic
literature, his understanding of discernment and other charisms is a consequence of his patristics research, illustrating the relation between spiritual
gifts and the church's unity.

Unity of the Church

The presence of God in the church manifests in diverse gifts of grace. These
gifts are given for the sake of strengthening the unity between its members
and with God, so it is of ecclesiological importance that these gifts are exercised rightly. Theologies of charisms concern the boundaries of communal
identity insofar as they determine who is responsible for exercising which
gifts and when.[47] The first chapter mentioned Robeck's observation that most
of Paul's discussions of grace gifts occur within his passages on the church.
Lists of gifts inform ecclesial practices and order.[48] Christian spirituality is
ecclesiological because it is communal, and so disagreements on spirituality have communal implications. Part of the motivation of ecumenists when
studying spirituality is to seek consensus on practices. Robeck contends that
if the ecumenical movement is a prophetic movement, but there is no consensus on what constitutes prophecy, then churches will be unable to fulfill
their prophetic calling. He cites Hans Reudi-Weber, former WCC director
of biblical studies, who asserted that there was worrisome little reflection
on prophecy in ecumenical circles despite the frequent use of prophetic language in the movement.[49] Protestantism identifies prophetic gifts with the

Spiritual Ecumenism

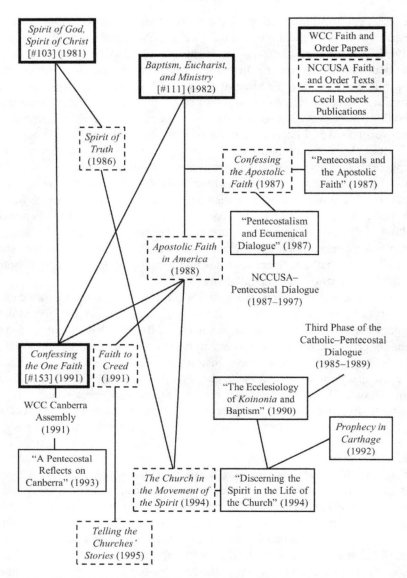

Figure 5.1 The Genesis of Robeck's Ecumenical Thought. *Source*: By the author.

act of proclaiming the Word in sermons and in social witness,[50] Catholic and Orthodox traditions follow a later patristic pattern of folding the charism into the episcopal office, and Pentecostals see prophecy as a spontaneous event. Robeck advocates the study of the early church for its integral understanding of charisms and ecclesiology.[51]

156   Chapter 5

Challenges to church unity in the patristic era stemmed from political pressures and false teachings, and they were further aggravated by prophetic activity. Robeck's research is not in heresiology, so he does not spend extended time on particular schismatic groups, but the groups are examples of spirituality becoming a source of division. Montanism is a common focal point for discussions on spiritual gifts and ecclesiology in the early church. Scholars compare the movement to contemporary independent movements either for the sake of condemning the contemporary movements as heretical or for the sake of championing the contemporary movements as continuing a prophetic heterodoxy against an oppressive institutional orthodoxy. Robeck himself is reticent to make these comparisons due to the historical distance between Montanists and later charismatic groups.[52] There is also considerable variation across the space and centuries in which Montanism was active, making it difficult to make any determinative assessment with the ancient group as a reference point. At any rate, it is clear that Robeck, in his patristics research, is sympathetic to certain schismatic groups while ultimately upholding the judgments of early catholicism.

The church relied on spiritual gifts for guidance and comfort to weather the storm of controversies. Prophecies were given to exhort the faithful during persecutions, and many of the prophecies were recorded and circulated to other congregations. Robeck lists examples from Cyprian during the Decian persecution, where Cyprian gave instructions to the congregations under his episcopacy on what to do with the lapsed who sought to be readmitted to the church. Disagreements over how to readmit—or even whether to do so—were dividing churches. Cyprian admonished the congregations according to instructions he received from God through prophetic visions.[53] Insight received from spiritual gifts contributed to the teachings and practices that guided the church.[54]

Patristic studies on charisms trace declines of charismatic activity. A recurrent question is whether the development of ecclesiastical structures and a firm concept of Tradition extinguished the more ecstatic gifts, or at least marginalized their place in the church's life. Humm lists "a cluster of comorbid movements" that accompanied the decline, including a rise in asceticism, the formalization of liturgical structure, and a constrained orthodoxy.[55] Robeck is not critical of the development of the early episcopal system as a means of preserving the apostolic deposit and the unity of the church, which is why he acknowledges contemporary value in patristic literature. The communion of churches is a consequence of the Spirit indwelling them, yet human leadership also links them. On the other hand, Robeck does not ascribe authority to the literature, seeing the early church leaders as no more inspired than contemporary leaders.[56] Ecclesiastical offices are not opposed to the charismatic ministry of the church, but the charismatic ministry also requires critical discernment among the faithful of the messages they have received from church leaders.

Robeck's patristics research is motivated by his Pentecostal confession, in part to edify his Pentecostal community in their use of spiritual gifts, but also to justify their claims of apostolicity. Laura Nasrallah interrogates the Christian historiography of the early church. The study of origins is a project of persuasion and validation. The nature of charisms especially lends itself to historiographical questions of truth and progress, for it is believed that gifts of grace are perceptible phenomena that originate from outside of history.[57] She is critical of the colonialist underpinnings of Weberian models of routinization and Victor Turner's cyclical offshoots of the oppressed, both of which are standard frameworks in the study of the early church and of Pentecostalism.[58] She observes that scholars often study Montanism to explain historical developments of canons and offices, thereby contrasting civil, rational orthodoxy with liminal and ecstatic behaviors of the disenfranchised.[59] Robeck at times employs this same rhetoric, yet he does not employ the binary between charisma and orthodoxy that Nasrallah condemns. Along with Humm,[60] he acknowledges that early catholicism was at least as charismatic as the schismatic groups it deemed heretical. As mentioned previously, Robeck contends that the development of orthodoxy and ecclesiastical structures was not an attempt to oppress ecstatic spirituality; it was an attempt to preserve the newfound social liberation afforded by the Spirit's work in the Christian community.

Similar to the previous section, Robeck's patristics research would go on to influence his understanding of spiritual gifts in the church's unity. The tension between magisterial authority and charisms is seen in his controversial and well-known essay, "An Emerging Magisterium? The Case of the Assemblies of God."[61] In the essay, after an excursion into patristic thought on Tradition, he asserts that the preservation of a community and its confessional identity is dependent on equitable discernment practices, from which his church was deviating. His critique of his own denomination in the essay nearly caused him to be defrocked;[62] it was more controversial than any of his ecumenical work. More recently, two essays of Robeck's that have appeared in Faith and Order papers concern spiritual gifts and their relation to ecclesial decision-making.[63] The two Faith and Order studies examine how churches arrive at their teachings for the sake of informing future ecumenical reflection on how churches can achieve consensus. His essays detail how Pentecostal denominations have understood the role of the Spirit in these institutional processes, making the unity of the church a pneumatological, charismatic matter.

158   *Chapter 5*

CHARISMATIC ECUMENISM

The spiritual dimension of unity in the early church can also be seen in the contemporary church. Bilateral dialogues and the reconciliation of memories are text-driven enterprises, and councils of churches manifest an institutional dimension. Spiritual ecumenism, however, often occurs without such media, making the method difficult for ecumenists to quantify. A common recourse is to study spiritual ecumenism as it occurs within particular movements and events, including the Charismatic movement. Originating no earlier than the 1960s, the movement has proven to be a widespread and, at times, problematic renewal effort. It distinguishes itself from other renewal movements in that it seeks the cultivation and right use of spiritual gifts within the local church. The catholicity of God's presence in the church means that no Christian community is without charisms, yet the particular historical renewal called "the Charismatic movement" presumes a normative measure of charismatic activity.

The movement defines itself as an ecumenical endeavor insofar as it is the product of and catalyst for exchange between churches. It has moved beyond its origins, but few would deny that the Charismatic movement is a Pentecostal influence on other churches. The promise and problems of the exchange have become a field unto itself. The 1975 Nairobi Assembly of the WCC initiated a sub-unit on Renewal and Congregational Life, which examined, among other subjects, the Charismatic movement. WCC's interest in the movement was a result of the Catholic–Pentecostal dialogue that began three years prior.[64] The study project on the Charismatic movement received an "unprecedented response" from churches prior to the *Baptism, Eucharist, and Ministry* study.[65] It was clear that the subject was one to which churches globally had devoted significant attention.

Discourse surrounding the Charismatic movement's ecumenical import can betray a form of elitism, wherein Pentecostals boast of their contributions to church unity. It can also spotlight the relations of Pentecostal churches with other churches, centering Pentecostalism within the ecumenical landscape. It should be remembered, however, that Charismatics in Protestant, Catholic, and Orthodox churches outnumber "Classical" Pentecostals globally, meaning that much of the interchurch engagement in the Charismatic movement occurs without direct involvement from Pentecostal churches. Several bilateral dialogues have attested to the contributions of the Charismatic movement to relations between the two partners, including the Evangelical–Catholic,[66] Catholic–Baptist,[67] Lutheran–Catholic,[68] Methodist–Catholic,[69] and Baptist–Methodist[70] international dialogues. The unitive implications of the Charismatic movement are not a Pentecostal hypothesis but a lived experience to which non-Pentecostal churches testify. Yet churches also testify to the fact

Spiritual Ecumenism 159

that the Charismatic movement has proven a common challenge that churches must face together, as described in the Lutheran–Reformed,[71] Anglican–Baptist,[72] and Anglican–Methodist[73] international dialogues. Similar to the patristic era, spiritual gifts motivate reflection on the church's ministry and unity.

Robeck's study of the Charismatic movement is for its ecclesiological nature. He stresses that the renewal is not an external force on the church but is part of the church and that the renewal has awakened within participants an ecclesiological vision of the singular Body of Christ. The fellowship that constitutes the church hinges upon a common experience of the Spirit (1 Cor. 12:13).[74] He also studies the movement as a form of internal critique within the field of ecumenical studies. Despite his decades of contributions to councils of churches and dialogues, he resists the tendency to portray them as normative forms of ecumenism. A methodological study of the Charismatic movement shifts focus away from Spirit baptism—a pneumatological experience that goes beyond the questions addressed in this book—and instead attends to the ecclesiological considerations of the movement, particularly the charismatic nature of the church's unity and its order.

Charismatic Unity and Division

The Charismatic movement has been a locus of reflection on and experience of unity in the church. Robeck uses the movement as a catalyst for his thought on koinonia. He asks how Christians should conceive of a communion ecclesiology that encompasses the diversity of not only Pentecostal churches but also the Charismatic members of Protestant, Catholic, and Orthodox churches.[75] The question is not meant to exclude non-Charismatics from the communion but to highlight the fellowship that constitutes the church across divisions. The experience should then inform doctrine on the church. Discussions of unity in the Charismatic movement are often centered on orthopathy, where the affective reception of divine grace forms believers as part of the church, though it should be stressed that orthopathy never exists apart from orthodoxy and orthopraxy, concerns that are more prevalent in ecumenical discourse. The Charismatic movement is a laboratory for spiritual ecumenism as believers discern what preserves or impairs the church's fellowship.

The Charismatic movement brings Christians together in several contexts, including deliverance ministries, discipleship classes, and service programs, but the most common context is that of worship and prayer gatherings. Participants in Charismatic gatherings spend time praying for each other or for a common cause. Robeck identifies the ecclesiological significance of such practices. Through intercession, believers affirm their place in the church alongside those for whom they are praying. Additionally, those for whom people pray move from the periphery of the people's consciousnesses.[76] May

Ling Tan-Chow describes this process in the Singaporean Charismatic context. Gatherings of prayer for their country encourage the sharing of resources for the churches' common mission and pulpit swaps between congregations.[77] Of course, the Charismatic movement is not unique in its advocacy of common prayer, but it follows a similar pattern as other movements of spiritual ecumenism.

Charismatic gatherings foster communion between participants through encounter. Robeck describes the transformative effects of spiritual encounter. The interpersonal exchange occurs between the believer and the Spirit, and the interface is socially mediated. The church becomes the context in which believers anticipate the presence and manifestation of the Spirit. Here, Robeck specifically speaks of Pentecostalism as a spirituality of direct encounter,[78] but his comments also apply to the Charismatic movement. He describes the movement as a process of recognition wherein believers recognize in each other the presence of the Spirit, crossing confessional boundaries in ways that few other experiences of spiritual ecumenism have done.[79] The aforementioned WCC consultation asserted that the Charismatic movement expanded the ecumenical movement. Churches are often separated, not by theology, but by a lack of communication. The Charismatic movement addresses this by bringing believers together in spiritual gatherings.[80] Former WCC General Secretary Philip Potter at the consultation confirmed that the Charismatic movement made conversations between Protestants, Catholics, and Orthodox easier.[81]

The spiritual encounter between believers is transrational, but it also raises the believers' consciousness of their communion with each other. Robeck refers to this as a form of recognition. His use of the term is related to the legal use in ecumenical discourse of the validity of ministries, though here it refers to an acknowledgment of the Spirit's presence in another community that arises from experience.[82] The Charismatic movement offers space for divided Christians to recognize in each other the same Spirit. For example, the WCC initiated a study on the Charismatic movement nearly two decades before it began holding consultations with Pentecostal churches. Furthermore, the WCC study report reveals a greater openness to the Charismatic movement than to Pentecostals. Insufficient data exists to measure the impact of the study on member churches of the WCC, but one can wonder whether the prolonged effects of the Charismatic movement made member churches more open to their Pentecostal peers. Robeck argues such when he says that the movement improved relations between Pentecostal and other churches.[83] He even offers a litmus test: how likely a church is to respect and work with Pentecostals is a reflection of how well the church treats its own Charismatic members.[84] Participation in shared spiritual settings contributes to the sharing of spiritual practices, paving the way for mutual recognition.

The ecumenical nature of the Charismatic movement has been variously received. Peter Hocken reports that it is the first renewal movement of Protestant provenance that the Catholic Church embraced[85]—though it is more accurate to say that the ecumenical movement was the first. Efforts to contextualize the renewal within Catholicism inadvertently distanced Charismatic Catholics from their non-Catholic peers while constraining the movement as one renewal stream among many. Hocken describes the domestication of the Catholic Charismatic Renewal in the West during the 1980s. What was once heralded as a radical experience in ecumenism just a few years earlier was not mentioned in the *Directory for the Application of Principles and Norms on Ecumenism* in 1993 and *Ut unum sint* in 1995.[86] The absence from these texts is striking. Robeck was present as a fraternal delegate at the meeting in Rome of the Ecumenical Commissions of Episcopal Conferences and the Synods of Eastern Catholic Churches that authored the *Directory*.[87] Additionally, when *Ut unum sint* was released, the United States Conference of Catholic Bishops named Robeck as a theological expert to interpret the encyclical for the general public.[88] The Catholic Church did not associate the Charismatic Renewal with their ecumenical relations with Pentecostal churches. There are recent signs of a desire to recover the ecumenical roots of the movement locally and globally, including the formation of the Christian Unity Commission of the Catholic Charismatic Renewal International Service, half of whose commission members are non-Catholic.[89]

The question remains whether the transdenominational Charismatic movement revolves around Pentecostal churches as its center of gravity. Robeck contends that "the Charismatic Renewal must be understood as a logical extension of the Pentecostal Movement."[90] He employs a common narrative in saying that Pentecostal churches are a byproduct of Christians either leaving or being expelled from their churches after attending Charismatic revivals.[91] Those who remained in their original churches now constitute the contemporary Charismatic movement. He appeals to a statement in a Lutheran–Catholic joint document, which explains that "the Pentecostal movement is present in many other churches in the form of the charismatic movement, creating new commonalities and communities across confessional boundaries."[92] This line of reasoning motivated the inclusion of Lutheran, Reformed, Baptist, Anglican, and Orthodox ministers in Pentecostal bilateral dialogue teams because of their Charismatic status. It also lies behind the common phrase, the "Pentecostal/Charismatic movement," encompassing over 600 million Christians from an array of confessions as part of a common renewal movement. Pentecostal churches would appear to have had a disproportionate influence on others.

The influence is not unidirectional. Robeck identifies instances where the Charismatic movement shaped his own Pentecostal denomination. He refers

162   *Chapter 5*

to the AG's "Statement of Fundamental Truths."[93] Robeck narrates changes to the AG's Statement in the latter twentieth century in its articulation of the doctrine of Spirit baptism. He contends that such changes are a consequence of the theology of spiritual gifts developed in the wider Charismatic movement.[94] The academic and ministerial interactions in the movement impacted how doctrine was taught in the AG.[95] However, this complicates Robeck's prior understanding of the movement. If it were solely an extension of Pentecostalism into other churches, then Pentecostal churches would not be influenced, yet his example of the AG shows that the Charismatic movement has shaped Pentecostal churches.[96] One can wonder whether a sharper conceptual distinction is warranted between Pentecostal churches and the Charismatic movement.

Robeck praises the movement for having created communities and bonds of communion across denominational and social divisions.[97] It should be acknowledged, however, that this is not a universal experience. The impact of the Charismatic movement has stirred up strife in some churches, which is partially why many churches conducted studies on the movement in the 1970s and 1980s. Abuses of spiritual gifts and elitism toward non-Charismatics cause power struggles in congregations. In response to those who extol the ecumenical value of the renewal, John Odeyemi pushes back by saying that, though Charismatic revivals cross confessional borders, they do not always go beyond common prayer; in fact, they often serve as sites of proselytism.[98] As mentioned in the previous chapter, proselytism is a denial of koinonia, which contrasts with claims of fostering koinonia through the Charismatic movement. Additionally, disagreements over the place of charismatic experiences in the local church have led to schisms.[99] In such instances, renewal is a pretext for division rather than a method toward unity. The question remains whether the spiritual practices of the Charismatic movement can contribute to ecumenical work.

Charismatic Order

Similar to the discussion on patristic charismatic theology, controversies surrounding the operation of spiritual gifts within the church should not lead to a denial of the gifts' place in the church. Instead, they require communal discernment on their right use in building up the church. Robeck argues that the early church offers insight into how to reconcile competing understandings of spiritual gifts.[100] He here speaks primarily of the gift of prophecy, but his literature on charisms elsewhere is equally informed by patristic thought. In an NCCUSA Faith and Order consultation on discernment, he acknowledges that the charismatic presence of the Spirit in the church results in questions of power, authority, and truth among the church's members.

Spiritual Ecumenism 163

The task is then to order charisms so that believers can receive the fullness of the Spirit in their individual and communal lives.[101] Connie Ho Yan Au's study on the Charismatic movement in England examines the formational elements of the movement, wherein participants were trained in the proper exercise of spiritual gifts. The confessionally diverse range of educators and participants prompted the need for deliberation between divergent theological understandings of the church and its ministry.[102] Spiritual ecumenism brings Christians together in prayer, and out of this experience, they reflect together on what communal forms their spirituality should take.

The ecumenical movement has provided space for churches to discern together how best to exercise gifts of the Spirit in their ministries, though these spaces are usually not at an institutional level. The WCC consultation on the Charismatic movement gathered responses from churches on the nature of the unity they were experiencing through the movement. Responses also voiced concerns that the movement had raised, prodding churches to revisit their teachings on charisms.[103] The consultation offered a list of discernment criteria for churches to use when gauging the proper use of spiritual gifts.[104] Unfortunately, the reception process of *Baptism, Eucharist, and Ministry* soon overshadowed the discussion. Subsequent ecclesiological reflection of the WCC has been anemic on the church's charismatic nature. Veli-Matti Kärkkäinen critiques *The Nature and Purpose of the Church* for its lack of mention of charismatic ministries such as divine healing, exorcism, or prophecy as part of the church's ministry and mission, despite their prominent place in churches in many regions.[105] The latter *TCTCV* text fares no better, thus missing an opportunity to address a divisive ecclesiological debate. Even before Robeck's formal ecumenical ministry began, he recognized the need for communal discernment in the Charismatic movement on the exercise of gifts for the sake of unity.[106] The movement is a space for discernment on topics that ecumenists overlook elsewhere.

Similar to other points of doctrinal contention, common methods and authorities are needed for churches to seek consensus on spiritual gifts. For Robeck, after scripture, the best place to start is the early church. His articulation of spiritual ecumenism is part of his theology of the church's apostolicity. He notes that, at the Pentecost event, the Spirit was poured out on all those present, not only the apostles, empowering them to share in the same commission as the apostles.[107] The charismatic ministry of the church preserves the apostolic deposit insofar as believers continue to receive and operate spiritual gifts. This, in his mind, is the goal of the Charismatic movement.[108]

Patristic witness to the apostolic faith testifies to the church's reliance on the gifts, and it offers guidance on how to exercise them in the life of the local church, which is why Robeck values patristic insight on these questions. A response submitted to the WCC consultation from the Malankara

164 — *Chapter 5*

Orthodox Syrian Church is instructive. The church reports that it sought to encourage its Charismatic members into higher leadership positions, yet the effort struggled because the Charismatics "manifest[ed] some Montanist tendencies."[109] The report's allusion to a controversy of the early church is a way of appealing to patristic thought on proper Christian spirituality. Insufficient data exists on Charismatic Malankara Orthodox to assess the report, but two things are apparent—that there were controversies on how the church's charismatic ministry should be manifest in the community; and that, despite these controversies, the Malankara Orthodox Syrian Church believed its Charismatic members would contribute to the well-being of the community in leadership positions.

Robeck does not distinguish between hierarchical and charismatic gifts in his literature, mostly because the language is foreign to his Pentecostal tradition, though he affirms both as being given to the church by the Spirit.[110] He hesitates to place much significance on the charisms given to particular offices lest those positions come to be seen as monopolizing revelation from the Spirit. One can identify an unresolved tension in his thought between the God-given role of church leadership and the democratization of spiritual gifts.[111] The presence of God in the church is meant to offer new forms of social relations, not sacralize existent ones.[112] Robeck appeals to Cyprian when he says that the whole community and not lone individuals are to operate gifts.[113] He does not address Cyprian's theology of episcopal oversight of the community, which is a pressing question for ecumenical theology, but he is attempting to offer ways for Christians to benefit mutually from their exercise of charisms.

To address competing understandings of spiritual gifts, Robeck advocates for the communal exercise of discernment for the sake of constructing ecclesiology together on the nature of spiritual gifts. Spiritual ecumenism is of assistance here because it permits communal deliberation beyond that afforded within the confines of councils of churches and bilateral dialogues. As mentioned before, he defines discernment as "prayerful reasoning" and "spiritual revelation" to acknowledge its charismatic nature.[114] All Christians are endowed with spiritual gifts, and so all Christians must discern together the right exercise of the gifts.[115] Most papers that Robeck presented in Faith and Order consultations of the NCCUSA and WCC were on the topic of discernment, drawing from his research in patristics and the Charismatic movement. Discernment occurs at the intersection of dialogue and spiritual ecumenism. It is a manifestation of the koinonia that believers enjoy, and it strengthens the bond between them.[116] Spiritual encounters between believers and the Spirit are preconditions for discussions in ecumenical spaces on how the church is meant to be in the world. For Robeck, ecclesiastical structures and spirituality rely on each other, which is why renewal efforts, such as the

Charismatic movement, are needed to ensure that communities are attuned to the Spirit's leading.[117] Robeck's promotion of the ecumenical value of the Charismatic movement is not as a finished product but as a method toward ecclesiological convergence.

SPIRITUAL ECUMENICAL METHODOLOGY

The use of spiritual ecumenism as a method toward church unity has ecclesiological implications. However, these implications are not commonly seen in the practices of spiritual ecumenism. Ecumenical prayer services can serve as a cover for churches that wish merely to be seen as ecumenically committed. The feeling of comradery in gatherings can convince believers that they have achieved unity while their divisions remain untouched. Perhaps churches value the method initially because they believe that it is safer and less costly than others. For spiritual ecumenism to serve as an ecumenical method, it must change churches. Christian spirituality is a process of conversion of believers toward God and each other, and their communion with each other manifests in the Spirit's bestowal of gifts and order. Spirituality, in Robeck's words, can rightly be called pneumatological ecclesiology.

According to this study's thesis, for spiritual ecumenism to serve as an ecumenical method, it must rely on shared ecclesiology between divided churches and result in ecclesiological convergence. The sharing of spiritual practices in ecumenical gatherings occurs as an expression of the participants' partaking in a common spiritual heritage of the church, and the gifts manifested are a sign of their communion. Furthermore, as problems inevitably arise from differing understandings of spirituality and the use of spiritual gifts, believers discern together how to order their practices rightly so that they preserve the communion between believers. Insofar as the church's order is a gift of the Spirit to encourage the use of other gifts, the common understanding and exercise of charisms constitutes ecclesiological convergence.

Charismatic Ecclesiology

The ecumenical method of spiritual ecumenism relies on the sharing of spiritual practices between divided Christians. They are capable of partaking in these practices out of a recognition that they are encountering the same God as part of the same fellowship of believers. Prayer is central to Christian spirituality and ecumenism as a form of participation in divine economy.[118] *Ut unum sint* uplifts common prayer as the "most complete expression" of Christian love.[119] The communion between believers and God is characterized by love, which is also the guiding principle of the exercise of charisms. Robeck

166   *Chapter 5*

appeals to the encyclical in his call for more opportunities for Christians to pray with each other.[120] Prayer gatherings often serve as starting points for other ecumenical ventures. For example, it was hoped that the 2008 launch of the Brazilian Encristus project would bring together Catholics and Pentecostals for prayer and ultimately lead to dialogue in the country;[121] a formal working group began in 2021. It is worth noting that the Brazilian endeavor is at a more developed stage than the United States dialogue mentioned in chapter 2. Spiritual ecumenism brings together Christians who otherwise would have remained isolated.

As Robeck argued previously, the church's charismatic nature is where the principle of unity in diversity is most visible. The plurality of spiritual gifts active in the church's life is a sign of God's presence, resulting in many forms of spiritual encounter. As such, diversity typifies Christian spirituality. The method of spiritual ecumenism, to be consistent with this understanding of charisms, does not seek uniformity. If the Charismatic movement sought to unite churches by making them share a common culture, then Charismatic renewal would be the antithesis of the unity seen at Pentecost. Nonetheless, the ecumenical method seeks unity by ordering diversities such that they build up the community together. Harding Meyer reminds that churches bring their understandings of unity into the ecumenical movement for them to converge.[122] Along these lines, Robeck raises questions of the preservation of the apostolic faith and of the freedom to listen to the Spirit's leading.[123] Whether it be the gift of prophecy or other charisms, divergent understandings of gifts should be discerned so that all gifts can function in their proper place.

The diversity of spiritual traditions in the church is an expression of its catholicity.[124] The ecumenical movement, in seeking a fuller understanding of ecclesial catholicity, encourages Christians to experience the church's diversity. Participation in other churches' liturgical practices and musical heritage characterizes ecumenical prayer gatherings. Ecumenical songbooks gather hymns out of liturgical solidarity with churches globally, just as councils of churches from different countries each year prepare the materials for the Week of Prayer for Christian Unity. The ecumenical laboratory of Taizé is shared outside the community through its growing body of songs, and the dissemination of Eastern iconographic traditions enriches the spiritual lives of Catholic and Protestant churches. Prejudice alone would dismiss the Charismatic movement from being upheld in a similar regard. The movement serves as a platform for the exchange of musical and prayer traditions across regions and cultures. In fact, even people who are skeptical of Charismatics will still attend gatherings for the music. The movement confirms the *TCTCV* statement that liturgy is a visible paradigm of koinonia, for in worship, believers stand in communion with God and others across time and space.[125]

Spiritual Ecumenism 167

One of the reasons that spiritual ecumenism is prized is because of the potential level of participation within churches. Ecumenism is often lamented as the domain of ecclesiastical hierarchs and intelligentsia, but every believer is capable of prayer. Regardless of ordination status, education, age, class, or ability, each and every Christian alive on the planet labors as an ecumenist whenever they pray for the unity of the church. Potter identifies the mobilization of laity as the driving force and goal of the ecumenical movement; he looks to the Pentecost event as their source of empowerment.[126] The Spirit's bestowal of grace gifts to each member incorporates them into the church and equips them for the church's ministry, including its ministry of reconciliation. Robeck adds that the charismatic dimension of the church must be cultivated.[127] Movements of spiritual ecumenism are one way that churches direct attention to all their members so that, together, they can be renewed for their common calling.

Unfortunately, ecumenical reflection on spiritual gifts is relegated to bilateral dialogues with Pentecostal churches, which could give the impression that Pentecostals relentlessly foist the topic onto their dialogue partners. The previous chapter, however, saw this to be far from the case. The Catholic Church chose the topic of charisms in the sixth phase of the Catholic–Pentecostal dialogue, Reformed churches proposed the Reformed–Pentecostal dialogue to address spiritual gifts in the church's mission, and the Lutheran World Federation initiated its dialogue with Pentecostal churches because they sought to engage better with their own fellow Lutherans. Outside of these dialogue commissions, there is little contemporary interconfessional dialogue on divergent understandings of the church's charismatic nature. This does not mean there are no longer problems or debates on spiritual practices. Instead, the lack of dialogue suggests that churches are addressing these conflicts without consulting each other. Au advocates conciliar practices as a way for churches to coordinate their spiritual lives together, drawing on her experience with the WCC and the Hong Kong Christian Council.[128] In a book review years ago, I critiqued Au for her discussion of the conciliar implications of Charismatic renewal. After further research, I now recognize the insight of and agree with her claims, which guided my argument in this chapter, and I can say her book warrants greater attention than has been given by scholars thus far. Spiritual ecumenism in the Charismatic movement brings churches together at the local level to discern how to exercise their God-given gifts in the world today, leaving their leaders and scholars struggling to catch up in the conversation.

The charismatic nature of the church is also a matter of apostolicity. The WCC consultation affirmed that the church experiences the resurrection of Christ in the operation of spiritual gifts.[129] The Pentecost event is a Christological event in that the apostolic community received the promise of the

168 *Chapter 5*

Father as confirmation of the Son's glorification. Robeck locates the church's apostolicity as residing in its members, and God's presence preserves apostolicity in the community in the fullness of the Spirit's work.[130] Ecumenists work toward the renewal of the church so that divided communities together can receive the fullness of God's gifts. Though the Charismatic movement is a movement of spiritual ecumenism, Potter in the WCC consultation proclaimed that "the whole ecumenical movement has been in fact a Charismatic Renewal."[131] Furthermore, "the member churches of the World Council of Churches need the Charismatic Renewal for their own renewal."[132] Many ecumenists doubtlessly will not give as glowing an endorsement of the Charismatic movement as did the WCC general secretary, but the concern for ecclesial renewal remains a task of the ecumenical movement, while it is remembered that renewal and unity can come only through believers' conversions to God.

Spiritual ecumenism testifies to the charismatic constitution of the church. The experience of koinonia in ecumenical prayer gatherings informs the ecclesiology that emerges from ecumenical work. Robeck defines the church as a product of the Spirit,[133] which is why its communion is charismatic.[134] Participants in the WCC consultation—including those who did not identify as Charismatic—reported that the Charismatic movement "granted us a new experience of the church. This new experience can properly be described as a social experience of God."[135] Pneumatological ecclesiology guides ecumenists in seeking convergence because it is a source that all can access equally. The report equates the church with the social experience of God, potentially blurring the line between the church and Christian spirituality, yet this confirms the reliance of ecclesiological convergence on the sharing of spiritual practices, inevitably leading to questions of resultant church order.

Ecclesiastical Order

Christian spirituality takes communal form in the church. The presence of God in the church constitutes its ecclesiality, and God gives to the church its order and practices to sanctify its members. Meyer explains that the visibility of the church's unity implies that the unity is manifest in the empirical reality of the church.[136] Part of this empirical reality is the communal practices of the church that preserve its communion, which is why research in ecumenical methodology studies the operation of spiritual gifts. Not all occurrences of common prayer contribute to the ecumenical project. The WCC consultation reported that the Charismatic movement has caused problems of authority and order among churches.[137] The discussion of the patristic era also noted instances where charismatic activity led to divisions. The ecumenical method of spiritual ecumenism requires that Christians, when they are brought

Spiritual Ecumenism 169

together in spiritual gatherings, discern together how to receive in common the gifts they have been given to preserve their communion with each other. Without the sharing of spiritual practices, ecclesiological convergence cannot occur.

Language of ecclesiastical order could appear to be oppositional to the approach of spiritual ecumenism, stoking fears of constraining the free movement of the Spirit. A response to *TCTCV* from an Anglican–Pentecostal consultation in England questions whether one should ever attempt to order the gifts of the Spirit's renewing work in the church.[138] However, Robeck's assessments of patristic and Charismatic spiritualities demonstrate the reliance of the church's ministry on the proper use of gifts. Pentecostal critiques of other churches' neglect of particular charisms are themselves an argument for how spiritual gifts should be ordered in the life of the church. Benjamin Crace has recently echoed this concern in his proposal of dialogue with the Coptic Orthodox church. The Coptic tradition's understanding of charisms in public ministry is a potential source for mutual reflection with Pentecostals. However, he contends that the Coptic restriction of particular spiritual gifts to clergy and monastics is inconsistent with the apostolic witness in scripture and with patristic teaching, concluding that reconciliation between Pentecostals and Coptic Orthodox will need to account for the operation of these charisms within the church's life.[139] Spiritual ecumenism raises questions over who can exercise which gifts and when.

The ephemeral nature of spirituality requires a reference point by which Christians can discern their spiritual practices together. Scripture serves as the first authoritative source on such questions, but churches have also found value in the patristic witness as early Christians grew in their understanding of the apostolic faith. Robeck acknowledges that Tradition is not only the doctrines of the church but also the prayer and worship practices by which Christians commune with previous generations.[140] The relationship between spiritual renewal and the early church is akin to the neo-patristic synthesis of twentieth-century Eastern Orthodoxy. The renewed attention to patristic texts informed Orthodox spiritual theology, consequently shaping ecumenical ecclesiology through figures such as Georges Florovsky, Dumitru Stăniloae, and John Zizioulas. Robeck likewise turns to patristic thought for its spiritual theology in his work on ecumenism, subsequently shaping ecclesiological reflection beyond his own church tradition within the ecumenical movement. The Charismatic movement does not normally draw from patristic literature, but it seeks to recover the spirituality of the early church for contemporary church unity, embodying the tension of continuity and change that defines renewal.

The focus on the charismatic nature of the church distinguishes the Charismatic movement from some other movements that pursue spiritual

170   *Chapter 5*

ecumenism. Christian communities have adopted various disciplines (such as Ignatian or hesychastic spiritualities) regardless of confession. It is also increasingly common for religious orders to exist across ecclesiastical lines. However, the forms of prayer life in these movements do not seek to be universal because they foster particular charisms for their respective vocations. On the other hand, the Charismatic movement understands itself as the renewal and reordering of charisms within the Christian community according to an apostolic pattern. The liturgical movement of the twentieth century is perhaps the most similar transdenominational spiritual movement that positions itself as normative. Proponents do not advocate the movement because they believe it to be "superior" or "holier" than other liturgical forms but because they believe it retrieves gifts from Tradition to renew and unite the church. As such, there is a universalizing element of the liturgical reforms across cultural and confessional distinctions to express their common catholicity through time and space. Similarly, the contemporary reception of Tradition through the Charismatic movement pertains to the nature of the church itself. Charismatic spirituality should not be listed alongside Athonite, Benedictine, or Franciscan traditions as comparable streams of renewal; otherwise, it would unite only Charismatics within each church rather than churches as wholes. The charismatic reordering of the Christian community is not for a privileged few but is meant to promote the well-being of the whole. Charismatic renewal is normative insofar as it is apostolic.

A normative claim does not monopolize spiritual ecumenism or deny the value of other movements, nor does it presume that the Charismatic movement presents a unified vision of the church. Even a cursory familiarity with the movement bewilders with its diversities. As a movement of spiritual ecumenism, it brings Christians together to seek from God the source of their unity and discernment on how to live out their unity in concrete, visible ways. A renewal is neither spiritual nor ecumenical if it does not change the values, structures, and practices of churches. The method of spiritual ecumenism results in ecclesiological convergence through the conversion of believers toward each other, and this change in hearts is seen through their change in actions. *TCTCV* identifies the Spirit as the source of the church's gifts and order.[141] The text goes on to argue for the need to evaluate ecclesiastical structures in light of God's gifts.[142] Robeck's study of the Charismatic movement and patristic literature resists a dichotomy between personal and institutional understandings of ecumenical change. The church's spirituality is not separate from its organizational life.

Spiritual ecumenism, being more than a preface to ecumenical work, informs the means and goals of this work. The spiritual dimension of ecumenism prompts Robeck to endorse organic union as a model of church unity. Models are beyond the scope of the present study on methods, but his thought

Spiritual Ecumenism 171

illustrates how spiritual ecumenism results in ecclesiological convergence. He values the concept of reconciled diversity for its acknowledgment of a diversity of ecclesial gifts, yet he concludes that organic union is more consistent with the church's charismatic nature.[143] Restorationist ecclesiology seeks congruity between the nature of the church and its visible form, as seen in the early church.[144] It is insufficient to say that the church is one in the Spirit without being one in practice. The validity of his argument is not the concern of the present study, but only its acknowledgment that Christian spirituality has communal implications.

Robeck's argument is primarily an internal discussion within Pentecostal circles on the method of spiritual ecumenism. He is critical of Pentecostal voices that uphold spiritual ecumenism—more commonly termed in Pentecostal literature as "ecumenism of the Spirit"—as an alternative form of ecumenism that eschews the institutional dimension of communion.[145] Instead, he argues that the communion of believers in the Spirit takes in the church "visible, structural support."[146] Benvenuti likewise observes that Robeck critiques Pentecostals who see prayer as the only needed response to racialized ecclesiastical divisions, covered in the second chapter.[147] The above analysis of ecumenical methodology shows that the organizational practices of churches are meant to foster spiritual encounters with God. Order and charisms are gifts from the same Spirit. The charismatic nature of the church blurs the common distinction between the church's structure and spiritual reality, making spiritual practices a part of the church's visible unity that ecumenists seek.[148] As seen in the patristic era, disagreements on spiritual practices can result in ecclesiastical divisions, so churches today seek consensus on how to receive their order and gifts.

Charismatic theology especially reveals the ecclesiastical implications of spiritual ecumenism. The presence of charisms in the church is inherently a perceptible phenomenon meant to guide and grow the faith of the church in its sanctification. Pneumatology becomes a matter of studying the experienced—even evidential—acts of the Spirit, including the Spirit's work in renewing and preserving the church's unity. To argue that the church's spiritual reality has no implications for the church's visible life or structures is symptomatic of a weak pneumatology. Regardless of the goals advocated, the ecumenical method of spiritual ecumenism presumes the desire for ecclesial change to reverse divisions. Why should Christians long to pray with each other and then not long for their churches to be with each other?

The conversion that occurs through spiritual ecumenism leads to the sixth chapter on Christian Forums. The ecumenical method relies on the sharing of testimonies as the primary form of communication in the gatherings. Spiritual ecumenism entails the conversion of Christians to each other through their encounter, establishing a connection between individual and ecclesiastical

172   *Chapter 5*

transformation. Testimonies in Christian Forums situate the self and one's community within the larger context of salvation history, narrating the work of God to reconcile the world. The reconciliation that occurs in the method, similar to spiritual ecumenism, relies on the presence of Christ and its visible witness in the lives of Christians. Robeck was an architect of the most controversial methodological development of ecumenism thus far in the twenty-first century—the Global Christian Forum.

NOTES

1. Kroesbergen, "Radical Change"; Chammah J. Kaunda, "The Day of Prayer and Its Potential for Engendering Public Ecclesiology Ecumenism in Zambia," *Religions* 9, no. 12 (2018): 1–13; Chammah J. Kaunda, "The Nationalization of Prayer and Prayerization of the Nation," in *Competing for Caesar: Religion and Politics in Post-Colonial Zambia*, ed. Chammah J. Kaunda and Marja Hinfelaar (Minneapolis, MN: Fortress Press, 2020), 39–56.

2. *UR*, §8.

3. Gesa Elsbeth Thiessen, "Ecumenism in Praxis: Critical Observations on the Week of Prayer for Christian Unity," in *Apostolic and Prophetic: Ecclesiological Perspectives* (Cambridge: James Clarke, 2011), 94.

4. Wolfgang Vondey, "Pentecostal Participation in Ecumenical Dialogues: Bilateral and Multilateral, Local and Global," in *Pentecostal Theology and Ecumenical Theology: Interpretations and Intersections*, ed. Peter D. Hocken, Tony L. Richie, and Christopher A. Stephenson, Global Pentecostal and Charismatic Studies 34 (Leiden: Brill, 2019), 87.

5. *TCTCV*, §67.

6. Thiessen, "Ecumenism in Praxis," 95.

7. *TCTCV*, §16.

8. *UUS*, §33.

9. Walter Kasper, *A Handbook of Spiritual Ecumenism* (Hyde Park, NY: New City Press, 2007), §30.

10. Kasper, §11.

11. Mayer, "Instrument," 530.

12. *UR*, §6.

13. *TCTCV*, §51.

14. Robeck, "Pentecostal Ecclesiology," 253.

15. Robeck, "The Church," 150, 151.

16. Robeck, "Pentecostal Ecclesiology," 253.

17. Robeck's theological hermeneutic also shapes his understanding of ecumenism, but the field of theological hermeneutics goes beyond the scope of the present study.

18. Cecil M. Robeck, Jr. in discussion with the author, November 29, 2022.

19. A notable exception was when Robeck, due to his patristics and ecumenical research, was asked to support the campaign to have Irenaeus be declared a Doctor of

Spiritual Ecumenism 173

the Catholic Church. Pope Francis in 2022 conferred on Irenaeus the title of "Doctor of Unity." Cecil M. Robeck, Jr. in correspondence with the author, February 3, 2022.

20. Benvenuti, "Reconstruction," 82–84, 199; Muszczyński, "Ekumenizm," 99, 186, 187.

21. William Weinrich, in a review of the book, criticizes Robeck for relying on feminist scholarship in his attention to women's empowerment in the early church, which reveals the mixed reception of Robeck's patristics research and how, despite these controversies, Robeck advocated for the contemporary relevance of patristics. William C. Weinrich, "Review of Cecil M. Robeck, Jr., *Prophecy in Carthage: Perpetua, Tertullian, and Cyprian,*" *The Catholic Historical Review* 82, no. 3 (1996): 495, 496.

22. Robeck, *Prophecy in Carthage*, ix.

23. John Panagopoulos, ed., *Prophetic Vocation in the New Testament and Today*, Novum Testamentum Supplement 45 (Leiden: Brill, 1977); John Panagopoulos, *Η Εκκλησία των Προφητών: Το προφητικό χάρισμα εντη Εκκλησία των δυο πρώτων αιώνων* (Athens: St. Vassilopoulos, 1979).

24. Robeck, "Foreword," xii, xiii.

25. Cecil M. Robeck, Jr., "Written Prophecies: A Question of Authority," *Pneuma* 2, no. 2 (1980): 26–45; Cecil M. Robeck, Jr., "Prophetic Authority in the Charismatic Setting: The Need to Test," *Theological Renewal* 24 (1983): 4–10; Robeck, "Irenaeus;" Cecil M. Robeck, Jr., "Les dons prophétiques : Une perspective pentecôte," in *Pentecôtisme et prophétie (1)*, ed. Jean-Claude Boutinon and Romuald Hanss, Collection d'études pentecôtistes 5 (Léognan, France: SFE, 2019), 3–35; Cecil M. Robeck, Jr., "A Pentecostal Perspective on Prophetic Gifts," *Asian Journal of Pentecostal Studies* 23, no. 1 (2020): 109–37.

26. Robeck, "Irenaeus," 111.

27. Alan Humm, *Psychology of Prophecy in Early Christianity: Prophetism and Religious Altered States of Consciousness* (Piscataway, NJ: Gorgias Press, 2009), 106.

28. Robeck, "Pentecostal Ecclesiology," 253.

29. Cecil M. Robeck, Jr., "The Gift of Prophecy in Acts and Paul, Part II," *Studia Biblica et Theologica* 5, no. 2 (1975): 41; Robeck, "Les dons," 18.

30. *Didache* 11, 13; *The Shephard of Hermas* 43, cited in Cecil M. Robeck, Jr., "Prophecy, Prophesying," in *Dictionary of Paul and His Letters*, ed. Gerald F. Hawthorne and Ralph P. Martin (Downers Grove, IL: InterVarsity Press, 1993), 758; Cecil M. Robeck, Jr., "The Prophet in the *Didache*," *Paraclete* 18, no. 1 (1984): 16–19; Cecil M. Robeck, Jr., "Prophecy in *The Shepherd of Hermas*," *Paraclete* 18, no. 2 (1984): 12–17.

31. Ignatius, *To the Philadelphians* 7, cited in Robeck, "Les dons," 25.

32. Robeck, "Canon," 67–72.

33. Tertullian, *Against Praxeas* 8.5, cited in Robeck, *Prophecy in Carthage*, 124–27.

34. Tertullian, *Against Marcion* 5.8, cited in Laura Nasrallah, *An Ecstasy of Folly: Prophecy and Authority in Early Christianity*, Harvard Theological Studies 52 (Cambridge, MA: Harvard University Press, 2003), 141.

174 *Chapter 5*

35. "The fact that the Montanists apparently did not fully understand the nature of Christian prophecy may have deprived them of the ability to dialogue responsibly with any other Christians." The publication predates the beginning of Robeck's academic interest in ecumenics, which suggests a development in his thought. Cecil M. Robeck, Jr., "Montanism: A Problematic Spirit Movement," *Paraclete* 15, no. 3 (1981): 28, 29.

36. Cyprian texts are cited from G.W. Clarke, ed., *The Letters of St. Cyprian of Carthage*, 4 vols., Ancient Christian Writers: The Works of the Fathers in Translation 43, 44, 46, 47 (New York: Newman Press, 1984).

37. Humm, *Psychology*, 182.

38. Cyprian, *Epistles* 39.1, 4; 40; 48.4; 63.1; 66.5, 10, cited in Robeck, *Prophecy in Carthage*, 156–65.

39. Cyprian, *Epistle* 43.5, cited in Robeck, 151.

40. Robeck, 204.

41. Robeck, "Prophecy, Prophesying," 760.

42. Robeck, "Canon"; Robeck, "An Emerging," 168.

43. "Experience in Christian Faith and Life," §73–116; Joint Consultative Group between the World Council of Churches and Pentecostals, "Recommendations of the Joint Consultative Group of the World Council of Churches and Pentecostals to the Ninth Assembly, Porto Alegre, Brazil, 2000–2005," 359; "Do Not Quench the Spirit," §75–98; "The Spirit of the Lord Is Upon Me," §76.

44. Hunter, "An Emmaus," 94.

45. Robert M. Grant, "Review of Cecil M. Robeck, Jr., *Prophecy in Carthage: Perpetua, Tertullian, and Cyprian*," *Church History* 62, no. 3 (1993): 378.

46. Benvenuti, "Reconstruction," 199.

47. Nasrallah, *An Ecstasy*, 26.

48. Nasrallah, 32, 61–94.

49. Robeck, "Les dons," 4, 5.

50. The sociopolitical function of prophecy often dominates ecumenical discourse. For example, see Charles Stedman Macfarland, *Christian Unity in Practice and Prophecy* (New York: The Macmillan Company, 1933).

51. Robeck, *Prophecy in Carthage*, x.

52. Cecil M. Robeck, Jr. in discussion with the author, November 29, 2022.

53. Cyprian, *Epistle 11*, cited in Robeck, *Prophecy in Carthage*, 177–87.

54. Robeck, "Canon," 73, 74.

55. Humm, *Psychology*, 4, 5.

56. Robeck, "Some Pentecostal," 230.

57. Nasrallah, *An Ecstasy*, 203.

58. Nasrallah, 14, 17.

59. Nasrallah, 7, 159, 202.

60. Humm, *Psychology*, 196.

61. Robeck, "An Emerging."

62. Cecil M. Robeck, Jr. in discussion with the author, November 29, 2022.

63. Cecil M. Robeck, Jr., "The Authority of the Holy Spirit in Pentecostal Churches: A Response to David A. Adesanya," in *Sources of Authority, Volume 2:*

Contemporary Church, by World Council of Churches Commission on Faith and Order, ed. Tamara Grdzelidze, Faith and Order Paper 218 (Geneva: World Council of Churches, 2014), 39–51; Cecil M. Robeck, Jr., "Word, Spirit, and Discernment," in *Churches and Moral Discernment, Volume 1: Learning from Traditions*, by World Council of Churches Commission on Faith and Order, ed. Myriam Wijlens and Vladimir Shmaliy, Faith and Order Paper 228 (Geneva: World Council of Churches, 2021), 137–45.

64. Jerry L. Sandidge, *Roman Catholic/Pentecostal Dialogue (1977–1982): A Study in Developing Ecumenism*, vol. 1, Studien zur Interkulturellen Geschichte des Christentums 44 (Frankfurt: Peter Lang, 1987), 446.

65. Walter J. Hollenweger, "Introduction," in *The Church Is Charismatic: The World Council of Churches and the Charismatic Renewal*, ed. Arnold Bittlinger (Geneva: World Council of Churches, 1981), 2.

66. "The Evangelical-Roman Catholic Dialogue on Mission, 1977-1984: A Report," 1985, VII.2.f.

67. "The Word of God in the Life of the Church: A Report of International Conversations Between the Catholic Church and the Baptist World Alliance (2006-2010)," 2010, §96.

68. "From Conflict," §14.

69. "The Denver Report: Report of the Joint Commission between the Roman Catholic Church and the World Methodist Council, First Series 1967-1970," 1971, §51; "Toward an Agreed Statement on the Holy Spirit (Honolulu 1981)," 1981, §20; "The Call to Holiness: From Glory to Glory. Report of the Joint International Commission for Dialogue between the World Methodist Council and the Roman Catholic Church 2016," 2016, §52.

70. "Faith Working through Love: Report of the International Dialogue between the Baptist World Alliance and the World Methodist Council," 2018, §96.

71. "Communion: On Being the Church. Report of the Lutheran–Reformed Joint Commission between the Lutheran World Federation (LWF) and the World Communion of Reformed Churches (WCRC), 2006–2012," 2014, §23–27.

72. "Conversations Around the World: The Report of the International Conversations between The Anglican Communion and The Baptist World Alliance, 2000–2005," 2005, §32.

73. "Into All the World: Being and Becoming Apostolic Churches. A Report to the Anglican Consultative Council and the World Methodist Council by the Anglican-Methodist International Commission for Unity in Mission," 2014, ix.

74. Robeck, "The Church: A Unique," 1, 2.

75. Robeck, "Pentecostal Ecclesiology," 252.

76. Robeck, "Pentecostal/Charismatic," 29, 30.

77. Tan-Chow, *Pentecostal*, 64.

78. Robeck, "The Authority," 44, 45.

79. Robeck, "The Holy Spirit and the Unity," 373.

80. "Towards a Church Renewed and United in the Spirit: WCC Consultative Group Paper," in *The Church Is Charismatic: The World Council of Churches and the Charismatic Renewal*, ed. Arnold Bittlinger (Geneva: World Council of Churches, 1981), §I.2.

176 Chapter 5

81. Philip Potter, "Charismatic Renewal and the World Council of Churches," in *The Church Is Charismatic: The World Council of Churches and the Charismatic Renewal*, ed. Arnold Bittlinger (Geneva: World Council of Churches, 1981), 86.

82. Robeck, "Discerning the Spirit," 31; Robeck, "Can We Imagine," 67.

83. Robeck, "Charism(ata)," 163, 164.

84. Robeck, "A Pentecostal Assessment," 14.

85. Peter D. Hocken, *Azusa, Rome, and Zion: Pentecostal Faith, Catholic Reform, and Jewish Roots* (Eugene, OR: Wipf & Stock, 2016), 87.

86. Peter D. Hocken, "The Contributions of the Charismatic Movement to Christian Unity," in *Pentecostal Theology and Ecumenical Theology: Interpretations and Intersections*, ed. Peter D. Hocken, Tony L. Richie, and Christopher A. Stephenson, Global Pentecostal and Charismatic Studies 34 (Leiden: Brill, 2019), 49, 50.

87. Robeck, "John Paul II," 10.

88. Robeck, 17.

89. "Christian Unity Commission," Catholic Charismatic Renewal International Service, last modified June 9, 2021, https://www.charis.international/en/christian-unity-commission/.

90. Robeck, "Pentecostals and Charismatics," 251.

91. Robeck, "A Pentecostal Assessment," 13.

92. "From Conflict," §14; Robeck, "Can We Imagine," 68.

93. The birth of denominationalism in the United States required denominations to distinguish their identities from each other while maintaining unity within their own communions. A common way to do so was the authoring of texts that served as doctrinal charters. Examples include the Southern Baptist Convention's "Baptist Faith and Message," the United Church of Christ's "Statement of Faith," and the African Methodist Episcopal Church's use of John Wesley's "Articles of Religion." These texts offer guidance for instructing congregations and are doctrinal benchmarks that ministers uphold to remain in good standing with their denominations.

94. Robeck, "An Emerging," 198, 199.

95. Robeck, 213.

96. For a larger survey of discussions from the second half of the twentieth century on Charismatic influences on Pentecostal churches, see Frank D. Macchia, "God Present in a Confused Situation: The Mixed Influence of the Charismatic Movement on Classical Pentecostalism in the United States," *Pneuma* 18, no. 1 (1996): 33–54.

97. Robeck, "Can We Imagine," 68.

98. John Segun Odeyemi, *Pentecostalism and Catholic Ecumenism in Developing Nations: West Africa as a Case Study for a Global Phenomenon* (Eugene, OR: Wipf & Stock, 2019), 22.

99. For discussion on the nature of causality in these schisms, see Lukas Soko and H. Jurgens Hendriks, "Pentecostalism and Schisms in the Reformed Church in Zambia (1996–2001): Listening to the People," *HTS Theological Studies* 67, no. 3 (2011): 1–8; Cecília L. Mariz and Carlos Henrique Souza, "Carismáticos e pentecostais: Os limites das trocas ecumênicas," *Contemporânea: Dossiê Desafios Contemporâneos da Sociologia da Religião* 5, no. 2 (2015): 381–408.

100. Robeck, *Prophecy in Carthage*, x.

Spiritual Ecumenism

101. Robeck, "Discerning the Spirit," 35, 38.
102. Au, *Grassroots Unity*, 98–140.
103. "Responses of the Churches," in *The Church Is Charismatic: The World Council of Churches and the Charismatic Renewal*, ed. Arnold Bittlinger (Geneva: World Council of Churches, 1981), 40–66.
104. "Towards a Church Renewed," §5.
105. Veli-Matti Kärkkäinen, "The Nature and Purpose of the Church: Theological and Ecumenical Reflections from Pentecostal/Free Church Perspectives," in *Pentecostalism and Christian Unity: Ecumenical Documents and Critical Assessments*, ed. Wolfgang Vondey (Eugene, OR: Pickwick Publications, 2010), 239, 240.
106. Robeck, "Written," 44, 45.
107. Robeck, "The Authority," 43.
108. Robeck, "Charismatic Movements," 153.
109. "Responses of the Churches," 42, 43.
110. Robeck, "Discerning the Spirit," 36.
111. Cecil M. Robeck, Jr., "A Pentecostal Perspective on Leadership," in *Traditions in Leadership: How Faith Traditions Shape the Way We Lead*, ed. Richard J. Mouw and Eric O. Jacobsen (Pasadena, CA: De Pree Leadership Center, 2006), 139–60; Robeck, "The Leadership"; Robeck, "Authoritative," 204.
112. Robeck, "A Pentecostal Perspective on Leadership," 142.
113. Robeck, "Discerning the Spirit," 47.
114. Robeck, "Authoritative," 209–14.
115. Robeck contends that discernment might be the most important charism for the life of the church. Robeck, "The Holy Spirit and the Unity," 366, 369.
116. Robeck, "Discerning the Spirit," 34.
117. Robeck, "The Authority," 51.
118. Tan-Chow, *Pentecostal*, 76.
119. *UUS*, §21.
120. Robeck, "Evangelization," 64; Cecil M. Robeck, Jr., "Evangelicals and Catholics Together," *One in Christ* 33, no. 2 (1997): 160.
121. Ari Pedro Oro and Daniel Alves, "Renovação carismática católica: Movimento de superação da oposição entre catolicismo e pentecostalismo?," *Religião e Sociedade* 33, no. 1 (2013): 136.
122. Meyer, *Ökumenische Zielvorstellungen*, 17.
123. Robeck, *Prophecy in Carthage*, x.
124. Kasper, *A Handbook*, §11.
125. *TCTCV*, §67.
126. Potter, "Charismatic," 82.
127. Robeck, "Can We Imagine," 67.
128. Au, *Grassroots Unity*, 199–203.
129. "Towards a Church Renewed," §2.1.
130. Robeck, "The Holy Spirit and the Unity," 379.
131. Potter, "Charismatic," 81.
132. Potter, 85, 86.
133. Robeck, "The Church: A Unique," 1.

178 Chapter 5

134. Robeck, "Pentecostal Ecclesiology," 252.

135. "Towards a Church Renewed," §2.2.

136. Meyer, *Ökumenische Zielvorstellungen*, 22.

137. World Council of Churches Sub-unit on Renewal and Congregational Life, "Report of the Consultation on the Significance of the Charismatic Renewal for the Churches," in *The Church Is Charismatic: The World Council of Churches and the Charismatic Renewal*, ed. Arnold Bittlinger (Geneva: World Council of Churches, 1981), 204.

138. "Report on the Anglican-Pentecostal Consultation," in *Churches Respond to The Church: Towards a Common Vision, Volume 2*, by World Council of Churches Commission on Faith and Order, edited by Ellen Wondra, Stephanie Dietrich, and Ani Ghazaryan Drissi, Faith and Order Paper 232 (Geneva: World Council of Churches, 2021), §6.

139. Benjamin D. Crace, "Towards a Global Pneumatological Awareness: A Comparative Account and Assessment of the Charismata in the Coptic Orthodox Church," *Journal of Pentecostal Theology* 30, no. 1 (2021): 140, 141, 144.

140. Robeck, "Worship," 93, 95.

141. *TCTCV*, §16.

142. *TCTCV*, §26.

143. Cecil M. Robeck, Jr. in discussion with the author, November 29, 2022. Robeck, "Can We Imagine," 61–66.

144. Robeck, "The Challenge," 317.

145. Cecil M. Robeck, Jr. in discussion with the author, November 29, 2022.

146. One might be tempted to dismiss Robeck's thought as a capitulation to Catholic or other ecumenical voices, but this paper in which the claim was made was delivered at his first dialogue session with the Catholic Church before he had conducted any research on ecumenics. He could have acquired this notion only from his biblical and patristics background. Cecil M. Robeck, Jr., "The Holy Spirit and the New Testament Vision of Koinonia" (Second session of the third phase of the international Catholic–Pentecostal dialogue, Sierra Madre, CA, 1986).

147. Benvenuti, "Reconstruction," 94.

148. Au, *Grassroots Unity*, 198.

Chapter 6

Testifying to Christ within Christian Forums

The Indonesian Christian Forum (Forum Umat Kristen Indonesia [FUKRI]) is the national platform for relationship building and dialogue on social issues among Christians. The FUKRI gathers leaders from the eight national Christian ecclesial bodies—the National Council of Churches and Catholic episcopal conference; the evangelical, Baptist, and Pentecostal fellowships; and the Salvation Army, Adventist, and Orthodox churches. In addition to this confessional diversity, the ecumenical movement in Indonesia is shaped by the country's approximately 6,000 inhabited islands and 700 spoken languages. The FUKRI is an attempt to offer coordination and communication. Leaders gather monthly to discuss the place of Christian churches in the country's pluralistic society. Previous topics for the Forum have covered the Busan Assembly of the WCC, the 500th anniversary of the Reformation, and the nature of Christian mission in contemporary Indonesia.[1] Without the framework of the FUKRI, many of the eight national ecclesial bodies would have had no ongoing relationship.

Christian Forums are one of the newest ecumenical methods to have drawn attention from scholars and practitioners. The Global Christian Forum (GCF) and the subsequent formation of national and local Christian Forums were heralded as signs of either progress or regress in the ecumenical movement. The Forum method seeks to further the ecumenical agenda by reconciling disconnected churches and strands of the ecumenical movement. It pursues this end through the gathering of a diverse array of church communities and through the signature use of testimonies ("faith stories") in gatherings.[2] While all Christian communities employ storytelling, much of the theological understanding of the ecumenical method comes from Pentecostal testimonial practices. The proliferation of shared spaces for encounters between

179

180   *Chapter 6*

Christians and the adoption of a spiritual practice for communal discourse builds on methodological reflection from the past century of ecumenism.

The emergence of the GCF sparked debates over potential conflicts with other ecumenical methods and the theological self-understanding of Christian Forums. Authors often refer to the use of testimonies as an influence from Pentecostal spiritual practices, but no scholar has written on the ecclesiological nature of testimony as Pentecostals and non-Pentecostals alike employ in the ecumenical method. Also, the explicit focus on Christians as individual believers contrasts with the notion that churches are the primary actors in ecumenical engagement. How does the transformational encounter between people reconcile communities?

There have been repeated calls for theological and programmatic articulation of the GCF project, with questions surrounding the contribution of sharing testimonies to the unity of the church.[3] There is a consensus among scholars that Forums must engage ecclesiology if they are to make any substantive contributions to the ecumenical movement, but there is not yet consensus on the ecclesiological nature of Forums. Dagmar Heller has even asserted that the GCF does not seek convergence.[4] Yet, as I have argued, if ecclesiology is the elemental theological dynamic of ecumenism and if ecclesiological convergence occurs in the work of ecumenism, then the status of Christian Forums as an ecumenical method hinges upon their pursuit of convergence. As I have also argued, if Christian Forums contribute to ecclesial unity, then they contribute to convergence only if they are based on the ecclesiological principles shared between churches. The ecumenical method of Christian Forums relies on a shared understanding of the church's pointing to and participation in God's reconciling work, and as churches develop common ways of testifying to this reconciling work, they converge in their recognition of each other as fellow believers.

The recency of the ecumenical method's emergence results in fewer sources of information available for researchers than other topics in ecumenics. This chapter occasionally notes gaps in existent literature that would otherwise have been useful for assessing the validity and scope of claims that some authors make. I restrict my argument to what can be known presently, trusting that future scholarship will continue to mold the priorities and principles beyond how they are presented here. Additionally, saving this method for the end of the book is not meant to portray Christian Forums as the culmination of other methods. Forums intersect with other methods in theory and practice, so it is beneficial to analyze Forums now after having studied the previous topics. If anything, literature often portrays Forums as gateways to other forms of ecumenical relationships. The progression of the topics also follows Robeck's career, which placed him in the leadership of the GCF after he began contributing to other projects.

Christian Forums 181

RECONCILIATORY ECCLESIOLOGY

Little ecclesiological reflection has been published on the Christian Forum method thus far. It is, therefore, beneficial to identify ecclesiological principles that pertain to the method from an oft-cited source to aid broader ecumenical discourse. The entwinement of the church's attestation to God with its reconciling work is described succinctly in the opening paragraph of *Lumen gentium*. The conciliar text famously states that the light of Christ shines on the countenance of the church and, as such, the church resides in Christ "as a sacrament or a sign and instrument" of the intimate union with God and the unity of humankind.[5] The presence of God in the church is a constitutive dimension of the Christian community's ecclesiality. The previous chapter saw this in the manifestation of the church's charismatic nature. To speak of the light of Christ on the countenance of the church can be taken as an image of the ecclesial presence of Christ. The church's nature and mission are consequences of the work of Christ, and the church stands as a sign of communion between God and people because it points to its origins in God.

Sacramental ecclesiology is a wide and diverse field that could take the book beyond its driving question of ecumenical methodology. The conciliar text uses two key terms that explicate the meaning of the church as a sacrament and that control the present discussion—sign and instrument. The church is a sign of unity because it is a product of God's reconciling humanity. Signification implies a form of participation in that to which the sign points—in this case, the church partakes in the divine life by means of the incarnation and humanity's incorporation into the triune communion. The ecumenical movement has defined its goal as visible unity because witness must be perceptible if it is to point to God, emphasizing the importance of the church's function as a sign.

TCTCV builds on *Lumen gentium* in saying that the church bears witness to divine economy by reflecting divine communion in the church's life.[6] Ecclesial sacramentality incorporates the empirical reality of the church as part of its nature. Discussions on the materiality of the presence of Christ in the church naturally focus on the sacraments, with churches currently holding varying understandings of this presence. One could also expand the concept to include the divinization of the whole created order through its sanctification in the incarnation and the abiding presence of the Spirit of Christ. Yet, the incarnation upholds humanity as a preeminent expression of the materiality of the Body of Christ insofar as people partake in the divine nature.

The church is also an instrument of unity insofar as it has been given the ministry of reconciliation. The Toronto Statement, when speaking of the unitive purpose of the WCC, describes the act of bearing witness to Christ as the *raison d'être* of the church.[7] It carries out this mission in extending the grace

182   *Chapter 6*

it has received to the world. Reconciliation occurs as a process of interpersonal encounter, which is where faith is born, where the Word is encountered, and where people are granted an opportunity to commune with God.[8] The biblical image of the church as the people of God prioritizes people in the definition of the church. Neither liturgies, offices, nor doctrines encounter God, for they are not persons. These other things are ordered to facilitate and sustain communion with God and the Christian community. The church is more than its members, but it never exists apart from them. *TCTCV* affirms that the church is a means of this communion, and it asks whether the frailty of the church's members undermines its ability to point to God.[9]

Responses to *TCTCV* express generally positive regard for the document's sacramental ecclesiology while noting that many churches—such as Pentecostal ones—do not use sacramental terminology.[10] "Sacramental" is used in this chapter inclusive of differing understandings of ordinances by focusing on the church's function as sign and instrument. Debates continue on sacramental rites, yet the responses reveal consensus on the notion that the church is an effective sign of God's reconciliatory presence and action. The sacramental nature of the church places people in relationship with God and each other, and "any manifestation of the Church is only significant in its referring function" to the divine reality beyond the church itself.[11]

The referential function of sacramental ecclesiology intersects with the practice of testimony. "Testimony" is not understood here in an exclusively Pentecostal sense, as is often studied in theological literature, but rather as a technical term denoting the narrative construction of experience-based truth claims. The rhetorical act occurs between the speaker and audience when the speaker testifies to something outside both the speaker and audience that can be experienced. Testimony presumes a referential capability of communication such that language has meaning beyond itself. Because it is an act of communication, it raises questions of epistemology and rhetoric. The multifaceted nature of testimony drew the attention of francophone philosophers toward the end of the twentieth century, including Paul Ricoeur and Emmanuel Levinas, in their studies of the referential use of language.[12] Subsequent authors tested their theories in other fields wherein testimony occurs, such as legal settings and journalism.

When the testimony is of a religious nature, these questions concern communal meaning, authority, and the identity of the religious community. The second chapter spoke of narrative as a form of identity construction for churches as communities ascribe significance to experiences that are integrated into a coherent scheme. These stories place the self in the context of one's surroundings and relationships. On the other hand, testimony is a narrative that decenters the self by speaking of an externally experienced reality. It arranges ideas and events into a story, making it a useful tool for speaking of transcendent religious experiences. Testimony is the theological mode of historical narrative. It speaks of persons and events to ascribe religious significance to them, ultimately making claims about the divine actor in the story. If testimony to an external reality beyond the speaker is impossible, then the church likewise cannot serve as a sign ofo a divine reality beyond itself.

Testimony constructs communal identity even when it points outside the community. All societies utilize forms of storytelling to impart wisdom, structure worldviews, and ascribe communal meaning to experiences. The preeminent form of Christian testimony is the scriptural witness, around which the church has formed its identity. Christian worship also revolves around stories of God's work in salvation history.[13] The church's Tradition perpetuates apostolic testimonies of the life of Christ as a way to manifest Christ's presence in the church. Ancient hagiographic practices tell stories of saints—not for the sake of imparting biographic details but for the sake of pointing believers to the divine source of their holiness. Not all stories are testimonies. Testimonies employ religious symbols for the sake of appealing to, expanding, or subverting authoritative sources of the community, and they are told to influence the hearer, who interprets and assesses the narrative. Testimonies are told according to the relationship that exists between the speaker and the audience, establishing an interplay between personal testimony and communal identity. How a person tells a religious story has implications for how the speaker and community are to understand their relationship with each other and God.

The reconciliation of Christians through the sharing of testimonies has been called the "charism"[14] of the GCF. Literature often refers to these as "faith stories" to distance the method from its Pentecostal origins, but I retain the more technical and widely used "testimony" to illuminate the field of testimonial studies and the practice's functions in faith communities. The stories are meant to point to the reconciling work of God in Christ as experienced in the Christian life. The initial proposal for the Forum explains that the "proposed Forum is possible because of the unity that is already given in Christ. It is called for because of our common faith in a reconciling God whose church knows that it is summoned to become God's reconciled and reconciling people."[15]

The GCF has always had a basis in reconciliatory ecclesiology. On the other hand, scholars orbiting the GCF have recognized the need to reflect ecclesiologically on the method. The GCF Committee formed an ad hoc Theology Working Group in 2012 to author a short statement on the principles of the GCF. The goal of the document was to articulate theological "and especially ecclesiological"[16] insights learned from the method thus far. However, any honest assessment of the document would conclude that it does not

184   Chapter 6

offer substantive ecclesiological insight. Claims made about the church could apply to any dimension of the ecumenical movement, leaving the nature of Christian Forums unspecified.

The remaining questions concern the contribution of Christian Forums to the advancement of ecclesiological convergence. To adapt Raiser's argument, the question is not whether Forums have an ecclesial nature but whether the relationships fostered in Forums are ecclesial in nature.[17] Similar to all other dimensions of the ecumenical movement, the theological understanding of the Christian Forum method develops alongside changes in the movement at large. Questions also surround the significance of testimonies for church unity. If the method adopted the practice from particular church communities, how can one say that the method's basis is in a shared ecclesiology when not all church traditions use testimonies in the same ways?

Robeck was a leading mind behind the formation of the ecumenical method. The principles he advocated for are a direct result of his ecumenical career as he moved between communities and institutions that had no contact with each other. He realized that the communities needed to recognize their common faith in Christ and to believe the others' faith was genuine before any further ecumenical work could be tried between them. Robeck does not speak of sacramental ecclesiology in his writings on the GCF or testimony. He asserts that the materiality of the church is in its people.[18] The relationships between believers are where the unity of the church is tangible and visible—thus, where the church testifies to the reconciling work of God. Additionally, as the introductory chapter explained, the ability to follow the thought and actions of one ecumenist across organizations and decades of ecumenical history offers insight into the interrelation of ecumenical methods. A study of Robeck's thought and work contributes to answering the ecclesiological questions surrounding Christian Forums.

GLOBAL CHRISTIAN FORUM

Apologists of the GCF champion from a variety of angles the Christian Forum model of ecumenical engagement. Its detachment from previously existent organizations enables the foregrounding of new relationships between divided churches. The GCF is called a catalyst and methodology rather than an organization that seeks consensus or action.[19] Its engagements with spiritual ecumenism for dialogue among churches and councils are hoped to be a crucible for reflection on ecumenism at large. Advocates project their aspirations onto the fledgling ecumenical project, proclaiming it will succeed where, they believe, other methods have failed.[20] Others are more cautious, seeing the need to combine narrative encounter with theological reflection.[21] The sharing of testimonies reconciles divided Christians and advances ecclesiological convergence insofar as the church is both a sign and instrument of God's reconciling work. This is seen in the origin and development of the GCF.

Origin of Methodological Principles

The origins of the GCF coincide with Robeck's introduction to the WCC. Increased attention to churches outside the WCC in the 1990s strained the coherency of the Council, which was already reeling from the Canberra Assembly. The *Common Understanding and Vision* (*CUV*) policy statement sought to offer stability and direction through integration. Raiser's election as general secretary followed the trajectory of themes in his recently published and still-often-cited *Ökumene im Übergang*, wherein he describes ongoing challenges for the ecumenical movement as a form of renewal and transition.[22] The broadening of the vision of the WCC included the appointment of Huibert van Beek to the Office of Church and Ecumenical Relations. He oversaw the consultations with Pentecostal and African Instituted Churches mentioned in the third chapter. Robeck was invited to contribute to Faith and Order and the Canberra Assembly as part of these initiatives. He worked alongside van Beek during this decade to plan what would become, at the 1998 Harare Assembly, the Joint Consultative Group (JCG) between Pentecostals and the WCC, discussed in the third chapter.[23]

Raiser was concurrently developing the idea for an ecumenical forum to deliberate on pressing issues of the day, akin to the World Social Forum.[24] The forum would help facilitate relations of the WCC with non-member churches, including the Catholic Church, though calls for a Special Commission on Orthodox Participation in the WCC also revealed the need for creative ways of managing conflict between member churches.[25] Raiser convened in 1998 a meeting at Bossey on a Proposal for a Forum of Christian Churches and Ecumenical Organizations. At the meeting were forty representatives of WCC member churches, regional ecumenical organizations, national councils, service organizations, the Vatican, and Robeck.[26] They agreed on the value of a forum and defined the three methodological variables that have come to characterize the Christian Forum ecumenical method: (1) the forum would be detached from any existent church or ecumenical body to foster a common space for dialogue, (2) the forum would invite half of its attendees from outside the WCC member churches and Catholic Church, and (3) the forum would use the sharing of testimonies as the primary medium of discourse.

These three variables were tested following the 1998 meeting. However, in the dozens of published historical accounts found during my research, not once do the authors name the origin of the variables. The peculiarity of

186   *Chapter 6*

the three methodological variables contrasts with the actors who initiated the GCF and their original intentions. The forum idea that Raiser proposed was to be a WCC-sponsored gathering with fellow ecumenical organizations and partners. Why would these organizations and churches suddenly abandon this approach by creating a space divorced from their own networks? Additionally, initial conversations on the forum were as concerned with Orthodox and Catholic Churches as they were with broadening the scope of Protestant interlocutors. Why would the committee suddenly shift its approach by allocating half of the space to a constellation of churches who were never singled out in prior conversations about the forum? Furthermore, the forum was intended to gather major service organizations and churches to deliberate on pressing social issues of the day. Why would these hierarchs suddenly abandon their desire for formal, technical, and scholarly discussions and opt instead for a Pentecostal spiritual practice with which most had little to no personal experience? The trajectory of the ecumenical forum's development is inexplicable without the presence of the sole Pentecostal attendee at the 1998 consultation.

Robeck attended the consultation at the request of Raiser due to Robeck's previous contributions to the Faith and Order Commission, Canberra Assembly, and conversations leading to the *CUV*, in addition to his work with the NCCUSA, Conference of the Secretaries of Christian World Communions (CSCWC), Catholic–Pentecostal dialogue, and Reformed–Pentecostal dialogue. More than being a token Pentecostal, he was one of the most diversely experienced people sitting at the table. Robeck's insight into the various portions of the ecumenical movement would be a welcome addition to the conversation on the movement's future. He acknowledges, though, that his presence was not always welcome. He recalls his previous invitation to speak to the NCCUSA Governing Board on the possibility of engaging Pentecostal churches, where he was explicitly told that some saw Pentecostals as a threat to the aspirations of the council.[27] He speaks of conflict and avoidance between churches that cause distance between the WCC and some churches. Experiences of conflict between churches resulted in ignorance, fear, and distrust.[28] On the other hand, he does not blame the WCC members alone.[29] He argued that any viable endeavor to reconcile the divide would have to fashion a new table, not simply inviting people to a WCC table.[30]

Robeck also suggested that the proposed forum should include equal numbers from non-WCC churches and from member churches and the Catholic Church.[31] Invitations to the leadership of ecclesial bodies and organizations would aid long-term efforts in ecumenical engagement.[32] The pattern creates a "bilateral structure in a multilateral context."[33] It is common for ecumenical projects to establish quotas to enhance the purpose of the event. Bilateral dialogues ensure equal numbers of the two parties at the table lest either dominates the conversation, and the WCC maintains its 25 percent rule for Orthodox representation lest the non-Orthodox members drown out their voices. Such measurements are not intended to be accurate representations of church demographics. The GCF is no different in this regard when it limits the participation of the Catholic Church and WCC member churches to half of the attendance.

Robeck's final and most controversial suggestion was the use of testimonies as part of the forum.[34] He drew inspiration from traditions of Pentecostal narrative theology that often differ from the theological methods used in ecumenical theologizing.[35] The appeal is consistent with those, such as Walter Hollenweger, who called for "bilingual" modes of discourse in the ecumenical movement to account for oral theology.[36] Robeck has championed the use of stories in many of his projects, including the JCG and Faith and Order.[37] His decades of contributions to multilateral dialogue and leadership of bilateral dialogues reveal his valuing of scholarly reflection, but he acknowledges its limitations. Testimony, as mentioned before, employs religious symbols and integrates events into a coherent narrative that situates the self and community in a larger context, which conveys meaning and significance of truth claims through appeal to lived experience—or, in Robeck's words, it "brings down the highfalutin ideas to see how they play out in real life."[38] This use of testimony is stripped of the practice's liturgical, educational, and evangelistic dimensions, as would be employed in Pentecostal communities, and instead is used as proof of credible witness.[39] It enables recognition of one's own faith in the other, establishing a relationship between speaker and audience as part of a common ingroup while giving flesh to perceived differences that can then be worked out. The trust built in the exchange would facilitate contentious conversations.

Robeck's proposals were rejected by everyone at the 1998 meeting as a cheap imitation of ecumenism. The turnaround came when Raiser was eventually convinced, who then worked to bring the others on board with Robeck's idea.[40] Published accounts of the GCF's formation skip over this developmental pivot. The absence of Robeck from these accounts is likely due to the desire to place greater significance on the actions of communities over individuals. On the other hand, it also erases the contributions of Pentecostals from this episode of ecumenical history, which would have been impossible had it not been for the generations of Pentecostal ecumenical work that preceded it. The resultant picture is that of self-proclaimed ecumenical "insiders" reaching out to the "outsiders." Literature on the GCF often portrays the method as the condescension of ecumenists to the level of Pentecostal and other churches, but it is more accurate to say that the formation of the GCF is part of the struggle of Pentecostal and other ecumenists to achieve parity in ecumenical spaces.

188 *Chapter 6*

It was decided to try a trial run of Robeck's proposals. He and van Beek identified and invited attendees from non-WCC member churches for an event held in 2000 at Robeck's home institution, Fuller Theological Seminary, in Pasadena, California. The multidenominational evangelical seminary was selected due to its strong historic engagement with Pentecostal churches, the ecumenical movement, and a global student body. The event included the sharing of testimonies rather than academic papers. Robeck explains that the approach empowers novices and destabilizes professionals, creating a broad and equitable table founded on new ways of speaking and listening.[41]

A subsequent meeting was held in 2002, again at Fuller, with Robeck as co-chair. It tested on a larger scale the method of sharing testimonies, which has been called "the single most powerful tool of the Forum in building and deepening relationships."[42] Robeck advocated to Pentecostals around this time the need for places where church leaders can meet each other and form relationships with those from other churches, especially those historically seen as enemies.[43] He sees the GCF as such a space.[44] Some of the testimonies were conversion stories or about encounters with missionaries, which led to discussions of proselytism. Copies of "Evangelization, Proselytism and Common Witness"—the report of the recently concluded fourth phase of the Catholic–Pentecostal dialogue—were distributed among participants as an example of progress in addressing these conflicts globally.[45] The meeting marked a milestone in the forum's development. The name "Global Christian Forum" was adopted, and after the meeting, the World Evangelical Alliance (WEA) was invited as a formal partner.[46]

The 2002 meeting concretized the vision of the GCF and its method. Robeck served on its Continuation Committee, which was "the heart of [the] GCF" in determining its function.[47] The committee's subsequent meeting with the Pontifical Council for Promoting Christian Unity stressed that the GCF should not replace WCC Assemblies or create another bureaucracy. The GCF maintains a bare minimum of structure, relying heavily on the committee for guidance. Robeck and other committee members met with the CSCWC the following year to confirm that a separate space was indeed needed.[48] He continued to serve on the committee to advise the activities of the GCF, from which he retired after the 2024 Fourth Global Gathering in Accra.[49] He was also the only remaining original member of the team who carried out the vision of the ecumenical forum after 1998. His leadership of the GCF intersected with his roles in the JCG and the Faith and Order Commission, offering coordination between high-profile ecumenical efforts of the first quarter of the twenty-first century. Konrad Raiser initiated an ecumenical forum, and Huibert van Beek oversaw its unfolding, but the GCF as it functions today would never have come into existence without the thought leadership of Cecil Robeck.

Development of Forum Method

The Continuation Committee agreed that preparatory work was needed before an international forum could be held. Regional meetings in various countries were held after the model that Robeck designed at the Fuller consultations.[50] Robeck advised or co-moderated many of these meetings. Sarah Jones depicts each meeting as "a microcosm of the global Christian family" in its attempts to bridge confessional divides.[51] The 2006 GCF event in Bangkok resulted in the Christian Conference of Asia and the Federation of Asian (Catholic) Bishops' Conferences extending an invitation to the Evangelical Fellowship of Asia (now Asia Evangelical Alliance) to join their triennial Asian Movement for Christian Unity gatherings.[52] The pan-Asian gatherings since then have addressed issues of climate change and Christian mission. The GCF regional meeting in Nairobi also facilitated new relationships between the All Africa Conference of Churches, Organization of African Instituted Churches, and Association of Evangelicals in Africa, whose Nairobi offices now meet regularly for prayer and fellowship.[53]

The 2007 Global Gathering in Limuru, Kenya, was the first global forum. Robeck refers to his experience at the Limuru gathering as "a vision coming true." The cultural and denominational diversity of participants led him to describe the event as "a new Pentecost."[54] Daniel Okoh, then-president of the Organization of African Instituted Churches, says that the Gathering was the first global ecumenical event that African Instituted Churches were asked to take a leading role in planning, and he affirms the value of testimonies as a form of communication at the event.[55] Robeck's role was described as "indispensable" in garnering support from many church leaders and organizations.[56] The only two groups that declined invitations were the AG in the United States and the World Assemblies of God Fellowship.[57] The event won the approval of the CSCWC and WEA, who held their meetings in Nairobi around the same time, and the Pentecostal World Fellowship (PWF) soon thereafter joined the leadership of the GCF.[58] Not everything was equally successful. A paper delivered by Pentecostal scholar Cheryl Bridges Johns, of whom Robeck speaks highly,[59] was received by some attendees as an offensive "counter-dialogue."[60] She called for new wineskins for a new era of ecumenism, asserting that the "'mainstream' ecumenical paradigm . . . is no longer viable."[61] This tension between churches and between ecumenical methods has motivated conversations surrounding the GCF.

The 2011 Global Gathering in Manado, Indonesia, expanded the understanding of testimonies to include a more expressly communal dimension.[62] As mentioned above, testimonies speak of the self within one's larger context. Communities likewise narrate their self-understandings in their relation to the works of God in history. It became clearer how the sharing of testimonies

190   *Chapter 6*

contributed to understanding and dialogue between communities when they were able to share their communal narratives. A form of this was the inclusion of presentations on world Christianity from researchers. A presentation by David Sang-Bok Kim, then-president of the WEA, surveyed trends in global evangelicalism, though some considered his remarks as harsh and offensive toward other churches.[63] Larry Miller around this time spoke of the recent conclusion of the "Healing Memories" study from the Lutheran–Mennonite dialogue, mentioned in the second chapter, which saw how the sharing of stories revealed the need for renewal and forgiveness between the two traditions.[64] The GCF gained structure in 2012 with the naming of the "four pillars"—the Pontifical Council for Promoting Christian Unity (now DPCU), WCC, PWF, and WEA.[65] Miller's and Robeck's work with the CSCWC augmented the confessional aspect of the GCF's leadership.[66]

The original idea for the Forum was to discuss common issues facing churches. The GCF identified persecution and proselytism for topical Forums. A consultation was held in 2015 in Tirana, Albania, due to the experience of persecution there during the soviet era.[67] The Lausanne–Orthodox Initiative, to which Robeck had previously contributed, also influenced the selection of Albania as the host for the event due to the developing relationships between Evangelicals and Orthodox in the country.[68] The event was an opportunity for Christian communities to hear first-hand of persecution in many countries and the interventions of ecumenical partnerships. A report was given from the Indian National United Christian Forum on ongoing work between the national council, evangelical fellowship, and Catholic episcopal conference on fostering resistance in the face of persecution.[69] Shahan Sarkissian, Armenian Archbishop of Aleppo, reported that he "could not ask for a better Christian forum to describe the discrimination and persecution that [his] church is suffering from today."[70] The event called for the strengthening of communion between churches in the face of persecution and martyrdom.[71] In 2017, a consultation on mission addressed best practices in mission collaboration and the need for the healing of memories between Christian communities that have suffered proselytism.[72]

After these events, the PWF World Missions Commission established a Task Force for Religious Liberty, which was merged shortly thereafter with the World Assemblies of God Fellowship's preexistent Commission on Religious Liberty to become a joint Pentecostal Commission on Religious Liberty.[73] Though the PWF webpage for the commission names the objective of working with "other evangelical initiatives,"[74] the AG webpage names "mainline Protestant denominations and even the Roman Catholic and Orthodox Churches"[75] as partners in mission. It is doubtful whether such a posture would have come to fruition without the GCF.

These consultations raised concerns among ecumenical actors. A meeting of the four pillars ahead of the 2018 Global Gathering agreed that the GCF's mission of broadening and deepening relationships did not extend to the conducting of programs.[76] Robeck concurs that it is not the place of the GCF to issue statements or decisions. Because it is not a membership organization, its statements would have neither authority nor weight. Such actions are more meaningful and effective when undertaken in other ecumenical bodies. However, he fears that, without a space outside of the WCC to discuss divisive issues, the conversations will struggle to include non-member churches.[77] He speaks from decades of personal experience as an ecumenist from a non-member church.

The 2018 Global Gathering was held in Bogotá, Colombia. Kathryn Johnson, representing the Lutheran World Federation, spoke at the Gathering on the value of testimonies in the recognition of Christians. Every believer has a relationship and story with Jesus. These stories make Christians aware of the presence of Christ in one's own life and that of others.[78] She recalls an encounter at a GCF meeting:

A testimony was given to the importance of testimonies by someone for whom this was a cherished part of praising God. An Orthodox priest offered a challenge: in his tradition[,] they rather told stories of holy people, in order to provide an example to others and, even more, to bear witness to Christ. The Pentecostal retort was swift: "What do you think our testimonies are for?"[79]

The stories testify to the work of Christ. Leonid Kishkovsky offers an interpretation of the ecumenical method from within the Orthodox tradition when he says that testimony connects personal faith to the Christian community, serving as "a witness to the presence of the Kingdom of God in our midst."[80] He draws on the example of Seraphim of Sarov. The Russian mystic taught that a goal of the reception of the Spirit is to be better able to recognize the presence of Christ in every person.[81] K.M. George adds that both bearing witness to Christ and recognition of the witness are acts inspired by the Spirit.[82] When divided Christians witness the work of Christ in their lives, they are better able to see the same work in the lives of others.

Beyond the GCF, the Christian Forum method has borne fruit in addition to that seen above. Robeck attributes the formation of the PWF's Christian Unity Commission in 2019, mentioned in the third chapter, to the experience of PWF leadership in the GCF.[83] The ability of ecclesiastical leaders to encounter and listen to leaders of other church traditions opened the door for increased dialogue and partnership at a formal, structural level. Sarah Jones reports that the Anglican Communion has begun to use the sharing of testimonies in meetings that are potentially fractious, rooting the gathered parties

192 Chapter 6

in their common life in Christ.[84] Elsewhere, the WEA now has an office in the WCC's Ecumenical Centre headquarters in Geneva, thanks to the work of the GCF. Future research will assess the impact of the Forum method on various communities and their relationships between each other as the method undergoes reception within churches.

RECEPTION OF THE CHRISTIAN FORUM METHOD

GCF leaders at the Limuru Global Gathering called for the localization of the ecumenical method if any significant progress was to be made. Robeck also sees the need to incorporate Christian leaders in the lower strata of ecclesiastical institutions.[85] Regional and national Christian Forums have emerged between confessional bodies as a result of consultations. These smaller entities should not be judged against the standard of the GCF as though it were the Platonic ideal of the ecumenical method. These Forums differ from each other due to the confessional demographics, ecumenical histories, and political contexts of the locations. The GCF newsletter gives updates on some of these Forums, and a couple of essays have been published, but no research has conducted transnational surveys of the Forums. Local ecumenism generally suffers from a dearth of scholarship due to the lack of institutional and financial support such projects receive and due to the assumption that "bigger is better," yet ecumenism matters insofar as it impacts local Christian communities where unity and division are experienced. The reception of the Christian Forum method is part of the method's refinement and the advancement of the ecumenical movement, and so it warrants future study. Robeck himself has had limited involvement with some of these regional Forums, including his local Southern California Christian Forum.

Regional Christian Forums

Churches in South and Southeast Asia were among the first to establish Christian Forums. The National United Christian Forum of India was formed in 2009 as a partnership of the national council, Catholic episcopal conference, and evangelical alliance to address the persecution of Christians as a religious minority in the country. This threefold partnership of comparable ecclesial bodies would repeat itself through the formation of other Forums, including the United Forum of Churches in Bangladesh in 2011. The Indonesian Christian Forum (FUKRI), mentioned in this chapter's introduction, was launched at the 2011 Manado Global Gathering of the GCF. Each of these Forums has served as platforms for church leaders to discuss issues facing their communities in their countries, which retrieves the initial impetus for an ecumenical forum for churches to dialogue informally.

The most-studied offshoot of the GCF is the Fórum Pentecostal Latino-americano e Caribe (Foro Pentecostal Latinoamericano y Caribeño [FPLC]), founded in 2011. Transnational Pentecostal networks in the region have always been entwined with the ecumenical movement.[86] The idea for the FPLC sprang from the 2010 GCF regional meeting in Costa Rica. It is narrower than the GCF in gathering Pentecostal churches, so its interest in the present study is limited. The FPLC encourages dialogue and encounters between ecclesiastical leaders and scholars in the region, especially those outside of Pentecostalism.[87] Robeck was invited to address the FPLC on Pentecostal participation in the ecumenical movement at the centenary of the 1916 Panama Missionary Congress. The group has also released edited collections on Pentecostal ecumenical engagement, inadvertently making Portuguese one of the most commonly used languages for published literature by Pentecostals on ecumenics.

Christian Forums in Europe appear to be organizing themselves by language. Examples include the Nederlands Christelijk Forum launched in 2013, the Polish Christian Forum (Polskie Forum Chrześcijańskie) in 2016, and the Forum Chrétien Francophone in 2018. Mariusz Muszczyński drew inspiration from his role in the Polish Forum for his dissertation on Robeck. A smaller spin-off in 2021 is the Forum Chrétien Romand, which gathers churches and ministries in Romandy, the francophone region of Switzerland. The Forum is especially significant because it gathers the Geneva offices of various international ecumenical and nonprofit organizations. A *deutschschweizer* counterpart is currently under development.

Scholarship on local ecumenism struggles to glean knowledge on some regions due to inequitable access to information technology and dissemination of published material. Little information was found in my research on Christian Forums in Africa or the Caribbean. Sarah Jones reports that national Forum experiments were to be conducted in Kenya, Ghana, and Zimbabwe,[88] though no further references were found to such entities. News articles from the past few years have cited the activities of ecumenical bodies named the Tanzania Christian Forum (Jukwaa la Wakristo Tanzania) and the Fórum Cristão Angolano.[89] Additionally, the GCF newsletter in 2014 spoke optimistically of an emergent Foro Cristiano Cubano, though no details have been provided since.[90]

David Sang-Ehil Han is currently pioneering an experimental bilateral Christian Forum in Cleveland, Tennessee, between Catholic priests and Pentecostal pastors. The project is in collaboration with Nathan Smith of the Glenmary Home Missioners. The goal is to grow relations between the two communities at the local level to receive the fruit of half a century of

194 Chapter 6

international dialogue. Most of these clergy have had no prior contact despite the progress of relations between their church traditions. While bilateral dialogue is rightly the domain of scholars, the idea behind the Forum project is to enact a form of communication that local leaders can engage. If successful, the project may be promoted in dioceses across the United States.[91]

Further transnational research is needed on Christian Forums as they develop. Such studies ought to examine not only the activities of the Forums but, more importantly, the strengthened ecclesiastical relationships that are fostered through the Forums. In keeping with the intent of the ecumenical method, Forums are not administrative entities that conduct programs, so there is little reason to expect them to grow organizationally. Ecumenists should instead expect other forms of ecumenical engagement to grow, which is the marker for success. With little information available on other local Christian Forums, it benefits the present study to attend to an example with which Robeck has had more direct involvement.

Southern California Christian Forum

Robeck's career brought him into contact with ecumenical networks in his local Los Angeles area. One of these networks, due to Robeck's influence, became the Southern California Christian Forum (SCCF) in 2015. The SCCF prides itself as the geographic origin of the Christian Forum method at Fuller's campus in Pasadena, California. The story of the SCCF's formation serves to illustrate many of the prevailing debates on the Forum method seen above in a smaller setting where ecumenical actors are brought into closer contact with each other.

It is important to acknowledge from the outset that I have served as part of the SCCF for the past seven years in various capacities. As such, I have a vested interest in portraying the SCCF in a positive light, yet a study of ecumenical methodology and Robeck would be incomplete without accounting for his contributions to local ecumenism. My role in the SCCF also grants me a more intimate knowledge of the Forum method than many scholars who have written on the GCF from a distance. I stick as closely as possible to the available information from archival materials and personal interviews to avoid prejudicing the discussion. I do not resolve disagreements on particularities of the SCCF's activities but mention them as ongoing questions in the field while reserving my analysis for the ecclesiological basis and convergence of the ecumenical method.

Robeck's contribution to the SCCF occurred during its transition from being the Southern California Ecumenical Council (SCEC).[92] Ecumenical organizations in the United States at the turn of the twenty-first century suffered from decreasing denominational financial support and rising political polarization. Several organizations responded by transforming into either interfaith networks or social service enterprises, each of which is easier to justify to donors than ecumenical work. The SCEC's sister Northern California Ecumenical Council became the Northern California Interreligious Conference in 2000. At the centennial of the SCEC in 2012, member churches witnessed the same pressures mounting, leaving the council's leadership to search for solutions. The intent here is not to assess the soundness of the decisions made but to report the changes as they occurred. The consensus of the SCEC board was that before them lay the choice between reinventing the organization or watching its flame die out.

The SCEC began its discernment process with the election of Alexei Smith as president in 2012. Smith serves as the Ecumenical and Interreligious Officer of the Roman Catholic Archdiocese of Los Angeles. The Catholic Church at the time held observer status in the SCEC, yet he was elected president because it was feared that the destabilization of Protestant commitments to ecumenism would make the council fall apart. Smith's diocesan office raises the status of the SCCF in garnering support from denominational heads. The board hired its Executive Director, Gabriel Meyer, to aid the leadership transition. Meyer was, in many ways, an unconventional choice; he had neither formal theological training nor experience in service organizations. He is a retired journalist with correspondence experience in the Holy Land, Balkans, and Sudan, bringing him into close contact with the extremes of religious conflict. Additionally, as a Charismatic Eastern Catholic, he is intimately familiar with the diversity of the Christian faith. He previously contributed to the 1977 Kansas City Charismatic Renewal Conference and helped found a Charismatic residential community, a popular expression of lay spiritual ecumenism during the era. He sought to contribute to the SCEC in its desire to build relationships between religious communities who had no contact with each other.

The SCEC established a task force to review ongoing trends in the ecumenical movement in the United States and abroad. The task force interviewed church leaders and scholars in Southern California on the importance of ecumenism for their communities. Some reported that a greater focus on relationships was needed for ecumenical work, while others said that their churches were too busy trying to survive to concern themselves with ecumenism. The task force, during this process, contacted a Catholic priest who was involved with the national Evangelicals and Catholics Together initiative; he recommended that the SCEC look into the GCF as a model of ecumenical engagement. Smith already had a working relationship with Robeck as co-chairs of the local Catholic–Evangelical dialogue in Los Angeles. Robeck met with the board to talk about his experience with the GCF and what it sought to accomplish. He acknowledged that the SCEC needed to broaden in

196 Chapter 6

order to survive. He did not advocate for the replacement of the SCEC, but he acknowledged the Christian Forum as a viable model worth considering.

The historical arc of the century-old ecumenical body warrants observation.[93] The reconfiguration into the SCCF in 2015 was the latest iteration of numerous forms for the organization that each responded to changing contexts. Preceding the Christian Forum model, the body operated as the SCEC since 1982, the Southern California Council of Churches since 1957, the Southern California Council of Protestant Churches since 1943 before the inclusion of the Greek Orthodox church, and the statewide California Council of Churches since 1937. The statewide body followed national trends in the American ecumenical movement toward conciliation, foreshadowing the transition of the national federation of churches (FCC) into the national council (NCCUSA). The prior embryonic California Church Federation was birthed in 1913 under the leadership of Edwin Ryland, the founder of the Los Angeles Church Federation (LACF), discussed in the second chapter for its opposition to the Azusa Street Revival. The SCEC was an organizational descendant of the ecumenical body that first rivaled American Pentecostals. Over a century later, faced with pressing methodological questions, the organization sought counsel from a spiritual descendant and historian of the revival it once opposed.

Robeck was asked to lead a trial run of a Forum meeting on Fuller's campus for the SCEC. It was received positively by most, though he recalls that one board member stormed out of the event early, calling it fake ecumenism. By the end of 2015, the board agreed that a transition to a Forum model was the best path forward that would preserve a programmatic dimension to the ecumenical movement in Southern California. The SCCF, since then, has operated primarily through hosting ministerial retreats and monthly Bible studies for attendees from diverse confessional backgrounds. Similar to other regional Christian Forums, it has moved beyond the initial sharing of testimonies to engage in other topics. Participation hinges upon engagement with ecumenical officers and ecumenically minded lay leaders. A perennial problem is finding partner churches and institutions to host events due to the decreasing commitments to ecumenism in the region. Michael Kinnamon, scholar of conciliar ecumenism and the SCCF's most loyal critic, observes that a struggle of Forums is their ability to raise ecumenical action or to engage churches beyond the individual participants.[94] The SCCF has sought to circumnavigate this through resourcing lay leaders to engage their own churches, with varying degrees of success.

The SCCF is likely the only Christian Forum with a Faith and Order Commission, chaired since 2008 by Lutheran minister Ray Kibler, a former student of Robeck. The commission was founded following the 1957 Oberlin Conference on Faith and Order as part of a national movement to localize multilateral dialogue in the reception of ecumenical discourse and texts. Specifically, the original organizers in 1961 sought to contribute to the NCCUSA's own new commission in reflecting on the ecclesiological significance of councils of churches.[95] The SCCF Commission, in some ways, is a return to the origins of the Faith and Order movement before commissions were integrated into councils. It is also a way to support the work of the SCCF with theological reflection, an aspect that others see the GCF as lacking. Kinnamon notes, however, that, without a conciliar structure, the commission struggles to recruit official representatives and to gain a voice in the theological reflection of churches in the region.[96]

The SCCF inherited many of the functions of the SCEC because it stands as the sole regional ecumenical entity. It organizes the annual Week of Prayer for Christian Unity service in partnership with denominations and local churches, though it often struggles to find denominational heads who care enough about ecumenism to help plan the event. The SCCF in 2021 also acted as consultants in the planning of the bilateral Catholic–Pentecostal Forum in Cleveland mentioned above. Engagement with lay leaders has placed the SCCF in a mentorship position to train local ecumenists in leading their congregations to engage in the work of ecumenism. It initiated in 2022 a partnership with the Pacific Network for Mission Education to build up the SCCF's internship program for university students who seek ecumenical formation as part of their studies. The SCCF stands as an example of methodological innovation in the ecumenical movement as Christians respond to the changing circumstances of churches. It carries out its work from the conviction that, even when churches do not prioritize their relations with each other, the gospel call to unity remains.

RECONCILIATORY ECUMENICAL METHODOLOGY

The emergence of Christian Forums foregrounded tensions within the ecumenical movement concerning the goals and work of ecumenism. It would be wrong to suggest that these tensions did not already exist. Suspicion and arrogance of some churches over others do not hinder the ecumenical movement, for the movement exists to bring these churches together to address their conflicts. The GCF and other Forums are experimental in engaging leaders of these traditions to facilitate their relations. The method assumes that interpersonal encounter serves as a transformative source of ecclesiological reflection. The Christian Forum method is capable of pursuing church unity because of the method's basis in ecclesiology. The use of testimonies relies on the nature of the church as both a sign and instrument of unity, without which participants would not be able to recognize the work of Christ in each

198   *Chapter 6*

other. Consequently, as churches develop common ways of testifying to this reconciling work, they converge in their recognition of each other as fellow believers.

Communion

The ecclesiological basis of Christian Forums was introduced as pertaining to sacramental ecclesiology. The church serves as a sign and instrument of communion because of the presence of Christ in the church. This does not imply that consensus exists on the church's sacramentality, or even whether it is appropriate to use the term "sacrament" when speaking of the church. The focus on Robeck and his Pentecostal tradition would certainly disqualify such an approach. Instead, the argument is that the prior recognition of the church's testifying to God's work to reconcile the world informs the work of ecumenism, even while churches do not yet agree on how this testifying occurs. This was seen in prior chapters. Churches disagree on practices of catholicity while still supporting councils of churches, disagree on the nature of discernment while still engaging in bilateral dialogues, and disagree on charisms while still promoting movements of spiritual ecumenism. Ecumenical methods are the means by which ecclesiological convergence is sought, and this is no less true for the church's function as an effective sign of God's reconciliatory presence and action. The work of ecumenism is possible because some form of ecclesiological consensus already exists.

The Christian Forum method presumes that the church is a sign of communion between God and people. The testimonies that participants share are not supposed to be about themselves or their communities but about how God was present in the stories. As Han explains, testimonies make speakers and hearers aware of the work of God in drawing creation together with himself in salvation history.[97] The method also presumes that speakers and hearers share in the communion that God has extended to the church. Kathryn Johnson's affirmation of the method above relied on the fact that interlocutors each have stories of encounters with Jesus. These testimonies are examples of the light of Christ on the countenance of the church. There would be no point in having participants testify to something they have not experienced or that they do not believe their interlocutors would also understand. The stories reveal the presence of Christ in the lives of participants and, consequently, in the communion shared between participants, a topic returned to below.

To argue that Christian Forums have theological presuppositions challenges the way that some authors have presented the method as a space without an agenda. Huub Vogelaar presses the issue by asking: What, theologically speaking, is an open space?[98] Promoters of Christian Forums employ the slogan that the method creates a neutral space for divided Christians to encounter each other as equals without obligations. The phrase intends to assure skeptics of the lack of ulterior motives on behalf of other attendees, and it implies that other methods are ideologically biased. However, as stated from the outset of this book, neutrality is a fiction. There is no neutral vantage point from which one can speak of God or engage other people. The ecclesiological basis of ecumenical methodology is the reason why the work of ecumenism results in ecclesiological convergence. If Christian Forums were truly and purely void of theological presuppositions, then they could not advance Christian unity. Van Beek argues that Forums are not vacuums because they operate as gatherings of people who bring their ecclesial traditions and shared faith into the space.[99] Participants in Forums engage the church as it exists as the people of God.

The prioritization of the church as the people of God emphasizes the diversity that constitutes the church. The plurality of stories told in Christian Forums is an example of the church's diversity insofar as the Christian faith is seen lived out in innumerable cultures, places, and positions in society. Robeck sees Christians as the most material existence of the church. The diversities of Christian lives are part of the materiality that serves as a sign and instrument of reconciliation. Testimonies reveal the fullness of the gospel in history. A persistent tension for the method is the divergent uses of testimony within churches. The above vignette of the exchange between the Pentecostal and Orthodox clergy illustrates the different ways that Christian communities seek to point their members to God. When one uses the term "testimony" in a technical sense as defined above, it can be claimed that all church traditions utilize testimonies to God within the lives of faith communities, but the method has had to expand beyond the originally Pentecostal understanding of testimony. In the previous chapter, spiritual ecumenism is often practiced as introducing Christians to the diversity of liturgical and spiritual traditions within the global church to broaden believers' understanding of ecclesial catholicity. One could argue that the adoption of testimonies in Forums is one such form of spiritual ecumenism, yet it appears in the literature that the intent of the ecumenical method is not to focus on the plurality of testimonial forms but rather on their common divine referent.

The spiritual dimension of Christian Forums occurs through interpersonal interactions. As also claimed in the previous chapter, Christian spirituality takes a communal form in the church. Believers can engage in many spiritual practices on their own, but they cannot testify to themselves. The church's existence as a sign is such that its witness is meant to be perceived by others. The act of sharing testimonies is a spiritual practice that reveals God to the hearer. It relies on the ability of a speaker and hearer to talk of God in comparable ways. Angelo Maffeis argues that the existence of a common language between interlocutors is the clearest evidence that prior consensus

200   *Chapter 6*

is needed for dialogue to occur.[100] Christians would not be able to recognize their common faith in each other's stories if they did not have common ways of speaking of their faith.

Nonetheless, disagreements on the value of the Christian Forum method reveal that communities do not always use the same language or symbols when speaking of their faith. The method of bilateral dialogue also reveals that language is not always the problem; sometimes Christians are simply making conflicting statements. Robeck advocates testimonies as a way to give flesh to these differences, which can then be examined more fully together. Testimony employs religious symbols and integrates events into a coherent narrative, which conveys the meaning and significance of truth claims through an appeal to lived experience. It enables participants to learn about other churches when they speak of the embodiment of theological articulations in concrete situations.[101] Calixto Moreno sees this as a strength of the ecumenical method. Participants are encouraged to speak in the terms and priorities of their own churches. The encounter of communities changes the way that their stories are told and enables each to recognize commonalities with the other. In these different stories, participants grow in their awareness of the common work of the Spirit who brings Christians together.[102] The diversity of histories among churches is a testament to the reconciling work of God in which Christians participate.

Sacramental ecclesiology concerns the positioning of believers in relationship with each other, God, and the world. It defines the church in its function as an effective sign of God's reconciliatory presence and action in bringing about communion. The Christian Forum ecumenical method operates on the shared assumption among participants that the church testifies to the work of God in history. Otherwise, no "faith stories" could be shared at gatherings. These stories position the church in its referential nature to God and in its partaking in divine economy in the various historical situations in which churches find themselves. Testimonies are part of the sacramental nature of the church. They contribute to the reconciliation of Christians by revealing their preexistent relation to each other as a result of the work of Christ. Christians can testify of their common reception of divine grace because of the communion they share with each other and God. Communion thereby serves as a prerequisite for mutual recognition.

Recognition

The Christian Forum ecumenical method results in ecclesiological convergence through the mutual recognition of Christians as fellow believers. The field of ecumenics has long regarded recognition as an ecclesiological concept. The New Delhi declaration defines visible unity as requiring that "ministry and members [be] accepted by all," and the Toronto Statement affirms recognition as a goal of the ecumenical movement because it is an expression of churches growing into a common understanding of the nature of the church.[103] Christians cannot claim to hold a common vision of the church while denying each other's membership in the church. Paul Avis asserts that the first synodical stage is mutual acknowledgment. It is a form of "spiritual intuition," where Christians discern the presence of Christ in each other. The recognition of communities as each belonging to Christ is the precondition for their ability to dialogue and act together.[104]

Robeck explains that the WCC in the late twentieth century acknowledged the need to promote recognition through Faith and Order studies on apostolic faith and ecclesiology, especially in light of the absence of most churches from the council.[105] It is not a coincidence that the GCF emerged during this same time period as part of the landscape of the ecumenical movement in its search for recognition between churches beyond the reach of the WCC. Robeck's career placed him in leadership positions within multilateral Faith and Order dialogue, global conciliar relations within the WCC's JCG, and the GCF. The ability to track his career between these initiatives illuminates the relationship between such ecclesiological concepts as recognition, conciliarity, and catholicity. The recognition promoted through Christian Forums is meant to enable ecclesiastical relations between churches in given regions through a renewed awareness of the catholicity of the Christian faith in its diversity. Reconciliation is the working out of what this recognition demands.

Avis adds that recognition needs objective criteria so the process does not dissolve into sentimentality.[106] The question of whether a community is Christian ought not to rely on whether another community happens to like them. There is also a fear that the desire for recognition could relativize the truth claims of churches. The Toronto Statement clarifies that the recognition sought is, first, a recognition of the headship of Christ of his church and only then of the belonging of other Christians to Christ.[107] Testimonies are not autobiographies because they are ultimately about the work of Christ in the person's life, and the goal of sharing testimonies is for the hearer to recognize in the story the presence of the same Christ they worship. Robeck realizes that communities need to recognize their common faith in Christ and to believe that the others' faith is genuine before any further ecumenical work can be tried between them. He advocates for the use of testimonies as a form of proof of a credible witness. The recognition of this credible witness then motivates work to overcome whatever barriers or prejudices exist.

However, there is a crucial difference between the recognition of churches and the recognition of individual Christians. The ecclesiological paradigm of Christian Forums foregrounds believers as the material dimension of the church because their relationships visibly testify to the reconciliation of the

202   *Chapter 6*

world in Christ. This addresses a potential objection to the argument sustained
in this book: can a church share ecclesiology with that which is not a church?
This is not a hypothetical situation. Ecclesial recognition is a question that has
driven the ecumenical movement to find creative solutions. At most ecumenical gatherings, there are likely communities present who do not recognize
the legitimacy of the claims of ecclesiality of all other attendees according
to theological or canonical standards. Ecumenists need the ability to speak
of ecclesiology without yet having achieved mutual recognition of churches.
Otherwise, no ecclesiological reflection could be undertaken in the ecumenical movement. Recognition of fellow believers as legitimate Christians is
often the recourse where ecclesial recognition is not yet possible, which the
Toronto Statement sees as an impetus for further ecumenical work.[108] Attention to Pentecostal churches highlights this need in the ecumenical movement. Vogelaar questions whether the inclusion of some Pentecostal groups
would push the theological limits of the GCF or "even damage the heart of
the gospel itself."[109] Robeck's attestation to the exclusion of some churches
from ecumenical projects further underscores the need for the promotion of
recognition. The work of ecumenism relies on the recognition of people as
Christians, lest the believers be excluded from ecumenical spaces, and the
growing inclusion of different ecclesial bodies within ecumenical spaces
mentioned above are examples of the advancement of recognition.

The relationships between believers are where the unity of the church is
tangible and visible—thus, where the church testifies to the reconciling work
of God. Reconciliation occurs as a process of interpersonal encounter, and
it is this reconciliation that forms the church. Scholars often describe the
function of Christian Forums as a form of spiritual ecumenism in the focus
on Christian relationships.[110] Participants recognize each other as members
of the same family of God, which is built on the foundation of the apostles
and prophets.[111] Olav Fykse Tveit even depicts the ecumenical movement as
having originated in the experience of individual Christians of each other as
fellow believers, who then called their respective churches to overcome their
divisions.[112] The existence and growth of the ecumenical movement itself is
evidence that interpersonal encounter changes communities.

The recognition is founded on the shared ecclesiological premise that the
presence of Christ constitutes the Christian community's ecclesiality. Even
where there is not yet recognition of churches, the recognition of Christ in the
presence of believers spurs ecumenical engagement. The previous discussion
among Orthodox scholars on the presence of Christ and Christian Forums
underscores the necessity of a conscious acknowledgment of the communion
shared between Christians. The sacramental nature of the church, as *Lumen
gentium* depicts, is a result of the light of Christ shining visibly on the church,
which is how the church can participate in the ministry of reconciliation.

Robeck blames the avoidance of churches of each other on the failure to recognize the work of God in each other.[113] GCF conversations on proselytism encouraged this recognition. The sharing of testimonies is intended to confirm for participants that they share the same faith. He argues that proselytism is due to ignorance of what God is doing in other churches and that the best way to end proselytism is to treat other Christians as peers.[114]

The experience of communion between believers sets the stage for dialogue on what separates them. Kuncheria Pathil argues this when he says that mutual recognition depends on the recognition and experience of Christ in other communities. He concludes that "any doctrinal or theological consensus is an explication and legitimation of this experience."[115] The Christian Forum method sees experience as a source that informs convergence.

On the other hand, Sarah Jones contrasts the GCF with Faith and Order when she says that the GCF foregrounds commonality between believers, while Faith and Order dialogue foregrounds doctrinal disagreements.[116] The chapter on conciliar ecumenism saw otherwise. Multilateral dialogue abandoned a comparative approach at the Third World Conference on Faith and Order at Lund in 1952. Since then, the assumption has been that progress in ecclesiological convergence can occur only from the starting point that the God-given nature of the church's unity precedes any and all ecumenical work. The *TCTCV* convergence text exemplifies this in its assumption that an articulation of a common vision of the church would spur renewal and concrete steps toward more visible unity. The Christian Forum method operates on a similar assumption as that of Faith and Order dialogue. Believers encounter and recognize each other as holding a common faith through the sharing of testimonies. Recognition then serves as the context for discernment through disagreements.

The historical development of Christian Forums challenges some understandings of the ecumenical method and its ecclesiological underpinnings. Some scholars have framed Forums as seeking to incorporate churches into the ecumenical movement,[117] which creates a curious dichotomy that is difficult to quantify between those who get to be called insiders and outsiders. If conciliar membership is the boundary, then it must be remembered that the WCC accounts for fewer than a quarter of churches who are members of national councils globally.[118] The ecumenical movement extends vastly beyond the reach of the WCC. It is also worth observing that the development of the GCF was possible only because of the decades of ecumenical work undertaken by churches outside the WCC. Robeck notes that Pentecostals are often annoyed by the identification of ecumenism with particular structures and churches.[119] Talk of marginal portions of the ecumenical movement often reflects the perception that particular churches are outside the "mainstream" of Christian churches.

The reconciliation of Christians who historically have been isolated from each other has raised questions regarding the ecumenical movement's self-understanding. The movement was never a homogeneous or unified phenomenon,[120] yet the Christian Forum method has caused some to declare a paradigm shift in the movement. Then-WCC general secretary Tveit asserts that it "would be utterly misleading to look at [the GCF] as an organization or a group with the mandate to pursue alternative ecumenism."[121] Meanwhile, GCF Committee member Han proclaims the GCF as "an alternative ecumenical paradigm for Pentecostal faith communities."[122] Han builds on the thought of Cheryl Bridges Johns in saying that "traditional ecumenism" is no longer viable, especially for non-Western churches.[123] It is worth noting that the SCCF was the only example found in the course of my research where a Christian Forum replaced an ecumenical body. Every other Forum built atop prior existent organizations—especially outside the West—thereby broadening and strengthening the "traditional" organizations' capacities for interchurch engagement. All of the national Forums have served as platforms for churches and organizations to address common issues facing their communities. The recognition of each other as Christians obliges them to pursue further measures of visible unity.

Pentecostals Han and Johns are not the only people who have championed Christian Forums over other methods. Annemarie Mayer, from her vantage point as a member of the Joint Working Group between the Roman Catholic Church and the WCC, explains the absence of Catholics from the council. After rehearsing the usual reasons, she asserts that the WCC is now less central to the ecumenical movement due to the presence of the GCF. Her implication is that, with the addition of global ecumenical spaces outside the WCC, the Catholic Church now has no compelling reason to join the council.[124] Such a claim misunderstands both the GCF and the WCC. Neither entity can fulfill the mission of the other, for the methods and ecclesiological principles of the two are distinct. Robeck's position on the question is clear: "I must say once again that the Forum is not an organization intended to replace the WCC. If it were, I would have nothing to do with it."[125] He is careful not to pit methods against each other.

If anything, one could argue that Robeck sees the reverse as true. A distinguishing characteristic of ecumenical methods is their temporary nature. Ecumenical prayer services are not needed in a united church, nor is the reconciliation of memories if there are no churches needing to be reconciled. No ecumenical body exists for its own self-preservation. Christian Forums are intended to be short-lived initiatives to meet a threshold of mutual recognition of believers and to establish communication between disparate parts of the global church.[126] Once the threshold is met, Forums are no longer needed. Meaningful inter-ecclesiastical relationships require more institutionalization

Christian Forums 205

and routinized practices than Forums can support. Robeck looks at the GCF—his vision come true of a new Pentecost—and says, "I hope it eventually dies."[127] He hopes churches will be able to enter into conciliar relationships within shared ecumenical bodies, but he acknowledges that this is not likely a short-term goal.[128] The church requires structures of mutual accountability for its unity to be visible and, therefore, a testimony to the reconciling work of God.[129] Recognition is merely the first stage of synodality.

The ecumenical method of Christian Forums finds its basis in the shared ecclesiological notion that the church is a sign and instrument of the reconciliatory work of God. When Christians testify to each other of God's work, they converge in their recognition of the presence of Christ in each other. The church exists as a people reconciled in communion whose lives testify to the work of God. This is a thin ecclesiology, yet the existence of conflicts between churches shows the need for work to promote recognition. Despite decades of dialogue on Christian missions, proselytism is prevalent in many countries. Despite generations of conciliar relations, churches still ignore each other when making decisions. Despite countless ecumenical assemblies and consultations, scholars still speak as though the church has centers and margins. Christian Forums advance ecclesiological convergence when Christians recognize their faith in the other. The sharing of testimonies permits believers to hear—in very different terms and stories—attestations to the common work of God. The recognition of fellow believers is, first, a recognition of the presence of Christ that causes the church to be an effective sign and instrument of communion, and then a recognition of other Christians as products and participants in this same reconciliatory work. The advancement of recognition constitutes ecclesiological convergence.

NOTES

1. Pontifical Council for Promoting Christian Unity and World Council of Churches Commission on Faith and Order, "Justice and Only Justice You Shall Pursue (Deuteronomy 16:18-20): Resources for the Week of Prayer for Christian Unity and throughout the Year 2019," 2018, 28, 29, https://www.oikoumene.org/sites/default/files/2020-09/Week_of_Prayer_2019.pdf.

2. Richard Howell and Casely Baiden Essamuah, eds., *Sharing of Faith Stories: A Methodology for Promoting Unity*, 2nd ed. (Farukh Nagar, India: Caleb Institute of Theology, 2018).

3. Centre for Intercultural Theology, Interreligious Dialogue, Missiology and Ecumenics (Centrum IIMO) of the Utrecht University, "The Global Christian Forum 1998–2007, and Beyond: An Evaluation Report," in *Revisioning Christian Unity: Journeying with Jesus Christ, the Reconciler at the Global Christian Forum, Limuru, November 2007*, ed. Huibert van Beek, Studies in Global Christianity (Eugene, OR:

206 *Chapter 6*

Wipf & Stock, 2007), 230; Sarah Rowland Jones, "The Global Christian Forum, A Narrative History: 'Limuru, Manado and Onwards,'" *Transformation* 30, no. 4 (2013): 239; Calixto Salvatierra Moreno, "La fé en los caminos de unidad de los cristianos: El Foro Cristiano Mundial," *Yachay* 57–58 (2013): 170.

4. Dagmar Heller, "Neue Entwicklungen in der Ökumene: Das Beispiel des 'Globalen Christlichen Forums,'" *Una Sancta* 64, no. 3 (2009): 217.

5. *LG*, §1.

6. *TCTCV*, §25, 27.

7. World Council of Churches, "The Church, the Churches, and the World Council of Churches: The Ecclesiological Significance of the World Council of Churches," 1950, §IV.6.

8. Maffeis, *Il dialogo ecumenico*, 109.

9. *TCTCV*, §27.

10. Maxim Vasiljević, "Sacraments and Sacramentality of the Church," in *Common Threads: Key Themes from Responses to* The Church: Towards a Common Vision, by World Council of Churches Commission on Faith and Order, ed. Ellen K. Wondra, Stephanie Dietrich, and Ani Ghazaryan Drissi, Faith and Order Paper 233 (Geneva: World Council of Churches, 2021), 129–52.

11. Vasiljević, 130, 152.

12. For examples, see Paul Ricœur, "L'herméneutique du témoignage," *Archivio di Filosofia* 42 (1972): 35–61; Paul Ricœur, "Le soi et l'identité narrative," in *Soi-même comme un autre* (Paris: Éditions du Seuil, 1990), 167–98; Emmanuel Levinas, "Truth of Disclosure and Truth of Testimony," in *Emmanuel Levinas: Basic Philosophical Writings*, ed. Adriaan T. Peperzak, Simon Critchley, and Robert Bernasconi, Studies in Continental Thought (Bloomington, IN: Indiana University Press, 1996), 98–107; Christophe Brabant, "The Truth Narrated: Ricoeur on Religious Experience," in *Divinising Experience: Essays in the History of Religious Experience from Origen to Ricoeur*, ed. Lieven Boeve and Laurence P. Hemming, Studies in Philosophical Theology 23 (Leuven, Belgium: Brill, 2004), 246–69; Philippe Gonzalez and Christophe Monnot, "Témoigner de son pâtir et de l'agir de Dieu : Les épreuves d'une communauté charismatique," in *Le corps, lieu de ce qui nous arrive : Approches anthropologiques, philosophiques, théologiques*, ed. Pierre Gisel (Geneva: Labor et Fides, 2008), 60–87.

13. Casely Baiden Essamuah, "Seeking Christian Unity through Faith Sharing: The Continuing Relevance of the Quest for Christian Unity," in *Sharing of Faith Stories: A Methodology for Promoting Unity*, ed. Richard Howell and Casely Baiden Essamuah, 2nd ed. (Farukh Nagar, India: Caleb Institute of Theology, 2018), 35.

14. Casely Baiden Essamuah, "A New Pentecost?: The Story of Peoples in the History of the Global Christian Forum and Its Contribution to World Christianity," in *World Christianity and Interfaith Relations*, ed. Richard F. Young, World Christianity and Public Religion 4 (Minneapolis, MN: Fortress Press, 2022), 256.

15. World Council of Churches, "Proposals Regarding a Forum of Christian Churches and Ecumenical Organisations," in *Revisioning Christian Unity: Journeying with Jesus Christ, the Reconciler at the Global Christian Forum, Limuru, November 2007*, ed. Huibert van Beek, Studies in Global Christianity (Eugene, OR: Wipf & Stock, 2007), 23.

Christian Forums 207

16. Global Christian Forum, "Our Unfolding Journey with Jesus Christ: Reflections on the Global Christian Forum Experience," 2013, 1, https://globalchristianforum.org/wp-content/uploads/2018/07/GFC-Our-Unfolding-Journey-ENG.pdf.

17. Raiser, *Ökumene im Übergang*, 175.

18. Robeck, "Roman Catholic-Pentecostal Dialogue: Some," 10.

19. Oxford Centre for Mission Studies, "The Global Christian Forum 1998–2007, and Beyond: An Evaluation Report," in *Revisioning Christian Unity: Journeying with Jesus Christ, the Reconciler at the Global Christian Forum, Limuru, November 2007*, ed. Huibert van Beek, Studies in Global Christianity (Eugene, OR: Wipf & Stock, 2007), 167.

20. Cheryl Bridges Johns, "When East Meets West and North Meets South: The Reconciling Mission of Global Christianity," in *Revisioning Christian Unity: Journeying with Jesus Christ, the Reconciler at the Global Christian Forum, Limuru, November 2007*, ed. Huibert van Beek, Studies in Global Christianity (Eugene, OR: Wipf & Stock, 2007), 93–101; David Sang-Ehil Han, "Changing Paradigms in Global Ecumenism: A Pentecostal Reading," in *Pentecostal Theology and Ecumenical Theology: Interpretations and Intersections*, ed. Peter D. Hocken, Tony L. Richie, and Christopher A. Stephenson, Global Pentecostal and Charismatic Studies 34 (Leiden: Brill, 2019), 111–30.

21. Huub Vogelaar and Greetje Witte-Rang, "The Global Christian Forum: Reconfiguration of the Ecumenical Scene. Tracks of Its History and First Evaluation," *Exchange* 39, no. 4 (2010): 390.

22. Raiser, *Ökumene im Übergang*.

23. Robeck, "An Ecumenical Journey," 59.

24. Vogelaar and Witte-Rang, "The Global," 379; Stefan Höschele, "Das Global Christian Forum: 'Forum' als Paradigma für die Zukunft der Ökumene?," in *Ökumene der Zukunft: Hermeneutische Perspektiven und die Suche nach Identität*, ed. Stephen Lakkis, Stefan Höschele, and Stefanie Schardien, Beiheft zur Ökumenischen Rundschau 81 (Frankfurt: Otto Lembeck, 2008), 120.

25. For a discussion of the Orthodox origins of the forum, see Metropolitan Kirill, "A Possible Structure of the World Council of Churches: Proposals for Discussion," *Ecumenical Review* 51, no. 4 (1999): 351–54.

26. Vogelaar and Witte-Rang, "The Global," 380; Robeck, "Growing Opportunities," 188.

27. Robeck, "A Pentecostal Assessment," 12.

28. Robeck, "Pentecostals and the Apostolic," 70; Robeck, "A Pentecostal Assessment," 11, 16.

29. Robeck, "A Pentecostal Assessment," 12.

30. Robeck, "An Ecumenical Journey," 60; Robeck, "Growing Opportunities," 188.

31. Robeck, "Growing Opportunities," 188.

32. Robeck, "Pentecostals and the Apostolic," 75.

33. Huub Vogelaar, "Das Global Christian Forum: Ein realistischer Weg der Ökumene?," in *Ökumene - überdacht: Reflexionen und Realitäten im Umbruch*, ed. Thomas Bremer and Maria Wernsmann, trans. Christian Föller, Quaestiones Disputatae 259 (Freiburg im Breisgau: Herder, 2014), 320.

208 *Chapter 6*

34. Robeck, "Growing Opportunities," 188.
35. Robeck and Sandidge, "Roman Catholic," 580.
36. Robeck, "A Pentecostal Assessment," 18, 34 n60.
37. Robeck, "Panel," 292; Joint Consultative Group between the World Council of Churches and Pentecostals, "Report of the Joint Consultative Group between the WCC and Pentecostals," 98.
38. Cecil M. Robeck, Jr. in discussion with the author, January 10, 2023.
39. Cecil M. Robeck, Jr. in discussion with the author, January 10, 2023.
40. Cecil M. Robeck, Jr. in discussion with the author, January 10, 2023.
41. Cecil M. Robeck, Jr., "Evangelism and Ecumenism One Hundred Years after Edinburgh, Part I," *The Lutheran Forum* 44, no. 2 (2010): 37; Robeck, "Ecumenism," 303.
42. Sarah Rowland Jones, "To Receive from Each Other, First Receive Each Other: Receptive Ecumenism and the Global Christian Forum," in *Receptive Ecumenism as Transformative Ecclesial Learning*, ed. Paul D. Murray, Gregory A. Ryan, and Paul Lakeland (Oxford: Oxford University Press, 2022), 76.
43. He presented the paper three months before the 2002 meeting at Fuller. The paper was published later as Robeck, "Pentecostals and Christian Unity," 320.
44. Martin Hoegger and Cecil M. Robeck, Jr., "A Pentecostal in the Ecumenical Boat: What Is the Place of the Church Fathers in Pentecostalism? Moral Discernment and the Issue of Homosexuality," World Council of Churches, last modified November 10, 2009, https://www.oikoumene.org/news/a-pentecostal-in-the-ecumenical-boat-what-is-the-place-of-the-church-fathers-in-pentecostalism-moral-discernment-and-the-issue-of-homosexuality.
45. Vogelaar and Witte-Rang, "The Global," 388.
46. Vogelaar and Witte-Rang, 380, 389.
47. Oxford Centre for Mission Studies, "The Global," 145.
48. Vogelaar and Witte-Rang, "The Global," 382, 392.
49. Cecil M. Robeck, Jr. in discussion with the author, January 10, 2023.
50. Huibert van Beek, "Das Christliche Weltforum und die Pfingstkirchen," *Ökumenische Rundschau* 60, no. 3 (2011): 270.
51. Sarah Rowland Jones, "The Global Christian Forum – A Narrative History," in *Revisioning Christian Unity: Journeying with Jesus Christ, the Reconciler at the Global Christian Forum, Limuru, November 2007*, ed. Huibert van Beek, Studies in Global Christianity (Eugene, OR: Wipf & Stock, 2007), 7.
52. The Asian Pentecostal Society has participated to varying degrees, but it is an academic network rather than an ecclesiastical organization. Jones, 15, 16.
53. Jones, 16; Jones, "The Global Christian Forum, A Narrative History," 231.
54. Cecil M. Robeck, Jr. in discussion with the author, January 10, 2023.
55. Larry Miller, ed., *Let Mutual Love Continue (Hebrews 13:1): Report of the Third Global Gathering, Bogotá, Colombia, 24–27 April 2018* (Bonn: Verlag für Kultur und Wissenschaft, 2021), 29.
56. Vogelaar and Witte-Rang, "The Global," 418.
57. Oxford Centre for Mission Studies, "The Global," 149.
58. Vogelaar and Witte-Rang, "The Global," 401; Jones, "The Global Christian Forum, A Narrative History," 228, 233.

59. Robeck, "Ecumenism," 300.

60. Huibert van Beek, ed., *Revisioning Christian Unity: Journeying with Jesus Christ, the Reconciler at the Global Christian Forum, Limuru, November 2007*, Studies in Global Christianity (Eugene, OR: Wipf & Stock, 2007), 43.

61. Johns, "When East," 93.

62. Global Christian Forum, "The Future of the Global Christian Forum: Guidelines from the Second Global Gathering," *Transformation* 30, no. 4 (2013): 295.

63. Vogelaar, "Das Global," 329.

64. Larry Miller, "A Journey with Jesus Christ: Moments of Revelation and Conversion," in *Sharing of Faith Stories: A Methodology for Promoting Unity*, ed. Richard Howell and Casely Baiden Essamuah, 2nd ed. (Farukh Nagar, India: Caleb Institute of Theology, 2018), 28.

65. Jones, "The Global Christian Forum, A Narrative History," 238.

66. Robra, "The World," 172.

67. Huibert van Beek and Larry Miller, eds., *Discrimination, Persecution, Martyrdom: Following Christ Together. Report of the Global Consultation, Tirana, Albania, 2–4 November 2015* (Bonn: Verlag für Kultur und Wissenschaft, 2018).

68. van Beek and Miller, 7.

69. van Beek and Miller, 39.

70. Quoted in van Beek and Miller, 70.

71. Robert Gribben and Larry Miller, "Global Christian Forum," in *The Oxford Handbook of Ecumenical Studies*, ed. Geoffrey Wainwright and Paul McPartlan (Oxford University Press, 2021), 484.

72. Gribben and Miller, 485; John Baxter-Brown, ed., *Call to Mission and Perceptions of Proselytism: A Reader for a Global Conversation* (Eugene, OR: Pickwick Publications, 2022).

73. This action is rare among CWCs. Churches typically maintain their autonomy by supporting ministries of a CWC while preserving their own comparable ministries. In this circumstance, the AG body surrendered part of its autonomy by merging its commission with that of the PWF out of the belief that it would enhance the member churches' ability to address Christian persecution.

74. "Pentecostal Commission on Religious Liberty," Pentecostal World Fellowship, accessed January 5, 2023, https://www.pwfellowship.org/pentecostal-commission-on-religious-liberty.

75. Since my research was conducted, the AG webpage was edited to align with the text of the PWF's webpage. The original AG webpage included a statement authored by Randy Hurst, special consultant to the AG World Missions executive director, from which the quote was pulled. "PCRL," World Assemblies of God Fellowship, accessed January 5, 2023, https://worldagfellowship.org/Commissions/PCRL. Access to the text can be found on the Internet Archive's Wayback Machine, https://web.archive.org/web/20221127092802/https://worldagfellowship.org/Commissions/PCRL.

76. Robra, "The World," 172.

77. Cecil M. Robeck, Jr. in discussion with the author, January 10, 2023.

78. Miller, *Let Mutual Love Continue*, 48.

79. Quoted in Miller, 49, 50.

210   *Chapter 6*

80. Leonid Kishkovsky, "Following Christ with Great Joy: Christians Called to Reconciliation," *Transformation* 27, no. 1 (2010): 58.

81. Kishkovsky, 60.

82. K.M. George, "Bearing Witness to Christ and to Each Other in the Power of the Holy Spirit: Orthodox Perspectives," *Transformation* 30, no. 4 (2013): 267, 268.

83. Cecil M. Robeck, Jr. in discussion with the author, January 10, 2023.

84. Jones, "To Receive," 83.

85. Cecil M. Robeck, Jr. in discussion with the author, January 10, 2023.

86. Several Pentecostal churches were founding members of the Consejo Latinoamericano de Iglesias (Conselho Latino-americano de Igrejas) in 1982. The WCC-sponsored gatherings with Pentecostals in the region since 1988, leading to the formation of the Comisión Evangélica Pentecostal Latinoamericana in 1990, which now appears to be defunct. Pentecostal scholars in 1998 formed the Red Latinoamericana de Estudios Pentecostales (Rede Latino-americana de Estudos Pentecostais) with the support of the WCC and in collaboration with the Comunidad de Educación Teológica Ecuménica Latinoamericana y Caribe and Ecumenical Association of Third World Theologians. It is difficult to overestimate the impact of the ecumenical movement on the promotion of Latin American Pentecostal scholarship, and these are perhaps the only regional Pentecostal academic networks in the world that have ecumenical engagement as a foundational purpose. David Mesquiati de Oliveira, "Instituições pentecostais latino-americanas para a unidade eclesial e para a produção acadêmica: O caso do FPLyC e da RELEP," in *As vozes da cooperação I: FPLyC, RELEP, FCM*, ed. Carlos Antonio Carneiro Barbosa and David Mesquiati de Oliveira, Coleção Pentecostalismo 3 (São Paulo: Editora Reflexão, 2017), 19–45.

87. Oliveira, 31, 32; Bernardo Campos, "Pentecostalismo y unidad en América Latina: 'Aspectos teológicos,'" in *Fuego que une: Pentecostalismo y unidad de la iglesia*, 2nd ed. (Lima: Foro Pentecostal Latinoamericano y Caribeño, 2020), 33–37.

88. Jones, "The Global Christian Forum – A Narrative History," 16.

89. Tanzania Christian Forum, "Tanzania: Joint Statement of the Extraordinary Meeting of the Tanzania Christian Forum," AMECEA: Association of Member Episcopal Conferences in Eastern Africa, last modified March 19, 2013, https://communications.amecea.org/index.php/2013/06/13/tanzania-joint-statement-of/; "Presidente do Fórum Cristão Angolano mostra-se apreensivo com seitas religiosas," Portal de Angola, last modified October 27, 2017, https://www.portaldeangola.com/2017/10/27/presidente-do-forum-cristao-angolano-mostra-se-apreensivo-com-seitas-religiosas/.

90. "Towards a Cuban Christian Forum," *Global Christian Forum News*, 2014, no. 2, p. 1, 2.

91. Nathan Smith in correspondence with the author, July 22, 2021.

92. Unless otherwise noted, all information for this oral history of the SCCF was received from discussions with Cecil M. Robeck, Jr. in discussion with the author on January 10, 2023, and with Alexei Smith and Gabriel Meyer in discussion with the author on January 13, 2023.

93. Dates provided are approximations based on archival materials that do not provide consistent timelines. Mention is also occasionally made to the inclusion of Nevada within some of these councils, but no discernible pattern was seen in when

and why the state is mentioned. Materials are held as part of the Southern California Ecumenical Council Collection, Archives, and Special Collections—David Allan Hubbard Library, Fuller Theological Seminary, Pasadena, California.

94. Michael Kinnamon, "Panel Presentation, National Workshop on Christian Unity" (National Workshop on Christian Unity, Christ Cathedral, Garden Grove, CA, 2022), 1.

95. The founding in 1961 also anticipated the intermittent regional Southwest Conferences on Faith and Order. "The General Secretary's Message," given by Forrest C. Weir at the 48th General Assembly of the Southern California–Southern Nevada Council of Churches, February 3, 1961, p. 6, box 2, Southern California Ecumenical Council Collection, Archives and Special Collections – David Allan Hubbard Library, Fuller Theological Seminary, Pasadena, California.

96. Kinnamon, "Panel Presentation," 2.

97. David Sang-Ehil Han, "The Global Christian Forum: A Pentecostal Story and Reflection," in *Sharing of Faith Stories: A Methodology for Promoting Unity*, ed. Richard Howell and Casely Baiden Essamuah, 2nd ed. (Farukh Nagar, India: Caleb Institute of Theology, 2018), 251.

98. Vogelaar, "Das Global," 332.

99. Huibert van Beek, "Editorial," *Transformation* 27, no. 1 (2010): 6.

100. Maffeis, *Il dialogo ecumenico*, 107.

101. Han, "The Global," 256.

102. Moreno, "La fé," 168.

103. World Council of Churches, *The New Delhi Report*, 116; World Council of Churches, "The Church, the Churches," §IV.5.

104. Avis, "New Paths," 49–51.

105. Robeck originally presented this paper in 1996 at a conference on Pentecostalism, which reveals his growing awareness of the need for practices that foster recognition, later influencing his contributions to the GCF. Robeck, "Pentecostals and Ecumenism," 346–48.

106. Avis, "New Paths," 49–51.

107. World Council of Churches, "The Church, the Churches," §IV.1, 4.

108. World Council of Churches, §IV.3–5.

109. Vogelaar, "Das Global," 331.

110. Andrzej Perzyński, "Exchange of Gifts: Experience of Global Christian Forum," *Łódzkie Studia Teologiczne* 26, no. 3 (2017): 58.

111. Moreno, "La fé," 166.

112. Miller, *Let Mutual Love Continue*, 42, 43.

113. Robeck, "Discerning the Spirit," 31; Robeck, "Lessons," 85, 86.

114. Robeck, "Taking Stock of Pentecostalism," 56; Robeck, "Pentecostals and Visible," 13.

115. Pathil, *Models*, 428.

116. Jones, "To Receive," 82.

117. Moreno, "La fé"; Huibert van Beek, "O Fórum Cristão Mundial e a busca pela unidade cristã," in *Pentecostalismos e unidade: Desafios institucionais, teológicos e sociais*, ed. David Mesquiati de Oliveira (São Paulo: Fonte Editorial, 2015), 13.

212   *Chapter 6*

118. Hawkey, *Mapping the Oikoumene*, 51.
119. Robeck, Jr., "Pentecostals and the Apostolic," 67.
120. Meyer, *Ökumenische Zielvorstellungen*, 11.
121. Quoted in Miller, *Let Mutual Love Continue*, 42.
122. Han, "Changing," 112.
123. It is unclear to which methods Han and Johns refer when critiquing "traditional" ecumenism. Both of their denominations—Church of God (Cleveland) and International Pentecostal Holiness Church—have historically contributed much to older ecumenical initiatives in the United States and abroad, including bilateral dialogues, Churches Together, church union negotiations, and councils of churches. Unless these two Pentecostal ecumenists are critiquing their own denominations, it is unknown what forms of ecumenical engagement they see Christian Forums as eclipsing. Han, 111, 113; Han, "The Global," 250.
124. Mayer, "Instrument," 547.
125. Hoegger and Robeck, "A Pentecostal."
126. Global Christian Forum, "Our Unfolding Journey," 5; Moreno, "La fé," 167.
127. Cecil M. Robeck, Jr. in discussion with the author, January 10, 2023.
128. Cecil M. Robeck, Jr. in discussion with the author, January 10, 2023.
129. Robeck, "Growing Up Pentecostal," 7; Hoegger and Robeck, "A Pentecostal."

Conclusion

The Karlsruhe Assembly of the WCC ended with a final gathering of commitment to the churches' future work. The participants prayed together before returning to their homes around the world as they looked forward to the next Assembly. Upon the departure of the thousands of delegates from Karlsruhe, the Assembly staff and stewards were left to clean up after the event. We spent the following day packing away the chairs on which WCC executives had sat while charting the next steps of the Council, washing the tables at which Christians who were not in communion with each other were able to break bread together, and gathering the translated documents used for the morning and evening common prayers. After the cleaning was finished at dusk, the stewards walked through the empty Assembly grounds that once were filled with all the tongues of Pentecost but now lay silent, and we marveled that such a historic event of the church could end so quickly. It reminded me of a statement that a fellow steward made weeks prior during our training for the event. She articulated on our behalf that, amid the labor we were soon to undertake, our only hope was that the Assembly would not be wasted effort. The labors of all those present at the gathering were an act of prayer for the unity of the church and an act of faith that God would unite it, yet the end of the gathering made us wonder whether our efforts had contributed to the church's unity and reconciliation—or, as this book has framed the question, whether the work of ecumenism truly results in ecclesiological convergence.

The purpose of this book was to determine how ecumenical methods contribute to the convergence of divided ecclesiologies. I have argued that methods employed in ecumenical work are an expression of shared ecclesiology between churches. The work of uniting churches relies on ecclesiological principles of what churches are called to be and do. Churches

214 *Conclusion*

undertake ecumenical work according to what they believe is consistent with their calling. Because ecumenical methods—by definition—are joint ventures between churches, they rely on an understanding of ecclesiology that is shared between the involved churches. Consequently, when churches further develop methods for ecumenical work, they converge in their ecclesiologies. Said differently, progress in uniting churches is seen when methods change.

IMPLICATIONS FOR THE STUDY OF ECUMENICAL METHODOLOGY

The preceding chapters identified changes for future research on ecumenical methodology, which are here summarized and synthesized. As mentioned from the outset, the present study is not in practical theology, so I do not offer new methodological principles. I have argued that the study of ecumenical praxis informs systematic theology. Ecclesiological construction benefits when scholars attend to the practices by which churches seek to relate to each other, for these practices are bonds of ecclesial unity on which ecumenists deliberate. The contribution of the study to the field of ecumenics is the notion that ecclesiological convergence occurs through ecumenical work. On the surface, this is a self-evident claim, yet theological reflection on ecclesial unity seldom attends to the process of convergence. Scholars of ecclesiology who examine doctrinal convergence within the ecumenical movement typically rely on texts to measure the extent to which churches have reached a consensus on the nature of the church. The prioritization of texts and verbal articulations of theology overshadows the equally important realms of practice and experience in Christian theologizing. Texts hold value for scholars only insofar as they point to convergence, which is change in ecclesiastical practices.

Theological inquiries on ecclesiological convergence in the ecumenical movement benefit from studying ecumenical methodology because it concerns the process by which churches seek unity. In the same way that convergence is the road to consensus, so methodology is the road to visible unity; and in the same way that convergence evidences real, albeit partial, concord as churches progress, so methodology evidences real, albeit partial, communion as churches move forward. At the same time, an enriched theological understanding of methodology prevents pragmatic approaches to ecumenical work. Ongoing methodological reflection throughout the ecumenical movement benefits from academic studies of convergence by using ecclesiology as a critical guide for the movement, fostering a creative and critical dialogue between theory and praxis.

Conclusion 215

If ecumenical praxis has ecclesiological implications, and if ecumenists seek ecclesiological convergence, then scholars should assess practices by the vision of the church that motivates the practices. My argument furthers Kuncheria Pathil's study on methodology introduced at the book's beginning. He argues that the changing conditions of the church prompt the need for changed methods, though he is less certain whether changed methods cause churches to change.[1] The study of Robeck's work confirms Pathil's tentative suggestion. A reciprocal relationship exists between ecumenical theory and praxis. Methodological reflection is a response to new situations of churches and a forward-looking enterprise that pursues more visible unity. The chapter on bilateral dialogue saw that the ecumenical method presumes an ecclesiology of renewal, for it points believers beyond their present circumstances while ensuring that they maintain their communion with previous generations through Tradition. Changes in dialogical methods influence how churches understand the tension of continuity and change within renewal. Studies of methodology can assess proposed methodological changes according to the ecclesiological principles that motivate the change.

The reconfiguration of ecumenical methodology also confirms the role of churches as primary actors in the ecumenical movement. The ecclesiological dynamic of the work of ecumenism should control inquiries in ecumenical research. Theologies of ecumenism have maintained that the unity of the church is the communion of believers with each other and with God. The divine source of the church precedes its existence and actions, and so ecumenists cannot create unity but only help make the church live out its God-given unity more visibly. This was seen in the third chapter on conciliar ecumenism. Member churches of a council precede the council itself. Churches foster conciliar relationships because these relationships occur prior to the churches' membership in a conciliar body. Consequently, ecumenists ought not assess churches by their ability to engage ecumenical methods but rather assess ecumenical methods by their ability to include churches as they presently exist. Otherwise, churches would not truly be primary actors.

The present study has focused on Robeck and Pentecostal churches, but the argument applies to all churches seen as "marginal" to ecumenism. The narrative construction of bodies and efforts as centers of the ecumenical movement betrays the notion that churches are primary actors. The ongoing identity negotiation of churches and their relations with each other brings practices of the ecumenical movement more in line with its theology of ecclesial unity. A koinonia already exists between "insiders" and "outsiders," which queries the very idea that the church could have margins; and if the church has neither centers nor margins, then neither does the ecumenical movement. To speak of any church or tradition as marginal to or outside of the ecumenical movement betrays the very self-understanding of the movement.

The ecclesiological basis of methods further problematizes discourse in the field of ecumenics. Mention was made in the preceding chapters of scholars who enshrine what they believe to be "traditional" principles of ecumenical engagement. The descriptor goes beyond pointing to a principle's commonality by attributing a normative character. However, as seen in the progression of changes and the diversity of debates on ecumenical methodology, it is difficult to absolutize any methodological principle by its age. There are Christians alive today who witnessed the birth of the first global bilateral dialogues, the genesis of councils of churches, and the widescale proliferation of ecumenical prayer services. The ecumenical movement is quite young in the grand scale of the church's history. Additionally, disagreements among practitioners of particular methods prevent much from being said about the methods in any normative sense. The academic study of ecumenical methodology first arose from the desire to understand the changes that have occurred historically and to guide ongoing changes responsibly.

The framing of practices and principles as "traditional" is less a qualitative assessment than it is a rhetorical move meant either to uphold a method as time-tested or to reject a method as antiquated. The chapter on bilateral dialogue saw this in Ellen Wondra's and Jelle Creemers's assertions that Pentecostals depart from traditional practices of representation and reception, while the chapter on Christian Forums cited David Sang-Ehil Han's and Cheryl Bridges Johns's arguments that traditional forms of ecumenical engagement are no longer viable. In both situations, a methodological principle is depicted as a standard to which churches are expected to conform, causing Pentecostal churches to stand as marginal nonconformists or innovative newcomers. The present study has sought to undermine understandings of ecumenical methodology that center some ecclesiologies and marginalize others. If methods are joint ventures, then they belong to all participants—no matter who the participants are.

Furthermore, the progressive pursuit of ecclesiological convergence requires changes in methodology. Each generation of the ecumenical movement differs from the previous one. The movement of today would be unrecognizable forty years ago, and their movement would be unrecognizable forty years prior to them. There has never been a traditional ecumenism. The relentless experimentation of methodological enterprises undermines attempts to juxtapose ecumenism as mature with Pentecostals as upstarts. Pentecostalism is at least as old as the ecumenical movement, if not older. Ecumenists infantilize Pentecostal churches by contrasting them with older church traditions, but a person could just as easily refer to the WCC as novel and to Pentecostal churches as archaic—after all, they are older than conciliar ecumenism. The ecclesiological basis of ecumenical methodology prevents any church from being seen as less capable of pursuing unity than others.

If no church tradition can rightly be positioned as marginal to the ecumenical movement, then there cannot be confessional ecumenical methods. This claim confirms the hesitations of Pathil and Nikos Nissiotis regarding attention to confessional differences in ecumenical work.[2] It does not suggest that confessional differences vanish when churches participate in ecumenical ventures. Divisions between churches often arise because the churches have competing understandings of the practices and structures meant to preserve unity. As Harding Meyer notes, however, churches bring their understandings of unity into the ecumenical movement for them to converge.[3] Likewise, dissatisfaction over ecumenical methods often arises because it is believed that the principles operative in the method are too closely dependent on the ecclesiology of a church tradition. Recurrent complaints that the systems of the WCC are "too Protestant" or "too Orthodox" point to the need for continuing reflection on ecclesiastical practices, while the WCC's foundation of national churches highlights yet more incongruities with the Catholic Church and independent churches. Authors similarly have spoken of the Pentecostal or Evangelical principles of Christian Forums even though these two communities are, at most, half of the participants at gatherings. If Evangelicals and Orthodox can both affirm the value of a model of ecumenical engagement, what does that reveal about their shared understandings of the church? The association between ecumenical practices and confessions points to the ongoing need to reconcile theologies of ecclesial unity.

Future studies of ecumenical methodology can use ecclesiology as a critical guide in assessing particular practices. The present book has argued that methods have ecclesiological implications because methodology has an ecclesiological basis. As such, reflection on the nature of the church can guide ecumenical praxis. This is especially valuable in studying the synergism between methods. Different approaches to ecumenical work result from different understandings of the church, and so any integrative vision of ecumenical methodology must account for the multifaceted nature of ecclesiology. The historical development of the ecumenical movement has in part been for the sake of resolving conflict between different portions of the movement.[4] Robeck's career testifies to the tensions that occur and the possibility of integration. The development of Christian Forums has conflicted with conciliar efforts, while movements of spiritual ecumenism risk overshadowing the importance of critical academic reflection. Even when one cannot speak of consensus as always having been achieved through Robeck's career, one still witnesses convergence through the strengthening of relations between churches. If methods spur ecclesiological convergence, then the multiplicity of existent methods testifies to the multifaceted nature

218   *Conclusion*

of ecclesiology. The unity of the ecumenical movement hinges upon the search for a coherent vision of the church. Systematic theology here plays an indispensable role in ecumenical scholarship by attending to coherency and consistency in Christian thought across communities. The study of ecclesiology seeks constructive and comprehensive accounts of the church for the sake of informing praxis in the diverse aspects of the church's life. Ongoing research on ecclesiology in the ecumenical movement can contribute to the work of uniting churches.

IMPLICATIONS FOR THE DOCTRINE OF ECCLESIOLOGY

As seen in the study on Robeck, research on ecumenical praxis holds value for theological construction in the search for ecclesiological convergence. Gillian Evans explains the importance of theological language in the project of ecumenism. The refinement of language used to speak of ecclesiology contributes to the construction of community insofar as community relies on communication and shared meaning.[5] She advocates for theology of ecumenism as a communal enterprise to ensure that it aids the work of ecumenism.[6] This is the project of dialogue, where divided churches learn to speak of the faith together, yet I have shown that dialogue is not the sole context in which churches refine their understandings of ecclesiology. Ecumenical methods contribute to the field of ecumenical theology because they are joint ventures that fashion and express community. Attention to methods also fulfills Paul Avis's four criteria for ecumenical theology.[7] Ecclesiology that attends to ecumenical methodology is *coherent* because it studies ecclesiological principles at the intersection of different communities, contexts, and practices; it is *credible* because it examines current practices and lived experiences of churches rather than mere ideas about the church; it is *critical* because it tests divergent ecclesiological claims against each other as they are negotiated in shared spaces; and it is *constructive* because it pursues the progression of methodological changes as ecumenists relentlessly inquire about next steps toward the future.

Ecumenics is a crucible for the field of ecclesiology. The ecumenical movement causes churches to revisit their self-understandings as they encounter other churches. The search for change implies the desirability of change toward that which churches believe they are called to be and do. Renewal, as an ecclesiological concept, is the act of churches changing. If ecclesiological convergence is a process of renewal within the ecumenical movement, then ecumenical praxis has ecclesiological significance. It was repeatedly affirmed in the preceding chapters that part of the empirical

Conclusion 219

reality of the church's unity is the communal practices that preserve communion. Even where there is not yet full communion, ecumenical methods are derived from the shared understandings of unity that presently exist between churches. The methods that ecumenists employ, if they foster communion, are part of what constitutes the church's fellowship and so are defining markers of ecclesiality. There is no church without practices that hold together a diverse fellowship. Robeck's career brought him into contact with diverse practices of ecumenism that are renegotiating what forms ecclesiastical relations should take today.

The diverse nature of ecumenical methodology is meant to support the diverse nature of the church. As explained in the first chapter, charisms are given to the church to order its life and sanctify its members. Even though gifts of grace are God-given, God continually leads the church to properly order that which it has received. The process of Christian communities improving the methods by which they relate to each other, because it is done under the guidance of the Spirit, is an act of the church ordering its gifts of grace to encourage a common life, for charisms ensure the vitality of the church's catholicity as the singular Body of Christ. The chapter on spiritual ecumenism saw this in its discussion of discernment in the proper exercise of spiritual gifts. Disordered charisms impair the life of faith in the Christian church, and deliberations on how to cultivate spirituality are ecclesiological inquiries on the proper function of discernment. Many of the methodological changes that occur in the ecumenical movement revolve around questions of discernment for the sake of preserving the church's catholicity and unity, whether in conciliar bodies, CWCs, or dialogue commissions. The practices of ecumenism concern the church's charismatic self-understanding in how the church is meant to receive the grace it has been given in the world today, and so these practices inform ecumenists' understanding of the unity they seek.

To suggest that ecumenical praxis informs the doctrine of ecclesiology is to argue that Christian communities construct their beliefs according to their experiences and deliberations thereon. This book selected Robeck due to his vantage point as a historian and Pentecostal scholar, both roles which prize the lived experiences of Christian communities. Ecclesiological studies of ecumenical methodology likewise are exercises in theology rooted in experience. History serves as the platform for divine economy wherein people receive revelation through works of grace. The manifest presence of God in the church is the starting point for any theological understanding of the Christian community, causing the church's experience of divine economy to be a source for its own self-understanding. The ecumenical movement, as one such work of grace, informs ecclesiology. The chapter on conciliar ecumenism saw this when churches recognized the conciliar nature of the church

220   *Conclusion*

because they experienced it. Later doctrinal consensus explicates experiences of common faith.[8]

Attention to experience and history causes theological studies on methodology to be more interested in the cultural, political, and socioeconomic conditions of the ecumenical movement than are other works on ecclesial unity. This was seen in Robeck's attention to social forces that shape the Christian life in the chapter on reconciling memories. The experience of believers in history is part of the church's historicity, and the existence of the church as a product of divine economy makes the church part of salvation history. As seen in the second chapter, divided churches reconcile their memories so that their self-narratives reflect a common understanding of the Christian community's reception of divine grace in history.

In light of the church's historicity, perhaps the greatest shift that occurs in the field of ecumenical ecclesiology is that for the related notions of apostolicity and Tradition. The two are experiences and theological concepts whose font is in the church's past. By gathering around the apostolic witness, believers gather around the collective memory of Christ, resulting in the church of today belonging to the same community that has persisted since Pentecost. However, if the reconciliation of divided churches is part of salvation history, then Tradition is more than the focal point for ecclesiological convergence; it must also inform the work of churches toward unity. Such is why Robeck prizes the Charismatic movement for its understanding of apostolicity. The movement recovers the spirituality of the early church for contemporary ecumenical work, wherein charisms order and empower the church. As discussed previously, *Tradition and Traditions* speaks of the Spirit's creative act in the transmission of the apostolic deposit, and the text claims that renewal is dependent on an adherence to Tradition.[9] If ecclesiological convergence constitutes ecclesial renewal, then the work of ecumenism is a form of the Spirit's creative work in the transmission of the faith.[10] Apostolicity is a mark of the church's unity because the apostolic faith offers the means by which churches overcome division. Similarly, the church's faithfulness to Tradition through time entails engaging these diverse means toward unity, and the continual change in these means is part of the church's search for what it means to be apostolic today. The historical existence of the church is of concern for scholars of ecclesiology.

Theological reflection on ecumenical methods historicizes ecclesiology by attending to the church's most material existence as the people of God. Christian doctrine on the church arises from the communion between believers, for the church is more than its members, but it never exists apart from them. The chapter on Christian Forums saw this in Robeck's advocacy for interpersonal encounter as a transformative source of ecclesiological reflection. Also, the WCC consultation on the Charismatic movement described the church as a

Conclusion 221

"social experience of God."[11] The existence of the Christian church as the people of God has ecumenical import. Churches are primary actors in the ecumenical movement, yet the movement faces the perennial problem of ecclesiastical recognition. For example, as noted previously, a majority of Christians globally belong to churches that do not recognize the ecclesiality of Pentecostal communities. Pentecostals are not the only Christians who face this challenge, but their presence in the ecumenical movement epitomizes the problem. The reinterpretation of ecclesiology that occurs through ecumenical engagement occurs as individual Christians encounter each other, including when their churches do not speak of each other as churches. Ecclesiological convergence culminates when churches are in full communion, and it begins when divided believers act together. The actions of these believers together—regardless of their present degree of communion—are a criterion by which ecclesiological claims gain credibility. The contribution of ecumenical methodology to the doctrine on the church is the notion that ecclesial communion exists visibly in history even while it is still not yet perfect.

FUTURE INQUIRY

The goal of ecumenists is to work themselves out of a job. Methodological research such as this book one day will no longer be needed when the church's unity is fully visible. Until then, the work of ecumenism is a constant discernment process. The present study has uncovered questions that will benefit future reflection on ecumenical methodology and ecclesiology.

An acknowledged limitation of the present study in systematic theology is its restriction to ecclesiology. Though ecclesiology may be the elemental theological concern of ecumenism, it is not the only theological concern. Doctrinal questions of Christology, pneumatology, anthropology, and other fields have divided churches in ways that are not directly related to methodology as is ecclesiology. The convergence that occurs through ecumenical work can pave the way for convergence in these other fields, yet the multifaceted nature of ecumenism includes space for sustained dialogue to resolve such disagreements. Churches acting together is never a replacement for consensus as a criterion of ecclesial communion. Ecumenics would benefit from further research on the relation of non-ecclesiological subjects to ecumenical methods.

Additionally, the biographical delineation of the study has hindered engagement with numerous methods with which Robeck has had no experience. Ecumenical models such as Churches Together, ecclesial covenants, comity arrangements, and church union negotiations are all methods that encourage ecclesiological convergence. Future research can examine these methods to

222   *Conclusion*

assess the nature of the convergence that is sought in them. Though Robeck was the best choice to answer this study's driving question, he is far from the only figure—Pentecostal or otherwise—who can give insight into theologies of ecumenism. The selection of other influential ecumenists will broaden the field's study of the movement's development.

The confessional lens of the book foregrounded methodological questions and changes in the ecumenical movement, but the discussion ought not end with Pentecostalism. Future studies would do well to study the movement from the vantage point of other ecclesial traditions. As repeated throughout the book, there is no such thing as an ecumenical method that is not shared, but the study of particular churches informs the larger movement by testing claims of theory and praxis within the experience of concrete, historical communities. The arguments in this study cannot be true if they are valid for Pentecostal churches alone. The future testing of methodological claims through the engagement of other churches accords with the purpose of the present book.

Finally, the question remains how ecumenical goals are clarified through the refinement of methods. Ecumenists name goals according to the systems, practices, and values that constitute a visibly united church. These goals then serve to orient the derivation of methods. However, if a reciprocal relationship exists between theory and praxis such that ecclesiological convergence occurs through the work of ecumenism, then the goals of the work ought also to be clarified. Future studies can examine this process of refinement as ecumenists come to agree on the desired outcomes of their work as they undertake it.

The ecumenical movement has sought the visible unity of the church. Ecumenists undertake their work with little consensus on what unity actually looks like. Divided Christian communities interface as their competing visions of ecclesial unity clash, just as different ecumenical bodies and initiatives negotiate their places within a larger movement predicated on values of diversity and inclusion. A coherent and comprehensive vision of the ecumenical movement is bound up with a common vision of the church—meaning that neither yet exists. The lack of clarity on goals, nonetheless, has not prevented the growth of the movement. Ecumenists in each generation and location discern the call of the gospel and what it asks of their churches. The pursuit of fidelity to the gospel without a clear understanding of what the future entails rightly qualifies the work of ecumenism as a Spirit-led process. Christ's prayer to the Father for the unity of believers was answered at Pentecost. The source of the church's communion in God means that communion exists prior to any ecumenical efforts, and as ecumenists undertake their work, they discern together the work of God in the church and how Christians ought to participate in it. The derivation of ecumenical methodology is part

Conclusion 223

of the search for ecclesiological convergence because it is these practices that make unity visible.

NOTES

1. Pathil, *Models*, 398.
2. Nissiotis, "Types," 54; Pathil, *Models*, 292.
3. Meyer, *Ökumenische Zielvorstellungen*, 17.
4. Meyer, 11.
5. Evans, *Method*, 113.
6. Evans, 19, 20.
7. Avis, "New Paths," 42, 43.
8. Pathil, *Models*, 428.
9. *Tradition and Traditions*, 27, 57.
10. The claim coincides with the assertion of the Holy and Great Council that Orthodox participation in the ecumenical movement "represents a consistent expression of the apostolic faith and tradition in a new historical circumstances [*sic*]." Holy and Great Council, "Relations," §4.
11. "Towards a Church Renewed," §2.2.

Bibliography

PRIMARY LITERATURE

Hoegger, Martin, and Cecil M. Robeck, Jr. "A Pentecostal in the Ecumenical Boat: What Is the Place of the Church Fathers in Pentecostalism? Moral Discernment and the Issue of Homosexuality." World Council of Churches. Last modified November 10, 2009. https://www.oikoumene.org/news/a-pentecostal-in-the-ecumenical-boat-what-is-the-place-of-the-church-fathers-in-pentecostalism-moral-discernment-and-the-issue-of-homosexuality.

Hunter, Harold D., and Cecil M. Robeck, Jr., eds. "Introduction." In *The Azusa Street Revival and Its Legacy*, 13–26. Cleveland, TN: Pathway Press, 2006.

Robeck, Jr., Cecil M. "A Pentecostal Assessment of 'Towards a Common Understanding and Vision' of the WCC." *Midstream: The Ecumenical Movement Today* 37, no. 1 (1998): 1–36.

———. "A Pentecostal Looks at the World Council of Churches." *The Ecumenical Review* 47, no. 1 (1995): 60–69.

———. "A Pentecostal Perspective on Leadership." In *Traditions in Leadership: How Faith Traditions Shape the Way We Lead*, edited by Richard J. Mouw and Eric O. Jacobsen, 139–60. Pasadena, CA: De Pree Leadership Center, 2006.

———. "A Pentecostal Perspective on Prophetic Gifts." *Asian Journal of Pentecostal Studies* 23, no. 1 (2020): 109–37.

———. "A Pentecostal Reflects on Canberra." In *Beyond Canberra: Evangelical Responses to Contemporary Ecumenical Issues*, edited by Bruce J. Nicholls and Bong Rin Ro, 108–20. Oxford: Regnum Books, 1993.

———. "African Pentecostal Contributions to Christian Unity." In *African Pentecostal Missions Maturing: Essays in Honor of Apostle Opoku Onyinah*, edited by Elorm Donkor and Clifton R. Clarke, 64–84. Eugene, OR: Wipf & Stock, 2018.

———. "An Ecumenical Journey I Never Imagined." In *Sharing of Faith Stories: A Methodology for Promoting Unity*, edited by Richard Howell and Casely Baiden Essamuah, 2nd ed., 51–64. Farukh Nagar, India: Caleb Institute of Theology, 2018.

226 Bibliography

———. "An Emerging Magisterium? The Case of the Assemblies of God." *Pneuma: The Journal of the Society for Pentecostal Studies* 25, no. 2 (2003): 164–215.

———. "An Introduction to Pentecostal Identity: Ecclesiology, Pneumatology, and Spirituality." In *Towards a Global Vision of the Church: Explorations on Global Christianity and Ecclesiology, Volume 2*, edited by Cecil M. Robeck, Jr., Sotiris Boukis, and Ani Ghazaryan Drissi, 297–310. Faith and Order Paper 239. Geneva: World Council of Churches, 2023.

———. "Authoritative Teaching in the Church." In *Towards a Global Vision of the Church: Explorations on Global Christianity and Ecclesiology, Volume 2*, edited by Cecil M. Robeck, Jr., Sotiris Boukis, and Ani Ghazaryan Drissi, 203–18. Faith and Order Paper 239. Geneva: World Council of Churches, 2023.

———. "Azusa Street: 100 Years Later." *Enrichment* 11, no. 2 (2006): 26–42.

———. "Azusa Street Revival." In *The New International Dictionary of Pentecostal and Charismatic Movements*, edited by Stanley M. Burgess and Eduard M. van der Maas, 2nd ed., 344–50. Grand Rapids, MI: Zondervan, 2003.

———. "Can We Imagine an Ecumenical Future Together? A Pentecostal Perspective." *Gregorianum* 100 (2019): 49–69.

———. "Canon, *Regulae Fidei*, and Continuing Revelation in the Early Church." In *Church, Word, and Spirit: Historical and Theological Essays in Honor of Geoffrey W. Bromiley*, edited by James E. Bradley and Richard A. Muller, 65–91. Grand Rapids, MI: Eerdmans, 1987.

———. "Catholic-Pentecostal Dialogue: An Update on the Fifth Round of Discussions." *Boletín Eclesiástico de Filipinas* 82, no. 854 (2006): 473–508.

———. "Charism(ata)." In *Dictionary of the Ecumenical Movement*, edited by Nicholas Lossky, José Míguez Bonino, John S. Pobee, Tom F. Stransky, Geoffrey Wainwright, and Pauline Webb, 2nd ed., 162–64. Geneva: WCC Publications, 2002.

———. "Charismatic Movements." In *Global Dictionary of Theology*, edited by William A. Dyrness and Veli-Matti Kärkkäinen, 145–54. Downers Grove, IL: InterVarsity Press, 2008.

———. "Christian Unity and Pentecostal Mission: A Contradiction?" In *Pentecostal Mission and Global Christianity*, edited by Wonsuk Ma, Veli-Matti Kärkkäinen, and J. Kwabena Asamoah-Gyadu, 182–206. Regnum Edinburgh Centenary Series 20. Oxford: Regnum Books International, 2014.

———. "Christians and Persecution: Making an Appropriate Response." In *The Suffering Body: Responding to the Persecution of Christians*, edited by Harold D. Hunter and Cecil M. Robeck, Jr., 62–81. Bletchley, UK: Paternoster, 2006.

———. "David du Plessis and the Challenge of Dialogue." *Pneuma: The Journal of the Society for Pentecostal Studies* 9, no. 1 (1987): 1–4.

———. "Developing and Maintaining a Pentecostal Ethos." *Quadrum: Journal of the Foursquare Scholars' Fellowship* 3, no. 1 (2020): 19–29.

———. "Dialogul dintre romano–catolici și penticostali: Câteva ipoteze penticostale." *Plērōma* 4, no. 1 (2002): 5–36.

———. "Discerning the Spirit in the Life of the Church." In *The Church in the Movement of the Spirit*, edited by William Barr and Rena Yocom, 29–49. Grand Rapids, MI: Eerdmans, 1994.

Bibliography 227

————. "Do Emerging Churches Have an Ecumenical Contribution to Make?" In *Towards a Global Vision of the Church: Explorations on Global Christianity and Ecclesiology, Volume 2*, edited by Cecil M. Robeck, Jr., Sotiris Boukis, and Ani Ghazaryan Drissi, 151–69. Faith and Order Paper 239. Geneva: World Council of Churches, 2023.

————. "Do 'Good Fences Make Good Neighbors'? Evangelization, Proselytism, and Common Witness." *Asian Journal of Pentecostal Studies* 2, no. 1 (1999): 87–103.

————. "'Do Not Quench the Spirit': Some Thoughts on the International Roman Catholic – Pentecostal Dialogue." In *Pentecostalism, Catholicism, and the Spirit in the World*, edited by Stan Chu Ilo, 131–48. Eugene, OR: Cascade Books, 2019.

————. "Doing Theology in Isolation." *Pneuma: The Journal of the Society for Pentecostal Studies* 12, no. 1 (1990): 1–3.

————. "Early Pentecostal Visions in the United States of Christian Unity, Retrenchment, and Evangelical Influences." In *Pentecostal Theology and Ecumenical Theology: Interpretation and Intersections*, edited by Peter D. Hocken, Tony L. Richie, and Christopher A. Stephenson, 3–23. Leiden: Brill, 2019.

————. "Ecumenism." In *Studying Global Pentecostalism: Theories and Methods*, edited by Allan Anderson, Michael Bergunder, André Droogers, and Cornelis van der Laan, 286–307. Berkeley: University of California Press, 2010.

————. "Evangelicals and Catholics Together." *One in Christ* 33, no. 2 (1997): 138–60.

————. "Evangelism and Ecumenism One Hundred Years after Edinburgh, Part I." *The Lutheran Forum* 44, no. 2 (2010): 33–39.

————. "Evangelization or Proselytism of Hispanics? A Pentecostal Perspective." *Journal of Hispanic/Latino Theology* 4, no. 4 (1997): 42–64.

————. "Facing Our Past." *Ministries Today* 13, no. 1 (1995): 40.

————. "Fifty Years of Catholic-Pentecostal Dialogue, 1972–2022: A Pentecostal Assessment." *Pneuma: The Journal of the Society for Pentecostal Studies* 44, no. 2 (2022): 220–50.

————. "First International Reformed-Pentecostal Dialogue." *Journal of Ecumenical Studies* 33, no. 3 (1996): 442.

————. "Foreword." In *Grassroots Ecumenism: The Way of Local Christian Reunion*, by Karen Petersen Finch. Hyde Park, NY: New City Press, 2022.

————. "Fuller's Ecumenical Vision." *Theology, News & Notes* 57, no. 2 (2010): 19–22, 28.

————. "Gifts (Charisms) of the Spirit." In *Towards a Global Vision of the Church: Explorations on Global Christianity and Ecclesiology, Volume 2*, edited by Cecil M. Robeck, Jr., Sotiris Boukis, and Ani Ghazaryan Drissi, 261–77. Faith and Order Paper 239. Geneva: World Council of Churches, 2023.

————. "Growing Opportunities for Pentecostal Ecumenical Engagement." *Pentecostal Education* 7, no. 2 (2022): 173–90.

————. "Growing Up Pentecostal." *Theology, News & Notes* 35, no. 1 (1988): 4–7, 26.

————. "Introducing Pentecostals to Lutherans." In *Lutherans and Pentecostals in Dialogue*, 31–57. Strasbourg, France: Institute for Ecumenical Research, 2010.

228 *Bibliography*

———. "Irenaeus and 'Prophetic Gifts.'" In *Essays on Apostolic Themes: Studies in Honor of Howard M. Ervin*, 104–14. Peabody, MA: Hendrickson Publishers, 1985.

———. "John Paul II: A Personal Account of His Impact and Legacy." *Pneuma: The Journal of the Society for Pentecostal Studies* 27, no. 1 (2005): 3–34.

———. "Le dialogue entre les pentecôtistes classiques et l'Église catholique." *Istina* 59 (2014): 151–60.

———. "Les dons prophétiques : Une perspective pentecôte." In *Pentecôtisme et prophétie (1)*, edited by Jean-Claude Boutinon and Romuald Hanss, 3–35. Collection d'études pentecôtistes 5. Léognan, France: SFE, 2019.

———. "Les pentecôtismes, entre passé et présent, et l'Église dans 300 ans." Translated by P.M. Desjardins. *Istina* 59 (2014): 139–49.

———. "Lessons from the International Roman Catholic–Pentecostal Dialogue." In *Pentecostalism and Christian Unity: Ecumenical Documents and Critical Assessments*, edited by Wolfgang Vondey, 82–98. Eugene, OR: Pickwick Publications, 2010.

———. "Letting the Riffraff In." In *From the Margins: A Celebration of the Theological Work of Donald W. Dayton*, edited by Christian T. Collins Winn, 329–33. Princeton Theological Monograph Series. Eugene, OR: Wipf & Stock, 2007.

———. "Martin Luther King, Jr. Day, 2010." *Ecumenical Trends* 39, no. 1 (2010): 7–9, 14.

———. "Montanism: A Problematic Spirit Movement." *Paraclete* 15, no. 3 (1981): 24–29.

———. "My Call to Ecumenism." In *Global Christian Forum: Transforming Ecumenism*, edited by Richard Howell, 66–72. New Delhi: Evangelical Fellowship of India, 2007.

———. "On Becoming a Christian: An Important Theme in the International Roman Catholic – Pentecostal Dialogue." *PentecoStudies: Online Journal for the Interdisciplinary Study of Pentecostalism and Charismatic Movements* 8, no. 2 (2008): 1–23.

———. "Panel Presentation on *The Church: Towards a Common Vision*." *Journal of Ecumenical Studies* 50, no. 2 (2015): 288–94.

———. "Pentecostal Churches." In *A Handbook of Churches and Councils: Profiles of Ecumenical Relationships*, edited by Huibert van Beek, 63–65. Geneva: World Council of Churches, 2006.

———. "Pentecostal Ecclesiology." In *T & T Clark Companion to Ecclesiology*, edited by Kimlyn J. Bender and D. Stephen Long, 241–58. London: Bloomsbury, 2020.

———. "Pentecostal Ecumenism: Overcoming the Challenges – Reaping the Benefits (Part I)." *Journal of the European Pentecostal Theological Association* 34, no. 2 (2014): 113–32.

———. "Pentecostal Ecumenism: Overcoming the Challenges – Reaping the Benefits (Part II)." *Journal of the European Pentecostal Theological Association* 35, no. 1 (2015): 5–17.

———. "Pentecostal Origins in Global Perspective." In *All Together in One Place: Theological Papers from the Brighton Conference on World Evangelization*, edited by Harold D. Hunter and Peter D. Hocken, 166–80. Sheffield, UK: Sheffield Academic, 1993.

Bibliography

———. "Pentecostal World Conference." In *The New International Dictionary of Pentecostal and Charismatic Movements*, edited by Stanley M. Burgess and Eduard M. van der Maas, 2nd ed., 971–74. Grand Rapids, MI: Zondervan, 2003.

———. "Pentecostal/Charismatic Churches and Ecumenism: An Interview with Cecil M. Robeck, Jr." *The Pneuma Review: Journal of Ministry Resources and Theology for Pentecostal and Charismatic Ministries and Leaders* 6, no. 1 (2003): 22–35.

———. "Pentecostalism and Ecumenical Dialogue: A Potential Agenda." *Ecumenical Trends* 16, no. 11 (1987): 185–88.

———. "Pentecostalism and Mission: From Azusa Street to the Ends of the Earth." *Missiology: An International Review* 35, no. 1 (2007): 75–92.

———. "Pentecostals and Charismatics in America." In *The Oxford History of Protestant Dissenting Traditions: The Twentieth Century. Traditions in a Global Context*, edited by Jehu J. Hanciles, 4:241–60. Oxford: Oxford University Press, 2019.

———. "Pentecostals and Christian Unity: Facing the Challenge." *Pneuma: The Journal of the Society for Pentecostal Studies* 26, no. 2 (2004): 307–38.

———. "Pentecostals and Ecumenism in a Pluralistic World." In *The Globalization of Pentecostalism: A Religion Made to Travel*, edited by Murray W. Dempster, Byron D. Klaus, and Douglas Petersen, 338–62. Oxford: Regnum Press, 1999.

———. "Pentecostals and the Apostolic Faith: Implications for Ecumenism." In *Confessing the Apostolic Faith: Pentecostal Churches and the Ecumenical Movement*, edited by National Council of the Churches of Christ in the USA, 61–84. Pasadena, CA: Society for Pentecostal Studies, 1987.

———. "Pentecostals and Visible Church Unity." *One World* 192 (1994): 11–14.

———. *Prophecy in Carthage: Perpetua, Tertullian, and Cyprian*. Cleveland, OH: Pilgrim Press, 1992.

———. "Prophecy in *The Shepherd of Hermas*." *Paraclete* 18, no. 2 (1984): 12–17.

———. "Prophecy, Prophesying." In *Dictionary of Paul and His Letters*, edited by Gerald F. Hawthorne and Ralph P. Martin, 755–62. Downers Grove, IL: InterVarsity Press, 1993.

———. "Prophetic Authority in the Charismatic Setting: The Need to Test." *Theological Renewal* 24 (1983): 4–10.

———. "Racial Reconciliation at Memphis: Some Personal Reflections." *Pneuma: The Journal of the Society for Pentecostal Studies* 18, no. 1 (1996): 135–40.

———. "Roman Catholic – Pentecostal Dialogue: Challenges and Lessons for Living Together." In *Pentecostal Power: Expressions, Impact, and Faith of Latin American Pentecostalism*, edited by Calvin Smith, 249–76. Global Pentecostal and Charismatic Studies 6. Leiden: Brill, 2010.

———. "Roman Catholic-Pentecostal Dialogue: Some Pentecostal Assumptions." *Journal of the European Pentecostal Theological Association* 21, no. 1 (2001): 3–25.

———. "Some Pentecostal Reflections on Current Catholic – Pentecostal Relations: What Are We Learning?" In *Towards Unity: Ecumenical Dialogue 500 Years after the Reformation. Essays in Honor of Monsignor John A. Radano*, edited by Donald Bolen, Nicholas Jesson, and Donna Geernhaert, 226–52. Mahwah, NJ: Paulist Press, 2017.

230   *Bibliography*

————. "Some Reflections from a Pentecostal/Evangelical Perspective." In *Faith and Order in Moshi: The 1996 Commission Meeting*, by World Council of Churches Commission on Faith and Order, edited by Alan Falconer, 135–40. Faith and Order Paper 177. Geneva: World Council of Churches, 1998.

————. "Southern Religion with a Latin Accent." *Pneuma: The Journal of the Society for Pentecostal Studies* 13, no. 1 (1991): 101–106.

————. "Specks and Logs, Catholics and Pentecostals." *Pneuma: The Journal of the Society for Pentecostal Studies* 12, no. 2 (1990): 77–83.

————. "Taking Stock." *One World* 210 (1995): 15–17.

————. "Taking Stock of Pentecostalism: The Personal Reflections of a Retiring Editor." *Pneuma: The Journal of the Society for Pentecostal Studies* 15, no. 1 (1993): 35–60.

————. "The Achievements of the Pentecostal - Catholic International Dialogue." In *Celebrating a Century of Ecumenism: Exploring the Achievements of International Dialogue*, edited by John A. Radano, 163–94. Grand Rapids, MI: Eerdmans, 2012.

————. "The Apostolic Faith Study and the Holy Spirit." In *Ecumenical Directions in the U.S. Today: Churches on a Theological Journey*, edited by Antonios Kireopoulos and Juliana Mecera, 77–102. Faith and Order Commission Theological Series. Mahwah, NJ: Paulist Press, 2012.

————. "The Authority of the Holy Spirit in Pentecostal Churches: A Response to David A. Adesanya." In *Sources of Authority, Volume 2: Contemporary Church*, by World Council of Churches Commission on Faith and Order, edited by Tamara Grdzelidze, 39–51. Faith and Order Paper 218. Geneva: World Council of Churches, 2014.

————. *The Azusa Street Mission and Revival: The Birth of the Global Pentecostal Movement*. Nashville, TN: Thomas Nelson, 2006.

————. "The Azusa Street Mission and the Historic Black Churches: Two Worlds in Conflict in Los Angeles' African American Community." In *Afro-Pentecostalism: Black Pentecostal and Charismatic Christianity in History and Culture*, edited by Amos Yong and Estrelda Y. Alexander, 21–41. New York: New York University Press, 2011.

————. "The Challenge Pentecostalism Poses to the Quest for Ecclesial Unity." In *Kirche en ökumenischer Perspektive*, edited by Peter Walter, Klaus Krämer, and George Augustin, 306–20. Freiburg, Germany: Herder, 2003.

————. "The Charismatic Renewal of the Church." *Theology, News & Notes* 30, no. 1 (1983): 2, 33–34.

————. "The Church." In *Pentecostals in the 21st Century: Identity, Beliefs, Praxis*, edited by Corneliu Constantineanu and Christopher J. Scobie, 141–57. Eugene, OR: Cascade Books, 2018.

————. "The Church: A Unique Movement of the Spirit." *Paraclete* 16, no. 4 (1982): 1–4.

————. "'The Color Line Was Washed Away in the Blood': A Pentecostal Dream for Racial Harmony." Costa Mesa, CA: Christian Education Press, 1995.

————. "The Earliest Pentecostal Missions of Los Angeles." *Assemblies of God Heritage* 3, no. 3 (1983): 3–4, 12.

Bibliography 231

————. "The Gift of Prophecy in Acts and Paul, Part II." *Studia Biblica et Theo-logica* 5, no. 2 (1975): 37–54.

————. "The Holy Spirit and the New Testament Vision of Koinonia." Presented at the second session of the third phase of the international Catholic–Pentecostal dialogue, Sierra Madre, CA, 1986.

————. "The Holy Spirit and the Unity of the Church: The Challenge of Pentecostal, Charismatic, and Independent Movements." In *The Holy Spirit, the Church and Christian Unity: Proceedings of the Consultation Held at the Monastery of Bose, Italy (14-20 October 2002)*, edited by D. Donnelly, A. Denaux, and J. Famerée, 353–81. Bibliotheca Ephemeridum Theologicarum Lovaniensium 181. Leuven, Belgium: Leuven University Press, 2005.

————. "The Leadership Legacy of William J. Seymour." In *We've Come This Far: Reflections on the Pentecostal Tradition and Racial Reconciliation*, edited by Byron D. Klaus, 39–65, 175–82. The Pentecostal Ministry Series 2. Springfield, MO: Assemblies of God Theological Seminary, 2007.

————. "The New Ecumenism." In *The Local Church in a Global Era: Reflections for a New Century*, edited by Max Stackhouse, Tim Dearborn, and Scott Paeth, 168–77. Grand Rapids, MI: Eerdmans, 2000.

————. "The Origins of Modern Pentecostalism: Some Historiographical Issues." In *The Cambridge Companion to Pentecostalism*, edited by Cecil M. Robeck, Jr. and Amos Yong, 13–30. Cambridge: Cambridge University Press, 2014.

————. "The Past: Historical Roots of Racial Unity and Division in American Pentecostalism." *Cyberjournal for Pentecostal-Charismatic Research* 14 (2004). www.pctii.org/cyberj/cyberj14/robeck.html.

————. "The Prophet in the *Didache*." *Paraclete* 18, no. 1 (1984): 16–19.

————. "*The Quiet Game*, Racism, and the Azusa Street Revival." In *The Pastor & the Kingdom: Essays Honoring Jack W. Hayford*, edited by Jon Huntzinger and S. David Moore, 63–91. Southlake, TX: Gateway Academic, 2017.

————. "Truth and Community: Insights from the Past and the Present." *Theology, News & Notes* 50, no. 1 (2003): 12–15, 19.

————. "Uncovering the Forgotten Story of the Azusa Street Mission." *Assemblies of God Heritage* 25, no. 4 (2006): 12–15.

————. "What Catholics Should Know about Pentecostals." *The Catholic World* 238, no. 1,428 (1995): 276–81.

————. "When Being a 'Martyr' Is Not Enough: Catholics and Pentecostals." *Pneuma: The Journal of the Society for Pentecostal Studies* 21, no. 1 (1999): 3–10.

————. "When I Grow Up, I Wanna Be...." *Fuller Focus* 17, no. 3 (2009): 30–31.

————. "William J. Seymour: An Early Model of Pentecostal Leadership." *Enrichment* 1, no. 2 (2006): 50–51.

————. "Word, Spirit, and Discernment." In *Churches and Moral Discernment, Volume 1: Learning from Traditions*, by World Council of Churches Commission on Faith and Order, edited by Myriam Wijlens and Vladimir Shmaliy, 137–45. Faith and Order Paper 228. Geneva: World Council of Churches, 2021.

————. "Worship in the Evangelical Tradition." *Ecumenical Trends* 30, no. 6 (2001): 93–96.

232   *Bibliography*

———. "Written Prophecies: A Question of Authority." *Pneuma: The Journal of the Society for Pentecostal Studies* 2, no. 2 (1980): 26–45.

———. "Yoido Full Gospel Church and Ecumenism." In *The Holy Spirit, Spirituality, and Leadership: Essays in Honor of Young-Hoon Lee*, edited by Wonsuk Ma and Robert Menzies. Oxford: Regnum Books International, forthcoming.

Robeck, Jr., Cecil M., and Frank Chikane. "Rebuilding a Broken Society: An Interview with Frank Chikane." *Theology, News & Notes* 48, no. 1 (2001): 20–27.

Robeck, Jr., Cecil M., and Young-gi Hong. "The Influence on the Churches in the World: Interview with Dr. Cecil Robeck." In *Charis and Charisma: David Yonggi Cho and the Growth of Yoido Full Gospel Church*, edited by Sung-hoon Myung and Yong-gi Hong, 27–33. Oxford: Regnum Books International, 2003.

Robeck, Jr., Cecil M., and Jerry L. Sandidge. "Roman Catholic and Classical Pentecostal Dialogue." In *The New International Dictionary of Pentecostal and Charismatic Movements*, edited by Stanley M. Burgess and Eduard M. van der Maas, 2nd ed., 576–82. Grand Rapids, MI: Zondervan, 2003.

———. "The Ecclesiology of *Koinonia* and Baptism: A Pentecostal Perspective." *Journal of Ecumenical Studies* 27, no. 3 (1990): 504–34.

———. "World Council of Churches." In *The New International Dictionary of Pentecostal and Charismatic Movements*, edited by Stanley M. Burgess and Eduard M. van der Maas, 2nd ed., 1213–17. Grand Rapids, MI: Zondervan, 2003.

Tennison, D. Allen, and Cecil M. Robeck, Jr. "Interview with Dr. Cecil M. Robeck, Jr." *Assemblies of God Heritage* 25, no. 4 (2006): 16–21.

PATRISTIC SOURCES

Cyprian. *Epistle* 11.
———. *Epistle* 39.
———. *Epistle* 40.
———. *Epistle* 43.
———. *Epistle* 48.
———. *Epistle* 63.
———. *Epistle* 66.
Didache.
Ignatius. *To the Philadelphians.*
Tertullian. *Against Marcion.*
Tertullian. *Against Praxeas.*
The Shephard of Hermas.

BILATERAL DIALOGUE REPORTS

"Bearing Fruit: Implications of the 2010 Reconciliation between Lutherans and Mennonites/Anabaptists. Report of the Lutheran World Federation Task Force to Follow Up the 'Mennonite Action' at the LWF Eleventh Assembly in 2010," 2016.

Bibliography

"Called to God's Mission: Report of the Third Round of the International Dialogue Between Representatives of the World Communion of Reformed Churches and Some Classical Pentecostal Churches and Leaders 2014-2020," 2020.

"Called Together to Be Peacemakers: Report of the International Dialogue between the Catholic Church and Mennonite World Conference 1998–2003," 2003.

"Church, Evangelization, and the Bonds of *Koinonia*: A Report of the International Consultation between the Catholic Church and the Evangelical Alliance (1993-2002)," 2002.

"Communion: On Being the Church. Report of the Lutheran–Reformed Joint Commission between the Lutheran World Federation (LWF) and the World Communion of Reformed Churches (WCRC), 2006–2012," 2014.

"Conversations Around the World: The Report of the International Conversations between The Anglican Communion and The Baptist World Alliance, 2000–2005," 2005.

"'Do Not Quench the Spirit': Charisms in the Life and Mission of the Church. Report of the Sixth Phase of the International Catholic-Pentecostal Dialogue (2011-2015)," 2015.

"Evangelization, Proselytism, and Common Witness: Report from the Fourth Phase of the International Dialogue between the Roman Catholic Church and Some Classical Pentecostal Churches and Leaders (1990-1997)," 1997.

"Experience in Christian Faith and Life: Worship, Discipleship, Discernment, Community, and Justice. The Report of the International Dialogue between Representatives of the World Alliance of Reformed Churches and Some Classical Pentecostal Churches and Leaders (2001-2011)," 2011.

"Faith Working through Love: Report of the International Dialogue between the Baptist World Alliance and the World Methodist Council," 2018.

"Final Report of the Dialogue between the Secretariat for Promoting Christian Unity of the Roman Catholic Church and Leaders of Some Pentecostal Churches and Participants in the Charismatic Movement within Protestant and Anglican Churches (1972-1976)," 1976.

"Final Report of the Dialogue between the Secretariat for Promoting Christian Unity of the Roman Catholic Church and Some Classical Pentecostals (1977-1982)," 1982.

"From Conflict to Communion: Lutheran–Catholic Common Commemoration of the Reformation in 2017. Report of the Lutheran–Roman Catholic Commission on Unity," 2013.

"Healing Memories: Reconciling in Christ. Report of the Lutheran-Mennonite International Study Commission," 2010.

Institute for Ecumenical Research in Strasbourg, France, David du Plessis Center for Christian Spirituality in Pasadena, California, and The European Pentecostal Charismatic Research Association in Zürich, Switzerland. *Lutherans and Pentecostals in Dialogue*. Strasbourg, France: Institute for Ecumenical Research, 2010.

"Into All the World: Being and Becoming Apostolic Churches. A Report to the Anglican Consultative Council and the World Methodist Council by the Anglican-Methodist International Commission for Unity in Mission," 2014.

234   *Bibliography*

"On Becoming a Christian: Insights from Scripture and the Patristic Writings with Some Contemporary Reflections. Report of the Fifth Phase of the International Dialogue between Some Classical Pentecostal Churches and Leaders and the Catholic Church (1998-2006)," 2006.

"Perspectives on Koinonia: Report from the Third Quinquennium of the Dialogue between the Pontifical Council for Promoting Christian Unity of the Roman Catholic Church and Some Classical Pentecostal Churches and Leaders (1985-1989)," 1989.

"The Call to Holiness: From Glory to Glory. Report of the Joint International Commission for Dialogue between the World Methodist Council and the Roman Catholic Church 2016," 2016.

"The Church as Community of Common Witness to the Kingdom of God: Report of the Third Phase of the International Theological Dialogue between the Catholic Church and the World Alliance of Reformed Churches (1998-2005)," 2005.

"The Denver Report: Report of the Joint Commission Between the Roman Catholic Church and the World Methodist Council, First Series 1967-1970," 1971.

"The Evangelical-Roman Catholic Dialogue on Mission, 1977-1984: A Report," 1985.

"'The Spirit of the Lord Is Upon Me': International Lutheran-Pentecostal 2016–2022 Dialogue Statement," 2022.

"The Word of God in the Life of the Church: A Report of International Conversations Between the Catholic Church and the Baptist World Alliance (2006-2010)," 2010.

"Toward an Agreed Statement on the Holy Spirit (Honolulu 1981)," 1981.

"Towards a Common Understanding of the Church: Reformed/Roman Catholic International Dialogue. Second Phase (1984–1990)," 1990.

"Word and Spirit, Church and World: Final Report of the International Dialogue between Representatives of the World Alliance of Reformed Churches and Some Classical Pentecostal Churches and Leaders (1996-2000)," 2000.

WORLD COUNCIL OF CHURCHES SOURCES

WCC Documents

Joint Consultative Group between the World Council of Churches and Pentecostals. "Report of the Joint Consultative Group between Pentecostals and the World Council of Churches." In *Resource Book, World Council of Churches 10th Assembly, Busan, 2013*, 151–63. Geneva: World Council of Churches, 2013.

———. "Report of the Joint Consultative Group between the WCC and Pentecostals." In *Resource Book, World Council of Churches, 11th Assembly, Karlsruhe, Germany 2022*, 97–105. Geneva: World Council of Churches, 2022.

———. "Report of the Joint Consultative Group (WCC–Pentecostals), 2000–2005, to the 9th Assembly of the World Council of Churches, Porto Alegre, Brazil." In *Towards a Global Vision of the Church: Explorations on Global Christianity and Ecclesiology, Volume 2*, edited by Cecil M. Robeck, Jr., Sotiris Boukis, and Ani

Ghazaryan Drissi, 341–63. Faith and Order Paper 239. Geneva: World Council of Churches, 2023.

Joint Working Group between the World Council of Churches and the Roman Catholic Church. "The Challenge of Proselytism and the Calling to Common Witness: A Study Document of the Joint Working Group between the World Council of Churches and the Roman Catholic Church," 1995.

Pontifical Council for Promoting Christian Unity and World Council of Churches Commission on Faith and Order. "Justice and Only Justice You Shall Pursue (Deuteronomy 16:18-20): Resources for the Week of Prayer for Christian Unity and throughout the Year 2019." 2018. https://www.oikoumene.org/sites/default/files/2020-09/Week_of_Prayer_2019.pdf.

"Responses of the Churches." In *The Church Is Charismatic: The World Council of Churches and the Charismatic Renewal*, edited by Arnold Bittlinger, 40–66. Geneva: World Council of Churches, 1981.

"Towards a Church Renewed and United in the Spirit: WCC Consultative Group Paper." In *The Church Is Charismatic: The World Council of Churches and the Charismatic Renewal*, edited by Arnold Bittlinger, 21–28. Geneva: World Council of Churches, 1981.

World Council of Churches. *Common Understanding and Vision of the WCC*, 1997.

———. "Constitution and Rules of the World Council of Churches," 2018.

———. *Consulta con las iglesias pentecostales: Lima, Perú 14 al 19 de Noviembre de 1994, Consejo Mundial de Iglesias*. Geneva: WCC Publications, 1994.

———. *Consultation with African Instituted Churches: Ogere, Nigeria, 9–14 January 1996, World Council of Churches*. Edited by Huibert van Beek. Geneva: World Council of Churches, 1996.

———. *Consultation with Pentecostals in the Americas: San José, Costa Rica 4–8 June 1996*. Edited by Huibert van Beek. Geneva: World Council of Churches, 1996.

———. "Message of the WCC 11th Assembly, 'A Call to Act Together,'" 2022.

———. "Proposals Regarding a Forum of Christian Churches and Ecumenical Organisations." In *Revisioning Christian Unity: Journeying with Jesus Christ, the Reconciler at the Global Christian Forum, Limuru, November 2007*, edited by Huibert van Beek, 23–25. Studies in Global Christianity. Eugene, OR: Wipf & Stock, 2007.

———. "Report of the Policy Reference Committee to the Porto Alegre Assembly," 2006.

———. *Report of the Proceedings of the Consultation between the World Council of Churches (Office of Church and Ecumenical Relations at the General Secretariat) and African and African-Caribbean Church Leaders in Britain at the New Testament Church of God, Harebills, Leeds, England, 30 November – 2 December 1995*. Edited by Roswith I.H. Gerloff and Huibert van Beek. Geneva: World Council of Churches, 1996.

———. *Signs of the Spirit: Official Report of the Seventh Assembly, Canberra, Australia, 7–20 February 1991*. Edited by Michael Kinnamon. Geneva: WCC Publications, 1991.

236   *Bibliography*

———. "The Church, the Churches, and the World Council of Churches: The Ecclesiological Significance of the World Council of Churches," 1950.

———. *The New Delhi Report*. New York: Association Press, 1962.

———. *Towards Common Witness*, 1997.

World Council of Churches Commission on Faith and Order. "The Dar es Salaam Report: Tenth Forum on Bilateral Dialogues, 'International Dialogues in Dialogue: Context and Reception,'" 2012.

World Council of Churches Sub-unit on Renewal and Congregational Life. "Report of the Consultation on the Significance of the Charismatic Renewal for the Churches." In *The Church Is Charismatic: The World Council of Churches and the Charismatic Renewal*, edited by Arnold Bittlinger, 201–12. Geneva: World Council of Churches, 1981.

WCC Faith and Order Papers

World Council of Churches Commission on Faith and Order. *An Ecumenical Exercise: The Southern Baptist Convention, the Seven-Day-Adventist Church, the Kimbanguist Church in the Congo, the Pentecostal Movement in Europe*. Edited by M.B. Handspicker and Lukas Vischer. Faith and Order Paper 49. Geneva: World Council of Churches, 1967.

———. *Churches Respond to* The Church: Towards A Common Vision, *Volume 1*. Edited by Ellen Wondra, Stephanie Dietrich, and Ani Ghazaryan Drissi. Faith and Order Paper 231. Geneva: World Council of Churches, 2021.

———. *Churches Respond to* The Church: Towards a Common Vision, *Volume 2*. Edited by Ellen Wondra, Stephanie Dietrich, and Ani Ghazaryan Drissi. Faith and Order Paper 232. Geneva: World Council of Churches, 2021.

———. *Common Threads: Key Themes from Responses to* The Church: Towards a Common Vision. Edited by Ellen Wondra, Stephanie Dietrich, and Ani Ghazaryan Drissi. Faith and Order Paper 233. Geneva: World Council of Churches, 2021.

———. *Confessing the One Faith: An Ecumenical Explication of the Apostolic Faith as It Is Confessed in the Nicene-Constantinopolitan Creed (381)*. Faith and Order Paper 153. Geneva: World Council of Churches, 1991.

———. *Councils, Conciliarity, and a Genuinely Universal Council*. Faith and Order Paper 70. Geneva: World Council of Churches, 1974.

———. *How Can Unity Be Achieved? Ecumenical Case Studies: Ghana, Korea, Rumania, Switzerland, Uruguay*. Faith and Order Paper 75. Geneva: World Council of Churches, 1975.

———. *Participating in God's Mission of Reconciliation: A Resource for Churches in Situations of Conflict*. Faith and Order Paper 201. Geneva: World Council of Churches, 2006.

———. "Report of Eighth Forum on Bilateral Dialogues." In *Eighth Forum on Bilateral Dialogues. The Implications of Regional Bilateral Agreements for the International Dialogues of Christian World Communions, John XXIII Centre, Annecy-le-Vieux, France, 14–19 May 2001*, 57–65. Faith and Order Paper 190. Geneva: World Council of Churches, 2002.

Bibliography 237

———. *Social and Cultural Factors in Church Divisions.* Faith and Order Paper 40. Geneva: World Council of Churches, 1951.
———. *The Church: Towards a Common Vision.* Faith and Order Paper 214. Geneva: World Council of Churches, 2013.
———. *The Roots of Our Common Faith: Faith in the Scriptures and in the Early Church.* Edited by Hans-Georg Link. Faith and Order Paper 119. Geneva: World Council of Churches, 1984.
———. *Towards a Global Vision of the Church: Explorations on Global Christianity and Ecclesiology, Volume 1.* Edited by Cecil M. Robeck, Jr., Sotiris Boukis, and Ani Ghazaryan Drissi. Faith and Order Paper 234. Geneva: World Council of Churches, 2022.
———. *Towards a Global Vision of the Church: Explorations on Global Christianity and Ecclesiology, Volume 2.* Edited by Cecil M. Robeck, Jr., Sotiris Boukis, and Ani Ghazaryan Drissi. Faith and Order Paper 239. Geneva: World Council of Churches, 2023.
———. *Tradition and Traditions: Fourth World Conference on Faith and Order, Montreal, Canada, 12–26 July 1963.* Faith and Order Paper 40. Geneva: World Council of Churches, 1963.
———. *What Are the Churches Saying About the Church: Key Findings and Proposals from the Responses to* The Church: Towards a Common Vision. Faith and Order Paper 236. Geneva: World Council of Churches, 2021.
———. *What Kind of Unity?* Faith and Order Paper 69. Geneva: World Council of Churches, 1974.

OTHER SECONDARY LITERATURE

Akinwale, Anthony A. "Christianity without Memory: An Evaluation of Pentecostalism in Response to Emeka Nwosuh." In *Tradition and Compromises: Essays on the Challenge of Pentecostalism*, edited by Anthony A. Akinwale and Joseph Kenny, 111–23. Aquinas Day Series 2. Ibadan, Nigeria: The Michael J. Dempsey Centre for Religious and Social Research, 2004.
Alencar, Gedeon Freire de. "Do carisma mobilizador ao burocratismo institucional: Conferência Mundial Pentecostal realizada no Brasil em 1967 e 2016." In *Pentecostalismos em perspectiva*, edited by David Mesquiati de Oliveira, Ismael de Vasconcelos Ferreira, and Maxwell Pinheiro Fajardo, 35–56. São Paulo: Edições Terceira Via, 2017.
———. *Ecumenismos & pentecostalismos: A relação entre o pescoço e a guilhotina?* São Paulo: Editora Recriar, 2018.
Au, Connie Ho Yan. *Grassroots Unity in the Charismatic Renewal.* Eugene, OR: Wipf & Stock, 2011.
Avis, Paul. "New Paths in Ecumenical Method." In *Reshaping Ecumenical Theology: The Church Made Whole?*, 39–59. London: T & T Clark, 2010.
Azusa Street Mission. "The Project." Accessed July 2, 2022. https://312azusa.com/the-project/.

238 Bibliography

Bauwelz, Joanicio Fernando. "Laboratório de diálogo ecumênico e inter-religioso na Diocese de Ponta Grossa, Paraná." *Caminhos de diálogo: Revista brasileira de diálogo ecumênico e inter-religioso* 9, no. 14 (2021): 128–37.

———. *Sobre a reconstrução do "nós": Laboratório de estudos sobre ecumenismo e diálogo inter-religioso.* Série teologia em diálogo 9. Porto Alegre: Editora Fi, 2020.

Baxter-Brown, John, ed. *Call to Mission and Perceptions of Proselytism: A Reader for a Global Conversation.* Eugene, OR: Pickwick Publications, 2022.

Beek, Huibert van. "Das Christliche Weltforum und die Pfingstkirchen." *Ökumenische Rundschau* 60, no. 3 (2011): 267–75.

———. "Editorial." *Transformation* 27, no. 1 (2010): 3–7.

———. "O Fórum Cristão Mundial e a busca pela unidade cristã." In *Pentecostalismos e unidade: Desafios institucionais, teológicos e sociais*, edited by David Mesquiati de Oliveira, 13–26. São Paulo: Fonte Editorial, 2015.

———, ed. *Revisioning Christian Unity: Journeying with Jesus Christ, the Reconciler at the Global Christian Forum, Limuru, November 2007.* Studies in Global Christianity. Eugene, OR: Wipf & Stock, 2007.

Beek, Huibert van, and Larry Miller, eds. *Discrimination, Persecution, Martyrdom: Following Christ Together. Report of the Global Consultation, Tirana, Albania, 2-4 November 2015.* Bonn: Verlag für Kultur und Wissenschaft, 2018.

Benvenuti, Sherilyn Rae. "The Reconstruction of a Pentecostal Social Ethic of Racial Reconciliation: The Work of Cecil M. Robeck, Jr., H. Vinson Synan, and Leonard Lovett." Ph.D. dissertation, University of Southern California, 2000.

Bertalot, Renzo. "Metodologia ecumenica." *Studi Ecumenici* 1, no. 1 (1983): 41–60.

Birmelé, André. *La communion ecclésiale : Progrès œcuméniques et enjeux méthodologiques.* Cogitatio Fidei 218. Paris: Cerf, 2000.

Bittlinger, Arnold. *Papst und Pfingstler: Der römisch katholisch-pfingstliche Dialog und seine ökumenische Relevanz.* Studien zur Interkulturellen Geschichte des Christentums 16. Frankfurt: Peter Lang, 1978.

Bordeianu, Radu. *Dumitru Staniloae: An Ecumenical Ecclesiology.* Ecclesiological Investigations 13. London: T & T Clark, 2011.

Boukis, Sotiris, Ani Ghazaryan Drissi, and Krzysztof Mielcarek. "'Towards a Global Vision of the Church': The Faith and Order Commission's Work on 'Broadening the Table of Ecclesiological Dialogue.'" *International Review of Mission* 108, no. 2 (2019): 401–14.

Boutilier, Gene. "Rev. Gene Boutilier Remarks, Centennial of Southern California Ecumenical Council, Thursday, September 27, 2012, Pasadena, California." Southern California Christian Forum internal document, 2012.

Brabant, Christophe. "The Truth Narrated: Ricoeur on Religious Experience." In *Divinising Experience: Essays in the History of Religious Experience from Origen to Ricoeur*, edited by Lieven Boeve and Laurence P. Hemming, 246–69. Studies in Philosophical Theology 23. Leuven, Belgium: Brill, 2004.

Buda, Daniel. "The World Council of Churches' Relationships with Pentecostalism: A Brief Historical Survey and Some Recent Perspectives on Membership Matters." *International Review of Mission* 107, no. 1 (2018): 81–97.

Bibliography

239

Bujak, Janusz. "The Teaching of Pope Francis About Synodality in the Context of Contemporary Theological and Ecumenical Reflection." Translated by Maciej Górnicki. *Collectanea Theologica* 91, no. 5 (2021): 147–73.

Campos, Bernardo. "Pentecostalismo y unidad en América Latina: 'Aspectos teológicos.'" In *Fuego que une: Pentecostalismo y unidad de la iglesia*, 2nd ed., 33–37. Lima: Foro Pentecostal Latinoamericano y Caribeño, 2020.

Cardoza-Orlandi, Carlos F. "Caribbean." In *A History of the Ecumenical Movement, Volume 3: 1968-2000*, edited by John Briggs, Mercy Amba Oduyoye, and Georges Tsetsis, 523–32. Geneva: World Council of Churches, 2004.

Centre for Intercultural Theology, Interreligious Dialogue, Missiology and Ecumenics (Centrum IIMO) of the Utrecht University. "The Global Christian Forum 1998–2007, and Beyond: An Evaluation Report." In *Revisioning Christian Unity: Journeying with Jesus Christ, the Reconciler at the Global Christian Forum, Limuru, November 2007*, edited by Huibert van Beek, 209–80. Studies in Global Christianity. Eugene, OR: Wipf & Stock, 2007.

Cereti, Giovanni. *Ecumenismo: Corso di metodologia ecumenica*. 2nd ed. Rome: Istituto di Teologia a Distanza, 1991.

Chircop, Lionel. "Re-Membering the Future." In *Reconciling Memories*, edited by Alan D. Falconer and Joseph Liechty, 2nd ed., 20–29. Dublin: The Columba Press, 1998.

Catholic Charismatic Renewal International Service. "Christian Unity Commission." Last modified June 9, 2021. https://www.charis.international/en/christian-unity -commission/.

Chunakara, Mathews George. *Ecumenism in Asia: Prospects and Challenges*. Tiruvalla, India: Christava Sahitya Samithi, 2014.

Clarke, G.W., ed. *The Letters of St. Cyprian of Carthage*. 4 vols. Ancient Christian Writers: The Works of the Fathers in Translation 43, 44, 46, 47. New York: Newman Press, 1984.

Cole, David Leon. "Pentecostal Koinonia: An Emerging Ecumenical Ecclesiology among Pentecostals." Ph.D. dissertation, Fuller Theological Seminary, 1998.

Crace, Benjamin D. "Towards a Global Pneumatological Awareness: A Comparative Account and Assessment of the Charismata in the Coptic Orthodox Church." *Journal of Pentecostal Theology* 30, no. 1 (2021): 123–44.

Creemers, Jelle. "Local Dialogue as a Means to Ecumenical Reception? The International and Dutch Pentecostal-Catholic Dialogues in Close-Up." *Exchange* 42, no. 4 (2013): 366–84.

———. *Theological Dialogue with Classical Pentecostals: Challenges and Opportunities*. Ecclesiological Investigations 23. London: T & T Clark, 2015.

Dangel, Silke. "Die ökumenische Arbeit der Pfingstbewegung und die Frage nach der konfessionellen Identitätskonstitution." In *Konfessionelle Identität und ökumenische Prozesse: Analysen zum interkonfessionellen Diskurs des Christentums*, 237–316. Theologische Bibliothek Töpelmann 168. Berlin: De Gruyter, 2014.

Daniels, III, David D. "Engaging Racial Equity: Toward a Pentecostal Political Theology of Race." *Pneuma: The Journal of the Society for Pentecostal Studies* 44, no. 3–4 (2022): 363–79.

240 *Bibliography*

———. "Future of North American Pentecostalism: Contemporary Diasporas, New Denominationalism, Inclusive Racial Politics, and Post-Secular Sensibilities." *Pneuma: The Journal of the Society for Pentecostal Studies* 42, no. 3–4 (2020): 395–414.

Djomhoué, Priscille. "Manifestations of Ecumenism in Africa Today: A Study of the Mainline and Pentecostal Churches in Cameroon." *International Journal for the Study of the Christian Church* 8, no. 4 (2008): 355–68.

Duchrow, Ulrich. *Konflikt um die Ökumene: Christusbekenntnis, in welcher Gestalt der ökumenischen Bewegung?* München, Germany: Christian Kaiser, 1980.

Eller, Daniel W., and Daniel D. Isgrigg. "Bibliometrics and Pentecostal Scholarship: A Review of Trends in *Pneuma*." *Pneuma: The Journal of the Society for Pentecostal Studies* 45, no. 1 (2023): 78–101.

Espinosa, Gastón. *William J. Seymour and the Origins of Global Pentecostalism: A Biography and Documentary History*. Durham, NC: Duke University Press, 2014.

Essamuah, Casely Baiden. "A New Pentecost?: The Story of Peoples in the History of the Global Christian Forum and Its Contribution to World Christianity." In *World Christianity and Interfaith Relations*, edited by Richard F. Young, 249–68. World Christianity and Public Religion 4. Minneapolis, MN: Fortress Press, 2022.

———. "Seeking Christian Unity through Faith Sharing: The Continuing Relevance of the Quest for Christian Unity." In *Sharing of Faith Stories: A Methodology for Promoting Unity*, edited by Richard Howell and Casely Baiden Essamuah, 2nd ed., 35–37. Farukh Nagar, India: Caleb Institute of Theology, 2018.

"Evangelical Perspectives from Canberra." In *Beyond Canberra: Evangelical Responses to Contemporary Issues*, edited by Bruce J. Nicholls and Bong Rin Ro, 38–43. Oxford: Regnum Books, 1993.

Evans, Gillian R. *Method in Ecumenical Theology: The Lessons So Far*. Cambridge: Cambridge University Press, 1996.

———. *The Church and the Churches: Toward an Ecumenical Ecclesiology*. Cambridge: Cambridge University Press, 1994.

Falconer, Alan D. "Remembering." In *Reconciling Memories*, edited by Alan D. Falconer and Joseph Liechty, 2nd ed., 11–19. Dublin: The Columba Press, 1998.

Finger, Thomas. "Reflections on an Ecumenical-Historical Experiment." In *Telling the Churches' Stories: Ecumenical Perspectives on Writing Christian History*, edited by Timothy J. Wengert and Charles W. Brockwell, Jr., 105–20. Grand Rapids, MI: Eerdmans, 1995.

Gabijan, Crescencia Cabilao. *Dialogue, Light, and Fire: Chiara Lubich and the Spirituality of Unity*. Manila, Philippines: University of Santo Tomas Publishing House, 2017.

George, K.M. "Bearing Witness to Christ and to Each Other in the Power of the Holy Spirit: Orthodox Perspectives." *Transformation* 30, no. 4 (2013): 267–72.

Global Christian Forum. "Our Unfolding Journey with Jesus Christ: Reflections on the Global Christian Forum Experience." 2013. https://globalchristianforum.org/wp-content/uploads/2018/07/GFC-Our-Unfolding-Journey-ENG.pdf.

———. "The Future of the Global Christian Forum: Guidelines from the Second Global Gathering." *Transformation* 30, no. 4 (2013): 295–96.

Bibliography 241

Góis Silva, Wallace de. "Igreja de Cristo Pentecostal no Brasil e unidade: Cooperação e tensões com grupos cristãos nos documentos históricos e teológicos." In *Pentecostalismos e unidade: Desafios institucionais, teológicos e sociais*, edited by David Mesquiati de Oliveira, 89–98. São Paulo: Fonte Editorial, 2015.

Gonzalez, Philippe, and Christophe Monnot. "Témoigner de son pâtir et de l'agir de Dieu : Les épreuves d'une communauté charismatique." In *Le corps, lieu de ce qui nous arrive : Approches anthropologiques, philosophiques, théologiques*, edited by Pierre Gisel, 60–87. Geneva: Labor et Fides, 2008.

Grant, Robert M. "Review of Cecil M. Robeck, Jr., *Prophecy in Carthage: Perpetua, Tertullian, and Cyprian.*" *Church History* 62, no. 3 (1993): 378–79.

Gribben, Robert, and Larry Miller. "Global Christian Forum." In *The Oxford Handbook of Ecumenical Studies*, edited by Geoffrey Wainwright and Paul McPartlan, 476–86. Oxford University Press, 2021.

Gros, Jeffrey. "Fifty Years and Running: Oberlin '57, Back and Beyond." In *Ecumenical Directions in the United States Today: Churches on a Theological Journey*, edited by Antonios Kireopoulos and Juliana Mecera, 57–76. Faith and Order Commission Theological Series. New York: Paulist Press, 2012.

———. "Presidential Address 2012. It Seems Good to the Holy Spirit and to Us: The Ecclesial Vocation of the Pentecostal Scholar." *Pneuma: The Journal of the Society for Pentecostal Studies* 34, no. 2 (2012): 167–84.

Han, David Sang-Ehil. "Changing Paradigms in Global Ecumenism: A Pentecostal Reading." In *Pentecostal Theology and Ecumenical Theology: Interpretations and Intersections*, edited by Peter D. Hocken, Tony L. Richie, and Christopher A. Stephenson, 111–30. Global Pentecostal and Charismatic Studies 34. Leiden: Brill, 2019.

———. "The Global Christian Forum: A Pentecostal Story and Reflection." In *Sharing of Faith Stories: A Methodology for Promoting Unity*, edited by Richard Howell and Casely Baiden Essamuah, 2nd ed., 247–56. Farukh Nagar, India: Caleb Institute of Theology, 2018.

Hawkey, Jill. *Mapping the Oikoumene: A Study of Current Ecumenical Structures and Relationships.* Geneva: World Council of Churches, 2005.

Hegertun, Terje. *Det brodersind som pinseaanden nødvendigvis maa føde: Analyse av økumeniske posisjoner i norsk pinsebevegelse med henblikk på utviklingen av en pentekostal økumenikk og fornyelse av økumeniske arbeidsformer.* Trondheim, Norway: Tapir Akademisk, 2009.

Heller, Dagmar. "Neue Entwicklungen in der Ökumene: Das Beispiel des 'Globalen Christlichen Forums.'" *Una Sancta* 64, no. 3 (2009): 210–18.

Hietamäki, Minna. *Agreeable Agreement: An Examination of the Quest for Consensus in Ecumenical Dialogue.* Ecclesiological Investigations 8. London: T & T Clark, 2010.

Hilborn, David. "Anglicans, Pentecostals, and Ecumenical Theology." In *The Many Faces of Global Pentecostalism*, edited by Harold D. Hunter and Neil Ormerod, 243–63. Cleveland, TN: CPT Press, 2013.

Hilborn, David, and Simo Frestadius, eds. *Anglicans and Pentecostals in Dialogue.* Eugene, OR: Wipf & Stock, 2023.

242   *Bibliography*

Hocken, Peter D. *Azusa, Rome, and Zion: Pentecostal Faith, Catholic Reform, and Jewish Roots*. Eugene, OR: Wipf & Stock, 2016.

———. "The Contributions of the Charismatic Movement to Christian Unity." In *Pentecostal Theology and Ecumenical Theology: Interpretations and Intersections*, edited by Peter D. Hocken, Tony L. Richie, and Christopher A. Stephenson, 43–64. Global Pentecostal and Charismatic Studies 34. Leiden: Brill, 2019.

Hollenweger, Walter J. "Introduction." In *The Church Is Charismatic: The World Council of Churches and the Charismatic Renewal*, edited by Arnold Bittlinger, 1–4. Geneva: World Council of Churches, 1981.

Holy and Great Council. "Relations of the Orthodox Church with the Rest of the Christian World," 2016.

Höschele, Stefan. "Das Global Christian Forum: 'Forum' als Paradigma für die Zukunft der Ökumene?" In *Ökumene der Zukunft: Hermeneutische Perspektiven und die Suche nach Identität*, edited by Stephen Lakkis, Stefan Höschele, and Stefanie Schardien, 117–33. Beiheft zur Ökumenischen Rundschau 81. Frankfurt: Otto Lembeck, 2008.

Howell, Richard, and Casely Baiden Essamuah, eds. *Sharing of Faith Stories: A Methodology for Promoting Unity*. 2nd ed. Farukh Nagar, India: Caleb Institute of Theology, 2018.

Humm, Alan. *Psychology of Prophecy in Early Christianity: Prophetism and Religious Altered States of Consciousness*. Piscataway, NJ: Gorgias Press, 2009.

Hunter, Harold D. "An Emmaus Walk That Leads to Rome? Little Known Convergences Emerge." *Plērōma: Studii Şi Cercetări Teologice* 20, no. 1 (2018): 89–95.

———. "Attacking Systemic Racism for the Common Good: Excerpts from the History of the 'Racial Reconciliation Manifesto.'" In *The Politics of the Spirit: Pentecostal Reflections on Public Responsibility and the Common Good*, edited by Daniela C. Augustine and Chris E.W. Green, 39–50. Lanham, MD: Seymour Press, 2022.

———. "Pentecostal Ecumenical Pioneers: Select Case Studies in Leadership." In *African Pentecostal Missions Maturing: Essays in Honor of Apostle Opoku Onyinah*, edited by Elorm Donkor and Clifton Clarke, 102–20. African Christian Studies Series 14. Eugene, OR: Pickwick Publications, 2018.

———. "WCC Consultations with Pentecostals." Pentecostal-Charismatic Theological Inquiry International. Last modified January 1, 2012. http://www.pctii.org/wcc/.

Indian Christian Day. "Home." Accessed June 29, 2022. https://indianchristianday.com/.

Jagessar, Michael N. *Full Life for All: The Work and Theology of Philip A. Potter. A Historical Survey and Systematic Analysis of Major Themes*. Serie Mission 19. Zoetermeer, The Netherlands: Boekencentrum, 1997.

John Paul II. *Orientale lumen*, 1995.

———. *Ut unum sint*, 1995.

Johns, Cheryl Bridges. "Remodeling Our Ecumenical House." In *Pentecostal Theology and Ecumenical Theology: Interpretations and Intersections*, edited by Peter D. Hocken, Tony L. Richie, and Christopher A. Stephenson, 131–53. Global Pentecostal and Charismatic Studies 34. Leiden: Brill, 2019.

———. "When East Meets West and North Meets South: The Reconciling Mission of Global Christianity." In *Revisioning Christian Unity: Journeying with Jesus*

Bibliography

Christ, the Reconciler at the Global Christian Forum, Limuru, November 2007, edited by Huibert van Beek, 93–101. Studies in Global Christianity. Eugene, OR: Wipf & Stock, 2007.

Jones, Sarah Rowland. "The Global Christian Forum – A Narrative History." In *Revisioning Christian Unity: Journeying with Jesus Christ, the Reconciler at the Global Christian Forum, Limuru, November 2007*, edited by Huibert van Beek, 3–36. Studies in Global Christianity. Eugene, OR: Wipf & Stock, 2007.

———. "The Global Christian Forum, A Narrative History: 'Limuru, Manado and Onwards.'" *Transformation* 30, no. 4 (2013): 226–42.

———. "To Receive from Each Other, First Receive Each Other: Receptive Ecumenism and the Global Christian Forum." In *Receptive Ecumenism as Transformative Ecclesial Learning*, edited by Paul D. Murray, Gregory A. Ryan, and Paul Lakeland, 74–85. Oxford: Oxford University Press, 2022.

Kalombo Kapuku, Sébastien. *Pentecôtismes en République Démocratique du Congo, Tome 1 : Conditions et pertinence de dialogue entre églises protestantes sur la mission aujourd'hui*. Paris: Les Éditions du Panthéon, 2015.

———. *Pentecôtismes en République Démocratique du Congo, Tome 2 : Propos et pertinence d'une éthique missionnaire*. Paris: Les Éditions du Panthéon, 2018.

Kärkkäinen, Veli-Matti. "*The Nature and Purpose of the Church*: Theological and Ecumenical Reflections from Pentecostal/Free Church Perspectives." In *Pentecostalism and Christian Unity: Ecumenical Documents and Critical Assessments*, edited by Wolfgang Vondey, 231–42. Eugene, OR: Pickwick Publications, 2010.

Kasper, Walter. *A Handbook of Spiritual Ecumenism*. Hyde Park, NY: New City Press, 2007.

Kaunda, Chammah J. "The Day of Prayer and Its Potential for Engendering Public Ecclesiology Ecumenism in Zambia." *Religions* 9, no. 12 (2018): 1–13.

———. "The Nationalization of Prayer and Prayerization of the Nation." In *Competing for Caesar: Religion and Politics in Post-Colonial Zambia*, edited by Chammah J. Kaunda and Marja Hinfelaar, 39–56. Minneapolis, MN: Fortress Press, 2020.

Kay, William K. "Anglican-Pentecostal Dialogue in the UK: An Analysis and Exhortation." *Journal of the European Pentecostal Theological Association* 34, no. 2 (2014): 160–71.

Kearney, Richard. "Myth and the Critique of Tradition." In *Reconciling Memories*, edited by Alan D. Falconer and Joseph Liechty, 2nd ed., 37–56. Dublin: The Columba Press, 1998.

Keshishian, Aram. *Conciliar Fellowship: A Common Goal*. Geneva: WCC Publications, 1992.

Kessler, Diane, and Michael Kinnamon. *Councils of Churches and the Ecumenical Vision*. Risk Book Series 90. Geneva: WCC Publications, 2000.

Kinnamon, Michael. "Assessing the Ecumenical Movement." In *A History of the Ecumenical Movement, Volume 3: 1968–2000*, edited by John Briggs, Mercy Amba Oduyoye, and Georges Tsetsis, 51–81. Geneva: World Council of Churches, 2004.

244   *Bibliography*

————. *Can a Renewal Movement Be Renewed? Questions for the Future of Ecumenism*. Grand Rapids, MI: Eerdmans, 2014.

————. "Panel Presentation, National Workshop on Christian Unity." Christ Cathedral, Garden Grove, CA, 2022.

————. *Unity as Prophetic Witness: W. A. Visser 't Hooft and the Shaping of Ecumenical Theology*. Shapers of Ecumenical Theology. Minneapolis, MN: Fortress Press, 2018.

Kishkovsky, Leonid. "Following Christ with Great Joy: Christians Called to Reconciliation." *Transformation* 27, no. 1 (2010): 55–62.

Koshy, Ninan. *A History of the Ecumenical Movement in Asia, Volume 1*. Hong Kong: Christian Conference of Asia, 2004.

Kroesbergen, Hermen. "Radical Change in Zambia's Christian Ecumenism." *Journal of South African Studies* 44, no. 2 (2018): 331–43.

Kurian, M. *Sarah Chakko: A Voice of Women in the Ecumenical Movement*. Thiruvalla, India: Christhava Sahithya Samithy, 1998.

Lapoorta, Japie Jimmy. *Unity or Division? The Unity Struggles of the Black Churches within the Apostolic Faith Mission of South Africa*. Kuils River, South Africa: J.J. Lapoorta, 1996.

Levinas, Emmanuel. "Truth of Disclosure and Truth of Testimony." In *Emmanuel Levinas: Basic Philosophical Writings*, edited by Adriaan T. Peperzak, Simon Critchley, and Robert Bernasconi, 98–107. Studies in Continental Thought. Bloomington, IN: Indiana University Press, 1996.

Lin, Judith C.P. "The Weight of the Cross: A Response to *The Church: Towards a Common Vision* from a Perspective of Persecuted Christians." In *Towards a Global Vision of the Church: Explorations on Global Christianity and Ecclesiology, Volume 1*, by World Council of Churches Commission on Faith and Order, edited by Cecil M. Robeck, Jr., Sotiris Boukis, and Ani Ghazaryan Drissi, 99–102. Faith and Order Paper 234. Geneva: World Council of Churches, 2022.

Lutheran World Federation International Consultation on Ecumenical Methodology. *Ökumenische Methodologie: Dokumentation und Bericht*. Edited by Peder Nørgaard-Højen. Geneva: Lutheran World Federation, 1978.

Maçaneiro, Marcial. "Na unidade do Espírito Santo: Observações sobre o diálogo internacional católico-pentecostal." In *Pentecostalismos e unidade: Desafios institucionais, teológicos e sociais*, edited by David Mesquiati de Oliveira, 99–117. São Paulo: Fonte Editorial, 2015.

Macchia, Frank D. "God Present in a Confused Situation: The Mixed Influence of the Charismatic Movement on Classical Pentecostalism in the United States." *Pneuma: The Journal of the Society for Pentecostal Studies* 18, no. 1 (1996): 33–54.

Macfarland, Charles Stedman. *Christian Unity in Practice and Prophecy*. New York: The Macmillan Company, 1933.

Maffeis, Angelo. *Il dialogo ecumenico*. Piccola Biblioteca delle Religioni 23. Brescia, Italy: Queriniana, 2000.

Mariz, Cecília L., and Carlos Henrique Souza. "Carismáticos e pentecostais: Os limites das trocas ecumênicas." *Contemporânea: Dossiê Desafios Contemporâneos da Sociologia da Religião* 5, no. 2 (2015): 381–408.

Mayer, Annemarie C. "An Instrument of the Ecumenical Movement: The Joint Working Group between the Roman Catholic Church and the World Council of Churches." *The Ecumenical Review* 70, no. 3 (2018): 526–52.

McCullum, Hugh. "Racism and Ethnicity." In *A History of the Ecumenical Movement, Volume 3: 1968-2000*, edited by John Briggs, Mercy Amba Oduyoye, and Georges Tsetsis, 345–71. Geneva: World Council of Churches, 2004.

McDonnell, Kilian. "Improbable Conversations: The International Classical Pentecostal/Roman Catholic Dialogue." *Pneuma: The Journal of the Society for Pentecostal Studies* 17, no. 2 (1995): 163–74.

Mendes, Felipe Lucas. "Ecumenismo na diocese de Ponta Grossa, a partir de uma visão católica e luterana." In *Sobre a reconstrução do "nós": Laboratório de estudos sobre ecumenismo e diálogo inter-religioso*, edited by Joanicio Fernando Bauwelz, 106–18. Série teologia em diálogo 9. Porto Alegre: Editora Fi, 2020.

Metropolitan Kirill. "A Possible Structure of the World Council of Churches: Proposals for Discussion." *Ecumenical Review* 51, no. 4 (1999): 351–54.

Meyendorff, Paul. "Apostolic Faith in Relation to the Historic Episcopate, Authority, and Primacy." In *Common Threads: Key Themes from Responses to* The Church: Towards a Common Vision, by World Council of Churches Commission on Faith and Order, edited by Ellen K. Wondra, Stephanie Dietrich, and Ani Ghazaryan Drissi, 33–39. Faith and Order Paper 233. Geneva: World Council of Churches, 2021.

Meyer, Harding. "Christian World Communions." In *A History of the Ecumenical Movement, Volume 3: 1968-2000*, edited by John Briggs, Mercy Amba Oduyoye, and Georges Tsetsis, 103–22. Geneva: World Council of Churches, 2004.

———. *Ökumenische Zielvorstellungen*. Bensheimer Hefte 78, Ökumenische Studienhefte 4. Göttingen: Vandenhoeck & Ruprecht, 1996.

Michel, Thomas, and J.M.R. Tillard. "Participation of the Roman Catholic Church in National Councils of Churches." Federation of Asian Bishops' Conferences Paper 97, 2001.

Miller, Larry. "A Journey with Jesus Christ: Moments of Revelation and Conversion." In *Sharing of Faith Stories: A Methodology for Promoting Unity*, edited by Richard Howell and Casely Baiden Essamuah, 2nd ed., 27–30. Farukh Nagar, India: Caleb Institute of Theology, 2018.

———, ed. *Let Mutual Love Continue (Hebrews 13:1): Report of the Third Global Gathering, Bogotá, Colombia, 24-27 April 2018*. Bonn: Verlag für Kultur und Wissenschaft, 2021.

Miller, Michael J. "God's Ecumenical Co-Pilot." The Catholic World Report. Last modified January 16, 2012. https://www.catholicworldreport.com/2012/01/16/gods-ecumenical-co-pilot/.

Moreno, Calixto Salvatierra. "La fé en los caminos de unidad de los cristianos: El Foro Cristiano Mundial." *Yachay* 57–58 (2013): 153–72.

Muszczyński, Mariusz. "Ekumenizm Cecila M. Robecka." Ph.D. dissertation, University of Opole, 2022.

Mwaura, Philomena Njeri, and Constansia Mumma Martinon. "Political Violence in Kenya and Local Churches' Responses: The Case of the 2007 Post-Election Crisis." *The Review of Faith & International Affairs* 8, no. 1 (2010): 39–46.

246   *Bibliography*

Nasrallah, Laura. *An Ecstasy of Folly: Prophecy and Authority in Early Christianity.* Harvard Theological Studies 52. Cambridge, MA: Harvard University Press, 2003.

National Council of Churches of Kenya. "NCCK Training Mediators." Last modified December 4, 2021. http://www.ncck.org/ncck-training-mediators/.

Newman, Joe. *Race and the Assemblies of God Church: The Journey from Azusa Street to the "Miracle of Memphis."* Youngstown, NY: Cambria Press, 2007.

Newsome, Maryalice. "The Impact of the Miracle in Memphis on the Racial Reconciliation Initiatives of the Assemblies of God Churches in the Greater Kansas City Area." Ph.D. dissertation, University of Missouri–Kansas City, 2004.

Nicosia, Paolo Salvatore. *Riconciliazione: Esperienze e modelli in contesti ecumenici.* Rome: Aracne Editrice, 2020.

Nissiotis, Nikos A. "Types and Problems of Ecumenical Dialogue." *The Ecumenical Review* 18, no. 1 (1966): 39–57.

Nørgaard-Højen, Peder. *Ökumenisches Engagement* und theologisches Erkennen: Beiträge zur ökumenischen Methodologie. Frankfurt: Peter Lang, 1998.

Odeyemi, John Segun. *Pentecostalism and Catholic Ecumenism in Developing Nations: West Africa as a Case Study for a Global Phenomenon.* Eugene, OR: Wipf & Stock, 2019.

Oliveira, David Mesquiati de. "Instituições pentecostais latino-americanas para a unidade eclesial e para a produção acadêmica: O caso do FPLyC e da RELEP." In *As vozes da cooperação I: FPLyC, RELEP, FCM,* edited by Carlos Antonio Carneiro Barbosa and David Mesquiati de Oliveira, 19–45. Coleção Pentecostalismo 3. São Paulo: Editora Reflexão, 2017.

Onyinah, Opoku. *Apostles and Prophets: The Ministry of Apostles and Prophets throughout the Generations.* Eugene, OR: Wipf and Stock, 2022.

Oredein, Oluwatomisin Olayinka. *The Theology of Mercy Amba Oduyoye: Ecumenism, Feminism, and Communal Practice.* Notre Dame, IN: University of Notre Dame Press, 2023.

Oro, Ari Pedro, and Daniel Alves. "Renovação carismática católica: Movimento de superação da oposição entre catolicismo e pentecostalismo?" *Religião e Sociedade* 33, no. 1 (2013): 122–44.

Oxford Centre for Mission Studies. "The Global Christian Forum 1998–2007, and Beyond: An Evaluation Report." In *Revisioning Christian Unity: Journeying with Jesus Christ, the Reconciler at the Global Christian Forum, Limuru, November 2007,* edited by Huibert van Beek, 141–208. Studies in Global Christianity. Eugene, OR: Wipf & Stock, 2007.

Palma, Marta. "A Pentecostal Church in the Ecumenical Movement." *The Ecumenical Review* 37, no. 2 (1985): 223–29.

Panagopoulos, John, ed. *Prophetic Vocation in the New Testament and Today.* Novum Testamentum Supplement 45. Leiden: Brill, 1977.

———. *Η Εκκλησία των Προφητών: Το προφητικό χάρισμα εντη Εκκλησία των δυο πρώτων αιώνων.* Athens: St. Vassilopoulos, 1979.

Pathil, Kuncheria. *Models in Ecumenical Dialogue: A Study of the Methodological Development in the Commission on "Faith and Order" of the World Council of Churches.* Bangalore: Dharmaram Publications, 1981.

Paul VI. *Dei verbum*, 1965.

———. *Lumen gentium*, 1964.

———. *Unitatis redintegratio*, 1964.

Pentecostal World Fellowship. "Pentecostal Commission on Religious Liberty." Accessed January 5, 2023. https://www.pwfellowship.org/pentecostal-commission -on-religious-liberty.

Perzyński, Andrzej. "Exchange of Gifts: Experience of Global Christian Forum." *Łódzkie Studia Teologiczne* 26, no. 3 (2017): 55–65.

Pieper, Lukas. *Paulos Mar Gregorios: Imaginationen des Ostens im Zeitalter der Ökumene*. Kirche - Konfession - Religion 81. Göttingen: Vandenhoeck & Ruprecht, 2021.

Plaatjies-Van Huffel, Mary-Anne. "A Critical Reflection of the Role of 'Context' in Discernment, Decision-Making and Reception." In *Leaning into the Spirit: Ecumenical Perspectives on Discernment and Decision-Making in the Church*, edited by Virginia Miller, David Moxon, and Stephen Pickard, 49–64. Pathways for Ecumenical and Interreligious Dialogue. Cham: Springer International, 2019.

Pontifical Council for Interreligious Dialogue, World Council of Churches, and World Evangelical Alliance. *Christian Witness in a Multi-Religious World: Recommendations for Conduct*, 2011.

Pontifical Council for Promoting Christian Unity. *Directory for the Application of Principles and Norms on Ecumenism*, 1993.

———. *The Bishop and Christian Unity: An Ecumenical Vademecum*, 2020.

Potter, Philip. "Charismatic Renewal and the World Council of Churches." In *The Church Is Charismatic: The World Council of Churches and the Charismatic Renewal*, edited by Arnold Bittlinger, 73–87. Geneva: World Council of Churches, 1981.

"Presidente do Fórum Cristão Angolano mostra-se apreensivo com seitas religiosas." Portal de Angola. Last modified October 27, 2017. https://www.portaldeangola.com/2017/10/27/presidente-do-forum-cristao-angolano-mostra-se-apreensivo -com-seitas-religiosas/.

Prior, John Mansford. "Jesus Christ the Way to the Father: The Challenge of the Pentecostals." Federation of Asian Bishops' Conferences Paper 119, 2006.

"Racial Reconciliation Manifesto." 1994. https://pccna.org/documents/1994manifesto.pdf.

Raiser, Konrad. *Ökumene im Übergang: Paradigmenwechsel in der ökumenischen Bewegung?* Kaiser Taschenbücher 63. Munich, Germany: Christian Kaiser, 1989.

"Report on the Anglican-Pentecostal Consultation." In *Churches Respond to* The Church: Towards a Common Vision, *Volume 2*, by World Council of Churches Commission on Faith and Order, edited by Ellen Wondra, Stephanie Dietrich, and Ani Ghazaryan Drissi, 383–87. Faith and Order Paper 232. Geneva: World Council of Churches, 2021.

Ricœur, Paul. "Le soi et l'identité narrative." In *Soi-même comme un autre*, 167–98. Paris: Éditions du Seuil, 1990.

———. "L'herméneutique du témoignage." *Archivio di Filosofia* 42 (1972): 35–61.

Robra, Martin. "The World Council of Churches and Pentecostals." *Ecumenical Review* 71, no. 1–2 (2019): 161–74.

248 *Bibliography*

Root, Michael. "Christian World Communions and the CUV Process." *The Ecumenical Review* 50, no. 3 (1998): 330–37.

Rosenior, Derrick. *Toward Racial Reconciliation: Collective Memory, Myth, and Nostalgia in American Pentecostalism*. Saarbrücken: VDM Verlag Dr. Müller, 2009.

Rusch, William G. *Ecumenical Reception: Its Challenge and Opportunity*. Grand Rapids, MI: Eerdmans, 2007.

Sanderson, Ross W. *Church Cooperation in the United States: The Nation-Wide Backgrounds and Ecumenical Significance of State and Local Councils of Churches in Their Historical Perspective*. Hartford, CT: Finlay Brothers Press, 1960.

Sandidge, Jerry L. *Roman Catholic/Pentecostal Dialogue (1977–1982): A Study in Developing Ecumenism*. Vol. 1. 2 vols. Studien zur Interkulturellen Geschichte des Christentums 44. Frankfurt: Peter Lang, 1987.

Santer, Mark. "The Reconciliation of Memories." In *Reconciling Memories*, edited by Alan D. Falconer and Joseph Liechty, 2nd ed., 30–36. Dublin: The Columba Press, 1998.

Sintado, Carlos A., and Manuel Quintero Pérez. *Pasión y compromiso con el Reino de Dios: El testimonio ecuménico de Emilio Castro*. Buenos Aires: Kairos, 2007.

Soko, Lukas, and H. Jurgens Hendriks. "Pentecostalism and Schisms in the Reformed Church in Zambia (1996–2001): Listening to the People." *HTS Theological Studies* 67, no. 3 (2011): 1–8.

"Spreads the Fire." *The Apostolic Faith*, vol. 1, no. 2, p. 4, October 1906.

Synan, Vinson. "Memphis 1994: Miracle and Mandate." 1997. https://pccna.org/documents/1994Memphis.pdf.

Tahun, Marthen. "Fractured Ecumenism and Attempts at Fence-Mending: Relations Between Pentecostals and Non-Pentecostals in Indonesia." In *Aspirations for Modernity and Prosperity: Symbols and Sources behind Pentecostal/Charismatic Growth in Indonesia*, edited by Christine E. Gudorf, Zainal Abidin Bagir, and Marthen Tahun, 139–69. Forum for Theology in the World 1. Adelaide, Australia: ATF Theology, 2014.

Tan-Chow, May Ling. *Pentecostal Theology for the Twenty-First Century: Engaging with Multi-Faith Singapore*. Ashgate New Critical Thinking in Religion, Theology, and Biblical Studies. Aldershot, UK: Ashgate Publishing, 2007.

Tanner, Mary. "The Achievement of Bilateral Dialogues and Some Implications for a Common Martyrology." In *A Cloud of Witnesses: Opportunities for Ecumenical Commemoration. Proceedings of the International Ecumenical Symposium, Monastery of Bose, 29 October – 2 November 2008*, by World Council of Churches Commission on Faith and Order, edited by Tamara Grdzelidze and Guido Dotti, 41–51. Faith and Order Paper 209. Geneva: World Council of Churches, 2009.

———. "The Relation between Multilateral Dialogues and Their Impact on International Bilateral Dialogues and on Regional Agreements, and the Ways in Which Bilateral and Regional Agreements Impact the Faith and Order Agenda." In *Eighth Forum on Bilateral Dialogues. The Implications of Regional Bilateral Agreements for the International Dialogues of Christian World Communions, John XXIII Centre, Annecy-le-Vieux, France, 14–19 May 2001*, by World Council of Churches

Commission on Faith and Order, 46–56. Faith and Order Paper 190. Geneva: World Council of Churches, 2002.

Tanzania Christian Forum. "Tanzania: Joint Statement of the Extraordinary Meeting of the Tanzania Christian Forum." AMECEA: Association of Member Episcopal Conferences in Eastern Africa. Last modified March 19, 2013. https://communications.amecea.org/index.php/2013/06/13/tanzania-joint-statement-of/.

"The Apostolic Faith Movement." *The Apostolic Faith*, vol. 1, no. 1, p. 2, September 1906.

Thiessen, Gesa Elsbeth. "Ecumenism in Praxis: Critical Observations on the Week of Prayer for Christian Unity." In *Apostolic and Prophetic: Ecclesiological Perspectives*, 89–105. Cambridge: James Clarke, 2011.

Third International Consultation for NCCs. "Reports from Working Groups." *The Ecumenical Review* 45, no. 3 (1993): 291–98.

"Towards a Cuban Christian Forum." *Global Christian Forum News*, vol. 2, no. 2, p. 1, 2, 2014.

Uytenbogaardt, Hans, and Guido Dotti. "Places of Memory." In *A Cloud of Witnesses: Opportunities for Ecumenical Commemoration. Proceedings of the International Ecumenical Symposium, Monastery of Bose, 29 October – 2 November 2008*, by World Council of Churches Commission on Faith and Order, edited by Tamara Grdzelidze and Guido Dotti, 200–209. Faith and Order Paper 209. Geneva: World Council of Churches, 2009.

Uzochukwu, Peter Uche. *Churches in the Family of God: A Proposal for Catholic Input towards Christian Unity in Africa*. Bloomington, IN: Xlibris, 2012.

Varghese, Alan. *Pentecostal Churches and Ecumenism in India*. Delhi: Indian Society for Promoting Christian Knowledge, 2015.

Vasiljević, Maxim. "Ecumenical Councils." In *Common Threads: Key Themes from Responses to* The Church: Towards a Common Vision, by World Council of Churches Commission on Faith and Order, edited by Ellen K. Wondra, Stephanie Dietrich, and Ani Ghazaryan Drissi, 69–83. Faith and Order Paper 233. Geneva: World Council of Churches, 2021.

———. "Sacraments and Sacramentality of the Church." In *Common Threads: Key Themes from Responses to* The Church: Towards a Common Vision, by World Council of Churches Commission on Faith and Order, edited by Ellen K. Wondra, Stephanie Dietrich, and Ani Ghazaryan Drissi, 129–52. Faith and Order Paper 233. Geneva: World Council of Churches, 2021.

Vischer, Lukas. "Comuniones mundiales, el Consejo Ecuménico de las Iglesias y el movimiento ecuménico." Translated by Rosa Herrera García. *Dialogo Ecuménico* 39, no. 123 (2004): 45–79.

Vogelaar, Huub. "Das Global Christian Forum: Ein realistischer Weg der Ökumene?" In *Ökumene - überdacht: Reflexionen und Realitäten im Umbruch*, edited by Thomas Bremer and Maria Wernsmann, translated by Christian Föller, 317–33. Quaestiones Disputatae 259. Freiburg im Breisgau: Herder, 2014.

Vogelaar, Huub, and Greetje Witte-Rang. "The Global Christian Forum: Reconfiguration of the Ecumenical Scene. Tracks of Its History and First Evaluation." *Exchange* 39, no. 4 (2010): 377–420.

Vondey, Wolfgang. "Pentecostal Participation in Ecumenical Dialogues: Bilateral and Multilateral, Local and Global." In *Pentecostal Theology and Ecumenical Theology: Interpretations and Intersections*, edited by Peter D. Hocken, Tony L. Richie, and Christopher A. Stephenson, 85–110. Global Pentecostal and Charismatic Studies 34. Leiden: Brill, 2019.

———. "Preface." In *Pentecostalism and Christian Unity: Ecumenical Documents and Critical Assessments*, edited by Wolfgang Vondey, ix–x. Eugene, OR: Pickwick Publications, 2010.

Weinrich, William C. "Review of Cecil M. Robeck, Jr., *Prophecy in Carthage: Perpetua, Tertullian, and Cyprian*." *The Catholic Historical Review* 82, no. 3 (1996): 494–97.

Weir, Forrest C. "The General Secretary's Message." Presented at the 48th General Assembly of the Southern California–Southern Nevada Council of Churches, February 3, 1961. Held in box 2, Southern California Ecumenical Council Collection, Archives and Special Collections – David Allan Hubbard Library, Fuller Theological Seminary, Pasadena, California.

Wengert, Timothy J., and Charles W. Brockwell, Jr., eds. "Preface." In *Telling the Churches' Stories: Ecumenical Perspectives on Writing Christian History*, xv–xxii. Grand Rapids, MI: Eerdmans, 1995.

West, Russell Wade. "That His People May Be One: An Interpretive Study of the Pentecostal Leadership's Quest for Racial Unity." Ph.D. dissertation, Regent University, 1997.

Wondra, Ellen K. "Ecumenical Reception." In *Common Threads: Key Themes from Responses to* The Church: Towards a Common Vision, by World Council of Churches Commission on Faith and Order, edited by Ellen K. Wondra, Stephanie Dietrich, and Ani Ghazaryan Drissi, 91–107. Faith and Order Paper 233. Geneva: World Council of Churches, 2021.

World Assemblies of God Fellowship. "PCRL." Accessed January 5, 2023. https://worldagfellowship.org/Commissions/PCRL.

Wuysang, Angie Olivia, and Marthen Tahun. "Autonomy, Splintering and Growing Ecumenism: Governance and Organisation in Pentecostal and Charismatic Synods in Indonesia." In *Aspirations for Modernity and Prosperity: Symbols and Sources behind Pentecostal/Charismatic Growth in Indonesia*, edited by Christine E. Gudorf, Zainal Abidin Bagir, and Marthen Tahun, 111–38. Forum for Theology in the World 1. Adelaide, Australia: ATF Theology, 2014.

戴觀豪．"「我將澆灌我靈予所有人」：　西摩的靈洗教義與普世合一." 華文五旬宗研究期刊 [Tai, David Kwun-Ho. "I Will Pour Out of My Spirit upon All Flesh: Seymour's Doctrine of Spirit Baptism and Ecumenism," *Chinese Journal of Pentecostal Studies*] 3 (2019): 56–79.

Index

Africa, 6, 10, 14, 33, 39, 49, 62, 72, 85, 100–3, 131–32, 139–40, 151–52, 185, 188–89, 193, 195. *See also* African Instituted Churches; All Africa Conference of Churches; Democratic Republic of the Congo; Kenya; South Africa; Zambia

African Instituted Churches, 100, 185, 189; Organization of African Instituted Churches, 189. *See also* Africa

Alencar, Gedeon, 13, 16, 90

All Africa Conference of Churches, 85, 189. *See also* Africa; regional ecumenical organizations

Anglicanism, 9–10, 66, 90; Anglican Communion, 89, 120, 136, 191; in bilateral dialogues, 43, 92, 120, 122, 133, 141, 159, 161, 169

apostolicity, 29–32, 35–37, 42–43, 57, 70, 98, 150, 156; and the apostolic faith, 30–31, 36, 39, 42, 62–63, 97, 100, 153–54, 163, 166, 169, 201, 220, 223n10; apostolic succession, 29, 45, 55n79, 101; and charisms, 20, 29, 36, 50, 150, 153, 157, 163, 166–70; and patristics, 30, 150, 153, 156, 163, 169; and Tradition, 29, 37–38, 42–43, 125, 134, 138–39,

153, 169, 183, 220, 223n10. *See also* Charismatic movement; patristics; Pentecost; restorationism; Tradition

Apostolic Pentecostalism, 66, 70, 89

Asia, 13–14, 40, 48, 57, 59, 62, 66, 72, 91, 96, 99, 102, 105–6, 130–32, 160, 167, 179, 189–90, 192–93, 208n52; Asian Movement for Christian Unity, 189. *See also* China; Christian Conference of Asia; Federation of Asian Bishops' Conferences; Hong Kong; India; Indonesia; South Korea; Taiwan

Assemblies of God (AG), 16, 18, 24n53, 65–67, 69, 71–72, 77–78, 87–90, 92, 95, 101, 122, 132, 157, 162, 189–90; World Assemblies of God Fellowship, 89–90, 189–90, 209n73, 209n75

Assemblies of God Theological Seminary, 67, 77

Assyrian Church of the East, 133

Au, Connie Ho Yan, 14, 163, 167

Avis, Paul, 9–10, 201, 218

Azusa Street Memorial Committee, 65–66, 82nn45–46, 82n49. *See also* Azusa Street Revival; commemorative sites; communal memory; history; local ecumenism; race and racism

252 *Index*

Azusa Street Revival, 61–68, 196; historical site of, 64–66, 82nn45–46, 82n49; as myth, 41, 61, 64–65, 67, 71, 74, 76–78, 81n44; and Pentecost, 62, 70, 75; in Pentecostal historiography, 41, 61–64, 77–78; and the Pentecostal/Charismatic Churches of North America, 20, 70–74, 76, 78; and race, 20, 61–68, 70–71, 77–78, 81n38, 154; Robeck's tour of, 65, 67, 78, 81n44, 82n49. *See also* communal memory; intra-Pentecostal ecumenism; Pentecostal/Charismatic Churches of North America; race and racism; reconciling memories

Baptism, Eucharist, and Ministry, 97, 158, 163. *See also* Faith and Order
baptism, water, 44, 46, 58, 86, 109n9. *See also* sacraments
Baptist churches, 33, 62–63, 66, 73, 90, 107, 179; Baptist World Alliance, 72, 92, 136, 141n14; in bilateral dialogues, 120, 123, 158–59, 161; Southern Baptist Convention, 11, 176n93
Beek, Huibert van, 100, 185, 188, 199
Benvenuti, Sherilyn, 17, 71, 151, 154, 171
Bertalot, Renzo, 4–5
bilateral dialogue, 8, 15, 17, 20, 27, 30, 34, 50, 90–91, 97, 117–40, 145n94, 145n114, 149, 158, 161, 164, 167, 186–87, 194, 198, 200, 212n123, 215–16; Anglican–Pentecostal, 92, 120, 141n15, 169; and confessional ecumenism, 8, 91, 117, 124, 135; Eastern Orthodox–Pentecostal, 111n44, 141n14; and identity negotiation, 90, 93, 120, 122–23, 139–40; Lutheran–Mennonite, 60, 76–77, 190; Lutheran–Pentecostal, 16, 20, 92, 120, 130, 132–33, 135, 139–40, 167; Reformed–Pentecostal,

16, 20, 34, 92, 120, 123, 130–35, 167, 186; Roman Catholic–Evangelical, 135, 141n11, 158, 195; Roman Catholic–Lutheran, 45, 117, 119, 145n94, 158, 161; Roman Catholic–Mennonite, 59, 75–76; Roman Catholic–Reformed, 59, 121, 135; Oriental Orthodox–Pentecostal, 169. *See also* confessionalism; multilateral dialogue; Pentecostals in dialogues; Roman Catholic–Pentecostal dialogue
Birmelé, André, 91, 119, 135, 145n94
The Bishop and Christian Unity: An Ecumenical Vademecum, 7, 119. *See also* Roman Catholic Church
Black–Asian relations, 65–66. *See also* Azusa Street Memorial Committee; race and racism
Body of Christ, 31, 33–34, 45–47, 52n28, 86, 105, 149, 152, 159, 181, 219. *See also* charisms; Christology; diversity; Pauline theology; people of God
Bone, Jeremy, x, 110n17
Brazil, 13, 62, 117, 122, 166. *See also* Latin America
Buda, Daniel, 101

Cardoza-Orlandi, Carlos, 7, 93
Caribbean Conference of Churches, 7. *See also* regional ecumenical organizations
Castro, Emilio, 10, 100
catholicity, 20, 38–39, 46–47, 50, 85, 89, 91, 103–6, 108, 139–40, 149, 158, 166, 170, 198–99, 201, 219. *See also* Christian World Communions; conciliarity; consensus; diversity
Cereti, Giovanni, 21n3
Charismatic movement, 20, 36, 45, 135, 150, 158–71, 195, 220; apostolicity, 36, 163–64, 166–70, 220–21; and Pentecostals, 12, 14, 30, 36, 121–23, 158–62, 166–67,

Index 253

169, 171, 176n96; renewal, 14, 36, 45, 158–59, 161–62, 168–70; and the WCC, 158, 160, 163–64, 167–68, 220–21. *See also* apostolicity; charisms; encounter; patristics; renewal; restorationism

charisms, 20, 29, 32–37, 44–45, 49–50, 52n28, 86, 103, 126, 131–32, 134, 138, 147–59, 162–71, 177n115, 183, 198, 219; diversity, 34, 44–45, 150, 166; divine presence, 32–33, 45, 148, 154, 158, 162; experience, 32–33, 36, 126, 162, 171; holiness and sanctification, 29, 32–33, 36, 171, 219; offices, 33, 155–57, 164, 169; order, 33–34, 44–45, 148, 151, 153, 159, 163, 168–71, 219–20. *See also* Charismatic movement; church order; diversity; discernment; divine economy; holiness; Holy Spirit; Pauline theology; prophecy; love; renewal; restorationism

Chikane, Frank, 102–3

China, 40, 96, 99, 105; China Christian Council, 96, 99, 105. *See also* Asia; Hong Kong; Taiwan

Cho, Yonggi, 132

Christian Conference of Asia, 13, 91, 189. *See also* Asia; regional ecumenical organizations

Christian Forums, 20–21, 50, 171–72, 179–81, 183–205, 212n123, 216–17, 220; recognition, 180, 184, 187, 191, 197–98, 200–5, 211n105; reconciliation, 180–81, 198–202, 204–5; regional and national, 179, 190, 192–97, 204. *See also* encounter; Global Christian Forum; recognition; reconciliation; Southern California Christian Forum; sacramental theology; testimony

Christian World Communions (CWC), 4, 20, 72, 88–93, 119, 121–22, 136, 209n73, 219; as different from councils of churches, 20, 88–91,

104–6, 111n39. *See also* catholicity; Conference of the Secretaries of Christian World Communions; Pentecostal World Fellowship

Christology. *See* Jesus Christ

Chunakara, Mathews George, 13

Chung, Hyun Kyung, 94

churches as ecumenical actors, 58, 94, 106, 180, 183, 186, 191, 194, 215, 221

Church of God (Cleveland), 66, 212n123

Church of God in Christ, 66, 70

church order, 20, 30, 32–33, 42, 44–45, 120, 148–51, 154, 159, 163, 165–66, 168–71, 182, 219–20. *See also* charisms; offices

"Classical" Pentecostal distinction, 122–23, 158

Clemmons, Ithiel, 70

Cole, David, 72, 126, 134

colonialism, 12, 40, 110n17, 147, 157

commemorative sites, 59–60

communal memory, 19, 29, 38, 40, 58–61, 69, 71, 74, 76, 220. *See also* commemorative sites; narrative

communication, 20, 45, 73, 91, 98, 105, 108, 116n120, 118–20, 129, 133–35, 160, 171, 179, 182, 189, 194, 204, 218. *See also* conciliarity; dialogue; discernment

communion, 4, 8, 20, 28, 32, 43–50, 72, 85–88, 90, 95–96, 98–99, 105–8, 118–19, 125–28, 134–35, 138, 148, 153, 156, 159–60, 162, 164–66, 168–69, 171, 181–82, 190, 198–200, 202–3, 205, 213–15, 219–22; and church order, 8, 45–46, 86, 156, 165, 171, 182; and diversity, 45, 48, 159; as participation in the divine life, 28, 44, 86, 105, 118, 148, 156, 181, 198, 222. *See also* communication; conciliar ecumenism; conciliarity; *concilio/consejo* distinction; consensus; recognition; visible unity

254   *Index*

conciliar ecumenism, 6, 16, 20, 47, 50,
79, 85–109, 110n22, 119, 153, 158–
59, 164, 167, 195–98, 201, 203–5,
212n123, 215–19; as different from
Christian World Communions, 20,
88–93, 104–5, 111n39; experience
in, 86–88, 103, 106–7; membership
in councils, 87–88, 94, 96–97, 99–
102, 104–8, 132, 138, 201, 203–4.
See also churches as ecumenical
actors; communion; *concilio/consejo*
distinction
conciliarity, 6, 8, 10, 20, 86–88, 91, 94,
98, 106–8, 109n9, 110n17, 201. *See
also* catholicity; communication;
communion
concilio/consejo distinction, 87–88, 94,
97, 103, 107, 110n17, 119. *See also*
communion; conciliar ecumenism
Conference of the Secretaries of
Christian World Communions
(CSCWC), 16, 89, 91–93, 104, 108,
111n45, 131–32, 186, 188–90. *See
also* Christian World Communions;
confessionalism
confessionalism, v, 7–14, 17–18,
40–41, 60, 62, 72–73, 88–94, 98–99,
104, 124, 131, 135, 147–48, 157,
160–63, 167, 170, 179, 189–90, 192,
196, 217, 222. *See also* bilateral
dialogue; dialogue; Christian World
Communions
Consejo Latinoamericano de Iglesias,
13, 210n86. *See also* Latin America;
regional ecumenical organizations
consensus, xii, 2–3, 5, 86, 98, 103,
109, 120, 131, 134, 138, 140, 154,
157, 163, 171, 180, 182, 184, 195,
198–99, 203, 214, 217, 220–22.
See also catholicity; communion;
convergence; dialogue
Consultation on Church Union, 60, 69.
See also race and racism
convergence, 2–4, 6, 8–9, 18–21, 27–28,
36, 49–50, 58, 60, 73–74, 76–77,

79, 86, 88, 97–98, 103, 108, 118,
120, 126, 131–35, 138–40, 148,
165–66, 168–71, 180, 184–85, 194,
198–200, 203, 205, 213–18, 220–23;
as changed practices, 3–4, 19–21,
103, 107, 118, 134, 214, 216; and
consensus, 2, 134, 198; as progress,
2, 3, 203, 214, 216. *See also*
dialogue; discernment; reconciliation
*Councils, Conciliarity, and a Genuinely
Universal Council* (*Councils*), 86.
See also conciliar ecumenism;
conciliarity; Faith and Order; World
Council of Churches
councils of churches. *See* conciliar
ecumenism
Creemers, Jelle, 14, 129, 136, 139, 216
Cyprian of Carthage, 45, 153, 156, 164

Dangel, Silke, 122
Daniels, David, 71
Dei verbum, 39. *See also* Second
Vatican Council; Tradition; *Tradition
and Traditions*
Democratic Republic of the Congo, 14,
62. *See also* Africa
dialogue, v, 2–4, 6, 8–10, 14, 17, 29, 43,
47, 70, 72, 85–86, 90, 93, 95, 108–9,
117–40, 147, 149, 153–54, 174n35,
179, 184–85, 189–91, 193, 200–1,
203, 205, 214, 218–19, 221; function
of documents, 3–4, 27, 36, 203;
observers of, 129, 135; representation
in, 97, 120, 122–24, 128, 133, 136–
37, 139. *See also* bilateral dialogue;
communication; confessionalism;
consensus; discernment; encounter;
Faith and Order; multilateral
dialogue; reception
Dicastery for Promoting Christian Unity
(DPCU), 123, 129, 190. *See also*
Pontifical Council for Promoting
Christian Unity; Roman Catholic
Church; Secretariat for Promoting
Christian Unity

Index 255

Didache, 152–53. *See also* patristics
Directory for the Application of Principles and Norms on Ecumenism (Directory), 7, 119, 138, 161. *See also* Roman Catholic Church
discernment, 2, 4, 9, 11, 19, 27, 30–31, 35, 39, 43, 46–48, 66, 71, 106, 133–40, 151, 157, 159, 162–67, 169–70, 195, 201, 203, 219, 221–22; changed practices of, 5–6, 20, 134–35, 137, 140; as a charism, 34, 153–54, 177n115; as practiced in dialogues, 20, 97, 99, 106, 109, 117–18, 130–31, 133, 149, 198; and prophecy, 153–54; as a topic of dialogues, 131, 133–34, 153–54, 162, 164. *See also* charisms; convergence; dialogue; prophecy; reception; recognition; spiritual ecumenism
diversity, xii, 5–8, 12–14, 18, 32, 34, 38–39, 44–50, 57–60, 62–63, 70–71, 85, 89, 92, 95, 99, 104, 121, 124, 128, 130, 140, 150, 154, 159, 163, 166, 170–71, 179, 181, 186, 189, 195–96, 199–201, 216, 218–20, 222. *See also* catholicity; charisms; recognition
divine economy, 28–29, 32, 43, 49, 58, 64, 74, 86, 165, 171, 181–82, 189, 200, 219–20. *See also* charisms; reconciliation; renewal; restorationism; revelation; salvation history
du Plessis, David, 30, 95, 103, 111n41, 121–22, 124, 129, 141n21

Eastern Orthodox churches, 2, 4, 6, 10–11, 16, 72–73, 92, 104, 155, 158–60, 169, 179, 190–91, 196, 199, 202, 223; in bilateral dialogues, 43, 87, 111n44, 122–23, 136, 141n14, 161; in the WCC, 5, 39, 95, 97, 102, 106–8, 185–87, 207n25, 217
ecumenical attitudes, 18. *See also* trust
ecumenical formation, 10, 18, 73, 90, 101, 197

ecumenical goals, 1–3, 5, 8, 19, 27, 34, 39, 41, 43–44, 46, 50, 58, 87–88, 101–2, 131, 137–39, 150, 163, 167, 170–71, 181, 197, 201, 205, 221–22. *See also* organic union
Ecumenical Institute in Bossey, 151, 185. *See also* World Council of Churches
ecumenical methodology: changes in, 1–6, 9–10, 14, 18–19, 40, 47, 50, 71, 99–100, 104, 170, 184, 195, 214–16, 218–20, 222; coherency within, 4, 7–10, 15, 89, 93, 110n22, 135, 149, 180, 184–85, 189, 204, 217–18, 222; temporary nature of, 5, 87, 204–5, 221
ecumenical theory, xii, 9–12, 88, 180, 214–15, 222. *See also* churches as ecumenical actors; insiders and outsiders; marginality; "traditional" ecumenism
Emmert, Athanasios, 122
encounter, 32, 65, 67–68, 107, 117, 122, 124, 128, 130, 136, 140, 148, 160, 164–66, 171, 179–80, 182, 184, 188, 191, 193, 197–200, 202–3, 218, 220–21. *See also* Christian Forums; dialogue; recognition; spiritual ecumenism
Encristus, 166. *See also* Brazil; Charismatic movement; spiritual ecumenism
England, 14, 163, 169. *See also* Europe
episcopacy, 8, 29, 43, 45, 55n79, 72, 97, 103, 106, 153, 155–56, 164. *See also* offices
Espinosa, Gastón, 64, 68
eucharist, 28, 75, 103, 118. *See also* sacraments
Europe, 1, 13–14, 17, 62, 75–76, 97–98, 132, 145n94, 163, 169, 190, 193, 195, 213. *See also* England
Evangelical Church Mekane Yesus, 132, 139–40
evangelicalism, 17, 49, 188, 190; and bilateral dialogues, 135, 141n11,

158, 195; and ecumenism, 95–96, 98, 107–8, 135, 141n11, 143n50, 158, 179, 188–90, 192, 195, 217; Evangelical churches, 69, 98, 107–8, 123, 135, 141n11, 143n50, 158, 190, 195, 217; Evangelicals and Catholics Together, 195; and Pentecostalism, 69, 73, 95–96, 98, 102, 123, 141n11, 190, 195. *See also* National Association of Evangelicals; World Evangelical Alliance

Evans, Gillian, 8, 126, 218

experience, xi–xii, 6, 8, 11, 15, 33, 36–38, 40, 58, 63, 68, 74, 92, 95, 97, 102–3, 106–7, 117, 119–20, 127, 134, 139, 147–48, 150, 152–53, 158–63, 166–68, 186, 189–92, 195, 202, 214, 218–22; of God, v, 1, 22, 29, 33, 37, 39, 126, 152–53, 159–60, 167–68, 171, 183, 198, 203, 219, 221; as source for theology, v, 3, 10, 18–19, 20, 42, 77, 86–88, 106, 152–53, 159–60, 163, 168, 171, 182–83, 187, 200, 203, 214, 218–20. *See also* spiritual ecumenism; Holy Spirit; testimony

Faith and Order, 27, 39–40, 86, 89, 96–99, 108, 119–20, 134–35, 157, 203; apostolic faith studies of, 30–31, 97, 100, 154–55, 201; NCCUSA's Commission on, 16–17, 30–31, 72, 97, 100, 114n89, 154–55, 162, 164, 197; Oberlin Conference of 1957, 196–97; and Pentecostals, 13, 16–17, 30–31, 72, 97–101, 108, 113n73, 114n89, 154, 162, 164, 185–88, 201; Southern California Commission on, 196–97, 211n95; World Council of Churches' Commission on, 7, 13, 16–17, 30–31, 36, 96–101, 105–6, 108, 113n73, 114n89, 155, 164. *See also* communication; conciliar ecumenism; dialogue; discernment; multilateral dialogue; Pentecostals in dialogues

faith stories. *See* testimony

Federal Council of Churches of Christ in America (FCC), 63, 196. *See also* conciliar ecumenism; National Council of the Churches of Christ in the USA

Federation of Asian Bishops' Conferences, 189. *See also* Asia

Florovsky, Georges, 169

Flower, J. Roswell, 95

Fórum Pentecostal Latino-americano e Caribe (FPLC), 193, 210n86. *See also* Christian Forums; Latin America

Francis, Pope, 173n19

Fuller Theological Seminary, ix–x, 16, 64, 81n44, 141n11, 188–89, 194, 196, 208n43

Gee, Donald, 95

Global Christian Forum (GCF), 16, 20, 172, 179–80, 183–95, 197, 201–5, 207n25, 211n105. *See also* Christian Forums; communion; recognition; reconciliation; testimony

gospel, 12, 32–33, 35, 37–38, 48, 57, 77, 117–19, 132–33, 197, 199, 202, 222

Gros, Jeffrey, 16, 30, 100

Han, David Sang-Ehil, 193, 198, 204, 212n123, 216

healing of memories. *See* reconciling memories

Heller, Dagmar, 180

Henn, William, 97

Hietamäki, Minna, 138

historical research, 17, 18, 20, 39–41, 59, 61, 64–65, 67–69, 71, 74, 77, 81n38, 219. *See also* communal memory; historicity; patristics

historicity, 5, 19, 28, 37, 39–42, 50, 58, 74, 139, 220–21. *See also* history; restorationism; Tradition

Hocken, Peter, 161

Index

holiness, 33–36, 42, 147, 170, 183, 191. *See also* charisms; Holiness movement; sanctification
Holiness movement, 33, 62
Hollenweger, Walter, 68, 123, 187
Holy and Great Council, 2, 223n10. *See also* Eastern Orthodox churches
Holy Spirit, v, 20, 28–30, 32–37, 39, 42, 44–46, 48, 63, 65, 86, 105–7, 118, 125, 136, 138, 148–54, 156–57, 159–60, 162–71, 181, 191, 200, 219–22. *See also* charisms; divine encounter; experience
Hong Kong, 62, 96, 99, 105, 167. *See also* Asia; China
Humm, Alan, 151, 153, 156–57
Hunter, Harold, 16, 70, 74, 100, 111n44, 124, 141n14, 154

Ignatius of Antioch, 152. *See also* patristics
India, 48, 57, 59, 62, 190, 192. *See also* Asia
Indonesia, 66, 72, 189; Indonesian Christian Forum (FUKRI), 179, 192. *See also* Asia
insiders and outsiders, 12–14, 187, 203, 215. *See also* ecumenical theory; marginality; Pentecostals, exclusion of; "traditional" ecumenism
intra-Pentecostal ecumenism, 16, 18, 20, 60–62, 64, 66–79, 89–91, 122–24, 186, 190, 193, 210n86. *See also* Azusa Street Revival; Pentecostal World Fellowship; Pentecostal/ Charismatic Churches of North America
Irenaeus, 45, 172n19. *See also* patristics

Jesus Christ, v, 29, 31–34, 37–39, 44, 46–49, 52n28, 58, 86, 105–8, 127, 138, 147–49, 152, 159, 167–68, 172, 181, 183–84, 191–92, 197–98, 200–3, 205, 219–22. *See also* Body of Christ

Johns, Cheryl Bridges, 25n56, 124, 146n124, 189, 204, 212n123, 216
Johnson, Kathryn, 191, 198
Joint Declaration on the Doctrine of Justification, 132, 145n94
Jones, Sarah Rowland, 189, 191, 193, 203

Kansas City Charismatic Renewal Conference, 195
Kärkkäinen, Veli-Matti, x, 123, 163
Kasper, Walter, 149
Kenya, 85, 189, 193; National Council of Churches of Kenya (NCCK), 85, 102. *See also* Africa
Keshishian, Aram, 6, 10, 87, 107
Kessler, Diane, 87
Kibler, Ray, ix, 196
King, Rodney, 65, 69
Kinnamon, Michael, ix, 47, 87, 110n22, 196–97
Koch, Kurt, 14
koinonia. *See* communion

Latin America, 13, 62, 69, 92, 117, 122, 166, 191, 193, 210n86. *See also* Brazil; Consejo Latinoamericano de Iglesias
Lausanne Committee for World Evangelization, 16, 135; Lausanne–Orthodox Initiative, 190
Levinas, Emmanuel, 182. *See also* Ricoeur, Paul; testimony
Lin, Judith, 99
local ecumenism, 15, 63, 72, 91, 192–94, 197
Los Angeles, 41, 61–67, 72, 75, 78, 81n38, 141n11, 194–95
Los Angeles Church Federation (LACF), 63, 196
love, v, xii, 1, 30, 38, 44–45, 47, 117, 119, 128, 133, 139, 148, 152, 165
Lovett, Leonard, 68, 70–71
Lubich, Chiara, 10
Lumen gentium (*LG*), 7, 138, 181, 202. *See also* sacramental theology; Second Vatican Council

258   *Index*

Lutheran churches, 61, 132–33, 139–40,
  196; in bilateral dialogues, 16, 20,
  45, 60, 76–77, 92, 117, 119–20,
  122–23, 130, 135, 140, 145n94, 158–
  59, 161, 167, 190; Lutheran World
  Federation (LWF), 6, 72, 120, 130,
  132, 139, 167, 191

Maçaneiro, Marcial, 139
Mackay, John, 91
Maffeis, Angelo, 8, 119, 199
marginality, 12, 189, 203–4, 215–17.
  See also ecumenical theory; insiders
  and outsiders; Pentecostals, exclusion
  of; "traditional" ecumenism
Mar Gregorios, Paulos, 10
Mayer, Annemarie, 204
McDonnell, Kilian, 121, 123, 125–26,
  141n21
Mennonite churches, 11; in bilateral
  dialogues, 59–60, 75–77, 92, 190;
  Mennonite World Conference, 60,
  89, 92
Methodist churches, 33, 61–63, 66, 72,
  77, 176n93; in bilateral dialogues,
  158–59; World Methodist Council,
  89, 104
Meyer, Gabriel, ix, 195
Meyer, Harding, 6, 8, 89, 116n120, 166,
  168, 217
Miller, Larry, 190
mission, 3, 5, 10, 14, 18, 27, 29, 32,
  34–36, 47–48, 57–58, 61–62, 64,
  70–72, 76, 78, 85, 88–90, 99, 101–2,
  105, 131–32, 143n50, 147, 152, 160,
  163, 167, 179, 181, 188–91, 193,
  197, 204, 205, 209n75
Missouri, 24n53, 67, 195
Moltmann, Jürgen, 47
Montanism, 152–53, 156–57, 164,
  174n35. *See also* patristics;
  prophecy
Moreno, Calixto, 200
multilateral dialogue, 30, 93, 96–99,
  105, 119, 130, 135, 187, 197. *See*

also bilateral dialogue; conciliar
  ecumenism; Faith and Order
Muszczyński, Mariusz, 17, 151, 193

narrative, 12, 14, 18–21, 37–41, 45,
  57–62, 64–65, 67–68, 70–79,
  81n44, 82n46, 101, 125, 130, 133,
  141n14, 161, 172, 179, 184, 187–91,
  194, 198–201, 205, 215, 220; and
  experience, 10, 68, 74, 77, 127,
  182–83, 187, 198, 200; narrative
  ecclesiology, 19–20, 41, 58–60,
  74–79. *See also* communal memory;
  reconciling memories; salvation
  history; testimony
Nasrallah, Laura, 157
National Association of Evangelicals
  (NAE), 69, 95–96. *See also*
  evangelicalism
National Council of the Churches of
  Christ in the USA (NCCUSA), 63,
  68, 87–88, 196; Faith and Order
  Commission of, 16–17, 30, 59, 72,
  97, 100, 114n89, 154, 162, 164,
  197; and Pentecostals, 16–17, 30,
  72, 94, 96–97, 100, 104, 114n89,
  186. *See also* conciliar ecumenism;
  Federal Council of Churches of
  Christ in America; Pentecostals in
  councils of churches; United States
  of America
National Workshop on Christian Unity,
  16. *See also* ecumenical formation
neutrality, 3, 10, 198–99
New Delhi declaration, 46, 200. *See*
  also World Council of Churches
Newman, Joel, 71
New Prophecy. *See* Montanism
Nicene Creed, 151. *See also* patristics
Nissiotis, Nikos, v, 15, 217
Nørgaard-Højen, Peder, 6, 127
North America, 69, 72–73, 97–99,
  132. *See also* North American
  Academy of Ecumenists; Pentecostal
  Fellowship of North America;

Index 259

Pentecostal/Charismatic Churches of
North America
North American Academy of
Ecumenists, ix, 17

Oduyoye, Mercy, 10
offices, 28–30, 33–34, 43–45, 66, 106,
151–53, 155–57, 164, 182, 195.
See also charisms; church order;
episcopacy
Onyinah, Opoku, 16
organic union, 49, 119, 170–71,
178n138. *See also* church order;
spiritual unity; visible unity
Oriental Orthodox churches, 4, 6, 10,
39, 57, 72–73, 87, 97, 104, 155,
158–60, 163–64, 190–91, 199, 202;
in bilateral dialogues, 77, 87, 169; in
the WCC, 5, 39, 95, 97, 102, 106–8,
185–87, 207n25, 217
orthopathy, xii, 159

papacy, 43
Pathil, Kuncheria, 5, 8, 93, 135, 203,
215, 217
patristics, 12, 17, 20, 28, 30, 33–34,
38–39, 45, 64, 74, 125–26, 133,
139, 150–57, 162–64, 168–71,
172n19, 173n21, 178n146. *See also*
apostolicity; restorationism; Tradition
Pauline theology, 33–34, 37–38, 44, 47–
48, 52n28, 58, 77, 150–52, 154, 159.
See also Body of Christ; charisms;
discernment; diversity; prophecy;
love
Pentecost, 29–30, 32, 38, 42, 45, 62–63,
67, 70, 75, 148, 152, 163, 166–67,
189, 205, 213, 220, 222
Pentecostal/Charismatic Churches of
North America (PCCNA), 20, 69–74,
76–79, 89; Azusa Street myth and,
20, 70–72, 76, 78; Christian Unity
Commission of, 16, 69, 72–73, 78;
Pentecostal Fellowship of North
America (PFNA), 69, 72, 78, 95;

"Racial Reconciliation Manifesto"
of, 70–71, 78; as response to race and
racism, 69–73, 77–78, 95. *See also*
Azusa Street Revival; intra-Pentecostal
ecumenism; race and racism
Pentecostals, exclusion of, 12, 63, 66,
98–99, 101–2, 105, 135, 186–87,
202. *See also* insiders and outsiders;
marginality
Pentecostals in councils of churches, 94,
101–2, 212n123. *See also* National
Council of the Churches of Christ in
the USA; World Council of Churches
Pentecostals in dialogues, 30, 90, 92,
141n11, 154, 161, 167, 212n123.
See also bilateral dialogue; Faith
and Order; National Council of the
Churches of Christ in the USA;
Roman Catholic–Pentecostal
dialogue
Pentecostal World Fellowship (PWF),
20, 89–93, 103, 105, 124, 129,
189–91, 209n73, 209n75; Christian
Unity Commission of, 16, 90, 97,
108, 122, 124, 129, 191; Pentecostal
World Conference, 30, 89, 91–92,
95, 106. *See also* Christian World
Communions; intra-Pentecostal
ecumenism
people of God, 19, 28, 32, 35, 43–44,
49–50, 182, 199, 220–21. *See also*
Body of Christ
persecution, 46, 99, 152–53, 156, 190,
192, 209n73
Plaatjies-Van Huffel, Mary-Anne, 5, 10
pneumatology. *See* Holy Spirit
Pontifical Council for Promoting
Christian Unity, 14, 123, 188, 190.
See also Dicastery for Promoting
Christian Unity; Roman Catholic
Church; Secretariat for Promoting
Christian Unity
Potter, Philip, 10, 160, 167–68
prayer, 20, 45, 63, 101, 126–28, 130,
134, 164–71, 189, 222; ecumenical

260   *Index*

prayer services, 1, 50, 147–49, 159–60, 162–63, 165–66, 168, 204, 213, 216. *See also* spiritual ecumenism; Week of Prayer for Christian Unity

Presbyterian churches. *See* Reformed churches

prophecy, 37, 73, 94, 121, 151–56, 162–63, 166; apostles and prophets, 38, 151–53, 202; as complement to discernment, 153–54. *See also* charisms; discernment

proselytism, 12, 97, 102, 126–27, 135, 143n50, 162, 188, 190, 203, 205

Protestantism, 17, 39, 49, 57, 70, 76, 92, 96, 98, 101–2, 107–8, 122–23, 130, 133, 139, 154, 158–61, 166, 186, 190, 195, 196, 217

purifying memories. *See* reconciling memories

Quakerism, 5, 62

race and racism, 17, 20, 40–41, 47, 60–73, 75, 77–78, 81n38, 82n46, 91, 95, 101, 124, 154, 171

Raiser, Konrad, 6, 100, 103, 118, 138, 184–88

reception, 12, 20, 29, 33, 35–37, 39–40, 43, 49, 64, 76–77, 97–98, 101, 110n17, 119–20, 127, 129–39, 152, 159, 163, 167–71, 182, 191–93, 197, 200, 216, 219–20. *See also* dialogue; discernment; recognition

recognition, 12, 20–21, 29–30, 34, 47, 57, 59, 64, 86, 95, 97, 101, 104, 106, 108, 126, 128, 137, 149, 160, 180, 184, 187, 191, 197–98, 200–5, 211n105, 221. *See also* Christian Forums; communion; dialogue; discernment; diversity; encounter; reception; testimony

reconciliation, 2–3, 8, 17, 19–20, 40–41, 44, 47–50, 58–60, 66–68, 70–71, 76–78, 126, 134, 138, 147, 154, 162, 169, 171–72, 179–86, 197–202,

204, 213, 217, 220; as divine act, 35, 47–49, 58, 71, 76, 78, 172, 180–85, 198, 200, 202, 205; as part of mission, 48, 58, 71, 76, 167, 181, 202; and repentance, 41, 49, 76. *See also* Christian Forums; convergence; divine economy; reconciling memories; sacramental theology; salvation history

reconciling memories, 19–20, 50, 57–61, 67–72, 74, 76–79, 125, 149, 158, 204, 220; and communal identity, 20, 67, 76, 78–79, 220; and communal memory, 19, 58, 60, 69, 74; and institutional changes, 49, 68, 72, 76, 78–79. *See also* commemorative sites; communal memory; narrative; reconciliation

Reformed churches, 5, 10, 66, 72, 99, 105–6, 132; in bilateral dialogues, 16, 20, 34, 59, 92, 120–23, 130–32, 159, 161, 167, 186; World Alliance of Reformed Churches, 120, 130–31; World Communion of Reformed Churches, 5, 34, 89, 120, 129–30, 136

regional ecumenical organizations, 13, 47, 106, 185. *See also* All Africa Conference of Churches; Caribbean Conference of Churches; Christian Conference of Asia; Consejo Latinoamericano de Iglesias

renewal, v, 6, 9, 14, 29–30, 35–38, 42–43, 45, 47–48, 50, 70, 75, 78, 85, 87, 103, 118–20, 126, 133–34, 137–40, 147, 149–50, 158–59, 161–62, 164, 166–71, 185, 190, 201, 203, 215, 218, 220; apostolicity, 35–36, 42–43, 138–39, 170, 220; change and continuity, 35–36, 42, 119, 138–39, 169, 215; dialogue, 14, 87, 118, 120, 133–34, 137–40, 215; restoration, 42–43, 70, 139; Tradition, 42, 119, 138–39, 170, 215, 220. *See also* Charismatic movement; charisms; divine economy; restorationism

Index

restorationism, 33, 37, 41–43, 50, 70, 86, 88, 133, 139, 150, 171. *See also* apostolicity; Charismatic movement; charisms; divine economy; historicity; renewal; Tradition

Reudi-Weber, Hans, 154

revelation, 37, 39, 64, 118, 134, 138, 152–53, 164, 198–99, 219. *See also* salvation history

Ricoeur, Paul, 59, 71, 182. *See also* communal memory; testimony

Robeck, Cecil, as scholar: of biblical theology, 18, 28, 31–32, 34, 37–38, 44, 48, 52n28, 77, 150–52, 154, 159, 172n17, 178n146; of patristics, 17, 20, 28, 30, 33–34, 38–39, 45, 64, 74, 125–26, 133, 139, 150–57, 162–64, 169–70, 172n19, 173n21, 178n146; of Pentecostal history, 18, 20, 33, 40–41, 60–69, 71, 74–78, 81n44, 95, 125–27, 154, 161

Robeck, Cecil, critiques of, 52n28, 75, 98, 124, 142n37, 154, 162, 164, 173n21

Robeck, Cecil, roles of: Assemblies of God minister, 16, 18, 24n53, 65–67, 69, 72, 77, 92, 95, 101, 157, 162; Azusa Street Memorial Committee co-founder, 65–66; bilateral dialogues leader, 16–17, 20, 27, 46, 120–21, 123–32, 136, 141n11, 141nn14–15, 142n37, 154, 178n146, 186; CSCWC participant, 16, 89, 91–92, 108, 111n45, 131–32, 186, 188, 190; GCF leader, 16, 20, 172, 180, 185–90, 201, 205; NCCUSA contributor, 16, 30, 72, 94, 97, 100, 114n89, 154, 162, 164, 186; PCCNA contributor, 16, 20, 69–70, 72, 74, 95; professor, 16–17, 64, 72, 98, 141n11, 126, 188, 196; PWF contributor, 16, 20, 108, 124, 191; SCCF contributor, 194–96; WCC contributor, 16–17, 20, 27, 47, 88, 94–103, 105, 107–8, 114n89, 157, 164, 185–88, 191, 201

Robeck, Cecil, understanding of: communication, 20, 73, 98, 102, 120, 127–28, 134, 144n69, 174n35, 188; discernment, 30–31, 34, 134–36, 151, 153–54, 157, 162–65, 177n115; prophecy, 37–38, 73, 94, 151–56, 162; race and racism, 20, 40–41, 47, 60–73, 75, 77–78, 91, 95, 101, 124, 154, 171; visible unity, 37, 42, 44–45, 48–49, 78, 89, 96–97, 126, 140, 170–71, 178n146, 205

Robra, Martin, 101

Roman Catholic Church, 4, 6–7, 10, 17, 22n15, 35, 39, 57, 62, 75–76, 87, 90, 92, 98–101, 105–8, 127, 133, 138, 147, 155, 158–61, 172n19, 179, 185–87, 189–90, 192, 195, 197, 204, 217; in bilateral dialogues, 39, 73, 75–76, 87, 90, 92, 119, 121, 133, 136, 158, 161, 166, 195. *See also* Dicastery for Promoting Christian Unity; Pontifical Council for Promoting Christian Unity; Roman Catholic–Pentecostal dialogue; Second Vatican Council; Secretariat for Promoting Christian Unity

Roman Catholic–Pentecostal dialogue, 16, 20, 34, 39, 44, 46, 92, 111n41, 120–31, 133–37, 140, 158, 167, 178n146, 186, 188, 193–94; influence on Pentecostalism, 121–23, 126, 129–30, 134, 140; national dialogues, 73, 166; patristics, 125–26, 139, 154; significance and studies of, 14, 120–23, 129, 136. *See also* bilateral dialogue; dialogue; Pentecostals in dialogues

Rosenior, Derrick, 71

Rusch, William, 100, 119

Ryland, Edwin. *See* Los Angeles Church Federation

262 *Index*

sacramental theology, 32, 103, 181–82, 184, 198, 200, 202. *See also* Christian Forums; communion; *Lumen gentium*; sacraments; testimony

sacraments, 33, 43, 45, 58, 86, 97, 101, 104, 120, 132, 181. *See also* eucharist; baptism, water

Salvation Army, 92, 179. *See also* Holiness movement

salvation history, 28, 37, 58, 78, 172, 183, 198, 220. *See also* divine economy; narrative; reconciliation; revelation

sanctification, 29, 32, 63–64, 168, 171, 181, 219. *See also* holiness; Holiness movement

Sanctified church. *See* Holiness movement

Sandidge, Jerry, 46, 128

Second Vatican Council, 30, 35, 87, 90, 100, 119, 121, 129, 136–37. *See also* Roman Catholic Church

Secretariat for Promoting Christian Unity, 90, 119, 122, 136. *See also* Dicastery for Promoting Christian Unity; Pontifical Council for Promoting Christian Unity; Roman Catholic Church

Seventh-Day Adventism, 90, 92, 147, 179

Seymour, William, 61–64, 67–68, 70, 77–78. *See also* Azusa Street Revival

Smith, Alexei, ix, 195

Society for Pentecostal Studies, ix, 17, 72, 129

South Africa, 49, 62, 102, 103. *See also* Africa

Southern California Christian Forum (SCCF), ix, 21, 192, 194–97, 204; Southern California Ecumenical Council (SCEC), 194–97, 210n93. *See also* Christian Forums

South Korea, 131–32. *See also* Asia

spiritual ecumenism, 15, 20, 31, 36, 46, 50, 101, 140, 147–72, 184, 195, 198–99, 202, 217, 219. *See also* discernment; encounter; experience; prayer

spiritual unity, 20, 50, 78, 171. *See also* visible unity

Spittler, Russell, 61

Stăniloae, Dumitru, 10, 169

Synan, Vinson, 68, 70–71

synodality, 4, 87, 96, 106, 137, 205

systematic theology, xi, 2, 4, 7–9, 17–18, 35, 37, 48–49, 117, 126, 214, 218, 221. *See also* consensus; dialogue; experience

Taiwan, 96, 99, 105, 106. *See also* Asia; China

Taizé, 149, 166

Tan-Chow, May Ling, 14, 159–60

Tanner, Mary, 16

Tertullian, 152–53. *See also* patristics

testimony, 1, 20, 32, 64–65, 102, 124, 130, 163, 171–72, 179–80, 182–85, 187–89, 191, 196–203, 205; and experience, 1, 49, 65, 158, 182–84, 198; and identity construction, 172, 182–83, 187, 189; as narrative, 64, 179, 182–83, 187; Tradition as, 37, 183. *See also* Christian Forums; experience; narrative; recognition; sacramental theology

The Church: Towards a Common Vision (TCTCV), 36, 58, 97–99, 109n9, 118, 134–35, 148–49, 163, 166, 169–70, 181–82, 203. *See also* convergence; Faith and Order

Tillard, Jean-Marie, 16, 86

Ting, K.H., 96

Toronto Statement, 181, 201–2. *See also* World Council of Churches

Tradition, v, 28–29, 37–40, 42–43, 50, 98, 119, 125, 133–34, 138–39, 153, 156–57, 169–70, 183, 215, 220, 223n10. *See also* apostolicity;

historicity; patristics; restorationism; *Tradition and Traditions*

Tradition and Traditions, 39, 220. *See also* Faith and Order; Tradition

"traditional" ecumenism, 135–37, 189, 204, 212n123, 216. *See also* ecumenical theory; insiders and outsiders; marginality

trust, 18, 126, 186–87. *See also* ecumenical attitudes

Tveit, Olav Fykse, 202, 204

Unitatis redintegratio (*UR*), 7, 44, 76, 134, 147. *See also* Second Vatican Council

United States Conference of Catholic Bishops, 17, 73, 161. *See also* Roman Catholic Church

United States of America, 16–19, 27, 33, 60, 62–63, 68–69, 72–74, 92, 95, 101, 145n94, 161, 166, 176n93, 189, 194–96, 212n123. *See also* Federal Council of Churches of Christ in America; Missouri; National Council of the Churches of Christ in the USA; National Workshop on Christian Unity; United States Conference of Catholic Bishops

Ut unum sint (*UUS*), 7, 125, 149, 161, 165

Uzochukwu, Peter, 6, 10

Vischer, Lukas, 89

visible unity, 1–2, 44–46, 48–50, 93, 97, 126, 138, 140, 170–72, 181, 200–5, 214–15, 221–23; as historical, 5, 37, 45, 221; and the materiality of the church, 44, 168, 184, 202; and practices, 4–5, 45, 78–79, 96, 126, 166, 171, 223; restoration of, 42, 171. *See also* communion; ecumenical goals; historicity; organic union; sacramental theology; spiritual unity; testimony

Visser 't Hooft, Willem, 10

Vogelaar, Huub, 198, 202

Vondey, Wolfgang, 16

Wainwright, Geoffrey, 16

Waldensians, 75

Watanabe, Bill. *See* Azusa Street Memorial Committee

Week of Prayer for Christian Unity, 147, 149, 166, 197. *See also* prayer; spiritual ecumenism

Wesley, John, 33, 176n93

West Angeles Church of God in Christ, 66

white–Black binary, 60, 70, 77. *See also* race and racism

white normativity, 17, 68–69. *See also* race and racism

Williams, J. Rodman, 122

Wondra, Ellen, 135–36, 216

Wood, George, 65

World Council of Churches (WCC), 4–5, 20, 30, 47, 62, 68, 87–89, 93–108, 124, 129, 147, 154, 160, 163–64, 167–68, 181, 185–92, 201, 203–4, 216–17, 220; Amsterdam Assembly, 1, 95; Busan Assembly, 1, 102, 111n39, 132, 179; Canberra Assembly, 47, 94–96, 99–100, 185–86; Commission on World Mission and Evangelism, 102, 143n50; *Common Understanding and Vision of the WCC* (*CUV*), 88, 99, 101, 185–86; *Constitution and Rules*, 93–94; Evanston Assembly, 95; Faith and Order Commission, 7, 13, 16–17, 30, 36, 96–101, 105–6, 108, 114n89, 164; Harare Assembly, 97, 100, 185; Joint Consultative Group between the WCC and Pentecostals (JCG), 16, 93, 99–104, 185, 187–88, 201; Joint Working Group between the Roman Catholic Church and the WCC, 100, 143n50, 149, 204; Karlsruhe Assembly, ix, 1, 4, 103, 213; Nairobi Assembly, 158,

189; New Delhi Assembly, 39; and Pentecostals, 16, 39, 93–95, 97–105, 108, 114n89, 129, 160, 185–88, 201, 210n86; Porto Alegre Assembly, 93, 111n39; Uppsala Assembly, 116n120, 121. *See also* conciliar ecumenism; conciliarity; Faith and Order; New Delhi declaration; Pentecostals in councils of churches; Toronto Statement

World Evangelical Alliance (WEA), 143n50, 188–90, 192. *See also* evangelicalism

Zambia, 14, 147, 149. *See also* Africa

Zizioulas, John, 16, 118–19, 169

About the Author

Josiah Baker is the administrative assistant of the Southern California Christian Forum. He presently serves as the secretary of the North American Academy of Ecumenists, where he chairs its bibliography committee, and as a co-leader of the Ecumenical Studies Interest Group of the Society for Pentecostal Studies. He previously served as the interim chair of the Southern California Commission on Faith and Order and as a steward at the Karlsruhe Assembly of the World Council of Churches. He has offered presentations for the National Workshop on Christian Unity and the American Academy of Religion and has published journal articles in English, French, Spanish, German, Portuguese, and Italian. His research interests are in ecumenical methodology, Pentecostal hymnody, and world Christianity. He earned his BA in Biblical and Theological Studies at North Central University in Minneapolis, Minnesota, as well as his MDiv and PhD in systematic theology at Fuller Theological Seminary in Pasadena, California. He is a fourth-generation member of the Assemblies of God from the Southern Missouri District and a fifth-generation Pentecostal.

www.ingramcontent.com/pod-product-compliance
Lightning Source LLC
Chambersburg PA
CBHW021711090325
23067CB00002B/23